The Madman in the White House

The Madman in the White House

Sigmund Freud, Ambassador Bullitt, and the Lost Psychobiography of Woodrow Wilson

Patrick Weil

Harvard University Press

CAMBRIDGE, MASSACHUSETTS · LONDON, ENGLAND

2023

An earlier version of this book was published in French as *Le Président est-il devenu fou?: le diplomate, le psychanalyste et le chef d'Etat*, © 2022 Éditions Grasset, Paris.

Printed in the United States of America

First printing

Publication of this book has been supported through the generous provisions of the Maurice and Lula Bradley Smith Memorial Fund.

Library of Congress Cataloging-in-Publication Data

Names: Weil, Patrick, 1956– author.
Title: The madman in the White House: Sigmund Freud, Ambassador Bullitt, and the lost psychobiography of Woodrow Wilson / Patrick Weil. |
Includes bibliographical references and index. |
Identifiers: LCCN 2022037088 | ISBN 9780674291614 (cloth)
Subjects: LCSH: Freud, Sigmund, 1856–1939. Thomas Woodrow Wilson, twenty-eighth President of the United States. | Wilson, Woodrow, 1856–1924—Mental health. | Bullitt, William C. (William Christian), 1891–1967. | Censorship—United States—History—20th century.
Classification: LCC E767.F73 W4513 2023 | DDC 973.91/3092 [B]—dc23/eng/20220830
LC record available at https://lccn.loc.gov/2022037088

To the memory of Aya
— Alice Roth (1912–2011) —
who lived a century through love

Contents

The Madman in the White House

Introduction

AS SPRING DAWNED on the morning of March 21, 1920, many close observers of President Woodrow Wilson wondered if he had gone mad. The day before, despite their pleas, the president had instructed his fellow Democrats in the Senate to vote against ratifying the Treaty of Versailles. This was a shocking reversal of Wilson's earlier efforts. For the first six months of 1919, he lived in a "temporary White House" on the right bank of the Seine in Paris. There he worked tirelessly to negotiate the treaty, which he and millions of others saw as a framework for lasting worldwide peace.

Those negotiations followed, of course, the conclusion of the First World War. Eighteen million had died, almost 10 million of them civilians. Another 21 million were wounded, many horribly mutilated for the rest of their lives. In response, Wilson convinced the Allies to approve the creation of a League of Nations, a global organization designed to prevent future wars. In addition, Wilson and the leaders of the United Kingdom had agreed to a defense pact with France, pledging that they would act together in self-defense at any sign of German aggression against her French neighbor. This in effect created a new collective security apparatus with the United States at its center. Wilson and the Allies had anticipated the United Nations and NATO decades before their time.

Returning to Washington from Paris in July 1919, buoyed by the prestige and popularity of the peace he had negotiated, Wilson envisioned ratification of the Versailles Treaty as a formality. But this proved gravely wrong. Many in the Senate worried that the treaty would commit the United States to defend others subject to aggression, with the result that Congress would be stripped of its constitutional prerogative to declare war. For months Wilson obstinately refused to hear this concern or do anything that might assuage it. His position never wavered, right up until the final defeat of the Versailles Treaty in the Senate; the treaty with France and the United Kingdom became a casualty of the impasse. Immediately upon the completion of the Senate vote, the whole world understood that although the Treaty of Versailles would formally enter into force, without US participation it provided little guarantee of an enduring peace.

In Paris, the press emphasized Prime Minister Georges Clemenceau's failed bet on a transatlantic alliance with the United States. French General Ferdinand Foch, the supreme allied commander who led the Allies to victory, predicted a new war would eventually break out and told a friend, "If we are not careful, our army will be significantly inferior in 1940 than it was in 1914."[1] In Washington, Wilson's followers unanimously held him responsible for the treaty's collapse, whether or not they supported its terms. Foreign policy "idealists" believed the treaty the president had signed betrayed his promise of "peace without victory"—it looked like a classic victor's peace, forced on the vanquished to the benefit of her enemy. Rather than provide for the universal self-determination Wilson called for, the treaty was full of annexations that saw the Allies swallowing up former territories of the defeated; rather than welcome Germany into a new world order centered on law, the treaty imposed humiliating and onerous financial burdens in the form of harsh reparations. "Realists," in contrast, thought that Wilson's main promises had been fulfilled. The treaty set out a collective-security framework that could prevent future wars. In line with the goal of self-determination, some new nation-states were born, including Poland. Germany would have to pay for the damages it caused, but contrary to popular belief the country—still the largest in Europe, and unencumbered by foreign debt aside from the reparations bill—had emerged from the war in relatively good economic shape.

Regardless of their differences, idealists and realists blamed the president for the failure of the peace—whether because the treaty itself was fatally flawed or because Wilson had assured its ruin in the Senate. Some attributed Wilson's fatal stubbornness to a stroke he suffered in fall 1919, which left him at death's door for weeks and permanently paralyzed the left side of his body. But others thought his behavior had deeper roots.

Many of the participants in the conference—including Clemenceau, British prime minister David Lloyd George, and Lloyd George's war secretary, Winston Churchill—attributed Wilson's failure to his psychology. This belief was shared by his American collaborators, including Robert Lansing, the secretary of state, and Wilson's closest adviser, Colonel Edward House. But only the young British economist and peace conference delegate John Maynard Keynes, in the enduringly influential 1919 book *The Economic Consequences of the Peace,* publicly evoked Wilson's "Freudian complex." Keynes was in the idealist camp—the group that saw the treaty as abandoning the principle of a law-based peace among states acting as equals. "The President's psychology was essential to explain how it came about, in spite of the President's sincerity, that a perfidious peace was enacted," Keynes wrote in a letter.[2]

William C. Bullitt, a journalist, diplomat, and fellow idealist, had joined Wilson in his fight to "create a world adequate to the needs of mankind."[3] After serving in the US delegation and coming away with an opinion similar to Keynes's, he resolved to torpedo the treaty in the Senate. Early in September 1919, the elegant twenty-eight-year-old appeared at a Senate hearing where he revealed that Wilson had deceived senators about the negotiations and further testified that top foreign policy officials—including Secretary of State Lansing—feared the treaty would draw the United States into a new war. Before the senators, Bullitt argued that if the United States ratified the treaty, it would indeed find itself at war again in short order, enjoined to fight on behalf of Eastern European states sure to be overrun by the new Bolshevik government in Russia.

Bullitt became a hero both for Wilson's Republican opponents and the liberals who had once supported Wilson. His revelations—arriving just before the treaty debate began on the Senate floor, while Wilson still enjoyed momentum—had seismic effects and earned him tremendous publicity. Activists urged him to seek office in his own right. Yet, though Bullitt had no doubt that he had been right to testify against the treaty, he had no interest in staying in politics. Disgusted by Washington, he withdrew into writing and existential limbo. In 1923 he divorced his first wife and married Louise Bryant, a fellow writer, social high-flier, and the widow of John Reed, the socialist journalist and author of *Ten Days that Shook the World.* Three years later Bullitt published an autobiographical novel, *It's Not Done.* An unexpected hit, the book sold 200,000 copies and was reprinted seventeen times.

Despite his successes, Bullitt remained traumatized by the tragedy of Versailles. He took up the torch of psychology and decided to write about Wilson's personality in an effort to make sense of what had happened. To help him in his task, he called on none other than Sigmund Freud, the founder of psychoanalysis. At the end of 1926, Bullitt went to Vienna and presented himself at Freud's door. Bullitt became Freud's patient. On Freud's couch, he shared facets of his life story but also discussed Wilson, about whom he was writing a play. The project received considerable praise from dramatists, but Bullitt was forced to abandon the work when he could not find a theater willing to show it.

Three years later, Bullitt came to Freud with a new idea. At the time, the Great Depression had hit the world and Europe's precarious peace was imperiled by the rise of fascism. The role of the United States in the world had expanded, yet its diplomacy remained embarrassingly underdeveloped. So Bullitt decided to write a book on diplomacy, a subject he intended to approach scientifically—through studies in geography, economics, history, and, finally, psychology. For Bullitt, the psychology of leaders was what mattered most. The book was to include portraits of the key personalities of the Paris Conference: Clemenceau, Lloyd George, Wilson, and other heads of state, as well as important figures from the American delegation, such as House and Herbert Hoover, the agricultural official and future president who ensured that Americans and their allies stayed fed during the war while the Germans succumbed to famine. Bullitt also intended to feature Vladimir Lenin, the Bolshevik leader, who had not been at the conference but whom Bullitt had met during secret talks in 1919. The book would conclude with a radical call for parliamentary government in the United States. The structure of the US government was overly dependent on a single individual, he thought—the president. A parliamentary system was better suited for a democracy.

Freud was intrigued. He had confided to Bullitt that he, too, had some ideas about Wilson that he would like to put to paper. Bullitt asked Freud to contribute to his book. Freud agreed, but only if Bullitt could gather the hard historical evidence they would need, including archival resources and interviews with the people who knew Wilson best. If Bullitt could gather this material for him, and if it proved appropriate, Freud was eager to collaborate.

Excited by the project, Bullitt dedicated himself to the task after returning to the United States. He obtained access to important personal archives. He carried out interviews with Wilson's confidantes: Cary Grayson, the president's doctor; Ray Stannard Baker, Wilson's biographer; Joseph Tumulty, his secretary; Bernard Baruch, his economic adviser; Colonel House; and others. Each confessed to Bullitt secret information or interpretations about Wilson that have been unknown until today.

Once assembled, the material seemed sufficiently impressive to Freud. In October 1930, he and Bullitt decided on a new course: instead of appending an additional chapter to Bullitt's diplomacy book, they would coauthor a complete book dedicated exclusively to Wilson. For months in Vienna, Freud and Bullitt studied and analyzed Wilson's life and personality. The president, they concluded, could not help but put himself in situations where he would suffer, be humiliated, enraged, and ultimately fail. To a psychoanalyst, this predilection for repeated cycles of self-destruction was a clear sign of neurosis, with the potential to provoke irrational thoughts and behaviors of the kind that appeared to be in evidence during the peace treaty negotiations.

In April 1932, after two years of work, the two men signed each chapter of a 389-page manuscript. By the end of their collaboration, Freud had developed an affection for the diplomat-turned-biographer. He was smart, he knew international politics, and he even had innovative ideas about psychoanalysis. They had become friends. When Bullitt wrote Freud, he would address him as "Dear Freud"—a rare expression of familiarity, as Freud was known reverentially to his circle as "professor." The coauthors looked forward to publishing their interpretation of Wilson's personality and its decisive role in the crisis that was then threatening world peace—an interpretation bolstered by the authority of the founder of psychoanalysis.

But if Bullitt had lost his admiration for Wilson, he never truly abandoned Wilson's vision. Amid the unfolding global catastrophe, he yearned to return to the center of the action and see that, this time, American values of democracy, liberty, and free enterprise won out. A liberal internationalist to his core, Bullitt found a new vehicle for his ideals in the 1932 Democratic presidential nominee, Franklin Roosevelt. Bullitt hoped to secure a job in Roosevelt's administration and recognized that further public criticism of Wilson—whose reputation was sullied after Versailles but on the mend posthumously in the 1930s—would render him persona non grata in the Democratic Party. With Freud's blessing, Bullitt chose to postpone publication of their book.

Over the next ten years, Bullitt served Roosevelt as one of his most prized diplomats. In the fall of 1933, Bullitt conducted alongside Roosevelt the negotiations that led to US recognition of the Soviet Union. He went on to become the first US ambassador in Moscow. Surrounded by a young guard that included George Kennan—future author of the vaunted "long telegram" laying out the foreign policy doctrine of Soviet "containment"—Bullitt cultivated a trademark style that blended dazzle with professional rigor. He loved diplomacy and geopolitics, but he was also a devotee of theater, parties, socialites. And socialists. Bullitt was a strident anti-Communist but not because he opposed leftist ideas. He had sympathy for socialist policies and tried to cultivate left-wing allies capable of appealing to those who might otherwise succumb to Communism, which Bullitt associated with dictatorship and cultism. In his private life, emancipated women played a major role and contributed to his successes: Inez Milholland, the feminist and suffragist; Ernesta Drinker, a writer and journalist who became his first wife; Bryant, the revolutionary journalist and his second wife; Missy LeHand, Roosevelt's assistant and chief of staff; Cissy Patterson, editor of the *Washington Times-Herald* and scion of the owners of the *Chicago Tribune.*

In August 1936 Bullitt became ambassador to France. From Paris, he coordinated the US embassies in Europe in an effort to save the increasingly tenuous peace. In September 1938, he went against the grain of elite opinion and convinced Roosevelt that the Munich Agreement would not satisfy Hitler and would instead lead to war. With the help of others—in particular the French businessman and statesman Jean Monnet—Bullitt organized the mass production of US fighter planes to supply the French army. When the French government fled Paris in June 1940, Bullitt stayed behind to protect the City of Light from destruction. He was among those who recognized the true nature of the new Vichy regime—its ambition to become the finest province of a Nazi Europe and to see Britain defeated. Bullitt had enormous influence on the early course of the war: after returning to the United States, he convinced Roosevelt to target North Africa as a possible site for a US offensive, providing the blueprint for Operation Torch, the first Allied landing of the conflict.

Soon, however, diplomacy was reduced to an auxiliary of war, and Roosevelt cast Bullitt aside. Bullitt nonetheless persisted in trying to shape national policy. On January 29, 1943, he warned the president in a famous memorandum that the United States should not, in its zeal to defeat Hitler, make undue concessions to Stalin. The consequences, Bullitt predicted, would be terrible for hundreds of millions of Europeans and Chinese, who were liable to become Soviet victims in due course. In appraising the memorandum's farsightedness, Kennan wrote that "it had no counterpart as a warning of that date." Indeed, Bullitt had been enormously prescient in foreseeing the postwar situation. As early as September 1939 he wrote, "To my mind, Mr. Hitler has already lost this war completely. I rather imagine that he thinks he can finish the French and British quickly enough to turn around and smash the Bolshies; but that isn't going to happen and in the end the Bolshies will gradually eat like a cancer to Berlin. Then the next stage will be of finishing off Stalin Khan."[4]

Bullitt worried that, like Wilson in 1919, Roosevelt would win the war and lose the peace. But Roosevelt was not listening. Frustrated, Bullitt decamped to Europe and, in April 1944, joined the Free French Army under Charles de Gaulle. Bullitt proved an able officer, serving and advising the esteemed General Jean de Lattre. By the close of the war, Bullitt had become something of a French national hero.

When he returned to Washington, D.C., in fall 1945, Bullitt continued his fight against Communism. He had no official position, but he nonetheless played a crucial role in foreign affairs. Through journalism, campaigns to sway his powerful friends, and freelance diplomacy, he found his way to the frontlines of the Cold War. He was a key negotiator in bringing about armistice in Korea. He contributed decisively to the return of Emperor Bao Dai to the throne of Vietnam, securing French and US support and thereby arraying American power against Ho Chi Minh's Communists. And he was indefatigable in his efforts to stave off Chinese Communism. When Chiang Kai-shek and his Nationalists lost China, Bullitt moved to Taiwan to advise Chiang.

In the early 1950s, Bullitt became an informal adviser to Vice President Richard Nixon; he was in some respect the original Henry

Kissinger, well before Kissinger arrived on the national scene. Although Bullitt died before Nixon became president, his influence lingered. Nixon held Bullitt up as a model. "The foreign service reporting is an utter disaster," he complained in 1971, because they described every little thing that happened without assessing the bigger picture. "The great ambassadors of the past such as Bullitt, put their view out."[5]

But it was not Bullitt's diplomatic record that would be his legacy. In December 1966, feeling death approaching, Bullitt finally published the Wilson biography nearly thirty years after Freud's death. The work was met with howls of protest. Many questioned whether Freud was really a coauthor. Bullitt died in Paris in February 1967 before reading any of the reviews, which were often severe. Wilson's reputation seemed untouchable at the time, while the influence of Freud and psychoanalysis had precipitously declined. Few reviewers agreed with the recent assessment of historian Adam Tooze, who has called the Wilson book a "compelling psychobiography" of a president "trapped in an imaginary world of language woven by his domineering Presbyterian father." Of course, others had written biographies of Wilson and his fellow presidents, but no one had written anything like that—no one except Bullitt and Freud.[6]

BEFORE HE PUBLISHED the Wilson biography in 1966, Bullitt removed or otherwise edited some 300 passages. Many of these focused on an ingenious link the authors had forged between Wilson's ineptitude and his Christ complex. Bullitt was a passionate Christian, and Freud, though he did not share Bullitt's faith, saw in the figure of Christ hope for a peaceful future. Although it is impossible to say so with certainty, I believe—and defend this belief in the later chapters of this book—that Bullitt thought this discussion would be excessively controversial and potentially dangerous, not least because it was steeped in shocking claims about Wilson's sexuality. Earlier than many other cold warriors, Bullitt perceived a global war afoot between Communists and Christians, and he was loath to give the former ammunition against the latter.

But while the published book omitted these key points of analysis, Bullitt preserved them. He kept the original manuscript all along, perhaps hoping that the public would one day discover what he and Freud truly thought of Woodrow Wilson. That day has come. My book reveals for the first time the content of the original Freud and Bullitt manuscript—a manuscript everyone thought had disappeared.

As a student, I read the Freud-Bullitt book published in 1967 in French translation. Even that version, though redacted, makes a convincing case that the psychology of leaders matters in the conduct of political affairs—that personality is very often at the heart of policy. But I did not take particular interest in Bullitt until the summer of 2014, when I found the 1966 US edition of the book in a New York shop. While reading, I took special note of the treatment of Colonel House, Wilson's adviser, on whom I was conducting research in the context of his relationship with Clemenceau. Seeking out correspondence between House and Bullitt, I discovered that Bullitt's archives were at Yale's Sterling Memorial Library, the same location as House's. Now I was pursuing Bullitt, too. The search took me to archives in Washington, D.C., Edinburgh, London, and Paris; Louisville, Kentucky; Staunton, Virginia; and West Branch, Iowa. By the winter of 2015, I had before me the original manuscript, signed by Freud and Bullitt at the bottom of each of its chapters. Some scholars were aware of it but presumed it lost or destroyed. At any rate, no one alive had seen it.

I decided to investigate how the original work was conceived, to measure the contribution of the father of psychoanalysis and to understand why the published version appeared as it did. I also needed to check the rigor of the historical details on which the two authors based their biography of Wilson—in particular, the negotiations surrounding the Treaty of Versailles, the Senate debate, and Wilson's role in both. I quickly concluded that to understand the fate of the Freud-Bullitt manuscript, I also had to follow Bullitt throughout his diplomatic life, from 1917, when he joined the State Department, to his death in 1967. This story begins with the Great War and the political wrangling surrounding its conclusion, focusing on the psychology of the president who saw the United States through the conflict and the subsequent peace process. From there it illuminates Bullitt's research into Wilson's life and work and his discussions with Freud before turning to Bullitt's diplomatic efforts in the Soviet Union and France and his wartime exploits. Finally, we join Bullitt in his personal Cold War, which overlapped with his return to the Wilson book.

This book, then, is a journey across the twentieth century. The Freud-Bullitt manuscript was born, nourished, delayed, modified, and cut for reasons having to do with Bullitt's intimate relationship with the great international events of the twentieth century and with the giants of his time: Lenin, Stalin, Roosevelt, Hoover, de Gaulle, Churchill, Chiang, and of course Wilson. Bullitt worked with them all, not to mention others less well-known but no less important for having been forgotten.

Bullitt's service alongside Wilson decisively influenced the project with Freud. The relationships Bullitt developed with others in Wilson's sphere facilitated his inquiry into what exactly had happened at the Paris Peace Conference—how it was that Wilson came to abandon many of his ideals and then his treaty. Later, Bullitt's return to a diplomatic career and his dedication to the fight against Communism help explain why the manuscript's publication was further postponed. These factors also shed light on most of the cuts that Bullitt made before the book was finally published. Until his death, he feared the potentially devastating effects of the original manuscript.

This manuscript emerged from the anger of its two authors. Freud and Bullitt were amazed at the discrepancy between the Wilson who bestrode the earth as a peaceful colossus in 1918 and early 1919 and the man who gave in so readily once the peace conference began. And why did Wilson—who understood that the treaty was far from perfect but thought that it might later be revised—seemingly do everything possible to kill it in the Senate? There was so much to explain to a public that, by the 1930s, had come to see Wilson as a heroic victim of isolationist US politicians and European imperialists.

Bullitt and Freud showed that Wilson was indeed a victim, but a victim of his own psyche. In assessing their research, I realized that there was much I had not understood about the Treaty of Versailles and the Senate ratification process, to say nothing of many of the tragic events that came after. Wilson bore considerable responsibility for those tragedies, as becomes clear when one peers behind the obscuring veil of a mythologized past. Even at a distance of ninety years, Freud and Bullitt's call to recognize the signs of pathological personality in our leaders has lost none of its urgency.

1

The American Collapse of the Treaty of Versailles

WHEN PRESIDENT WOODROW WILSON RETURNED to the United States on July 8, 1919, he was convinced that he would easily overcome all domestic opposition to the treaty he had negotiated in Paris. The peace, signed with Germany in the Hall of Mirrors of the Palace of Versailles, bore the strong imprint of the United States. Wilson's Fourteen Points, the framework for a lasting peace that he had presented to the US Congress in January 1918, had been accepted by the Allies and by Germany. The restoration of Belgian sovereignty, the return of Alsace-Lorraine to France, the dismantling of the Ottoman Empire, the adjustments of borders in the Balkans and Italy—all these territorial dimensions of the Fourteen Points were integral to the Treaty of Versailles. The Austro-Hungarian Empire also disintegrated and was forced to recognize the independence of its peoples in accordance with the principle of self-determination that had become Wilson's talisman.

Finally, and above all, the League of Nations, the cornerstone of the Fourteen Points, was placed at the head of the treaty. Wilson was especially proud of this contribution, which he considered decisive for the stability and security of all states. The league would be a forum for adjudicating international disputes and would provide mechanisms for preventing war. In cases of military aggression, economic sanctions would be applied immediately, and league members would be enjoined to collective defense, putting their own forces on the line to protect any member states that had been attacked.

Getting to this point hadn't been easy. Hostilities had ceased with the armistice of November 1918, but Wilson aimed for much more: not just the formal end of the Great War, but an end to all wars, for all time. The American president had spent the entire spring of 1919 negotiating daily with the Italian, British, and French prime ministers—Vittorio

Emanuele Orlando, David Lloyd George, and Georges Clemenceau. Along with Wilson, they comprised the so-called Council of Four or Big Four. The challenge was to draft a peace treaty that would secure a lasting peace while satisfying the Big Four's security, territorial, and financial interests and obtaining Germany's agreement.

Lloyd George and Clemenceau had been especially intractable. Having come to power in the middle of the war, both promised outright victory, not negotiated peace.[1] During arduous talks, Wilson was forced to make numerous concessions never contemplated in the Fourteen Points—concessions that allayed fears in Britain and France while deepening resentments in Germany. The British Empire would gain control of the German naval fleet and most of Germany's colonies. For fifteen years, France would be granted occupation of the left bank of the Rhine, the river comprising most of its border with Germany, and ownership of the Saar, a coalmining region straddling the French-German frontier. Thereafter, the Saar region would choose its destiny in a referendum. The treaty finally obliged Germany to not only pay reparations for damage done to civilian populations and property, but also to assume the cost of military pensions and compensation granted to soldiers' families during the war; for that purpose, Germany would be required to acknowledge its sole responsibility for "all loss and all damage suffered by Allied governments and associates and their nationals." But, recognizing that the resources of the vanquished were not unlimited, the treaty included some flexibility as to how much Germany would owe. A league commission, presided over by the United States, would determine the exact cost of the reparations. And Wilson thought that the league, once established, would compensate for the treaty's deficits.

By the summer of 1919, when the Senate began debate over ratification, a majority of Americans favored severe treatment of Germany. They were also in favor of maintaining alliances with England and France. The Republicans, Wilson's opposition in Congress, largely agreed. Henry Cabot Lodge, the powerful Massachusetts senator who served as majority leader and chair of the Foreign Relations Committee, wanted "a League among the Nations with whom the United States had been associated in the war."[2] What gave Lodge and his allies pause, however, was Article X of the League of Nations Covenant, the clause committing members to defense of each other's independence and territorial integrity. A separate Treaty of Guarantee—also under consideration in the Senate—would require the United States and Britain to defend France in case of German aggression. Wasn't that good enough? When it came to defending all league members from any aggression, Lodge and many others, including most Senate Republicans and some Democrats, were circumspect.

After Wilson introduced the treaty in the Senate on July 10, Republicans insisted on reading its hundred pages line by line, a process that took two weeks. Then the Foreign Affairs Committee organized six weeks of public hearings, at which thirty-three witnesses testified and presented documents, amendments, and resolutions.[3] On August 19, Wilson, sensing that opposition to the treaty might be growing as time dragged on, invited the Foreign Affairs Committee to a meeting at the White House. Aside from the transfer to Japan of Shantung, a German colony in China, the territorial clauses of the Versailles Treaty provoked little concern among the senators. Most of the discussion turned on the possibility that the United States might be pressed into a war by virtue of Article X, which would oblige the country "to respect and preserve as against external aggression the territorial integrity and existing political independence of all Members of the League." Wilson tried to assuage the senators by assuring them that any action would require the "unanimous consent" of the league's Executive Council, of which the United States was to be a permanent member. Furthermore, "Congress" would be "absolutely free to put its own interpretation upon [Article X] in all cases that call for action." Wilson described Article X as "the very backbone of the whole Covenant," yet he also said that it imposed only "a moral, not a legal obligation." It was "binding in conscience only, not in law"—though, he added, a "moral obligation" was "of course superior to a legal obligation."[4] It was a confusing assertion, not a clarifying one. The senators' perplexity only increased when they questioned Wilson about agreements the Allies—France, Italy, Russia, Britain, and Japan—had signed in secret before the United States joined the war. These treaties allocated territorial rewards in case of victory. Wilson told the senators, implausibly, that he had no knowledge of the secret treaties.

To shore up support for the treaty, Wilson went on tour, visiting sixteen states to address the American people directly. Considered by many contemporaries to have been the most powerful speaker the United States had ever produced, Wilson knew that he could court public opinion far more effectively than he could sway the opposing senators. He had a talent for turning people around, a power of reasoning embellished by his impressive rhetorical skills, which often united the inspirational tone of Theodore Roosevelt—with its echoes of the founding era—and the kinds of policy specifics that defined the speeches of Wilson's predecessor in office, William Howard Taft.[5]

Senate Republicans planned a rejoinder. They would bring in another witness—an insider, a diplomat who had taken part in the Paris Peace Conference itself and who would speak damningly of what Wilson had agreed to. Their first choice was William Bullitt, who had provided intelligence to Wilson and the others representing the United States at the conference. A few months earlier, on May 17, Bullitt had tendered his resignation in a letter to President Wilson that became public a few days later. "I am sorry that you did not fight our fight to the finish," Bullitt wrote, "and that you had so little faith in the millions of men, like myself, in every nation who had faith in you." Bullitt had counted himself an idealist of Wilson's stripe, a liberal who believed that international law could secure permanent peace. The Treaty of Versailles achieved nothing of the sort, he concluded. "Our government has consented now to deliver the suffering people of the world to new oppressions, subjections, and dismemberments—a new century of war." The renewal of conflict was assured by the treaty itself, Bullitt wrote. The "unjust decisions of the conference" with regard to territorial control and reparations were sure to provoke hard feelings and hostilities. What is more, the resulting conflicts would embroil the United States, thanks to Article X. "It is my conviction that the present League of Nations will be powerless to prevent these wars," Bullitt wrote, "and that the United States will be involved in them by the obligations undertaken in the Covenant of the League."[6]

The Foreign Relations Committee issued a subpoena for Bullitt's testimony, and after a few days of searching, the summons reached him in the woods near Fort Kent, Maine, where he was staying with his wife Ernesta. Returning from an errand, she found her husband lying in bed.

"Are you ill?" she asked, observing later that "he looked white and queer." He handed her the telegram from Senator Lodge. "If I tell what I should," he said, "my career will be ruined."[7]

But when it came time to testify, on September 12, 1919, Bullitt did not shrink from the limelight. Indeed, he had long hoped for an opportunity to speak before the Senate and only suffered briefly from cold feet. Once in the chambers, he swore to tell the truth and said all that he knew.[8] He spoke for three hours and provided extensive documentation of his experiences and what he had witnessed. At the end of his testimony, the journalists in the room rushed out to report on the day's events, knowing that the hearing would make the front page of every newspaper in the United States and would shake the world. Lodge was exultant. His last witness exceeded his expectations.[9] Bullitt had revealed key details that would help Lodge revise or derail the Treaty of Versailles in the Senate.

Bullitt's Revelations

Bullitt knew the peace conference and the European security situation better than anyone. After joining the State Department in fall 1917, he had coordinated what was commonly known as its Enemy Desk.[10] He would gather information from the Central Powers—Germany and Austria-Hungary—for Colonel Edward M. House, Wilson's main personal and political adviser, or for the president himself. At the peace conference, Bullitt served as chief of the Division of Current Intelligence Summaries. Every morning, he scoured sources and delivered his syntheses personally to Wilson, Secretary of State Robert Lansing, and the three other commissioners representing the United States at the conference. Bullitt retained numerous documents and drafts related to the treaty and the league; it was these that he provided to the senators, along with his own observations. The Wilson administration had deliberately kept senators in the dark, hoping to present them a fait accompli. Bullitt saw to it that they knew the facts.

Among the most important facts of which the senators knew nothing was Bullitt's secret mission to Russia and Wilson's response to it. A few weeks after Bullitt arrived in Paris for the peace conference, Colonel House directed him to travel to Moscow and meet with

Vladimir Lenin. The leader of the Bolsheviks, who had taken power in October 1917, saw an opportunity to obtain Allied recognition of his government. This was crucial because, in early 1919, the Bolsheviks were engaged in a bloody civil war with remnants of the tsar's regime and with others jockeying for control in Russia. Bullitt's task was to negotiate Russia's terms of entry into the new world order.

For the Allies, any such talks were enormously contentious, thanks to the Bolsheviks' perceived betrayal at Brest-Litovsk in March 1918. The Treaty of Brest-Litovsk, negotiated directly between Russia and the Central Powers, had ended the war in the east, freeing Germany to focus its might on the Western Front. This caused understandable consternation among the Allies. Upon entering the war, the United Kingdom, France, and Russia—the so-called Triple Entente—had each agreed not to conclude a separate peace. Yet the Bolsheviks did not feel bound by the tsar's promises.

Following the Allied victory, Clemenceau, alongside British secretary of war Winston Churchill, argued for intervening in the Russian Civil War in support of anti-Bolshevik forces. But Wilson and Lloyd George opposed, deeming the idea too risky.[11] All over Europe and the United States, the Bolshevik Revolution had politically powerful supporters who approved of a rebellion against what they considered an exploitative, domineering, and imperialist order that had sent millions of soldiers and civilians to die for their rulers' profit. As Wilson saw it, there was not a Western country that could safely deploy troops to Russia without creating troubles at home. After Brest-Litovsk, the United States had agreed to join its allies in deploying troops to the northern Russian towns of Arkhangelsk and Murmansk to prevent munitions previously sent to Russia from falling into German hands and to preserve the economic blockade against Germany.[12] But directly supporting the White Russians in their war against the Reds was a step too far.

Philip Kerr, personal and political secretary to Lloyd George, provided Bullitt with a list of conditions upon which he thought it would be possible for the Allied governments to establish normal relations with the new Russia. Hostilities would have to cease on all fronts of the Russian Civil War. All Russian parties claiming the authority of the state must be allowed to remain in control of whatever territories they occupied at the time, meaning that the Bolsheviks and the

White Russians would each keep their lands. The Allies would then agree to trade relations with the various governments succeeding Imperial Russia and would reopen supply routes.[13]

Negotiating secretly with the Bolsheviks, on the sidelines of Versailles, was a bold move. But Bullitt was determined to succeed. On March 11, the day he arrived in Moscow, he held face-to-face discussions with Lenin. For three days after that, Bullitt conducted negotiations with the Russian minister of foreign affairs, with Lenin nearby. Lenin eventually agreed to a proposal including all the points that Lloyd George and Kerr had charged Bullitt with obtaining. And Bullitt won additional concessions: political opponents of the Bolsheviks would be granted amnesty, and the tsar's successor governments would recognize full responsibility for paying the former empire's foreign debts. Lenin gave the Allies until April 10 to sign the agreement.[14] On March 25 Bullitt returned to Paris. That night, excited by Bullitt's debriefs, Colonel House called on Wilson, and the president invited Bullitt for an appointment the following afternoon.

The morning of the twenty-sixth, before his appointment with Wilson, Bullitt breakfasted with Lloyd George, Kerr, and General Jan Smuts, who represented South Africa at the Paris conference. All found Bullitt's report of the utmost importance; every indication was that they found the terms of Lenin's proposal entirely acceptable. However, that same morning, the influential editorialist Wickham Steed denounced the Allies' apparent readiness to accept the evil of Bolshevism. All the English-speaking attendees at the conference read Steed's rebuke in Paris's *Daily Mail*; he accused the Allies of accepting the plague of Communist dictatorship in exchange merely for the prospect of business opportunities in Russia.[15] Lloyd George, who was very sensitive to the press, decided he could not openly promote Lenin's proposal, but he still hoped it would win the day. He authorized Kerr to tell "Wilson that if he wanted to bring Lenin's proposal before the Council of Four, [Wilson] could count upon [Lloyd George's] support for consideration of it and probably acceptance of it."[16]

But before Bullitt could meet with Wilson, the president canceled the appointment, claiming a headache. The meeting was rescheduled for the following day, then canceled again. Wilson carried on refusing to meet with Bullitt until Lenin's April 10 deadline passed.

The new Russian state therefore never committed to laying down arms in the civil war and a fortiori was not included in the Treaty of Versailles or the League of Nations, which required signatories to recognize the borders of all member states. Wilson, it seems, had been convinced that the Bolsheviks would soon lose control of Moscow to the White Russians, who had wrested a hundred miles from the Bolsheviks in the previous week. Yet the opposite happened. The Bolsheviks quickly regained territory and by summer were moving toward victory across the area previously controlled by White Russians and toward possible expansion beyond the borders of Russia.

The Senate was therefore forced to confront a grave question: if, in the near future, Bolshevist armies spread into the rest of Europe, wouldn't the United States be at war? Bullitt laid before the senators Wilson's own draft of the league covenant, written on the president's typewriter. "So far as I know, in the final form of the League the only proposal of the president that remains more or less intact is Article X," Bullitt told the senators. It was hard to see how Wilson was not committing the United States to a war that seemed almost certain to arise, and not least because of the president's own miscalculations.[17]

Losing the War for Public Opinion

Wilson's refusal to act on Lenin's proposal was not the only revelation of Bullitt's testimony. Bullitt also told the senators about a conversation he and Secretary of State Lansing had in Paris, after Bullitt had submitted his resignation.

According to Bullitt's notes, Lansing had called parts of the treaty "thoroughly bad" and the League of Nations "entirely useless." Lansing thought France and Britain had gotten everything they wanted into the treaty, at the expense of ensuring dangerously high levels of resentment not only in Germany but also among colonized peoples—Irish, Arabs, Indians, and so on—who hoped that the league and treaty would assure them national self-determination. Instead, thanks to the Treaty of Versailles and various other treaties negotiated in Paris, many colonized peoples would remain under domination, if perhaps that of a new power. Nothing could be done to alter the unjust clauses the French and British imposed. Once the treaty was in place, the results would be potentially calamitous for the United States, thanks again to Article X of the league covenant, which guaranteed the territorial integrity of all member states. If the agreements did not draw the United States into war with the Russians, then they would draw the United States into some other war. "I believe," Lansing had told Bullitt, "that if the Senate could only understand what this treaty means, and if the American people could really understand, it would unquestionably be defeated, but I wonder if they will ever understand what it lets them in for." When Bullitt testified to these words, the senators responded with laughter.[18]

Hardly had the hearing concluded before Secretary Lansing judged Bullitt "a contemptible little traitor."[19] "If I happen to meet him—which I probably will not—I shall probably tell him what I think of him in terms straight from the shoulder," wrote William Phillips, an assistant secretary of state under Lansing.[20] The senators well understood that Bullitt was generating enemies among powerful men who were once his friends. As the hearing was wrapping up, Pennsylvania Republican Philander Knox asked, "What are your plans Mr. Bullitt?" He replied, "I expect to return to Maine and fish for trout, where I was when I was summoned by the committee."[21]

Bullitt's bombshell testimony was felt in Paris, where negotiations on assorted other treaties were continuing.[22] By revealing Lloyd George's support for his mission to Moscow, Bullitt succeeded in completely upsetting the British prime minister, who characterized the testimony as a "tissue of lies," at least as far as it related to him.[23] Clemenceau—the subject of an assassination attempt in February 1919—joked about Lansing, "I received my bullet at the conference; he his Bullitt only after he got home."[24] In the United States, it was the revelation of Lansing's opposition to the League of Nations that seemed most damning. This confidential information supplied "fresh capital for the political enemies of the Treaty and of the President," the *New York Times* reported.[25] Lansing decided to remain silent. There was enough truth in Bullitt's testimony that he could not flatly deny it.[26] Refusing to comment, the secretary of state himself left Washington for a fishing trip of his own, on Lake Ontario.

Wilson was in San Francisco, in the midst of his speaking tour, when he got news of Bullitt's testimony. Wilson's secretary, Joseph Tumulty, noted that his boss was "distressed and incensed beyond measure," but the president decided to make no comment. Lansing's long silence only heightened Wilson's feelings of betrayal. Nine days later—on September 21, while in Los Angeles—Wilson received a cable from Lansing, confessing that during his conversation with Bullitt he had "recognized that certain features of the treaty were bad, as I presumed most every one did," and that "the Senate and possibly the people, if they understood this, would refuse ratification."[27] Wilson turned to Tumulty and with a deep show of feeling said, "Read that, and tell me what you think of a man who was my associate on the other side and who confidentially expressed himself to an outsider in such a fashion? Think of it! This from a man whom I raised from the level of a subordinate to the great office of secretary of state of the United States. My God!"[28] At the end of his telegram, Lansing, clearly hoping to quell any tension, asked Wilson, "Do you think it would be wise for me to make a statement? . . . I wish to do everything I can to help in the ratification."[29] Wilson did not reply.

Perhaps in response to Bullitt's testimony and the wide coverage it was receiving, Wilson delivered his most compelling and thoughtful defense of the treaty during those days in California. With grand rhetorical flourish, he would tell his audience, "The treaty was not written, essentially speaking, at Paris. It was written at Chateau-Thierry, and in Belleau Wood, and in the Argonne." These were some of the war's major late-stage battles, where US soldiers had fought and died in large numbers. "Our men did not fight over there for the purpose of coming back and letting the same thing happen again," Wilson thundered, asserting that the Versailles Treaty and the League of Nations were the guarantors of peace that the world needed.[30] Indeed, Wilson claimed that, had the league been in place "in 1914, the war would have been impossible." The "absolute isolation and boycott" required by the league's sanctions regime would prevent war.[31] And, in any case, the United States would not be forced into war: "Not a single affirmative act or negative decision by the League of Nations can be validated without the vote of the United States," Wilson told his audience in San Francisco.[32] It was true: the decision to invoke Article X required the unanimous agreement of the Executive Council, the league's dispute-settlement organ.

As a permanent member of the council, the United States would have a de facto veto.

Even as Wilson was making powerful arguments—and affirming the US veto power more strongly than he did with the senators—his body was falling apart. Lansing's treachery does not seem to have helped. On the morning that Lansing's cable arrived, Admiral Cary Grayson, a surgeon who had been Wilson's personal doctor since the president entered the White House, began noticing "the first physical signs of the break in Mr. Wilson." Wilson had already suffered painful headaches and asthma that prevented him from sleeping, and an alarmed Dr. Grayson had even considered canceling the rest of the trip.

On September 22, while in Reno, Wilson complained of blinding headaches, breathing difficulties, and exhaustion, leading him to deliver the worst speech of his tour on the following day, in Salt Lake City. Wilson read aloud passages from a treaty reservation written by moderate Republican senators. A reservation is a state's tool for interpreting a treaty obligation narrowly, without actually rejecting the terms of the obligation. In this case, the senators were pro-treaty and pro-league but had concerns about infringements on US sovereignty—specifically, that the treaty could require the United States to join a war even in the absence of congressional approval as required by the US Constitution.[33] The audience, far from scandalized by these excerpts, erupted in applause. Wilson struggled to explain why he disagreed with the senators and the audience. Of course, he agreed "that in order for the United States to go to war it is necessary for Congress to act."[34] But the senators' reservation overstepped the bounds of constitutional nicety to strike at the moral heart of the league and the role the United States, or at least its president, had agreed to play in preserving peace. With the audience apparently unmoved, Wilson turned to calumny, falsely claiming that all signatories of the treaty including Germany had to agree to reservations. Wilson was trying to suggest that, by putting forth their reservation, the Republican senators were carrying water for the enemy—for the Germans. His case was neither clear nor convincing.

From there, Wilson's health and effectiveness worsened further. On September 25, in Pueblo, Colorado, Admiral Grayson noticed "drooling and a drooping on the left side of [Wilson's] face."[35] Under pressure from his doctor, the president reluctantly agreed to cancel the rest of the trip and was rushed back to the White House. On October 2, he awoke paralyzed on the left side of his body. Top medical specialists, led by the renowned neurologist F. X. Dercum, were assembled at the White House. The diagnosis was swift and secret: the president had suffered an ischemic stroke.[36]

During the days that followed, Wilson hovered between life and death. The possibility of his resignation or temporary replacement by the vice president was raised.[37] In Paris, Clemenceau quipped that the US Constitution "provides for a well president or a dead president but not for a sick president."[38] But, all joking aside, the French leader's mood was somber. The well-being of the treaty, no less than the president, was in doubt. As Wilson fought for his life, the White House was reorganized as a hospital ward.[39] He suffered a prostate infection, leading to a urinary blockage and high fever but could not undergo surgery in his condition. The best his attendants could do was apply hot compresses to reduce the swelling and temporarily relieve the blockage.[40] For weeks, Wilson "just lay helpless . . . He was lifted out of bed and placed in a comfortable chair for a short while each day."[41] He kept an electric light on a stand by his bed, and Grayson noted that when Wilson would awake and call the nurse, he would pick up the light and turn it toward a picture of his first wife, Ellen. He would look at the picture intensely for a few seconds before making his request of the nurse. This was a routine matter, done "literally hundreds of times."[42] Wilson's beard also grew to quite a considerable length during his illness. Two days before a visit from the prince of Wales—the future King Edward VIII—the president asked for a mirror before being shaven, looked closely at his own reflection, and turned to his doctor to recite his favorite limerick:

> Doctor,
> For beauty I am not a star,
> There are others more handsome by far,
> But my face I don't mind it
> For I am behind it
> It's the folks in front that I jar.[43]

Meanwhile, Britain, France, and Italy had ratified the treaty and were anxiously awaiting the US decision. Sixteen senators were intractably opposed to the treaty: fourteen Republicans and two Democrats. These "irreconcilables," as they were known, would vote against any version of the treaty, revised or not. The Senate Foreign Relations Committee had in fact passed forty-five amendments, but, unlike reservations, amendments were a nonstarter. To adopt them would have necessitated renegotiating the treaty with the other signatory countries, and there was no chance of Senate passage in any case—not with the irreconcilables, all the Senate Democrats, and nine "mild" reservationist Republicans opposed.

Appreciating that amendments were a dead end, Lodge gave his attention to reservations, four of them in particular. First, the United States must retain an unconditional right to withdraw from the league. Second, Lodge wanted to affirm that the league had no right to intrude in US domestic affairs. Third, the agreement had to guarantee the Monroe Doctrine, which held that European nations could not be allowed to intervene in the Western Hemisphere against US interests. The fourth and most important reservation would reaffirm the constitutional right of Congress to approve any military action, no matter what Article X said.[44]

The math was clear. To get a two-thirds majority as required to accept treaties, senators who fully supported the treaty needed to compromise and accept the reservations. It seemed like this is precisely what would happen. Hiram Johnson, the popular California senator and an irreconcilable treaty opponent, was convinced that his position had lost—that a settlement would emerge allowing "the President to shout in silence that he had a league of nations."[45]

But Johnson and other irreconcilables did not reckon on a reenergized Wilson. The president himself defeated the compromise that would have given him his treaty and his league, albeit in a somewhat stripped-down version. On November 18, Wilson wrote a letter stating that the reservations did not "provide for ratification but for nullification." He called for a "vote against the Lodge resolution of ratification."[46] The following day, the treaty without reservations garnered fifty-three yeas and thirty-eight nays, failing to meet the two-thirds threshold for passage. And with Wilson adamantly opposed, the treaty with reservations got only thirty-nine votes in favor, most of them from Republicans.

As Lodge predicted, Bullitt's testimony, and especially Lansing's hesitations about the treaty, poisoned ratification of the treaty without reservations.[47] Throughout the Senate debates, Lansing's confession was routinely invoked by the irreconcilables, destroying what remained of the secretary of state's credibility. He was forced to defend on the Senate floor a treaty he was on record demeaning, and the senators did not let him forget it.[48] For instance, on November 5, Missouri senator James Reed, a rare Democrat opposing ratification, recalled for his colleagues that in the fifty-three days since Bullitt's testimony, Lansing had not said a word publicly about it: "When it takes a man fifty-three days to deny a proposition of this kind, that is too long a preparation for the presentation of the simple truth."[49] On November 19, the day of the final vote, Connecticut Republican Frank Brandegee explained that his "no" was inspired by the secretary of state's question to Bullitt: "What does it let us in for?" "No man can tell," Brandegee added, "but I know this, that it lets you in for the first step, and the first step on the downward course is the fatal one, Mr. President."[50]

In Washington, the failure of ratification was celebrated by Wilson's opponents. A party broke out at the home of Alice Roosevelt, daughter of former president Theodore Roosevelt and a patron of Republican conviviality. For his part, Bullitt was secluded with Ernesta, his wife, in rural Vermont. He felt he had accomplished his mission. He had opposed the treaty and the league, feeling certain that the former would lead to further wars and that the latter would ensnare the United States in those wars. And, thanks to Wilson's stubbornness, Bullitt had won.

On the Verge

For the treaty's supporters, however, the struggle was not yet over. Wilson's advisers and allies mobilized for a new vote to get the treaty passed.

At this time, concern was rising again regarding the president's health. No one could see him without the permission of his wife, Edith. She acted as a gatekeeper, reading all the papers coming to the presidential office and deciding which ones should be given to her husband. Too sick to write his own State of the Union address, Wilson left the task to his stenographer, Charles Swem, under the direction of his secretary, Tumulty. Edith then corrected the draft, presumably under the dictation of her husband.[51] Rumors of a "boudoir government" circulated, and eventually Wilson agreed to a visit from a Senate delegation comprising Albert B. Fall, Republican from New Mexico, and Gilbert Hitchcock, the Nebraska Democrat and minority leader. With his wife at his (right) side, Wilson passed the test beautifully. He performed with his full intellectual capacity, convincing both senators that he could, despite his illness, remain in office.

On December 14, Wilson announced that he had "no compromise or concession of any kind in mind but intended . . . that the Republican leaders of the Senate shall continue to bear the undivided responsibility for the fate of the treaty." Wilson regretted that the Constitution did not provide for a popular referendum on the matter. So instead, on December 17, he drafted a letter to fifty-seven senators—listed by name—from thirty-eight states. It was a bizarre list including three Democratic senators who had supported him on the treaty as well as two Republican mild reservationists. A the same time, the letter omitted one irreconcilable, Nebraska Republican George Norris. Wilson was ready to challenge the senators to resign their seats and take immediate steps to seek reelection on the issue of treaty ratification.[52] He was convinced that the vast majority of voters supported him. Wilson promised that if a majority of the senators were reelected, he and Vice President Thomas Marshall would resign and turn the presidency over to a Republican chosen in advance as secretary of state, the position that, at the time, was next in the line of succession.

Fortunately for Wilson, he lacked the will and energy to pursue the plan, which could have raised fresh calls for his removal from office.[53] But he kept in mind the idea of a popular plebiscite on the issue of the league. In a letter read at the Democratic Party's annual Jackson Dinner on January 8, 1920, he told attendees that, "if the Senate wishes to say what the undoubted meaning of the League is, I shall have no objection." Failing that, Wilson proposed a "clear and single way out": "the next election [would take] the form of a great and solemn referendum" on the league.[54]

This statement encouraged a group of Democratic senators with mild reservations to pursue discussions with similarly disposed Republicans. By January 22, hopes for a compromise had never been higher, with Democrats even drafting amendments to the Lodge reservations—including the pivotal Article X reservation—which demonstrated their acceptance of the reservations in principle. Republicans also made some changes to the reservations. Lodge went so far as declaring, "The thing is going to work itself out."[55] Pressure from irreconcilable Republican senators forced Lodge to revert to his previous wording of the reservations, but his statement spoke for itself.[56]

The time seemed propitious for Lord Grey, the former British foreign secretary who had first conceived of the League of Nations, to provide some encouragement. In a letter published by the *New York Times* on January 31, he urged his countrymen and fellow Europeans to accept the US Senate reservations as expressing a desire for cooperation with the Allies—a desire that should be reciprocated. He further argued that nothing was more important for lasting world peace than US participation in implementing the treaty.

Yet Lord Grey's thesis was a blow to one of Wilson's main arguments—that the Lodge reservations would be unacceptable to the Allies.[57] In response, Wilson gave the coup de grâce to the last prospects of an accord. He reacted angrily, saying that if Grey had been in the United States following his statement, "his government would have been promptly asked to withdraw him." Lashing out against others who had wronged him in pursuit of the treaty, Wilson then asked for Secretary of State Lansing's resignation, ostensibly for having, a few months earlier, organized a cabinet meeting in the days following his stroke. Even among Wilson's sympathizers, Lansing's sudden firing raised doubts about the president's judgment and mental health.[58] Raymond Clapper, a United Press correspondent, wrote in his diary that Washington was "astounded at the President's action . . . Many believe he is on the verge of insanity."[59]

John Maynard Keynes, who had been a delegate of the British Treasury at the peace conference and would go on to be the twentieth century's most influential economist, had just published *The Economic Consequences of the Peace,* which painted a devastating portrait of Wilson. Here, behaviors long the subject of rumors and private assessments were aired in public. For Keynes, Wilson was a "blind and deaf Don Quixote" whose personality was a major cause of the treaty's flaws. Writing about Wilson's attitude during the peace negotiations,

Keynes described the most decisive moment "in the disintegration of the President's moral position and the clouding of his mind." This came when Wilson overruled his advisers and agreed that the pensions and separation allowances the Allies owed their soldiers' families could be fairly regarded as "damages" caused by German aggression. This "masterpiece of sophist's art" justified unsustainable reparations, Keynes argued.[60]

Several irreconcilables cited Keynes's book in the Senate. Knox singled out his arguments about the interdependence of economies and the cascading consequences that the ruin of Germany and Austria would have in Europe and the United States.[61] Paul Cravath, a New York lawyer who helped to coordinate Allied finances during the war and was a cofounder of the Council on Foreign Relations, felt that Keynes was charitable with his president. "Unless Wilson is stark'mad or unless Wilson is blinded by disappointment and anger, I believe that some [treaty] compromise will be accomplished," Cravath wrote to Keynes. "But none can forecast the conduct of a man like Wilson when his mental and moral peculiarities are accentuated and perverted by illness and disappointment."[62] Bullitt's friend Lincoln Colcord, one of the major political journalists of his era, was another pessimist. He thought Wilson had become unfit for office. "The President is unbalanced," Colcord wrote Bullitt. "He has his mind and all his faculties, but the factor of judgment does not function."[63]

In the wake of the Grey letter, the president remained inflexible. At the end of February, he resolved that fellow Democrats must reject any reservation "seeking to deprive the League of Nations of the virility of Article X." To accept such a reservation, Wilson believed, was an infringement on the very heart of the treaty. Either the United States entered the treaty without fear of assuming the moral obligation of world leadership, or it withdrew from the great concert of powers. One of the irreconcilable senators noted that, by refusing to compromise, "The President strangled his own child." The *Washington Post* labeled Wilson himself an "affirmative irreconcilable."[64] Senator James E. Watson, Republican of Indiana, wrote in his memoir that he suggested to Wilson that the only way to get the treaty passed was to "accept it with the Lodge reservations," leading Wilson to exclaim, with fire in his eyes, "Accept the treaty with the Lodge reservations? Never!

Never! I'll never consent to adopt any policy with which that impossible name is so prominently identified." Ominously, a number of the most influential Democrat-aligned papers that had backed the treaty, with or without the Lodge reservations, defected.[65]

On the morning of March 19, when the treaty with reservations came to the full Senate for a vote, Lodge seemed to have attracted enough Democratic support to reach the two-thirds majority needed for ratification. It took all the efforts of Hitchcock, the minority leader, along with two members of the cabinet sent by Wilson to the Capitol, to prevent only twenty-one Democrats from disobeying the president. A total of forty-nine senators voted in favor and thirty-five against, seven votes short of the two-thirds majority.[66]

Ten days later, Senator Hitchcock, the Democratic minority leader, and Bainbridge Colby, the new secretary of state, urged Wilson to send the treaty back to the Senate accompanied by reservations already accepted by Britain, France, Italy, and Japan. Doing so would put the burden on his Republican opponents and could make a profound impression on the country. Wilson rejected the proposal out of hand. "At present, the dead treaty lies very heavy on the consciences of those who killed it," he averred, "and I am content to let it lie there until those consciences are either crushed or awakened."[67]

The Versailles Treaty was not all that was mortally wounded; so was the Treaty of Guarantee—the military alliance between Britain, the United States, and France that Clemenceau called "the keystone of European peace." The Treaty of Guarantee was passed in Britain in the summer of 1919, but on the condition that the United States ratify the Versailles Treaty. The Treaty of Guarantee was therefore dead. "Its rejection," Clemenceau lamented, "amounted to an indirect invitation for the thwarted aggressor to try again."[68]

A Broken Piece of Machinery

Wilson apparently recovered enough to consider running for reelection in 1920, but ultimately he stepped aside. However, he still called for making the 1920 presidential race "a great and solemn referendum" on the League of Nations. Wilson believed right up to Election Day that James M. Cox, the Democratic candidate, would win. When his brother-in-law, Stockton Axson, voiced doubts, Wilson replied, "You pessimist! You don't know the American people. They always rise to a moral occasion. Harding will be deluged." Warren G. Harding, a conservative Republican with strong reservationist credentials, instead won in a landslide, with 60.3 percent of the popular vote against 34.1 percent for Cox and his pro-treaty running mate, Franklin D. Roosevelt. Many well-placed observers recognized that Wilson had gotten just the great and solemn referendum he was looking for. "I have never in my experience found the general electorate so bitter against an individual as they were against the president," Lansing wrote to House. "Wilson had become as unpopular as he had once been popular."[69]

The day Wilson left office in March 1921, Lansing made headlines by publishing his memoirs of the peace conference. Lansing's book caused a stir on Capitol Hill and became an instant bestseller. It was compared with Keynes's book, even if Lansing lacked the British economist's stylish prose and mordant wit.[70] "Mr. Wilson moves through its pages like a glacial object," one reviewer noted, "self-sufficient, dominating, one-purposed, a hardly human figure, egotistic, a sort of selfish superman, with one thought and only one—that of imposing his League upon the statesmen of the world while peace waited and the nations despaired."[71] A few weeks later, in place of the Treaty of Versailles, the Senate passed the Knox-Porter Resolution, which officially ended the war between Germany and the United States. President Harding signed it on July 2.

Wilson continued to follow American politics from his home on S Street in Washington D.C. He was pleased with the results of the 1922 midterm elections: Republicans lost seventy-seven seats in the House and seven in the Senate, which Wilson interpreted as a referendum in favor of himself. He confided as much to one of his visitors, Lloyd George's adviser Philip Kerr, who believed the former president had read the results "wrongly."[72] Throughout 1923, the idea that "the Sage of S street" might run again in 1924 was considered "a very probable possibility." Wilson encouraged the idea, refusing to commit himself to another candidate, even as he grew feebler by the day.[73]

On February 1, 1924, Grayson told his patient the truth: he was dying. Wilson breathed, "I am a broken piece of machinery. When the machinery is broken . . ." His voice petered out. There was a moment's silence, and then he said, "I am ready."[74] When he died on February 3, the only property he possessed was in Princeton, New Jersey—a cemetery plot, which he obtained when he had lived there as a professor and then as president of the university. But he had too many unhappy memories from Princeton and had told Edith he did not want to be buried there. Arlington Cemetery would not do either, he said, "because he could not forgive the despoiling of the estate of Lee"—that is General Robert E. Lee, whose wife had owned the land that became Arlington Cemetery and whom Wilson held in high esteem.[75] He was buried instead at Washington National Cathedral.

SINCE HIS SENATE TESTIMONY IN 1919, William Bullitt had turned his back on the world of politics. "There was no honest man in politics," he wrote. "You could not touch it and keep your principles. There were nothing except compromisers."[76] So the shock he felt on learning of the president's death surprised him, as did the memories it awakened.

Bullitt had joined Wilson to pursue the truth. Bullitt believed that only leaders who spoke honestly could maintain the public's trust in public institutions. From childhood, he associated truth with justice. As a youngster vacationing at his family's country house in Devon, Pennsylvania, near Valley Forge, he had absorbed the story of George Washington, who could not tell a lie. The mythical probity of the founding father had left a strong impression. "The Valley was as Washington had left it," he wrote. "There was no park. The doors of Washington's Headquarters hung open on sagging hinges. The windows were broken, the floors white with fallen plaster. But alone, unwatched, unheard, I could talk there with the mighty dead over the dwindling entrenchments, I would ride my pony imagining I was Mad Anthony Wayne or Lafayette: never George Washington. That would have been sacrilege."[77]

Asked later why he risked his career to testify, Bullitt responded that he was concerned by "the fate of millions of Russians dying of starvation and disease, thanks to the Western blockade." In the months and years that followed, he contributed money to fight famine in Russia and Austria. After Lloyd George lifted the Russian blockade and the Anglo-Soviet Trade Agreement was signed in March 1921,

Bullitt congratulated George Lansbury, then leader of the British Labour Party, who had put intense pressure on the prime minister. Bullitt had alienated many, but he did not care. He believed that he had to speak the truth for the good of Americans and others—that this was more important than his friendships or personal honor. "If I skimmed, my testimony would have no effect," he told Ernesta.[78]

And Bullitt knew that he was not alone, despite the hard feelings surrounding him. He closely guarded a letter from Harold Laski, an Englishman and Harvard political scientist who maintained close ties with American progressives and leaders of the British Labour Party. For Laski, Bullitt was an example to follow. "There is a footnote in the history of the future which marks you as the one American in Paris who realized the greatness of the opportunity," Laski wrote. "I do not speak lightly."[79]

2

The Making of William C. Bullitt

WILLIAM CHRISTIAN BULLITT JR. WAS BORN in Philadelphia on January 25, 1891, of wealthy and conservative patrician stock. The family traced back to Joseph Boulet, a French Protestant who fled Nîmes at the close of the Huguenot Wars in 1629 and settled in Maryland, where he changed his name to Bullitt. Joseph Boulet's descendants married into the families of Augustine Washington, the father of George Washington; Anne Henry, the sister of Patrick Henry; and Pocahontas and her husband, the tobacco planter John Rolfe. One descendant, Thomas Bullitt, surveyed the town site that became Louisville, Kentucky, home to several generations of Bullitts until William's grandfather moved to Philadelphia, where he was a major political reformer and author of the city's revised 1887 charter. Bullitt's mother, Louisa Horwitz, was the granddaughter of the most respected American surgeon of the time, Samuel Gross, immortalized in Thomas Eakins's painting *The Gross Clinic* (1875). Each of Bullitt's aunts established themselves in different European capitals: one in London, one in Rome, another in Paris. Horwitz also had a cousin in Berlin. Every summer, Bullitt would accompany his mother on visits to Europe.[1] Bullitt's family conversed in French, and young William also learned German.

On completing his secondary education at the private DeLancey School in Philadelphia, Bullitt chose to attend Yale because his family had no connections there and he wanted to make his own way in the world. He became chief editor of the *Yale Daily News* and president of the Dramatic Association, and he learned to box. He graduated with honors and was voted the most brilliant student of the class of 1912.[2] From there, he went to Harvard Law School, fulfilling his father's wish that William do "as he and his forbears had for many generations." But Bullitt was bored by the law and disliked "the slick cynicism fashionable in the school," typified by a comment he recalled from Professor

Joseph Henry Beale, who once told a student, "If you look for justice in law, you'll find the Divinity School three blocks to the left." After William Sr. died in March 1914, Bullitt dropped out of Harvard Law.

To help his mother escape the melancholy caused by her husband's death, Bullitt traveled with her across Europe. On July 28, 1914, the day Austria-Hungary declared war on Serbia, Bullitt and his mother were in Moscow. "A crowd poured down from Red Square past our corner rooms in the Hotel National shouting: Down with Austria! Hurrah for Serbia," Bullitt wrote.[3] Bullitt and his mother took one of the last trains to London through Warsaw and Berlin. Shortly thereafter, the pair traveled to Dinard, France, where Bullitt's grandmother died on August 24. He proceeded alone to Paris and stayed until October, through the First Battle of the Marne, which raged a mere thirty miles from the capital.

On September 15, after an extraordinary feat of French arms had thwarted the German advance, Bullitt wrote to a friend:

> Paris is tranquil as a becalmed sailboat. When it seemed inevitable that the Germans should be dining with us in a few days, the only sign of anxiety was the absence of one single smile on any face you met in the street. Now that the Germans are licked, at least temporarily, the only difference is that the smiles are there. There have been no mobs, no celebrations. For a while it was amusing to go out and watch the digging of trenches and the cutting of trees in the Bois, but that has become out of style. The only signs of war are the closed shops and thousands of soldiers everywhere, an occasional airplane and huge hordes in the churches. Sunday Notre-Dame and the streets about and the square in front were packed shoulder to shoulder and Jeanne d'Arc's banner and St Genevieve's were paraded. Quite a thrill.[4]

A Journalist in the War

In 1915, at the age of twenty-four, Bullitt returned to the United States to become a journalist. He first mastered touch-typing, then knocked on the door of the *Public Ledger*, the main Philadelphia newspaper at the time, without any introduction. He started at $10 a week as a district reporter working the twelve-hour nightshift in a waterfront section of the city largely populated by African Americans and recent immigrants. He phoned in stories about "raids, shootings, cutting scrapes, and Polish weddings, for a rewrite man to put into type."[5] Soon the *Public Ledger* made him a special correspondent aboard the Peace Ship, an expedition backed by Henry Ford. The expedition was inspired by Women's Peace Party cofounder Jane Addams, who had impressed on Ford and his wife Clara her dismay that 20,000 young men were dying in Europe every day "for little or no territorial gain and no worthy purpose."[6] Addams saw pacifism as a facet of feminism and war as a distinctively masculine vice. Peace negotiations, in her view, went hand-in-hand with the global attainment of women's suffrage.[7]

Ford agreed to finance an expedition to Europe for American pacifists and feminists. The plan was to pick up travelers in Norway, the Netherlands, and Denmark and then land in Stockholm to meet a delegation from Spain and Switzerland for a conference of neutral countries. On December 4, 164 Americans embarked on the *Oscar II.* The passenger manifest included Ford, a judge, business leaders, activists, students, journalists (including Bullitt), and the governor of North Dakota. Suffragists were there in force. Prominent among them was Inez Milholland, known for having led a Washington, D.C., suffrage parade from the back of a white horse during Wilson's March 1913 inauguration.[8]

The Peace Ship journey left Bullitt skeptical. Three days after the *Oscar II* set out, Wilson delivered his State of the Union address, asking Congress to strengthen the armed forces, especially the US Navy, and to invest in the merchant marine. The Peace Ship voyagers were divided about these requests and about the policy of war preparedness they implied. A small minority signed on to a call for Americans to oppose the policy, but no vote among the travelers was allowed.[9] Bullitt archly reported that, despite standing for democratic values, Ford and his fellows "feared democratic control of the peace expedition."[10] Upon arriving in Norway, Ford was ill and confined to his hotel room; on December 23, he decided to return home.[11] The ship continued to Stockholm without him. "His leaving caused much depression among the delegates," Bullitt wrote. Even the more optimistic passengers were now "less hopeful that the expedition will achieve anything toward peace in Europe."[12]

On his return to the United States on January 29, 1916, Bullitt immediately went to Boston to propose to his future wife. Ernesta Drinker was a daughter of the Philadelphia elite, whom Bullitt had met at a party at Yale. This was not the first time Bullitt had asked for her hand—intelligent and beautiful, with black hair and brown-green eyes that changed color depending on the light, she received numerous proposals. She regarded the bachelors of Philadelphia with horror and was unwilling to go along with the future of domesticity they promised. She initially rejected Bullitt, too, but they became comfortable companions. They sailed, swam, danced, and exchanged letters. They talked endlessly, shared books, and listened to music. There were still little things about him she didn't like; he would let slip an insensitive remark or behave tactlessly in public or find humor in something that pained her.

She said no again when he returned from Europe, but this time he changed her mind. They married on March 18 at Lehigh Chapel in Bethlehem, Pennsylvania. "We were happy, we were gay, daily we grew closer," Ernesta remembered. But it was difficult to adapt to "the difference in the male attitude to the married woman from the unmarried." She was the same person, but when unmarried she was "always a possibility, an invitation, a stimulus to competition." As a newly married woman, she was "removed from these horizons of eternal interest." Indeed, she felt as if she did not exist anymore. Distraught by the sudden change, she sought new ways to speak her mind. She decided to write and publish an "uncensored diary" of their honeymoon: a trip to the Central Powers, in the middle of the war.

The newlyweds disembarked in Belgium and found it devastated. In August 1914 Kaiser Wilhelm II's strategists had assumed that Belgium would be weak and passive, allowing a speedy German advance through the territory followed by a surprise assault against the French from across Belgian lines. The unexpectedly strong Belgian resistance disrupted this plan and contributed to the French victory at the Marne. German officers reacted by executing Belgian civilians, burning and pillaging towns, taking hostages, using civilians as human shields, and killing prisoners of war. The university town of Leuven was massacred. The Prussian general Moritz von Bissing told the Bullitts that

Leuven taught the residents of Brussels what would happen if they continued to defy the German invaders.[13]

Several weeks in Germany convinced Ernesta that the country was remarkably resilient. To crush Germany, to bring it to its knees or starve it out, seemed impossible. The Germans disliked Americans for their false neutrality, and the couple felt this enmity daily. At the beginning of the war, Wilson had declared that the United States would remain neutral in thought and deed. However, by letting Britain blockade German ports and mine the North Sea and by ordering the blacklisting of American companies doing business with the Central Powers, the United States made clear that it favored the Allies. The reasons were more pragmatic than ideological: the United States had a relatively small merchant fleet and relied on British ships to transport American passengers and goods. Bullitt was concerned that Germans saw him as a spy. It was not unusual for journalists to work informally for their governments during the First World War.[14] Alongside his reporting for the *Public Ledger,* Bullitt was gathering information that he would keep secret and deliver to the State Department after returning to the United States in fall 1916.[15]

The pair's arrival in Washington coincided with all the excitement of the coming presidential election. Theodore Roosevelt had returned to the Republican Party, after having divided it in 1912 by running against Republican incumbent Taft. Wilson's strategy was to rally the progressives who had supported Roosevelt four years earlier. With that in mind, he named Louis Brandeis, a progressive icon, to the Supreme Court. Wilson also signed the Federal Farm Loan Act, a controversial bill aimed at providing credit to rural farmers, and a child labor law. When railway workers were about to strike for an eight-hour workday, he convinced big business to support the Adamson Act, which delivered that protection for workers.[16] This record earned the support of the Roosevelt progressives, and Wilson was narrowly reelected.

Wilson's success also came on the back of a slogan: "He kept us out of the war." But on April 6, 1917, just a month after his second inauguration, the United States entered the conflict. Since the start of the war, US liberals—which is to say, one of Wilson's main bases of support—had opposed involvement on the grounds that Germany's collapse would mean a victory for the backward and authoritarian Russian Empire.

Their opinion shifted in February 1917. That month, the Romanovs fell, nominally placing Russia in the hands of a moderate socialist provisional government and inaugurating a period of disarray preceding the Bolshevik takeover. And Germany made the fateful commitment to a campaign of unrestricted submarine warfare, which threatened not only British but also US ships. For many American liberals, the Allied cause now appeared just and idealistic: a fight on behalf of democracy against Prussian militarism.

Imagining a Just Peace

It was the preeminent political writer Walter Lippmann who coined the phrase that crystallized Wilson's goal for Europe: "peace without victory." Lippmann had worked for Wilson since his reelection campaign, and on January 22, 1917, Wilson borrowed the phrase in a speech describing his aims.[17] In April, five days after the United States officially joined the war on the side of the French and British Allies, Lippmann gave House a plan for ideological mobilization at home. Wilson immediately endorsed it. He also began making speeches aimed at German and Austro-Hungarian imperial subjects. In these speeches, Wilson emphasized the importance of self-government, hoping to influence those subjects and weaken their will to fight by contrasting the aims of their masters with those of the United States.

Soon the State Department asked Bullitt to join its Enemy Desk with the task of coordinating these propaganda efforts.[18] Bullitt would gather information from the Central Powers to guide the president and his speechwriters. He also persuaded Wilson to quote German liberals in his speeches with the aim of detaching them from the Kaiser.[19] This effort at ideological mobilization was arguably the first major American contribution to the Allied war effort. Bullitt relished the work and found the State Department staff modest and efficient.

Meanwhile, Lippmann and Colonel House directed the Inquiry, a study group whose 200 experts in global affairs sought to prepare the United States for participation in the international peace conference that was bound to follow the end of the war. After the Soviet government revealed the existence of the Allies' secret treaties in November 1917, Lippmann spent three weeks, often working through the night, writing eight of Wilson's Fourteen Points, specifically those that dealt with concrete territorial issues—the sort that arose from the secret treaties. Then Wilson worked with House to add the general points, including guaranteeing freedom of the seas and establishing a League of Nations. On January 8, 1918, Wilson delivered the Fourteen Points to Congress. At 3 a.m. in Paris, Georges Mandel, Clemenceau's powerful chief of staff, received the Fourteen Points. Clemenceau demanded his sleep, but Mandel understood the gravity of what he was reading. "I will wake up Mr. Clemenceau" was all he said.[20] The speech made an equally strong impression in the Central Powers. Bullitt believed that, with his Fourteen Points speech, the president had effectively arrogated to himself leadership of liberals in Germany and Austria-Hungary. "The Liberals and Socialists of the Central Empires no longer suspect the President's good faith," Bullitt reported to a thrilled House.[21]

The Germans failed to end the war with a spring 1918 military offensive, but they were still on the attack in mid-July. Like most Americans, Bullitt assumed the war could not be won before the end of the year. Yet the German unraveling commenced on August 8 at Amiens, with the opening of a surprise Allied offensive. The battle lasted several days, but the Germans suffered enormous losses from the start; morale was crushed and soldiers surrendered in droves. General Erich Ludendorff, Germany's top strategist and military commander, called August 8 "the black day of the German Army." In the first week of September, the Austrian government issued its first peace note. To preserve the honor of the German Army, and to secure more favorable terms, Ludendorff asked his government to parlay directly with Wilson on conditions of armistice. While Wilson was exchanging letters with the Germans, House rushed to Paris and met with Lloyd George, Clemenceau, and Orlando. Confronted with their reservations about the Fourteen Points, House warned them about a separate peace with Germany.[22] After four days of tough negotiations, the British and French were ready to accept the Fourteen Points as the basis of the coming peace treaty, but they had one concern: the Fourteen Points mentioned reparations only in passing. After the immense costs of four years of war, the British and French demanded compensation. To fail in this regard would be to lose the support of an inflamed public.

Indeed, reparations were needed not only to provide financially after all that had been sacrificed, but also to punish the Germans. Even as it sued for peace, Germany had torpedoed the British steamer *Leinster* in the Irish Sea on October 16, killing 450 men, women, and children.[23] Retreating German forces had dynamited and flooded towns in Belgium and northern France, reducing factories, mines, roads, and railways to ashes.

Clemenceau proposed that the words "reparation for damage" be included in the armistice agreement as a "moral satisfaction," even if it would be only "implemented after the peace treaty was signed."[24] For the British, this did not go far enough. They insisted on being compensated not just for the material losses their enemies had inflicted. Their proposal that "compensation will be made by Germany for all damage caused to the civilian population of the Allies and their property by the aggression by Germany of Allied territory, by land, by sea, and from the air" was accepted, and the Allied memorandum approving the Fourteen Points as the basis for peace negotiations was transmitted to Wilson. On November 5 he forwarded the memorandum to the Germans, who also accepted, leading to the mutual signing of the armistice on November 11. Wilson was so thrilled that he decided to personally represent the United States at the peace conference in Paris, ignoring House's advice to stay in Washington. It was the first time a US president left the shores of the country while in office.

On December 3, Wilson sailed from Hoboken, New Jersey, aboard the USS *George Washington*. Bullitt was among the presidential retinue. The weather during the trip was warm and sunny. The president spent his evenings watching movies. After a few days, Bullitt noticed that none of the commissioners from the official US delegation nor any of the Inquiry specialists sailing with the president had held a meeting with him. None of them had any idea what they would be asked to do once they arrived in Paris. One evening Wilson told Jean-Jules Jusserand, France's ambassador to the United States, that he "meant nothing more by a League of Nations than an agreement by all the nations which sign the peace treaty to abide by its terms and to join in coercing any nation[s] which violate them." Bullitt could hardly believe that Wilson's ambitions for the league were so slight.

Soon thereafter Bullitt sat down beside the president at one of the film projections and suggested that "he ought to call together the members of the Inquiry and explain to them the spirit in which he was approaching the conference." Bullitt warned that their ignorance of the president's plans was making some of them skeptical, even cynical. Wilson took the advice. At noon the following day, he convened ten members of the Inquiry and in a "frank and engaging mood" clarified his position. Wilson said he believed in a League of Nations run by a council of ministers who would report to their governments. "War," he said, "must no longer be considered an exclusive business. Any war must be considered as affecting the whole world." Wilson expressed his belief in absolute economic boycott by the members of the league, cutting off any aggressor not only from goods but also from rail systems and from communications via telephone, telegraph, and postal mail. The German colonies should be administered by the league, he thought, and he would oppose any indemnity except for damages actually caused by Germany. "The conference broke up with the decentest sort of feeling," Bullitt noted in his diary. "All the soreness of the past week was gone."[25]

Wilson arrived in Paris on December 14, to an "an immense cry of love," according to a headline splashed across six front-page columns of *Petit Parisien*.[26] The whole world was on its way to Paris, the victors to demand reparations and redrawn borders; the Germans and the Austrians in the hope that the American president would secure a just peace; and representatives of the colonized, to collect on the promise of national self-determination. Wilson was treated as a prophet as much as a politician. "When Washington and Lincoln spoke, they spoke to America," the South African delegate Jan Christiaan Smuts noted. "When Wilson spoke, he spoke to the world."[27]

The beginning of the conference had been postponed due to the British elections on December 14. After a landslide in favor of his coalition, Lloyd George met with Wilson in London. There, Wilson got to know Smuts, a central figure in South African politics, who had once served as a Boer general. One of the architects of the union of South Africa, and of racial segregation within it, he was also the author of a pamphlet that influenced Wilson, "The League of Nations: A Practical Suggestion." Like Wilson, Smuts saw the league not as a court of arbitration but as a political forum—an association of "civilized" nations, rather than a cohort of the most powerful ones, in which the culture of war would give way to a culture of democracy.[28] Wilson also adopted Smuts's suggestions concerning the organization of the league, which would be based on a tripartite structure, with an executive council, general assembly, and secretariat.[29]

In Paris, Bullitt was an indispensable figure within the US diplomatic corps. As chief of the Division of Current Intelligence Summaries, he synthesized incoming telegrams and press reports in English, French, and German and debriefed each commissioner on their contents. This would take place each morning while they were dressing, shaving, or breakfasting. Bullitt met first with General Tasker H. Bliss at 9:00 a.m. At 9:20, he would meet with Henry White, an accomplished diplomat who came out of retirement to join the conference. Colonel House was next, at 9:40. Secretary of State Lansing followed at 10:00, and finally President Wilson himself at 10:30.[30]

Bullitt was not just a functionary, however. He was also involved in strategizing the US mission. In July 1918, in anticipation of eventual victory, Bullitt had drafted instructions sent to US embassies, asking them to report on the political forces in their respective countries that could be marshaled to back Wilson's plan.[31] From all reports, the main forces at play were the Labour Party in Britain and socialists on the continent, as well as a few liberals. For Bullitt, the movement for social democracy was about to occupy much the same place in twentieth-century politics as the movement for a democratic franchise had during the nineteenth century.[32] He pressed for broad cooperation among liberals, socialists, and labor organizations in all the belligerent countries as the best way to implement the president's program for a lasting world peace. But there was another motive, too: a European social democratic order might be able to head off the spread of Bolshevism, the main alternative to its left.

Frustration upon Frustration

It was with this strategy in mind that House dispatched Bullitt to meet with the continent's foremost socialists. In France, he held talks with the politicians Albert Thomas, Marcel Cachin, and Jean Longuet. In

Bern, he attended the Socialist International as the official representative of the American Commission to Negotiate Peace.[33]

All the socialist leaders of the ex-belligerent countries were in Bern: Cachin for the French socialists, Ramsay MacDonald for Labour, and Kurt Eisner for the German Social Democrats, the charismatic head of government in Bavaria who would be assassinated a few days after the Bern conference ended. The war had exacerbated the national and ideological tensions among them but also ignited a shared hope for an end to all wars. Collectively, they backed the league as proposed by Wilson, with one caveat: they wanted the league to include an assembly comprising delegates from national parliaments, representing all parties, including minority ones. This would ensure that the league was a real union of peoples, instead of ministers and diplomats. Bullitt and Cachin prepared a resolution announcing the proposal, MacDonald presented it, and the conference adopted it unanimously.[34]

Bullitt could not have been happier. His American colleagues were also impressed by his warm and confident relationship with senior socialist figures.[35] Bullitt returned to Paris from Bern armed with the socialist resolution, and House asked him to draw up amendments to the league covenant reflecting the socialists' wishes.[36] Bullitt's amendment was then transmitted to Wilson who, since February 3, had been presiding personally over the committee in charge of drafting the covenant. On February 14, he presented the draft covenant to 200 people assembled in a plenary conference. A "living thing is born," he announced, his hands resting on a bible.[37] The covenant was adopted unanimously—with Bullitt's amendment nowhere included.

The omission of the proposal undermined Wilson's standing among socialists, a major force in European politics. And he squandered an opportunity to democratize the league, which would likely have appealed to Republicans back home, concerned as they were to have a say in league decisions affecting the United States. Deeply disappointed, Bullitt considered resigning from the American delegation that day, while the treaty was still under negotiation. Colonel House, however, revived his spirits with a mind-blowing proposal: the secret mission to Russia.[38]

Even as "Bullitt obtained from Lenin terms far more favorable than anyone could have expected," the Russian offer went nowhere.[39]

Bullitt's cables to House boasting about the deal were picked up by French intelligence, and outraged officials leaked the information to the press.[40] Wilson, in Paris working on the treaty, received a cable from the White House reporting that "the proposed recognition of Lenin had caused consternation here."[41] Instead of backing the proposal, the president decided to support Herbert Hoover's recommendation that the Allies provide relief to Russia in exchange for a halt to Bolshevik military operations beyond certain borders—including "destabilization operations" abroad. The Bolsheviks rejected the Hoover plan.[42]

By this point, in April 1919, Wilson had other preoccupations besides Russia. His return to the United States for a short trip in mid-February, after the unanimous adoption of the league covenant, did not go well. On March 3, a few days after his meeting with the Senate Foreign Relations Committee, Lodge read a resolution signed by thirty-eight senators—enough to block ratification of the treaty—affirming their opposition to the draft of the Covenant. When Wilson returned to France on March 13, he was informed that Colonel House had agreed that the financial and territorial clauses be included in a preliminary treaty, while the league covenant would appear in the final treaty. Wilson bristled and immediately announced that there would be only one treaty, and it would include the league. To separate the league from the rest of the treaty, he feared, would give the Senate a chance to approve territorial claims and reparations clauses while later scuttling the league. Wilson considered House's position a deep betrayal. Even if House remained Wilson's adviser, their relationship was permanently marred. However, House did convince him of the need to accept some amendments suggested by former president Taft to placate opposition in the Senate. These included a requirement that the Executive Council agree unanimously in order to pursue any action as well as safeguards against the league's intervention in the domestic affairs of member states. The whole American delegation then turned to winning the approval of Clemenceau and Lloyd George.[43]

Lloyd George also had retreated from the Russian matter, never even mentioning the Bullitt mission to Wilson, and Lenin's April 10 deadline passed. A few weeks later, after the *Times* of London published a pamphlet signed by 200 British MPs urging Lloyd George not to recognize the Soviet government, the prime minister denied any involvement with Bullitt's mission. Adolf Berle, one of the US delegates, later remembered: "When Lloyd George refused all knowledge of his mission, when Wilson disavowed it, [Bullitt] was, as he thought, discredited by the people who had every right to congratulate him on having done what he was sent to do."[44] One consolation for Bullitt was that Ernesta had finally arrived in Paris from the United States. She might have come earlier but had stayed home to take care of Bullitt's mother. She died on January 20, after a severe attack of influenza.[45]

On Ernesta's first night in Paris, husband and wife dined together with a small group. She spent much of the evening talking about the Crusades with a shy fellow at the table. "Who is he?" she asked after the man had left. There was an incredulous sound from the others and a shout from her husband. Why, he was the most talked-about man in Europe, the most colorful figure of the conference: Lawrence of Arabia. She had never heard of him until that moment. "And I was so careful to put him at his ease," she said carefully. "Darling," Bullitt said, "you're marvelous." In the days to come, he had plenty of time to tell her everything that had happened in Paris since December, and she was proud of him. She thought he had been at his best during the Russian mission. All of his imagination, foresight, and energy came into play. His impudence was an asset, as were his sense of drama, fun, and self-importance, which "led him along paths others would have feared to tread."[46]

While waiting for the completion of the peace treaty, Bullitt moved on to other diplomatic causes, such as Zionism, which occupied his attention from the day he arrived in Paris. Over the course of several weeks, he advocated zealously on behalf of Chaim Weizmann and Aaron Aaronsohn, the Zionist delegates at the conference. He opened "all the doors that needed to be opened."[47] When Weizmann had readied a first draft of the Zionist proposal for a partition of Palestine, he told Aaronson to show a copy "strictly confidentially *only* to Bullitt."[48]

Bullitt also promoted Irish demands for independence, welcoming Edward F. Dunne, the former mayor of Chicago and governor of Illinois, and two other Irish American delegates in Paris and securing permission from Kerr for them to travel to Ireland. But Irish independence was a lost cause, certain to alienate the British. Wilson ignored the appeals of Irish American delegates and called them "mischief makers."[49]

Wilson seemed increasingly implacable, and his decisions kept reversing Bullitt's efforts. Bullitt rejoiced when Wilson decided to go home, leaving the rest of the commissioners to handle the treaty. "The President was fed up, he was refusing to sign the treaty," Bullitt announced to Longuet, the French socialist.[50] But soon enough the president changed his mind. He canceled his departure and remained in Paris to personally carry on the negotiations with France, Britain, and Italy.

On May 7, a treaty was finally presented to Ulrich von Brockdorff-Rantzau, the German minister of foreign affairs, at Versailles. Two days later, Berle and Bullitt read the text. They discovered that in the previous month Wilson had made a series of concessions on territorial and reparations issues. He had also agreed to guarantee the territorial integrity of member states.[51] Over the next few days, almost to a man, the US commission despaired of what the treaty had become.[52] As the journalist and US delegate Arthur Sweetser—once a strong Wilsonian—put it:

> No one in the American Commission regarded [the treaty] as a Peace of the Fourteen Points. The Saar (obviously a trading of Germans for reparations), the West Prussia and Silesian Boundaries, the selling off of Shantung to Japan, the prohibition against self-determination in German Austria—all seemed on the ragged edge of violating the Fourteen Points. Each case, taken by itself, was arguable, but, in their entirety, they produce a treaty which obviously did not accord with the liberal spirit which seemed to have been in the original Points.[53]

When Bullitt's letter of resignation became public on May 23, about twenty members of the US delegation met at the Hotel Crillon for a protest dinner, which also served as a farewell for Bullitt.[54] On May 27, the Bullitts left Paris for Oxford. Several colleagues and friends accompanied them to the train station to salute him. Oswald Villard, editor of the *Nation,* wrote him a heartfelt goodbye: "I hope that your cheerful countenance and never-failing good humor will still continue to radiate through the gloom in spite of all discouragements." In the magazine itself, Villard denounced all the "liberals" who had "succumbed to the temptation of power" and acknowledged "the courageous act of the only decent representative of the liberals—William C. Bullitt."[55] Herbert Croly, editor of the *New Republic*, wrote to Bullitt to tell him how much he admired his act of open protest against the treaty. Croly, too, made his opinion public in an editorial titled, "This Is Not Peace."[56]

A Wilsonian No More

After his resignation, Bullitt became a champion of those who had lost confidence in Wilson. The president had accrued many enemies. His support for amending the Espionage Act to outlaw criticism of the Constitution, government, and flag was widely reviled. And despair over the treaties he had signed in Paris only consummated the break. Lincoln Colcord, the journalist, wrote Bullitt that his gesture had made a big impact in the capital, and that forces in the Senate were following "with the keenest interest." There was a "shifting political situation," and Colcord urged Bullitt to "come home immediately."[57]

The Bullitts hastened their return, arriving in Philadelphia at the end of June. From there, Bullitt went to Long Island to work with Colcord on a new project: preparing the case against the treaty, using documents that Bullitt had transported from the Paris conference.[58] At this point, there was no plan for a hearing, but, through Hiram Johnson, Colcord reached out to the Republican senators. Later, when the subpoena for testimony arrived, Bullitt got over his jitters quickly. He knew what had to be done.

After his explosive Senate testimony, Bullitt's star rose still higher among disaffected liberals. Walter Lippmann exulted. "Wilson has begun to maunder," he wrote to a friend. "Billy Bullitt blurted out everything to the . . . delight of the Republicans. When there is an almost universal conspiracy to lie and smother the truth, I suppose someone has to violate the decencies." The *New Republic* praised him as one of the few who was not "too fearful of doing or speaking out to let their heart and conscience dictate their actions and speech." The *Nation* published Bullitt's testimony in full.[59]

The most daring word of congratulations came from Jack Reed, the impetuous and adventurous American journalist famous for his coverage of the 1913 Mexican Revolution and of the Bolsheviks. On their way to New Hampshire to stay at Croly's summer cottage, Bullitt and Ernesta stopped overnight at the Belmont Hotel in New York, where they received a phone call in their room. Ernesta picked up: "It's a Mr. Reed for you."[60] "God," Bullitt cried, "Jack Reed, he's crazy." It was indeed a dangerous choice by Reed, who was waiting downstairs in the lobby. Reed had just founded the Communist Labor Party, with the aim of replicating the Bolshevik triumph in America. But only a week after the party's founding, police went on strike in Boston, leading to a full-blown insurrection. Crowds surged through the streets looting, smashing store windows, and padlocking doors. Troops were called in and opened fire, killing five and wounding scores more. Then, on September 22, a nationwide steel strike began. During the ensuing manhunt for Communist leaders, Reed went into hiding.[61] He risked arrest to meet Bullitt, simply to tell him he had done a grand thing. Bullitt would never forget Reed's gesture.

After a few weeks at Croly's, Bullitt and Ernesta planned a restful fortnight in Windsor, Vermont. But they so loved "the quiet, the remoteness from active life, the rolling beauty of the autumn hills" that they decided to stay all winter. They hunkered down with open fires, falling snow, and only the sound of sleigh bells jingling on the roads. They tended to eleven puppies, drove their own sleigh behind fast horses, and skied at all hours of the day. Soon, the couple began to talk about a painful subject: having children. In just the first year after marrying, they had lost a premature baby and Ernesta had a miscarriage. Both felt the trauma deeply. For some time, Ernesta couldn't bear to go to houses with small children or to have sex. And Bullitt could not shake his "dynastic complex": children, he said, were the "sole excuse for existence." Now, invigorated by their New England winter and perhaps as well by Bullitt's daring in the halls of power, husband and wife once again shared the desire for a pregnancy. "I can't imagine being married to anyone but you," Bullitt told Ernesta. "Or ever loving anyone but you."

Yet, if Bullitt could appreciate an idyllic winter, he was also a man of action. He was rarely able to sit for more than a few minutes. "He would get up with a quick movement, walk briskly about the room, light a fresh cigarette or search for something he believed he wanted, then drop into his chair again," Ernesta wrote in her memoirs.[62] Bullitt could not get the treaty and surrounding political machinations off his mind. He contemplated writing a history of the peace conference and talked with Croly about works of history, politics, and economics he should read, to buttress his critiques of the league and the treaty. It was in this context that Bullitt jumped on an invitation to review Keynes's Wilson book in the first issue of the *Freeman,* a new radical weekly launched by the avant-garde publisher Benjamin W. Huebsch, who also printed Bullitt's Senate testimony.[63]

In his review, Bullitt hailed the British economist for writing a masterpiece but regretted that Keynes had in fact softened his portrait of Wilson. "In its original form," Bullitt argued, the book "marched like a Greek tragedy."[64] "What a great man came to Europe, and what a small one has gone home," Keynes had initially written. But the published passage read, "What a great man came to Europe in those early days of our victory!" Instead of needling Wilson as "under-equipped intellectually," the published Keynes described Wilson as "lacking the dominating intellectual equipment that would have been necessary." The five instances in which Keynes first described Wilson as "ignorant" were changed to "ill-informed." Wilson was no longer "unfertile" but "inadapted or "unresourceful." He was no longer a "vain man" but simply a "politician."[65] The *New York Times* took Bullitt's review as an occasion to draw an association between the two men: "the Bullitts and the Keyneses have got behind the words [of the treaty] and contemplated with moral revulsion the rotten heart."[66] This much was true, though the two diverged in their hopes for the future. Keynes still believed in a liberalism that Bullitt thought Wilson had killed off at Versailles. Instead Bullitt put his faith in the international labor movement, believing it could unite Social Democrats and Communists in spite of their differences and that an effective, nonviolent political left could be a home for partisans who might otherwise side with the violent Bolsheviks.

For Bullitt, any contributions to politics would have to come from outside of officialdom. Taking part directly was out of the question. In July 1920 his friend and former *Ledger* colleague Charles Sweeney conveyed to him an offer to become chairman of the National Committee of the Farmer-Labor Party. When Bullitt did not bother to reply, Sweeney wrote, "I go and want to make you the Lenin of America, and you say no 'I prefer my baronial estate.'"[67] Bullitt did provide the party a white paper on foreign affairs, perhaps suggesting his sympathy for the Farmer-Labor leadership, which included a number of his associates.

The next year saw Bullitt drifting still farther from his charged days as a political journalist and diplomat. He abandoned the idea of writing about the peace conference and instead focused on creating "a very great novel." He and Ernesta also found a bucolic place to live. En route to New York City, they stopped for a night at a friend's home in the Berkshires. He knew a farm nearby with 330 acres, 1,400 sugar maples, trout streams, and mountain views. The Bullitts immediately purchased it and decided to live there full-time, apart from one or two months during the winter in New York. Ernesta directed the property's renovation, adding a new dining room and converting an old cowshed into a drawing room. She hauled kegs of nails, buckets of paint, and mounds of cement. For the first time, she felt she was making something he liked; the home was her creation, her child. Antique-furniture auctions became a shared passion, as well as a kind of gambling—they knew nothing about antiques. Bullitt left Ernesta in charge of the money. He never saw a bill, much less paid one, in all the years of their marriage.

On the suggestion of Walter Wanger, a former colleague on the peace commission and now a film producer, Bullitt joined Famous Players—Lasky Corporation—later Paramount Pictures. The movies were perfect insofar as they would not remind him of his professional past. He planned to stay on with the studio until the house was paid off. Meanwhile, Ernesta went from one doctor to another to figure out why she could not get pregnant and to find a remedy that would allow her to secure "the supreme destiny of all women." In April 1921 the Bullitts gave a dinner for Albert Einstein and Chaim Weizmann, who were in the United States to build support for the Zionist cause. They borrowed a footman in livery to help their own butler for this memorable occasion.[68]

Officially, Bullitt stayed out of public life. But in March 1921, he felt he had to react to Lansing, Wilson's secretary of state, to denounce his hypocrisy.[69] In his newly published book *The Peace Negotiations,* Lansing revealed that he had sent a memorandum to the president just before the signing of the treaty, reading, "This war was fought by the United States to destroy forever the conditions which produced it. These conditions have not been destroyed. They have been supplanted by other conditions." Bullitt would not allow Lansing to pretend he had been on the right side of history. Whatever Lansing thought during the signing, he said something else during the Senate debate. As Bullitt noted in a letter published in the *New Republic,* Lansing had decided to tell the truth about the treaty only in 1921, when it could no longer make an impact. Bullitt himself had presented his fellow citizens with the facts when the treaty appeared certain to be approved, as well-placed observers understood. As Charles Nagel, Taft's secretary of labor, put it in a letter to Villard written after the release of Lansing's book, "Mr. Bullitt led the way."[70]

Bullitt was not about to let go of his resentments. His home life was also a disappointment, despite the pleasures of the farm. He simply could not envision a childless marriage continuing. Ernesta occupied herself with housekeeping. To boost her spirits, Bullitt suggested she write a play, but Ernesta did not believe she could. Players-Lasky gave her some outlines to support her first attempt and despite her initial hesitance, she finished and submitted a first draft after just a few weeks. Edward Sheldon, a dramatist and one of the most esteemed screenwriters of early cinema, found the work excellent.[71] With Sheldon's encouragement, Ernesta had found a possible route to fulfillment outside of the fruitless pursuit of a child.

3

An American in Paris and Vienna

AT THE END OF AUGUST 1921, as his marriage to Ernesta was failing, Bullitt met Louise Bryant, the young widow of John Reed. A year before, he had died in her arms from typhus and was buried a hero in the wall of the Kremlin. Like her husband, Louise was a chronicler of the Bolshevik triumph.[1] She sought Bullitt's help making a movie based on Reed's *Ten Days that Shook the World*, a firsthand report of the 1917 October Revolution that remains a journalistic classic. Fresh excitement took hold of the languishing Bullitt. It was not just the creative project that motivated him, it was Louise herself. They went to the theater a few times together in September and October. They talked. They fell in love. Louise dedicated a 1922 edition of Reed's book "To Billy Bullitt with my great respect and affection." She also added to the text a quotation from Lenin judging Bullitt to be "a man of honor."[2] In February of that year, they spent their first night together. When Louise went to Russia in June, she received letters from Bullitt every two or three days.[3]

In September Bullitt joined his new lover in Italy, where they spent the fall together. Ernesta had fallen ill and was convalescing in the French Riviera. In January 1923, Louise went to Rome to interview Mussolini, who had taken power months earlier. Bullitt had his own meeting to attend: he traveled to the French Riviera to propose a divorce. He hoped Ernesta would not fight it, which would "complicate everything hopelessly," he wrote to Louise. Nothing could dissuade him from his new love. While in Nice and Cannes, he met Cissy Patterson, then a journalist at the *New York Daily News*, who became infatuated with him. But Bullitt was not available.[4]

Ernesta rejected the divorce. Bullitt and Louise rejoined in Paris, then sailed back to New York at the end of January. They stayed at the Brevoort Hotel, a high-society locale where Louise renewed her friendship with the sculptor John Storrs and his wife Marguerite. Bullitt continued to press Ernesta to grant a divorce. "Ill and in despair," he wrote her imploringly on April 3, 1923, "I cannot go back to living with you. I don't want to. I don't believe I could even live with you if I wanted to. When I think now of having a child with you, I don't want it. It would be a ball + chain not a happiness." Ernesta knew, of course, that her husband loved another. If he could not join Louise, he wrote, "I will go to pieces in every way it is possible to go to pieces."[5] He was asking his wife to end their marriage, but he wrote as if she were still his best friend and confessor.

Eventually persistence paid off. On April 24, Ernesta appeared in court to initiate divorce proceedings as Bullitt had begged of her. Bullitt and Louise celebrated in grand style. At this point, she was in Italy to interview the soldier-poet Gabriele D'Annunzio and sun herself among the yellow roses of his garden for a few days.[6] It was D'Annunzio's oratory that had galvanized Italy to join the Allies in 1915. On the day of Bullitt's Senate testimony, September 12, 1919, D'Annunzio had captured the formerly Austrian city of Fiume, claiming it as a free state even as the Versailles Treaty had promised it to Yugoslavia. But Louise's articles did not talk much about politics. Instead, she described the parties D'Annunzio organized at Lake Garda. "During the festivities" of April 24, 1923, "a sensation was created by the arrival of William Christian Bullitt," she wrote. D'Annunzio rushed to him, embraced him, and took his celebration medal and pinned it on Bullitt's shirt, exclaiming, "I decorate you for high moral courage at Paris, when no one dared speak against Woodrow Wilson." Riding high, Bullitt shared with Louise the good news that he was now free to marry her.[7]

They spent the next two months in Istanbul, in a beautiful, if somewhat decayed, old spot Bullitt had rented in Anadolou Hissar, on the Asian side of the Bosporus. On June 6 Louise set out alone for Angora (later Ankara) to interview Mustapha Kemal Pasha, founder of the young Turkish republic, while Bullitt went to Paris for business. At the time she experienced a sense of abandonment: "All the happiness of discovering a new world broken by Bill going to Paris. I will remember his dear face forever—how delicate and full of sweet concern—when he stood on the other deck watching me off." But on the next page of her diary, she felt differently, like "Bill's slave." "He is looking for someone to adore," she continued.[8] She had a terrible trip to Angora, traveling in army trucks and sleeping in flea-ridden shanties. Nevertheless, she succeeded in interviewing Kemal Pasha and meeting the leaders of the new Turkish state. When Bullitt joined her on the Bosporus again at the end of June, she was ill with malaria, but happy.[9]

By September Louise was pregnant, and before the end of the year they married and settled in Paris in an elegant house rented from the novelist Elinor Glyn. Bullitt was about to become a father and spoke of it constantly over drinks and dinners.[10] But his passion for Louise was already fading. "Dear Darling Bill," she wrote him:

> I am awfully worrying about you. Please get the most thorough overhauling possible and please don't get too far away from me. You freeze me out of any nearness to you when you are ill. You know how I feel about you even when I'm having a baby. Yes, I even always feel that way. But you put up barriers I don't understand. I am really no good to you, dear, if I'm not worth something when everything's somehow wrong. I do so deeply love you.[11]

Louise sensed something was awry, and she was right. On February 5, 1924, in New York, Bullitt spent the evening with Ernesta. The day after, before embarking to London and then Paris, Bullitt wrote her. He had stayed up the whole night. "How I will miss you, my love," he told her, before musing in the postscript, "I don't now know how to address you . . . Mrs? Bullit."[12] She reciprocated, and he continued to send her messages in the same vein all the way to Paris.[13]

On February 24, Bullitt was beside Louise for the birth of their daughter, Anne Moen Bullitt, at their home in Paris. A little before midnight, after a daylong labor, "Louise made one great effort and the baby shot out into the doctor's hands." Then, "instantly one second old, she began to scream and beat the air with her fists and kick Louise's legs violently with her tiny feet." Bullitt had a theory: during the moment a child comes into the world, before the environment has any chance to leave its imprint, an infant can show you the person they will be as an adult. "I never received a more stunning impression of force and will than from that one second," he reflected. "When the doctor took her out of the bassinet, she grabbed the ribbon and would not let go. No sooner was she beside her mother than she snatched hold and began to suck terrifically. She starts life as a victor."[14]

Louise now lived a bourgeois existence, complete with servants and a nanny to take care of Anne. She embraced life in Paris. In the early 1920s, American artists and bohemians swarmed the city, where alcohol flowed freely in the absence of prohibition and intellectual life seemed more interesting than in the United States. As Anne grew to toddlerhood, Louise stopped working as a journalist. She published her last piece in the *Nation* in August 1925—"A Turkish Divorce," reporting on the end of Kemal's marriage, "killed presumably by the slow poison that has been fatal to so many romances—childlessness." Louise also tried to write a novel and some poetry. Bullitt was writing too. He had just finished the manuscript for a novel and was preparing to work on a second one. He attended horse races at the Auteuil Hippodrome, a ten-minute walk from their house. After the races, he would invite friends over. He enjoyed the wines, the parties, a whole new way of life for a man who, until recently, had savored the isolation of rural New England. Sunday lunch at the Bullitts became an institution. Notwithstanding the American artists, writers, and composers who had settled in the city, Paris boasted few American-style bars, and a great deal of entertaining was done at home. Memoirs of the period almost inevitably refer to gatherings at the Bullitts. In the evenings they hosted musical performances, often of the latest work by the American modernist and Parisian expat Georges Antheil. The composer himself would perform at the piano. Antheil remarked that Bullitt and Louise "seemed very happy together. They would reverently take us into a little nursery in the back of their house to pick up the covers over a little bed and present us their baby daughter."[15]

In the summer, the Bullitts enjoyed the farm in the Berkshires. Not long after purchasing it, Bullitt had hired a local couple, the Hartwells, who expertly handled the complicated management of the buildings, grounds, and animals, including an orchard, sugar bush, wood lot, and stables; horses, ponies, dairy cattle, and chickens. Mr. Hartwell introduced apple trees that became the mainstay of the farm. Eventually the farm's apple production was sold to a middleman, though Bullitt and his family kept a portion of the crop, which supplied his "apple diplomacy"—annual gifts of fruit boxes sent to friends all over the world.[16]

Bullitt's novel, *It's Not Done,* was published in March 1926, with a dedication to Louise. The work is a sometimes-bawdy satire of upper-crust society in Chesterbridge, Pennsylvania, a stand-in for Bullitt's own home of Philadelphia. Like Bullitt, the protagonist, Corsey, is a newspaper reporter who maintains love affairs with two women. Other characters, too, resemble figures in Bullitt's life. And Woodrow Wilson makes an appearance. When Corsey congratulates him for his speech declaring war, the fictional Wilson responds that he hates war, all wars. His only concern is "the peace he is going to make at the end of it." A friend tells Corsey to open his eyes, warning that "Wilson is just a middle-class Southerner with a colossal vocabulary and an even more colossal inferiority complex."[17]

The publisher Horace Liveright had turned down the book, telling Bullitt, "It will not sell 300 copies." But, released by Harcourt Brace, the novel swiftly found a large audience and was reprinted seventeen times.[18] It was a page-turner: Bullitt's friend Oswald Villard wrote him that the story "could have kept me up to 4 A.M." But Villard thought Bullitt was capable of something weightier. "I do not think the book is worthy of you," he wrote. "I look to you, with all your talent, to do a second one soon which will add greatly to your reputation. I know you can do it, and I know you can do it without stressing the sex note in every page."[19] Taking this criticism to heart, Bullitt abandoned his second novel and started working instead on a play about Wilson.

In the course of these dramas, Bullitt was repeatedly depressed. He began contemplating psychoanalysis in 1924, during a period when he was too sad to leave his bed. In September 1926, in the Berkshires, he fell from his horse. "Can you even *imagine* my ever falling off my horse?" he asked his friend, the painter George Biddle. "It dawned on me . . . I wanted to fall off my horse."[20]

Bullitt had been introduced to Freud's thought in 1910 by his Yale professor Roswell P. Angier, who had attended Freud's only lectures in America, at Clark University the previous year. Bullitt later recalled taking to the field of psychoanalysis "in such an absorbing manner, that I thought seriously of following [Angier's] suggestion that I should become a research psychologist."[21] When Bullitt decided he would himself try the talking cure, there was only one man for him to see. In late autumn 1926, Bullitt, Louise, and their daughter Anne returned to Paris. He promptly left his family there and traveled to Vienna, arriving in mid-November.

On Freud's Couch

Bullitt often told Biddle the story of how he met Freud. He had gone to 19 Berggasse, Freud's home. A man opened the door downstairs and told him that Freud was unwell and not taking visitors. Bullitt replied by giving the man his card and asking that the doctor be told that Mr. Bullitt had "called." "Freud must have been waiting at the top of the stairs," Bullitt recounted. "Down he came, running down the stairs, saying 'You're not Mr. William C. Bullitt, are you? Mr. Bullitt of Philadelphia? Oh, I have been so interested in your work, I have wanted to know you.'" As Biddle recalled it, Freud "was not taking new patients, but he would take Bill—on one condition only. 'I'll give you my word that I'll not see anyone else in this period, but you must give me yours that you won't desert me!'"[22]

Biddle "didn't believe a word of it," and Bullitt might well have exaggerated.[23] But it is probable that Freud had heard of him before their first meeting. Bullitt's letter of resignation to President Wilson had made headlines in the main Viennese newspaper, *Ostdeutsche Rundschau*, which opined that "Bullitt and his splendid and courageous letter will live forever in the history of mankind. Doubtless Wilson will also live, but Bullitt will unquestionably be infinitely better judged by the verdict of posterity than Wilson. Bullitt is our man, not Wilson."[24] And Bullitt's Senate testimony again garnered writeups in the Austrian and German press. Now, seven years later, a miserable Bullitt was in Vienna to start therapy, and he was not looking for attention. He shared his intentions with his brother Orville but asked him to keep them secret, and he complied. When Orville's wife asked him what his brother was doing in Vienna, he told her he had gone to hear the music.[25]

Bullitt never wrote about his sessions with Freud, and there is no record of what transpired. One can hardly guess how Freud behaved, given that he tailored his approach to each patient.[26] Abram Kardiner, a disciple, reported that Freud would talk to him when he was a patient, even exchanging gossip. But this would have been a great surprise to Freud's English patients, to whom he would listen while say nothing.[27] James Strachey, who would take on the gigantic task of translating and editing Freud's complete works in

English, described his experience of psychoanalysis with the master this way:

> Each day, except Sunday, I spend one hour on the Prof's sofa . . . and the "analysis" seems to provide a complete undercurrent for life. As for what it's all about, I'm vaguer than ever; but at all events it's sometimes extremely exciting; and sometimes extremely unpleasant—so I daresay there's *something* to it. The Prof. himself is most affable and as an artistic performer dazzling. . . . Almost every hour is made into an organic aesthetic whole. Sometimes the dramatic effect is absolutely shattering. During the early part of the hour all is vague—a dark hint here, a mystery there—; then it gradually seems to get thicker; you feel dreadful things going on inside you, and can't make out what they could possibly be; then he begins to give you slight lead; you suddenly get a clear glimpse of one thing; then you see another; at last a whole series of lights break in on you; he asks you one more question; you give a last reply—and as the whole truth dawns upon you the Professor rises, crosses the room to the electric bell, and shows you out the door.
>
> That's on favourable occasions. But there are others when you lie for the whole hour with a ton weight on your stomach simply unable to get out a single word. I think that makes one more inclined to believe it all than anything. When you positively feel the "resistance" as something physical sitting on you, it fairly shakes you all the rest of the day.[28]

Though Bullitt did not describe what psychoanalysis felt like to him, he must have agreed with Strachey that there was something to it. After finishing a session, he wrote Louise, "It is too silly! I wrote you a very depressed letter three hours ago and now everything is gay again. All because I thought a thought!!!! very bughouse indeed—but interesting . . . Don't worry about me. I have mental spasms occasionally, but everything is going amazingly well. Best love + a big hug."[29]

Certainly there was no lack of topics to discuss during his daily hour on the "sacred couch."[30] For one thing, there was his relationship with his two wives—Ernesta, the former but the closer confidante, and Louise, the mother of the child he desperately wanted and the woman with whom he seemed unable to live happily. From what Ernesta would later write in her unpublished memoirs, one can imagine some of what Bullitt shared with Freud. "He strove with all his driving energy, all his imagination, to stir my interest in sex to the high boiling point at which his own was always set, night and day, week in week out, in sickness and in health," Ernesta recalled. Yet she longed for a simple caress, a gentle arm around her, a kiss on her cheek, the comfort of her hand lying in his, the security of her head on his shoulder. The roles were reversed when it came to Louise, whose demands Bullitt could not satisfy.

Probably he told Freud of his first sexual experience. It had come on the Ford-sponsored Peace Ship in December 1915, with none other than the suffragist Inez Milholland. Milholland left a significant imprint on Bullitt. Milholland was generous, beautiful, courageous, and intelligent. Their liaison gave him the confidence to approach Ernesta when he returned to the United States, as he told her.[31] And Milholland's fearless pursuit of women's rights thoroughly impressed him. In 1916 she campaigned for Republican presidential nominee Charles Evans Hughes, who, unlike Wilson, favored the constitutional amendment for women's national suffrage. On October 22 of that year, Milholland collapsed in the middle of a speech in Los Angeles; her last public words were, "Mr. President, how long must women wait for liberty?" She died on November 25, "a martyr to the 'cause.'" Bullitt was devastated and later wrote to Milholland's mother, "Inez had and has a more profound influence on my life and actions than any living being. I feel her influence constantly and particularly when I have to make some decision that requires more courage than I possess. She was and will always be to me the greatest source of strength and inspiration . . . Inez was and is the greatest human being that I have ever known in my life."[32]

Milholland had believed in him. She had divulged to him her unusual, liberated way of life: she was married to a man who agreed that, even though wed, neither owned the other's bodies and sexual lives. She had even insisted that Bullitt meet her husband and shake his hand. This confidence was precious to Bullitt, who often felt that people did not like him. He had a vital need for friendship. "I had a friend," he said one day to Ernesta, describing a boy he recalled not from school or college but from his summer camp, Camp Pasquaney in New Hampshire, "a real friend who went around with me & and showed he liked me. It was wonderful!"[33] Lincoln Steffens, a muckraking American journalist who had joined Bullitt for the secret Moscow meetings in 1919, noticed a self-deprecating streak in him. The two men stayed in touch, and after Bullitt had completed the first draft of his novel, Steffens chastised him for criticizing his own work. "How do you judge your story like that?" Steffens asked. "It sounds to me as if you let some ass read your stuff and then taken his verdict." Bullitt even despaired about his newborn daughter.[34]

Bullitt believed his inferiority complex was "the result of his parents having had him circumcised when he was old enough to be aware of it without giving him any explanation." As a child, Bullitt was haunted by the idea that he was not like other boys and "that it was something to be horribly ashamed of."[35] Perhaps he noticed the difference when he compared himself to his older brother Jack. Jack was the child of his father's first wife, Emilie, and Bullitt looked up to him. "Even as a child he had wit," wrote Bullitt, who may also have been jealous of Jack's sexual conquests.[36] Bullitt was the son of his father's second wife, who was of Jewish origin. Had she imposed the circumcision, leaving her son to blame her for his own perceived inadequacies?

Ernesta described her mother-in-law as a generous person, warm and passionately fond of her two sons—William in particular. She was also a devoted Protestant, like her own parents and son William. Mrs. Bullitt had been ashamed of her Jewish background; she never spoke of it until her sons teased it out of her. Bullitt had a complex relationship with his heritage, which was somehow obvious to many. Ernest Hemingway, whom Bullitt met in Paris, referred to him as "a big Jew from Yale."[37] Perhaps Bullitt's Jewish ties had something to do with his Zionist advocacy. And at a time when European and American antisemites talked much of "Judeobolshevism," some of his colleagues may have seen his willingness to work with Bolshevists as a product of his Jewish origins. Certainly he faced hostility in the State Department. Hugh Gibson, who in 1919 became ambassador to Poland, wrote that he found Bullitt's behavior "contemptible and disgusting" and added, "perhaps my feeling is the more intense because I have known him to do other caddish things and lie about them."[38] At the time, "caddish" carried a double meaning, referring both to despicable people and to Jews. Yet Bullitt also embraced antisemitic prejudices. In July 1928, he jotted down a few thoughts on life for his daughter, including a paragraph on the life goals he associated with various peoples and the big questions that organized their pursuits: "Greek—To make beauty, to ensure beauty, to pursue beauty here on earth. 'Is it beautiful, harmonious?' Christian—to lay up treasures in heaven by serving God and the oppressed here on earth 'isn't it right?' Jewish—To get all the possessions possible on earth for one's self and one's family. 'What is there in it for me?'" Bullitt, like some self-hating Jews, felt compelled to articulate and prove how far he had traveled from his origins, a compulsion expressed through antisemitism. But this did not prevent him from cultivating relationships with Freud or Fritz Meyer, his Jewish doctor in Vienna, whom he helped to emigrate to the United States in 1936.[39]

During their months of therapy, Bullitt and Freud became something more than patient and healer. They became mutual admirers, intellectual compatriots, and friends. In April 1927, a few weeks after Bullitt's sessions ended, Freud wrote to thank him for a gift of books on American Indians and to encourage him in his writing. "No need to say that I am looking forward to your play on Wilson," Freud wrote. "I am sure you still appreciate him more than I do." The letter is signed, "Affectionately yours." In fact, Bullitt had already completed his play, *The Tragedy of Woodrow Wilson,* and dedicated it to "my friend Sigmund Freud . . . a man who, because he has acted always with both intellectual integrity and moral courage, is a great pathfinder for humanity."[40]

Separated into three acts, Bullitt's play shows Wilson as the figurehead of the "United States of the World"—inconstant, sensitive to flattery, and eager to leave his impression on the history of all peoples. Scenes from the Paris conference feature not a strategic thinker but something of a rube, ignorant of the damage he was doing and concerned primarily with personal and affective appeal. At one point, we see him agreeing to include Bohemia in the borders of Czechoslovakia without knowing that there were three million Germans in Bohemia. "That's curious," the Wilson character remarks when he realizes what he has done. "Masaryk never told me that," he says, referring to the Czech stateman Tomáš Masaryk. "If it is true, there must be good reasons for it. I like Masaryk."[41] The British and French premiers likewise are portrayed as taking advantage of Wilson's vanity and disinterest; they quickly appreciate that, so long as the treaty produces a League of Nations and Wilson's verbal promises are formally respected, he will cede on other issues. Eventually Wilson understands that he has been fooled and has betrayed his own promises of a just peace. After returning to the United States, a guilt-ridden Wilson delivers repetitive and mumbling speeches on behalf of the Treaty of Versailles before his stroke interrupts his campaign and he abandons the treaty to its fate.

The play received sympathetic readings. "It is a beautiful piece of work," Villard wrote, "understanding, effective, and admirably put together . . . Any producer ought to jump at it." Courtenay Lemon, a noted theater critic and a member of New York's prestigious Theatre Guild, praised Bullitt's "excellent review of Wilson," which he declared, "extremely readable to say at least." Lemon thought the work "would be just as interesting on the stage. In my opinion it is sound and just, and very well done and convincing." Yet the guild was unwilling to touch "so controversial" a subject.[42] Nor was anyone else. Whatever its qualities, the play went unperformed.

Sickness and Divorce

In June 1927 the Bullitts returned to the Berkshires. At the time, Louise was growing increasingly ill, having begun to feel unwell a year before.[43] She was also drinking more. One night she told Bullitt that she hated him for attempting to stop her. He "should love her whether she was drunk or not," she said.[44]

At times, Bullitt could not stand his wife's behavior. A January 1928 cocktail party was especially memorable.[45] Louise was invited to the Paris home of Bob McAlmon, publisher of James Joyce's *Ulysses*. Bullitt joined her and noticed, rather aghast, that it was a party of gays and lesbians. He asked Louise to leave; when she refused, he left without her. Louise returned home at five o'clock in the morning, accompanied by McAlmon and two guests, Gwen Le Gallienne and Yvette Ledoux. All were "thoroughly drunk," Bullitt reported, and subjected him to "a rude exhibition for half an hour."[46] This appears to have been the beginning of a close relationship between Louise and Le Gallienne, who at the time was suffering greatly from the breakdown of her own relationship with Ledoux, who had concluded that she preferred the company of men. Later, Louise would talk of the strong feelings she had for Le Gallienne, how she would sleep in her friend's arms. But she insisted their relationship was platonic.[47]

By March 1928 Louise was visiting London specialists in hopes of finding an explanation for her ailment, as well as some relief. The doctors diagnosed her with a rare disorder called Dercum's disease, characterized by painful fatty tumors forming under the skin. The day she was diagnosed, Louise thought about killing herself, and she wrote her will. That night, she considered leaving her husband—"he was so difficult"—and daughter as an alternative option. The idea of leaving would occur again in the following weeks when she returned to Paris.[48] But she did not go through with it.

In Paris, the Bullitts tracked down Dr. Dercum himself, the man who discovered the disease. Reached by telephone, Dercum did not need to see Louise in order to offer a grim prognosis. "Pray that she dies as soon as possible," he told Bullitt.[49] The couple decided not to admit defeat and to instead fight the disease. They bet that a great reduction in Louise's weight might have a favorable effect on her condition by eliminating the lumps of fatty tissue the disease was producing. Louise went to Baden-Baden, the famed spa town in southwest Germany, for treatment. A few weeks later, she returned home having lost thirty pounds.[50] But the remedy did not take.

"I had a dreadful summer, full of collapses," she wrote three months later, before embarking for France and thence to Baden-Baden to continue the cure. "I got thinner and thinner, but I weigh 104 and am still visible." She also fell deeper into her drinking habit. The only good news of the summer was that she had learned to drive a car. "I get so damned restless because I have been too feeble to carry out anything, but I find it's not tiring at all to dash around in a car if I'm driving."[51]

One event that summer exemplifies, perhaps better than any other, the collapse of Bullitt's and Louise's relationship. Indeed, the story would later form part of Bullitt's case in their divorce proceedings. That June, the pair attended Harvard-Yale crew races, watching from the yacht belonging to their host, the chairman of the Regatta Club. As the varsity race began, Louise, who had been drinking heavily, stood up at the edge of the yacht and appeared as though about to fall over the side. Bullitt caught her. In the divorce papers he noted, "She cursed me, saying that she had a right to fall overboard if she wanted to; that I was trying to restrict 'her liberty in every possible way.'" When they reached their hotel, she called him "a dirty little Philadelphia Jew whose only idea was to persecute her" and said "I was a miserable bourgeois and could not appreciate an artist like herself and could not appreciate her thoughts or anything she felt about life, and that she could not endure being near me any longer." Then "she took her clothes off and rushed through the hotel stark naked." She had become a blackout drunk. Not that Bullitt himself was immune to the temptation. In October 1928 he wrote her in Baden-Baden that he had stopped drinking and suggested that when she came back, they try not to drink before sunset.

The broken marriage left Bullitt in a liminal state. He remained attached to Louise, even as he pushed her away. In April 1929 he proposed looser terms for their relationship, suggesting that they live separately and meet when they wished. But he was in a sense dependent on her, indicating that he was incapable of writing if she was not well. A few days later, he sent a one-sentence letter: "Darling I miss you too much." The following day came another letter, which began, "Darling I miss you dreadfully." But only a week later, he demanded that she reform herself. After lunching with their daughter, Bullitt wrote to Louise, "She is going to have such a rotten life unless you get well and we are a real family again. You must, must get well, Louise. There is no life for either Anne or myself if you don't. We both need you—you your real self the way you used to be."[52]

There were other episodes like these. At one point, while in London to meet his cousin Lady Astor and share meals with Keynes and Kerr, Bullitt received a distressing cable from Louise. He responded despairingly:

> You needed to take a crack at me and invented an excuse. I suppose that when I left Paris, we were feeling much too easy and happy about each other. You had to smash things up somehow . . . Unfortunately, I am still so dependent on you emotionally that you can destroy me. And you always do . . . I don't know what to do; and I do know that I will not go on being demolished every two other weeks. I'll finally get a sense of self preservation. Love.

The next day, he sent a telegram saying he understood her completely and asking her to forget his earlier words.[53]

On and on, Bullitt proposed to his wife that she see Freud. "No human being can have the hellish experience you had as a child without having traces of the experiences buried deep. The drinking is just a symptom," he wrote. "I can't help you to find the baby's experience + you can't find them by yourself. Freud can help you to find them, but it will be your own intelligence + your own that will do the work."[54] When Louise finally wrote to Freud in April 1929, he replied that he was ready for her as soon as possible. "I know you are strong enough to settle your affairs yourself," he wrote, "but if you wish my advice I hope you will tell me everything necessary to form a reasonable judgment. With best sympathies."[55] Bullitt was enthusiastic and offered to pay for an extended stay in Vienna if she and Freud felt their meetings should continue.[56] In preparation for her introductory session, Louise left a note for herself: "Tell Freud—Bill has some sort of 'formula' for . . . 'being myself.' Never occurs to him I am bored by being made into his idea of a human being, a wife—or whatever it is."[57]

Louise later reported that when she met Freud, she told him of how her daughter Anne once said to her, "My mama is my friend." When asked if her daddy wasn't also her friend, she answered, "Oh, no, he is God." Freud was delighted. "That child is articulate," he said. "I have a theory that many children think that. Yours is the first to actually say it."[58] Louise did not continue with her analysis.[59]

Bullitt spent most of the summer of 1929 at a rented beach house in Villerville, Normandy. He made visits to the shore and took Anne to see the horse races in Deauville. And he worked on his play. He wrote Lawrence Langner, head of the Theatre Guild, that he would meet him in New York to hand over the manuscript of a play "considerably better" than his "Wilson."[60] Freud thought highly of *Gobi,* the new work. He described being swept away by the "passionate rhythm" of the play. "I see I was right for trusting your powers as writer," he wrote. On the back of his letter, he added, "The effect on the public may depend greatly on the way the play is represented. It ought to pass in a hurricane of passion, like an anxiety-dream."[61] In New York in mid-September, Bullitt submitted the manuscript as promised, along with Freud's laudatory comments. Courtenay Lemon, who had so enjoyed the Wilson play, recommended rejecting *Gobi* without further ado.[62]

In New York, Bullitt and Louise's marriage continued collapsing. One day, Louise knocked on their door at the Brevoort, and when Bullitt opened it, she "literally fell" into the room. He put her to bed in a drunken stupor and called a doctor. While waiting for him to arrive, Bullitt opened his wife's handbag and found five old letters to and from Gwen Le Gallienne and two more written that same day. When the doctor arrived and tried to call a neurologist, Louise drifted into the room naked. After she calmed down, they offered her the choice between a sanatorium or somewhere quiet and free of temptation. She refused both options and chose to go to San Francisco to visit her half-brother, a disabled veteran, and the only family member with whom she felt close.

While Louise was away, Bullitt took some time to think. Louise's intimacy with Gwen Le Gallienne upset him. He had refused to admit to himself that their relationship was physical. And Bullitt, too, was broken. He was stuck in a self-destructive but familiar pattern of behavior. As he explained to his friend Mura Dehn, a dancer and celebrated documentary filmmaker he met in Vienna, "he had this feeling that whatever course he set for himself he would carry out exactly according to his prearranged plan; he would let nothing whatsoever swerve him from it." This was not a self-congratulatory announcement of Bullitt's grit and determination. It was a description of pathology. The example he gave Dehn was that if he set out for a walk and told himself he would continue straight at a certain pace, he would continue no matter what obstacles he encountered, even if he fell into a chasm or leapt off a cliff.[63] At this point Bullitt had failed to publish anything for three years. He was also stuck on his wife's illness, unable to accept that Louise was incurably sick. He continued pushing weight loss while recommending that she seek Freud's cure for her neurosis.

Ultimately, the pair had to separate, though. The time came when Louise accused Bullitt of paying somebody to follow her. When Louise returned from California, he offered her the options of divorce or two years in an institution. She revolted and tried to kill herself with an overdose of sleeping pills. When she recovered, she joined Bullitt in Philadelphia where they decided to separate legally but did not get a divorce.[64] At the end of November, Louise sailed to Algiers via France. Against her expectations, while she was gone, Bullitt began divorce proceedings against her in Philadelphia.[65] As he put it in a letter to his friend Marsden Hartley, the celebrated modernist painter, "She is lost—not physically but emotionally. It is absolutely horrible . . . I did all I could, but it was hopeless because Louise has the delusion that I persecute her. God knows what will happen to her now. I hope she may be able to work out a life but I'm afraid she won't."[66]

In testimony delivered behind closed doors, Bullitt explained that Louise began drinking in the winter of 1926–1927, and as her drinking became heavier, her hostility toward him increased. He underscored the incidents justifying the divorce, including the public scenes resulting from her drunkenness. He repeatedly mentioned the relationship with Gwen Le Gallienne. His main concern, he maintained, was the damaging effect of her conduct on their child. Bullitt called his various French aides to testify, including his chauffeur and butler and the cook they brought with them to the Berkshires. Hortense DeJean, Anne's nanny, also testified. All of the witnesses corroborated Bullitt's words. As humiliating as the testimony was, it remained private. Louise was guaranteed a total absence of publicity so that there would be no damage to her reputation or public image.[67]

At first, Louise considered contesting the divorce. She planned to produce copies of successive telegrams Bullitt had sent her on October 13 and 15 while she was in San Francisco, both of which ended with his professions of "love."[68] Her lawyer advised her not to do it: "Could you not throw a veritable bombshell into the procedure by introducing your two love letters in evidence?" he asked. Doing so might lead to publicity for Bullitt's testimony, something Louise wanted to avoid. Ultimately the lawyer convinced her to agree to a divorce on the grounds of "indignities" rather than endure the embarrassment of a public legal drama.[69]

On March 24, 1930, the divorce, officially uncontested, was finalized before a master in Philadelphia's Court of Common Pleas. Bullitt was granted custody of Anne and agreed to an alimony payment of $300 every month for the rest of Louise's life, an amount worth more than

$5,000 today.[70] "I am sure now that we can be friends, deeply friends," Bullitt wrote her from France. "That is enough. And that is better than wounds, and lunacies, and horrors." He planned to call her on April 16, when he would be back in Paris, unless she instructed him not to.[71]

In the midst of the divorce proceeding, in mid-February, Bullitt had contacted Ernesta while sailing for Europe. When he arrived in London, he was "completely elated" to receive her response. He had suffered some uncertain moments "to say the least" while awaiting her reply. He probably hoped he could count again on her friendship and her listening ear; his letter concluded, "And now good night my love."[72] But in the weeks after arriving in Europe, he was alone and did not feel well, which was reason enough to see Freud again. Then, too, he had a new idea for an exciting project—further reason to meet Freud as soon as possible.

4

Sigmund Freud, Coauthor

WHY AND HOW DID FREUD DECIDE in the summer of 1930 to work on a psychological portrait of President Wilson? Eight years earlier, when the American journalist William Bayard Hale asked Freud to endorse his own psychobiography of Wilson, the good doctor noted that, while he admired much in Hale's work, he could never write such a book himself. But when Bullitt, another American journalist, came to him, Freud was ready to enlist.

Hale, Wilson's 1912 campaign biographer and once a trusted aide, had written Freud in 1922, seeking his endorsement for his new book, *The Story of a Style.* Described by its publisher as a "psychoanalytical study of Woodrow Wilson," the book focused on Wilson's rhetoric and what it revealed about his personality. "Mr. Wilson deals in words, spends his time, his life, with words; is what he is, and does what he does, by the instrumentality of words," Hale wrote. "Statement, argument, appeal."[1] He sent a copy of the book to Freud, along with a note in German. Replying in English, Freud blessed the work as possessing "a true spirit of psychoanalysis in it."[2]

Freud was taken with Hale's careful interpretations of Wilson's language. Hale noted how the president made recurring use of the consonants v, s, and p, and of certain "talismanic" words, as if each were clothed with mystical powers: words like "process," "counsel," and "punctilio"; "fountain," as in "fountain of learning" or "fountain of friendship." Repeated many times, some phrases came to "dominate the intellect." Wilson never shortened a sentence, and he loaded his with adjectives. Hale found that, in one sample of a published hundred words, Wilson used thirty adjectives against one "pure verb"—a ratio ninety times greater than he found in a sample of works from famous authors, such as Dickens, Poe, Shakespeare, Carlsyle, and Stevenson, whose samples averaged one adjective for every three verbs. In his 1898 biography of George Washington, Wilson mentions "the colony of Virginia" many times, inevitably pairing it with modifiers: "fair," "quiet," "robust," or "hale." Likewise the American continent is "great," "virgin," or "roomy," again and again. Hale argued that a man who has something to say has neither need nor time for many adjectives. Men of action needed only verbs. What was stable in Wilson, Hale concluded, were not facts and actions, which he often forgot or held only fragilely in his memory. What was firm was his attachment to symbolic words.[3]

Freud mused that Hale's "kind of higher and more scientific 'graphologie' would be sure to find a broad application in literary criticism." With his psychological interpretations of Wilson's language, Hale had "indeed opened up a new field of analytic research," which would later be called lexicology. And Freud shared in Hale's passionate denunciation of Wilson as a betrayer of the peace. "You need not to be ashamed of it," Freud wrote. "In a purely confidential way: I detest the man who is the object of your study. As far as a single individual can be responsible for the misery of this part of the world, he surely is."[4]

But Freud also expressed reservations. "I cannot overcome my objection that what you have done is a bit of vivisection," he wrote. "Psychoanalysis should not be practiced on a living subject, unless he submits to it, against his own will . . . I am not in the habit of killing my own patients." He cautioned further that "psychoanalysis should never be used as a weapon in literary or political polemics," especially against "a living personality." If nothing else, the analyst could not be sufficiently objective. "The fact that I am conscious of a deep ongoing antipathy towards the President is an additional motive for reserve on my side," Freud explained. However, he did ultimately authorize a public endorsement of the book.[5]

Like Bullitt, Freud once had high hopes for Wilson. On December 22, 1916, a few days after Wilson invited all belligerents to put forward their conditions for peace, Freud wrote to his Hungarian colleague Sándor Ferenczi, "I have to acknowledge that Wilson's intervention in favor of peace, announced today, that we have to take seriously enough, has its part in my mood, more oriented towards life."[6] At the time, Wilson was asking both sides to state their essential war aims, and not everyone was listening; but Freud was.[7] Two years later, with the November 1918 armistice approaching, Freud wrote to Ferenczi that he no longer expected anything from Wilson.[8] Then, the following February, Freud could write of "confidence in the President."[9] Freud wanted to believe in Wilson, but he wasn't sure about the American who seemed to think he could redefine the future of nations.

When disappointment came a few months later with the Treaty of Versailles, Freud noted the public's deep interest in psychoanalytical interpretation of Wilson's personality. In his *Economic Consequences of Peace,* a bestseller in Vienna, Keynes had noticed that during the final signing ceremony at Versailles, the German representative alluded in his speech to the gap between Wilson's Fourteen Points and the text of the treaty, which provoked a furious outburst from the president. Keynes interpreted Wilson's reaction thusly: "In the language of medical psychology, to suggest to the President that the treaty was an abandonment of his professions was to touch on the raw of a Freudian complex."[10] Freud told James Strachey that "he'd never enjoyed so much local celebrity as in consequence of this." At the time, Freud was not yet a household name. Outside of certain medical and intellectual circles, Freud was, as James Strachey wrote his brother Lytton in 1921, "entirely unknown. I went and asked for one of his books in a large book-shop, & they never heard his name."[11]

In the following years, Freud maintained his interest in Wilson. Theodor Reik, a psychoanalytic disciple, remembered walks through Vienna with Freud speaking bitterly of the former president. He would joke about the Fourteen Points and describe Wilson as a kind of Don Quixote, undone by his own idealism.[12] Then Bullitt arrived in 1926. While undergoing therapy, he was working on his play. The play Bullitt sent to the Theatre Guild in March 1927 was without a doubt influenced by conversations with Freud, and, given Freud's hearty appreciation of the play, it seems to have excited his imagination. Freud's bitterness gradually gave way to curiosity, to the point that he reportedly told Bullitt he was "interested in diagnosing the character of Wilson."[13]

It was a time for widespread reappraisal of the war. The armistice was a decade old when Freud changed his mind about another protagonist, Clemenceau.[14] And by spring 1930, when Bullitt began to toy with the idea of collaborating with Freud, participants on all sides of the Treaty of Versailles were settling scores, "re-fighting the war on paper."[15] In Germany, the army general and aspiring dictator Ludendorff attributed defeat to failures of civilian leadership. Prince Max von Baden, a pro-democracy nobleman, replied that if the Germans found themselves at a disadvantage in the negotiations, it was due to Ludendorff's strategic miscalculations.[16]

In the United States, the war of interpretation was at its peak. One of its casualties was Colonel House. In *Woodrow Wilson and the World Settlement,* published in 1922, the progressive journalist Ray Baker emphasized House's betrayal of Wilson. Baker noted the brief period of February 1919 when Wilson was in the United States, during which House went against his wishes and accepted a preliminary deal with the French and British on reparations and territorial changes that would have postponed approval of the League of Nations to a later, final treaty. Baker's interpretation was the dominant one until 1928, when the first two volumes of House's diaries appeared. In the diaries, House rejected this interpretation of events, explaining that he had Wilson's mandate to negotiate and, when Wilson reversed the agreement severing the league from a preliminary treaty, House did not object.[17] As such, he had neither betrayed Wilson nor usurped his authority. House characterized his decision as entirely well-meaning: peace was urgently needed—under armistice conditions, Germany remained embargoed and hungry—and would not be forthcoming without concessions to the British and French. Thus a compromise was necessary, and he was simply trying to reach one, while understanding that Wilson might balk and had every right to do so. While Baker's thesis was that House had weakened Wilson by negotiating behind his back, House contended that he had done no such thing and that it was instead Wilson who doomed the treaty with his own intransigence.

Then, in 1929, came Churchill's WWI memoir, *The Aftermath.* "If Wilson had simply been an idealist or a caucus politician, he might have succeeded," Churchill wrote. "His attempt to run the two in double harness was the cause of his undoing." To Wilson, "the differences in Europe between France and Germany seemed trivial, petty, easy to be adjusted by a little good sense and charity. But the differences between Democrats and Republicans in the United States! Here were really grave quarrels . . . peace and goodwill among all nations abroad, but no truck with the Republican Party at home. That was [Wilson's] ticket and that was his ruin and the ruin of much else as well." The European Allies had agreed to serious concessions to get the United States on board with the treaty; because of Wilson's failure, Europe was left to lift itself up as best as it could.

These reassessments came after a time of escalating tensions, as Germany spent the first half of the 1920s refusing to pay its war debts. In January 1923 France responded with fury by occupying the Rhineland, forcing the Americans to take a renewed interest in European affairs. The US Dawes Plan permitted Wall Street to lend Germany the money to pay reparations due France and Britain, which could then reimburse their debt to the United States. After years of friction, the Treaty of Locarno—signed in 1925 by Germany, France, Britain, Italy, and Belgium—guaranteed the borders in Western Europe and instituted Britain, which had distanced itself from France, as an arbiter of any disputes that might arise among the signatories.

At the time, Churchill was optimistic about the prospects of Locarno and the Treaty of Washington, a 1922 naval arms control deal signed by the United States, the United Kingdom, Italy, and Japan. However, he saw warning signs in demography—the population of France would soon be only half that of its German neighbor—leading him to conclude that "the anxieties of France and the resentments of Germany are only partly removed."[18] Further, Churchill's book was published before the stock market crash of October 1929 and could not have foreseen how the Great Depression would reopen and exacerbate the wounds of war and its aftermath. With the world's major economies in disarray, a new conflict seemed to loom on the horizon.

In this context, Bullitt wanted to write about diplomacy—in service of his country and with rigor. Until 1914 the United States had been protected by 3,000 miles of water off its east coast and 5,000 miles off its west coast. These oceans were mainly controlled by Britain, so that the United States could afford to be ignorant and inactive on the global stage without great consequences. Bullitt saw that, after the war, this arrangement was no longer valid. The United States had become the wealthiest nation in the world. It conducted trade without British protection and had become a creditor nation, its capitalists lending and investing everywhere on earth. Now was the time for a true internationalism—a Wilsonian vision unadulterated by compromise and delusion. America as a nation of global destiny was still alive for Bullitt, who wanted his country to play a cooperative and leading role by promoting the rule of law, democracy, free speech, and free enterprise across national borders.[19]

For Bullitt, the fate of mankind was determined over millions of years by geography, over hundreds of years by demography, over tens of years by economics, and year over year by psychology. In his new book, Bullitt intended to concentrate on this last element. He had interacted with key personalities of the peace negotiations and believed in their decisive roles as individuals. The book would start with the part that personalities played in the failure of the Paris Peace Conference. He wanted to draw portraits of the minds of the Big Four—Clemenceau, Lloyd George, Orlando, and Wilson—as well as Lenin. In addition, Bullitt would analyze the American delegation, including House, Hoover, and the Inquiry scholars. He intended to conclude with ideas for the future, namely the critical importance of Franco-German reconciliation and a call for greater US investment in a professional diplomatic service.

Above all, Bullitt wanted to lodge a brief on behalf of effective leadership and statesmanship—something Wilson had not provided. If Wilson had demonstrated anything, it was that the United States must abandon the presidential system itself because it left the country and the world far too reliant on the caprices of one person. This was a radical idea: disturbed by what he saw at the Paris negotiations, Bullitt wished to recommend that the United States scrap the office of the presidency and instead institute a system of parliamentary government.[20]

With this project in mind, Bullitt wrote to Freud to arrange a meeting on May 17, 1930.[21] They convened in Berlin, where Freud was receiving medical treatment after surgery on his jaw bones. (By this time, Freud was suffering almost constantly from the prosthesis he had received following an operation on his maxilla, which he underwent to treat a cancer several years earlier.) Bullitt shared his plan for the book and proposed that Freud write a chapter on Wilson. Freud was interested. Only a few months earlier, after reading Lytton Strachey's biography of Queen Elizabeth I, he became convinced that one could write a psychological biography with historical evidence. Freud wrote to Strachey to express his admiration: "you have approached one of the most remarkable figures in your country's history, you have known how to trace back her character to the impressions of her childhood, you have touched upon her most hidden motives with equal boldness and discretion, and it is very possible that you have succeeded in making a correct reconstruction of what actually occurred."[22] Yet, such a project could hardly be done on the fly. The author couldn't simply rely on impressions; like a historian, he needed facts.

Freud thought that if Bullitt were able to collect sufficient evidence, perhaps they could write something on Wilson together. It would not be a psychoanalysis, which was a process of self-inquiry conducted by a patient and analyst over an extended period. Rather, it would be a psychological interpretation conducted on the basis of biographical material. This was an extraordinary offer; Bullitt could not refuse a man he held in such high esteem, as a collaborator and a friend. And both men, of course, were interested in Wilson's enigmatic personality and his responsibility for determining the world's fate at Versailles.

Bullitt was optimistic that he could assemble the information they needed. He would go first to Colonel House. The two had met in London on May 7, just ten days before Bullitt visited Freud with his idea. House had seemingly put Wilson's psyche on a platter: "Wilson, after I had known him for a year or two, told me everything about his personal life and family, all things that men usually keep from each other," House said. "We were truly intimate."[23] Bullitt needed all the information House possessed. And Freud was ready to sift that information and come to terms with the personality it reflected.

5

The Failure of the First Atlantic Alliance

AN ENTHUSIASTIC BULLITT LEFT Freud in Berlin and, back in London, resumed his conversations with Colonel House. When Bullitt had first interviewed House, he was to be one of the figures included in a panoramic study of diplomacy. The new project with Freud focused exclusively on Wilson, but still the full cooperation of the president's most influential confidante was essential. Bullitt would read all the biographies, all the memoirs and histories published on Wilson's time at Princeton, at the Paris conference, and elsewhere. He would delve even further into the man's life, interviewing his closest friends and collaborators. And when it came to Wilson's political life, House in particular held a treasure trove of information. During the eight years he worked for Wilson, House kept meticulous records. Every evening, with rare exceptions, he would dictate the events of the day to his secretary, Miss Denton. The resulting corpus consumed more than 2,000 pages and most of the entries related to Wilson.[1] The majority of the notes were unpublished; Bullitt wanted access to everything.

Obtaining House's cooperation required rebuilding the trust that had been lost over the Versailles Treaty. House had supported its ratification and even taken a swipe at Bullitt, comparing him negatively to Keynes, whom House saw as "a sort of solidified Bullitt, with more mature judgment."[2] Before the peace conference, Bullitt—along with a clutch of other journalists, including Colcord, Cobb, Swope, and Lippmann—had constituted a kind of entourage for House, who seemed to share their views on what a postwar liberal international order should look like.[3] Indeed, when it came to establishing a Wilsonian vision of global peace on the basis of law and interstate cooperation, hardly anyone seemed more committed than House. In June 1917 he told Colcord he was willing to stake his job, his friendships, and his good name on the project's success:

> If I see that the Peace conference is going wrong, if I become convinced that liberalism is not coming through, and that there is no hope of its coming through, I have made up my mind to throw my whole life and career into the balance, to tell what I know, to have all the cards out of the table, to kick up a rumpus that will ring from end to end of the world—in short to turn on the crowd I have been playing with, and appeal to the people of the world. I know that such a course will sacrifice all my connections and friendships, would ruin my reputation with those whom I work with today, and would spoil my present and future efficiency; but nevertheless, I have decided that it must be done.[4]

For Bullitt and his fellow liberals, then, House's backing of the final treaty was a great betrayal. Bullitt recalled vividly a conversation with House the day after quitting the peace conference. The only thing House had to say was that the League of Nations would correct the injustices of the treaty, which Bullitt had gone to some lengths enumerating in his letter of resignation. House acknowledged that the league lacked the power to fix what ailed the agreement, but it would change nonetheless when the world was governed by radicals and socialists. House believed that, within ten or fifteen years, leftism would be ascendant across the major powers, including in the United States.

By the spring of 1930, much time had passed, and the two men, Bullitt and House, were willing to hear each other out. They met first in April, before Bullitt gained Freud as a coauthor, and three more times in late May and early June. They then embarked on the same boat from London to the United States, where they would have more time to talk.[5]

House shared his personal story. He had become interested in politics at the age of twelve. He remembered following the disputed presidential election of 1876 as a seventeen-year-old student at Hopkins Grammar School in New Haven, along with his classmate Oliver Morton Jr., son of Oliver Morton, the radical Republican senator from Indiana. House and Morton Jr. traveled to New York and Washington, attending important political events convened by both parties. After college, House entered business in his home state of Texas. Then, in 1892, he ran Democratic governor James Hogg's victorious reelection campaign. House ran successful bids by three more Democratic gubernatorial candidates in subsequent years, demonstrating his incomparable skills as a campaign manager. He was asked to run for the governorship himself but refused on the grounds that he could not withstand the Texas summer heat. House never served in the military, but Hogg commissioned him as a lieutenant colonel in Texas's state militia; gradually House came to be referred to by his rank.[6]

In 1911, when it became obvious that Theodore Roosevelt would run against his successor Taft and thereby split the Republican vote, Democrats saw an opportunity to win the presidency. House sought a candidate to support. "Why did you choose Wilson?" Bullitt asked. "I selected him very carefully," House answered. He "considered seriously" both William Gaynor, then the mayor of New York, and Wilson. "But Gaynor was not a man I could influence easily, he had many ideas of his own," House said. "I found at once I could easily control Wilson." Bullitt noticed that House was apt to take such care. He "never drinks alcohol, tea or coffee, never smokes," Bullitt wrote. He had "a quiet veiled voice, coming gently from the back of his throat." "'I see, I see,'" he would say, "'I know, I know,' producing impression of agreement without the slightest commitment. Very kindly, inscrutable, gentlemanly."[7]

At the beginning of Wilson's presidency, House filled high-ranking positions with his friends—William Gibbs McAdoo at the Treasury, Albert Burleson as postmaster general—and blocked the nomination of Louis Brandeis as attorney general.[8] On the domestic front, House used his political skills to parlay with members of Congress on Wilson's behalf and shield the president from office seekers and favor hunters. House also proved his acumen in international affairs, an area that did not greatly interest Wilson. The president twice asked him to be secretary of state, but House declined both times. "I did not want it because I had much more power and freedom as Wilson's personal representative," House told Bullitt. "Everything important was done through me . . . not only the business of the State Department but also of the War Department and of the Navy."[9]

In November 1918, on the eve of the armistice, it was House who obtained Lloyd George's and Clemenceau's agreement that the Fourteen Points would be the basis for peace negotiations. It was a great achievement for House and for Wilson, solidifying his role as the most influential world leader at the conference. However, House's relationship with Wilson deteriorated after the colonel apparently agreed to separate the league covenant from a preliminary treaty. "It was a great mistake for me to be peace commissioner. I should have stayed at the President's elbow just unofficially on the outside," House said. "Just when my influence was most necessary, I lost it."[10]

House and Wilson had agreed on the objective in Paris: to establish a League of Nations, which would foster peace based on the liberal model of cooperation among peoples. To achieve this goal, there were two options. Wilson could fight Clemenceau's and Lloyd George's reactionary pursuit of annexation and indemnities, with the support of their countries' liberals as well as labor activists, socialists, and eventually Bolshevists. Or Wilson could compromise his liberal ideals and achieve what he could with the two leaders. House thought both options worth pursuing, hence his alignments with liberals like Lippmann and Bullitt and his decision to dispatch Bullitt on the 1919 missions to Bern and Moscow.

Wilson, however, distrusted socialists and communists and rejected an alliance with the left. So House turned to Orlando, Clemenceau, and Lloyd George to negotiate the treaty.[11] Even as House focused on the president's objectives, as a true diplomat, he also took liberties when negotiating in the hope of reaching an acceptable compromise and convincing Wilson to accept it after the fact. House helped secure the agreement of the Allies and, in so doing, earned the gratitude of Lloyd George and Clemenceau.

Following the peace conference, House maintained good relations with the British and French leaders. He would travel to England and France every summer, seeing Lloyd George in London and Clemenceau in Paris or in the Vendée. Once, in June 1922, he asked Clemenceau if he regretted Wilson's presence in the Paris negotiations. "The old man thought for a moment," and replied

> After the armistice he noticed a tendency in Lloyd George and the English generally to antagonize the French, and an unwillingness to meet the French claims. He concluded if Wilson sat in the Conference the power of his great office might be invoked in France's behalf when matters concerning her interests came to the fore. He thought the results of the Conference justified this expectation and

> he gave several examples of where there was a clash between himself and George, and Wilson came to the rescue of the French.[12]

House agreed. France and Clemenceau owed much to Wilson personally. The president had supported Paris as the seat of the peace conference after having ruled out Lucerne and Geneva, both suggested by House, because of fears of Bolshevism in Switzerland.[13] Substantively, it was thanks to Wilson that Alsace-Lorraine was restored to France without a referendum; House would have preferred to incorporate Alsace-Lorraine into Switzerland and thereby create "an eternal barrier between Germany and France."[14] During the peace negotiations, Wilson would often tell Paul Mantoux, the French diplomat and interpreter, that, having been "raised in one of the Southern states devastated by the Civil War and submitted for years to a regime of constraint of the victors during the reconstruction, his sympathy had been, after 1871, to the populations [of Alsace-Lorraine] submitted despite their protests, to the domination of the victor."[15]

In addition, Wilson backed Clemenceau in opposing the merger of Austria and Germany, despite the expressed desire of representatives from both countries that they share a common republic.[16] Wilson had been shocked and infuriated by Germany's ambition to dominate Europe, without regard to self-determination. Now, ignoring the irony of rejecting self-determination for Austrians and Germans who yearned for unification, Wilson feared that merger would create "one of the most powerful countries of the world" and not only that but "a great Roman Catholic power." Further, Wilson supported Clemenceau's push for demilitarization of the Rhineland and approved of creating Poland, Romania, and Yugoslavia—all potential French allies.[17] Finally, at the end of the peace conference, when Lloyd George wanted to allow a German army of 200,000 men instead of 100,000 and to reduce the duration of the occupation of the Saar, Wilson again sided with Clemenceau.

A few days later, Wilson told the journalist Ray Stannard Baker, "As this conference has progressed, my regards for Clemenceau have risen. I don't agree with him in the least, but he is a strong, honest, courageous old man."[18] On June 28, 1919, when Wilson returned from Paris to Washington, D.C., Clemenceau accompanied him to the station. With a tremble in his voice and moisture in his eyes, Clemenceau told

Baker, "In saying goodbye to the President I feel that I am saying goodbye to my best friend."[19] Yet Clemenceau appreciated as well how much of the responsibility for France's successes lay with House, who had done so much of the negotiation himself. In a farewell letter to House a few months before Clemenceau's death in November 1929, the French leader wrote, "When you will come back to Europe next year, I may have changed planets. Wherever I go, I will not forget you, for you have given my country, without harming yours, a shoulder to lean on in perilous days."[20]

The basis for their mutual understanding was born in October 1918, when Clemenceau offered immediate approval of the Fourteen Points, permitting House and Wilson to score a domestic victory over Theodore Roosevelt, who had encouraged Lloyd George and Clemenceau to impose their own conditions on a defeated Germany. In exchange, harsh terms were agreed on for the armistice, so that the Germans could not resume war in the near future.[21] The second key moment was in mid-March 1919, when Lloyd George and Wilson proposed to Clemenceau a triple defensive alliance—the Treaty of Guarantee that would assure immediate intervention by Britain and the United States in the event of German aggression against France. Lloyd George proposed it in the alliance on the suggestion of his secretary Kerr, but House probably told Clemenceau he had suggested it to Kerr.

This so-called Atlantic Alliance—in particular, the US military guarantees—was already Clemenceau's main strategic objective. Clemenceau had been only half-satisfied by the league's collective-defense clauses and would have preferred a stronger body, with an international police force on land and sea. Wilson rejected this idea.[22] And in mid-March 1919, in an effort to win the Senate's approval of the treaty, Wilson suppressed the automatic solidarity embodied in the January 1919 draft covenant. He accepted that the league's nine-member Executive Committee—which included the United States as a permanent member—would decide unanimously, on a case-by-case basis, which sanction to carry out in instances of international aggression. This meant that the league would not in fact be a defensive alliance, because the United States and other Executive Committee members would have a veto over declarations of war.[23] But this also opened a window of opportunity to clinch a deal on a special treaty of guarantee with France, entailing automatic engagement.

Russia, an old ally, was now out of the picture, so the Atlantic Alliance was fundamental, in Clemenceau's eyes, to French national security. Without British and US defensive guarantees, the league and the treaty were worth little. Thus Lloyd George declared that in the event of a German attack, all British forces would be put at France's disposal, and Wilson pledged his full support in the name of the United States.[24] In doing so, they saved French approval for the amendments to the league. Thanks to these pledges, a seemingly reluctant Clemenceau abandoned his request for an independent Rhineland republic. He did, however, secure the temporary occupation of the left bank of the Rhine. In view of France's geographical distance from Britain and even more so the United States, there would always be a period, in the case of a German offensive, where France would have to defend herself alone.[25]

The Treaty of Guarantee would be impotent if the US Senate did not approve. For one thing, the British alone could not provide sufficient aid; Clemenceau was relying primarily on the umbrella of US power. For another, the language of the agreement necessitated US approval. On the eve of signing the treaty, Lloyd George slipped a word into it without Clemenceau's immediate notice: the treaty would become operative "only" if the Americans ratified it. So when the Senate failed to do so, the British Empire declined any obligation of solidarity with France.

Clemenceau felt cheated, and the French lost confidence in Britain.[26] But House agreed with Clemenceau that the unhappy situation in Europe was due primarily to the US failure to ratify the Versailles Treaty and the Treaty of Guarantee.[27] House thought that, in concert, the Versailles Treaty, the League of Nations, and the Treaty of Guarantee were a good basis for collective security and a fairer world. Versailles marked a significant advance for the right of self-determination, assuring sovereignty to several small nations. Germany would lose 12 percent of its territory, but much of it was populated by French, Walloons, Danes, and Poles; under the rubric of self-determination, they did not belong in Germany anyway. Still, Germany would remain the largest country in Europe, and the US presence on the league's Reparations Committee would have made it possible,

House argued, to reduce German indemnities in exchange for an effective guarantee of French borders. There was thus a great deal to like in the final package. House was thus deeply distressed when Wilson not only failed to bring Senate Republicans along but eventually did his best to derail ratification.

Bullitt began his conversations with House with a very different view, having decided that the territorial and reparations clauses of the Versailles Treaty were too unjust to be worthy of support—too great a breach of the liberal ideals of cooperation and self-determination to earn his backing, and too likely to produce further conflict in which the United States would be ensnared. But during his lengthy discussions with House, Bullitt came to better understand the colonel's realist vision of peace. And House was ready to find common cause with Bullitt, concluding that "Wilson first laid down the Fourteen Points and then laid down on the Fourteen Points."[28]

For House, too, Wilson's personality deserved further investigation. To be sure, House respected the president's canniness. "Wilson's acute mind was ever ready to take up the new and unusual, provided it was based in sound principles," House wrote to the historian Charles Seymour in 1922. "He had rare courage in this direction, which, together with his eloquence, made him particularly fit to become the spokesman of the world in the most trying time in history." Yet "he failed," House thought, "because he was temperamentally unfit to deal with the Senate."[29] House therefore was pleased that Freud should have taken an interest in the president. House was also happy to help Bullitt reevaluate his own—House's—place in history. When House and Bullitt landed in New York, House promised he would speak to Seymour. From his perch at Yale, the historian was in charge of the very papers Bullitt wished to see: House's unpublished diaries.

6

Princeton Nightmares

FREUD WOULD HAVE LOVED to have spoken with Wilson in person to better understand his personality and character. Not that Wilson was bereft of a legacy by which to know him. He left behind a voluminous corpus documenting his ideas and observations. Raised in and convinced of the value of the scriptures, he was steeped from an early age in the power of language and learned to choose his words carefully.[1]

Wilson conveyed precise meaning whether in casual conversation, correspondence, or prepared lectures. Wilson enjoyed the relationship between the orator and masses and experienced "an absolute joy in facing and conquering a hostile audience . . . or thawing out a cold one." Speaking to crowds "set my mind—all my faculties—aglow," he wrote. "I suppose that this very excitement gives my manner an appearance of confidence and self-command which arrests the attention. However that may be, I *feel* a sort of transformation—and it is hard to go to sleep afterwards."[2]

By the time he was a national political figure, Wilson was so covetous of his words that he had everything transcribed. During the 1912 presidential campaign, he hired a stenographer to do so. Charles Swem, then nineteen years old, would remain with Wilson throughout his two terms as president. The two worked with impressive speed and intensity. Every morning Swem would arrive at the White House at 9 o'clock and open Wilson's mail. The president dictated replies, and there would be no drafts or corrections. Wilson also dictated to Swem important letters, state papers, and diplomatic notes. The young stenographer went everywhere with the president, taking transcripts at his bedside, aboard ships, at the Peace Conference, and on the presidential campaign trail. At the end of his tenure, Swem had, by his own reckoning, written down 10 million of Wilson's words. Swem came to know the innermost workings of his employer's mind and considered himself "the great man's second self, the part that records what he considers best of him and worth recording."[3]

But these were crafted words, designed to show force of character and intellect, clarity of vision, courage of conviction, and capacity for leadership. Freud was focused on something else—not the seductive and self-interested power of a prepared speech or letter but the meanings that words conveyed when individuals spoke freely. The power of psychoanalysis to reveal the shrouded workings of the mind was itself rooted in open exchange between patient and analyst.[4] With the psychoanalyst sitting outside of view, the patient was asked to say everything that came to them, no matter how incoherent, absurd, immoral, or painful. You must speak, Freud wrote, "precisely *because* you feel an aversion to doing so."[5] A patient would often start treatment by telling the story of their life, then turn to stories of the day-to-day. At some point, they would begin to report their dreams. When recounting the content of a dream, the patient might suddenly say something that would provoke an idea, image, or reminiscence.[6] Speech, with its myriad meanings, could generate unexpected associations, until some scene from the past, long absent from a patient's consciousness, reappeared.

Sometimes an association arises without hesitation; the first idea or memory that occurs carries with it some sort of explanatory power that can help a patient understand their neurosis and thereby take control of it. Sometimes the patient produces a long chain of associations before arriving at understanding. "The longer and more roundabout the chain of associations the stronger the resistance" of the neurosis, Freud wrote.[7] In his landmark 1899 book, *The Interpretation of Dreams,* Freud tells of his many recurrent dreams concerning his own achievements. Through free association, the dreams bring him back to a scene from his youth, when he was seven or eight years old. "One evening before going to sleep," he remembers, "I disregarded the rules which modesty lays down and obeyed the call of nature in my parents' bedroom, while they were present. In the course of this reprimand, my father let fall the words: 'the boy will come to nothing.'" Freud interprets the recurrence of this scene, within dreams related to his successes, as a wish to tell his father, "You see, I have come to something."[8] A dream, he concludes, is always the expression of a wish or desire.

The association between dreams and the past was essential to Freud's thought and his therapeutic model. As he put it, to come to grips with oneself required "a *détour* through the pre-historic period of childhood."[9] The promise of psychoanalysis is that, through associations, the patient is able to regress to forgotten moments and connect these to present-day life, giving it new meaning. When, in the course of psychoanalysis, the moment of regression to the past ends, the memory of the scene remains vivid. Its meaning is reinterpreted and reintegrated in the adult mind, making the patient an active interpreter of the scene.[10] If the forgotten scene deeply structures the functioning and circulation of desires and other feelings, then its rediscovery—the present knowledge of the earlier scene—can yield some relief. Freud realized that this process of discovery could be facilitated by free association in the presence of a witness, and so psychoanalysis was born. This "talking cure," as one of Freud's first patients called it, led to an important further realization: only part of our mental life is conscious, while a significant part of it is unconscious.

The analysis could reveal these obliterated contents through the associations produced by dreams but also through slips of the tongue. A slip of the tongue, whether in speaking or writing, involves expressing something other than what one consciously intends. One has the intention of making a particular remark, but something interferes; an uncanny force interrupts and disturbs what one meant to say. This uncanny force is what Freud called the unconscious.[11]

The expression of the unconscious can take much more painful forms than a simple lapsus. It can involve the recurrence of an unhappy or uncomfortable situation in the course of everyday life. The patient acts as though compelled by another; in these cases, "We have the same relation to [the action] as we have to a psychical process in another person, except that it is in fact one of our own." These expressions of the unconscious through repetition and compulsion are important to notice, report, and interpret, as, for many, there can be no rest until one succeeds in understanding them. Access to that understanding creates the potential to live a freer, more active, and happier life, one less dependent on and subjugated to unknown and unmastered forces that cause suffering.

Wilson was not alive to report his dreams. And, even if he had reported them in writings or speeches, Freud could not have interpreted them. The analyst had to be present in the room with the patient to do the work of successive associations. But Bullitt and Freud were nonetheless lucky. They would be helped by Wilson's genuine openness to and intimacy with friends. "There are few great men given to letter-writing whose letters are frankly revealing," Edith Gittings Reid, a friend of Wilson's, noted. He was among these few.[12] Bullitt had already felt as much while reading biographies of Wilson by William Allen White, James Kerney, David Lawrence, and Ray Baker, as well as the memoirs of Joseph Tumulty, Wilson's White House secretary.[13]

Still, Bullitt needed more. He needed House's diaries, so he contacted Charles Seymour, the keeper of House's materials at Yale. As a historian, Seymour thought it critical that Bullitt's attitude toward historical research was "characterized by honesty." Duly impressed, Seymour advised House to help Bullitt as much as he could but not to allow unrestricted access to the diaries, as portions were better left confidential.[14] So House proposed that Seymour's assistant, Helen Reynolds, search the entire diary and extract everything dealing with Wilson that might be of interest for Bullitt's and Freud's work.[15] Then Bullitt would select what he wanted from the extracts, after which House would review them before letting him type them up for his own use.

At the end of July 1930, Reynolds gave Bullitt excerpts of House's diary. Bullitt also convinced her to let him read materials beyond her own selections. When House was informed, he was at first annoyed but eventually authorized Bullitt's access to wider segments of his diaries, provided all names were redacted.[16] Bullitt thanked House for the privilege. "No single episode illumines in a flash the problem my friend wishes to analyze," Bullitt wrote, referring to Freud, "but an accumulation of small incidents makes a mosaic."[17]

Bullitt noted Wilson's many declarations of friendship with House, which were reciprocated. House's December 22, 1913, diary entry states that Wilson "was solicitous of my welfare and came into my room to see that everything was properly arranged. He said he enjoyed talking with me because he did not have to think about what he was saying. He . . . was most affectionate in his manner." When House came back from his second trip to Europe on March 6, 1916, he noted that the president placed his arms around his shoulders and said, "I cannot adequately express to you my admiration and gratitude for what you have done. It would be impossible to imagine a more difficult task than the one placed in your hands, but you have accomplished it in a way beyond any expectations . . . my dear friend, you should be proud of yourself and not of me since you have done it all." Bullitt mentioned the gushing prose to Reynolds, who passed along his surprise to House. The colonel confirmed his closeness with Wilson. "As a matter of fact," House wrote to Reynolds, "I have never had a friend who opened his mind and heart to me more fully."[18]

What interested Bullitt most was the content of the confidences Wilson shared with House. Soon after they met in 1911, Wilson wrote House, "Every day I am confirmed in the judgment that my mind is a one-track road and can run only one train of thought at a time!"[19] House agreed. "The President's characterization of himself as 'a man with one track mind' is all too true, for he does not seem able to carry along more than one idea at a time," House wrote. Wilson also told House that "he always lacked any feeling of elation when a particular object was accomplished. When he signed the Tariff Bill"—the Revenue Act of 1913, major legislation lowering tariffs and establishing an income tax—"he could not feel the joy that was properly his, for it seemed to him that the thing was over and that another great work was calling for his attention, and he thought of this rather than the present victory."[20]

The diaries provided Bullitt with pieces of his "mosaic," but he needed yet more. If he was going to apply Freud's techniques—albeit, in attenuated form—he would have to understand the full course of Wilson's life. The biographies provided a good deal of information, but information alone was insufficient. Bullitt had to get into Wilson's mind. How do you get into the mind of a dead man? By talking with those who knew him best.

The Early Wilson

Bullitt's first interview was on July 9, 1930, with Dudley Malone in New York. Malone had been Wilson's campaign manager for the 1910 New Jersey gubernatorial election, and the two became close friends.

On the morning of election day, Malone was the only nonfamily member present at Wilson's home.[21] When Wilson took office as president in March 1913, he appointed Malone third assistant secretary of state, then collector of the Port of New York—one of the most powerful federal jobs of the time. Malone worked for Wilson during the 1916 presidential campaign as well. In September 1917, Malone stepped down from his post as collector, to protest Wilson's treatment of suffragists and their cause.[22] Later Malone married the feminist Doris Stevens. He remained a friend of Wilson's daughter, Jessie Woodrow Wilson Sayre, a liberal and also a militant for women's rights.

Malone helped Bullitt understand Wilson's passion for words—a passion that originated in childhood, that period of life so essential to the psychoanalytic enterprise. During the 1910 campaign, Malone explained, "Wilson was constantly talking about his father. He told me that his father taught him his use of words. He would sit on his father's knees, and they would play 'synonymous' using the old Worcester dictionary. Wilson on weekdays would get on the pulpit of his father's church and make speeches to the empty church or read from [Walter] Bagehot or other favorite authors. Wilson was very happy in his family. And I remember him say he missed not having a son." As far as Malone was concerned, Wilson "was very emotional, he had a white fire burning in him, if he had lived in the time of the Crusades he certainly would have gone."[23]

Indeed, Wilson was the son of a deeply Christian family. Born on December 28, 1856, in Staunton, Virginia, Thomas Woodrow Wilson was named in honor of his maternal grandfather Thomas Woodrow—a Presbyterian minister like Wilson's own father Joseph Ruggles Wilson, who was also a professor of rhetoric. Before Wilson was a year old, the family moved to Augusta, Georgia, where his father became pastor of the First Presbyterian Church. The father encouraged his son's love of words, directly and by example, yet the young Wilson was shy rather than loquacious, did not read before the age of nine, and did not write before he was eleven. Frail, with poor eyesight, he was also kept out of many sports.[24]

In researching Wilson's background, Bullitt encountered a genuine mystery: Wilson seemed to have no memory of the Civil War, yet the election of Abraham Lincoln apparently was firmly embedded in his mind. "My earliest recollection is of standing at my father's gateway in Augusta, Georgia, when I was four years old, and hearing someone pass and say that Mr. Lincoln was elected and there was to be war," Wilson said in a 1909 speech. "Catching the intense tones of his excited voice, I remember running in to ask my father what it meant."[25] Wilson's father sided with the South.

In May 1870, General Robert E. Lee came to Augusta. This, too, was a memorable day for Wilson. Forty years later, while president of Princeton University, he described "the delightful memory of standing, when a lad, for a moment by General Lee's side and looking up into his face." In Lee he found "a gentle figure—a man whom you remember, not as a man who loved war, but . . . a man whom men did not fear, but loved." Lee had "sacrificed himself for the things that were the nearest . . . He thought of the neighbors." By conviction, he chose to serve the South, even if he knew the cause was lost. "What has been the result?" Wilson asked his audience. "It has been that the South has retained the best asset, her self-respect." As Wilson put it, "A boy never gets over his boyhood . . . So, I am obliged to say again and again that the only place in the country, the only place in the world, where nothing has to be explained to me is the South." Lee was a "national hero," according to Wilson, which meant "there are no sections in this country anymore." All his life, Wilson would remain faithful to Lee.[26]

At the end of 1870, Wilson's father moved the family to Columbia, South Carolina, where he became a theology professor. At the age of fourteen, Wilson entered private school. He studied writing, history, and Latin and did badly, "not because he was not bright enough but because he was apparently not interested." He instead organized a baseball club, and, though he played the game poorly, was elected president of the club, writing its bylaws and creating a parliamentary procedure for its operation. All his life, "he was drawing up constitutions for various organizations, and finally a covenant for the nations of the world," Ray Baker wrote.[27]

During the winter of 1872–1873, Wilson had a religious awakening—a foundational experience that came courtesy of Francis J. Brooke, a ministry student "on fire with zeal." Brooke studied with Wilson's father and held religious meetings in his quarters. The meetings became so popular that they were moved to the seminary's chapel. It was during one of these meetings with Brooke that Wilson experienced his "religious turning." From that moment forward, he felt a direct connection with God. Every day he would say grace before meals, pray morning and evening, and read his Bible. As he put it, "So far as religion is concerned, argument is adjourned." When he was president, Wilson visited the chapel where he had his epiphany. He paused at the doorway and said, "I feel as though I ought to take off my shoes. This is holy ground." He added, "I have never heard greater speaking in my life than I have heard from that rostrum."[28]

Wilson and Brooke became friends, and the former followed the latter to Davidson College, outside Charlotte, North Carolina. Wilson remained at best an average student; his true interest was in the debating society. If he was not especially fond of classes, though, he was at this stage becoming a highly skilled speaker and writer.

In fall 1875 Wilson enrolled at Princeton. Here he had an intellectual awakening to pair with his earlier religious one. Inspiration came in the form of "The Orator," an 1874 *Gentleman's Magazine* article describing how British prime minister William Gladstone had risen to leadership through daily debating tournaments in the House of Commons.[29] After reading the story, Wilson wrote to his father that "he had found that he had a mind."[30] The discovery broke his shyness and convinced him that he would be like Gladstone: he, too, would debate and conquer through his moral earnestness and choice of words. He, too, would lead through oratory. Wilson went on to head a debate group at Princeton, where he stood out as a man of principle. Once, he was assigned to defend protectionism, which he strongly opposed; he refused the assignment and left the debate competition.[31]

Wilson's father "had moments of regret that his brilliant son had not chosen the ministry." But the two were close, and the elder did not dissuade his son from his vocation.[32] Indeed, Joseph Wilson encouraged his boy. "I am greatly pleased to know that extemporaneous speaking is your forte," he wrote in a letter to Wilson after he had moved on to the University of Viriginia Law School. "By all means cultivate the gift or rather the assemblage of gifts. It is rare, and as valuable as rare. It is the diamond among those accomplishments which ensure the future of a public man."[33] Despite his gifts and his success, Wilson never believed he truly lived up to the confidence his father had in him—or his father's model. "I wish I could believe that I had inherited that rarest gift of making great truth attractive in the telling and of inspiring with great purposes by sheer force of eloquence or by gentle stress of persuasion," Wilson wrote. He always felt inadequate in comparison to his father. "If I had my father's face and figure, it wouldn't make any difference what I said," he quipped.[34]

At Christmas in 1879, Wilson returned to Staunton, Virginia, his birthplace, where some of his cousins attended the Augusta Female Seminary (now Mary Baldwin University). He fell in love with one of them, Hattie Woodrow, the daughter of his mother's beloved brother, also Thomas Woodrow. Wilson began a "somewhat ardent correspondence" with Hattie, but his health collapsed in December 1880. This was a source of deep discouragement. "How can a man with a weak body ever arrive anywhere," he asked despondently. He convalesced at his family's home, now in Wilmington, North Carolina, and worked hard on the law. In summer 1881, he asked Hattie for her hand in marriage and was refused.[35] Shortly thereafter, he stopped signing his name "T. Woodrow Wilson" and declared that he would sign as "Woodrow Wilson" from then on. "I need a trademark in advertising my literary wares," he explained. "Thomas W. Wilson lacks something—Woodrow Wilson sticks in the mind."[36]

In June 1882 Wilson moved to Atlanta. He was admitted to the bar in October but did not enjoy practicing law in exchange for money, which he found incompatible with "the best interest of intellectual life."[37] Instead that interest would be served in academia. In 1883 he enrolled at Johns Hopkins, where he pursued a PhD in political science. That same year, in April, he met Ellen Louise Axson, the daughter of another Presbyterian minister, and fell in love. They decided to marry, but not before Ellen went off to study art in New York.

At Johns Hopkins, Wilson wrote a thesis in which he aspired to explain American political institutions according to their actual functioning rather than the ideals ascribed to them.[38] He took aim at the Constitution's framers as men so afraid of despotism that they designed a government in which power was fragmented and seemed to reside nowhere. By the mid-1880s, congressional committees bargained behind closed doors, and the power of the president, the sole representative of the people, had declined to not much more than routine. But a constitution "is accountable to Darwin not to Newton," Wilson wrote: it has to evolve over time. Impressed by the British parliamentary system, he urged creating a new form of government in which all authority—legislative and executive—lay with a Congress designed to be accountable to the public, legislating on the basis of open debate.[39] The thesis was published in book form as *Congressional Government* in 1885, the same year Wilson and Ellen married.

Though the work of a fresh graduate, Wilson's book attracted attention and elevated him to the highest level of constitutional scholarship. Bryn Mawr College, which had just opened in 1885, wanted to recruit him. Wilson hesitated; he did not favor higher education for women, even if he recognized that its time had come. Eventually he accepted the position. Together with Ellen at Bryn Mawr, Wilson found a sense of security. He was never away from his home for more than a day without writing Ellen. "You are the only person in the world—without *any* exception—to whom I can tell *all* that my heart contains," he wrote. "I am the only one who can rest him," she once told a friend.[40] She gave birth to their first girl in 1886, their second the following year, and a third the year after that.

Wilson made a powerful impression at Bryn Mawr, but when Wesleyan made him an offer with a higher salary, he didn't delay. "I have for a long time been hungry for a class of men," he wrote his friend Robert Bridges, a Princeton professor.[41] And soon enough he moved on once more, with Bridges's support. Princeton was Wilson's dream; he joined the faculty in 1890.

Among the reports on Wilson's emotional life contained in House's diaries were curious references to the president's time at Princeton. On December 12, 1913, Wilson told House that he had not slept well the night before—he had nightmares concerning his Princeton years. "These terrible days have sunk deep into his soul," House wrote, "and he will carry their mark to his grave." The following January, House noted that whenever they had no governmental business to discuss, somehow or other Wilson would drift into discussing "his life at Princeton and his troubles there, showing . . . how deeply the iron entered his soul."[42] "It was not until well into his second term that

Wilson got over talking about his experience in Princeton," House told Bullitt.[43]

What had gone so wrong? Why the repeated nightmares, the anxiety and obsession? Whatever happened at Princeton seemed to distract Wilson even from his role as president of the United States. It was as if he was bound, against his will, to a compulsion to repeat the past.

A Stubborn Heart

Wilson had a chair at Princeton and was surrounded by love: his wife, three daughters, and his father, who had come to live with them after the death of his wife, Wilson's mother.[44] Wilson also developed an intimate friendship with a fellow faculty member, John Grier Hibben, a former Presbyterian minister who joined Princeton a year after Wilson as an instructor in logic. They would meet almost every day and trusted each other completely. Their wives, too, became friends. But Wilson was overworking "outrageously," to the point of doubting the meaning of his life. He suffered headaches, stomach pain, and general nervousness. In 1896 he had a breakdown and lost the use of his right hand. He learned to write with his left hand and found relief in solitary travel to England, where he would tour the countryside, most often by bicycle.[45] "I am so tired of a merely talking profession!" he told his brother-in-law Stockton Axson, "I want to *do* something."[46]

The occasion to act came on June 9, 1902, when Wilson was elected president of Princeton University. Full of happiness, he declared, "I feel like a new prime minister getting ready to address his constituents."[47] This was the moment to fulfill his dreams of leadership: "He was Gladstone at last," Bullitt commented.[48] Wilson obtained full and independent power to appoint and dismiss professors, develop systems of discipline, impose compulsory church attendance, and implement other sorts of university policy. Faculty and trustees enthusiastically supported Wilson's major pedagogical policy, which saw the university shift from classroom teaching to a tutorial model "resembling Oxford but better than Oxford." Better, Wilson thought, because the tutors would be appointed not for life but for five-year terms.[49] Wilson raised enough funds to recruit fifty tutors and keep the new system going for three years.

By the end of 1905, Wilson was highly popular at Princeton, yet he still felt unhappy. In February 1906 he was again close to a nervous breakdown. One morning in May of that year, he woke up blind in his left eye. Hibben found him doctors in Philadelphia and the two visited together. A Dr. Stengel recommended that Wilson take a long break and slow down his work.[50] With Ellen and the three children, he departed for a few months of rest in England.

Wilson returned to Princeton in fall 1906. It was at this point that his real troubles began. Andrew West, dean of the graduate college, had just been offered the MIT presidency. West was frustrated and prepared to leave: unlike Harvard and Yale, which had well-established graduate colleges, Princeton had only forty graduate students, who studied in professors' homes. After Wilson and the Princeton board of trustees pledged to erect a graduate college, West agreed to stay. But, as would become clear soon, the problem was hardly solved.[51]

In truth, Wilson was little concerned with the graduate school. He was focused on another issue: classism on campus. He wanted to abolish the upper-class clubs that were at the heart of student life. The university had never provided a dining hall, so instead students jockeyed for admission to one of the twelve elegant clubhouses in town, which came complete with lawns and tennis courts. The clubs accommodated only juniors and seniors and then selectively, most often the sons of the wealthy.[52] Students left out after junior year arrived felt humiliated and ostracized and often left the university. For Wilson, this was the perpetuation of an aristocracy that had no place in a democratic society.[53] He proposed instead grouping students in residential colleges like those at Oxford or Cambridge. Each college would have a dining hall for socializing and recreation.[54] Moved by Wilson's arguments, the board of trustees endorsed his recommendations on June 10, 1907.

But Wilson was in for a rude awaking. Some faculty felt contempt because they had not been consulted, leading to opposition. At a faculty meeting on September 26, Hibben not only voted against Wilson's proposal but seconded a motion against it brought by another professor, one Henry van Dyke. Still, the faculty on the whole were supportive, voting eighty to twenty-three to back the plan.[55] But alumni, nostalgic for their time in the clubs, were almost unanimously opposed and refused to support financially the expensive project of developing residential colleges. Wilson responded harshly. Sometimes he made light of alumni sentiment, but his moralizing streak was irrepressible: "if we are right, they must be wrong," he said at one point. Characteristically, Wilson personalized the fight, rejecting any compromise on what he called "nothing less than the most critical work of my whole administration."[56] When the board of trustees met on October 17, their opinion had changed. With alumni unwilling to support the proposal, they formally requested that Wilson withdraw it.[57]

Wilson considered resigning but instead took to the road to address and convert the alumni in a series of speeches in the East and Midwest. This effort at persuasion failed miserably and Wilson had another breakdown. "Tortured by nerves, neuritis, sick headaches and sour stomach," he sought rest in Bermuda in January 1908.[58] Ellen Wilson attributed the breakdown to "the loss of a friend he took to his bosom"—that is, Hibben.[59] After returning to Princeton on February 27, he remained obsessed with Hibben. A year later Wilson wrote to Mary Peck, a friend he had made in Bermuda, "What a fool I am to go back to that so often! Can my heart never be cured of its hurt?" A few months later, he would write again how his "stubborn heart" would not heal from the wound of Hibben's betrayal.[60]

Wilson had lost the board in part because he was still doing nothing about the graduate college. For Grover Cleveland, former US president and a member of the board, this represented a serious breach of Wilson's pledge to West.[61] Then, a new opportunity arose in May 1909. William Procter—an alumnus and head of Procter & Gamble—proposed a $500,000 donation for the graduate college, provided the trustees raised an equal sum. The only condition was that the graduate school not be in the center of the campus because the grounds there did not offer enough space for future expansion. West, who agreed that the college should be in a remote location, was grateful. But Wilson would not hear of it. He demanded that the graduate school be sited in the middle of campus and further argued that he could not accept that the educational policy of the university would "be determined by those who give money."[62]

Yet this principled justification belied the underlying issue: the facts suggest that what Wilson really could not accept was the challenge to his power that West represented. "West must be absolutely eliminated," Wilson told his supporters. He would make no "concession of any kind that would not entirely eliminate West from the situation."[63] Wilson's anger was utterly out of proportion with the substance of the dispute. Indeed, he did not actually object to the remote location preferred by Procter and West. At one point, Wilson proposed building two graduate colleges, one on campus and one elsewhere.[64] When Moses Taylor Pyne, chairman of the board of trustees, announced at a board meeting on January 13, 1910, that Procter had accepted this proposal, Wilson gave up the game: he replied that the location dispute was less important than the fact that Procter was trying to carry out Dean West's and not Princeton's ideals.

From the board's perspective, Wilson's obstinacy was unfathomable. During the meeting, he was forced to acknowledge that he had supported West's plan before becoming its enemy, even writing a laudatory preface to a report West had written on the development of a graduate college. Faced with further evidence of his irrational position, Wilson replied that he had not read the document before approving it. But the truth was that he had personally corrected proofs of the report. Wilson's contradictions lost him the board's faith in his integrity and ability to continue governing the university.[65]

Wilson responded by launching a publicity campaign in which he claimed the board was persecuting him for his efforts to democratize Princeton by replacing dinner clubs with residential colleges. It was this version of the story that the *New York Times* published on February 3, in an editorial emphasizing Wilson's struggle against social "exclusiveness" and for "real democracy." As Bullitt later discovered, the editorial—though unsigned and therefore representing the perspective of the newspaper—was in fact written by Wilson. A few days later, Procter withdrew his offer.[66]

Wilson continued giving speeches and writing letters defending "his political reputation as an enemy of the plutocratic snobbery."[67] At an alumni meeting in Pittsburgh on April 16, Wilson asked, "Which should have precedence, the Princeton family judgment, or the common judgment of the country?" He answered, "By the standard of the country will the college be judged." The judgment was severe: "The colleges . . . serve the classes, not the masses. They serve certain strata, certain visible uplifted strata, and ignore the men whose need is dire" while "looking to the support of wealth rather than to the people."[68] The Pittsburgh speech stirred up excitement all over the country, but it infuriated the Princeton community. A new twist came on May 18, with the death of Isaac C. Wyman, a wealthy Princeton alumnus. Wyman's will directed that his whole estate, worth an estimated $2 to $4 million, be dedicated to endowing a graduate college at Princeton University. West was named as one of the two executors of the will. Wilson knew that the board of trustees would not refuse the gift, that West would be acknowledged as the leader of the graduate college, and that he had lost.

Wilson did not resign from Princeton until October, but he had unofficially moved on months earlier by throwing in his hat for the Democratic nomination for governor of New Jersey. He got it due in part to the support of George Harvey, owner of *Harper's Weekly,* who thought Wilson safely conservative. For one thing, Wilson opposed women's suffrage. He saw a woman's place as in the home and had an aversion to what he called "masculinized women" who agitated for voting rights. In June 1909, he had also spoken out against labor unions, which he accused of undercutting business profits.[69] On June 23, 1910, in a final push for the nomination, Wilson promised fealty to New Jersey Democratic Party boss James Smith, saying that if he were nominated and elected governor, he would not start "fighting or breaking down the Democratic state organization."[70] From a man so idealistic about open government, this was a staggering promise. It was also an empty one. Immediately after winning office in November 1910, Wilson backed Smith's opponent in a race for the US Senate. Wilson went on to build a coalition of state Democrats and Republicans who wanted to reform election laws and regulate trusts, a further blow to the New Jersey Democratic machine.[71]

Wilson barely settled into the governor's office before launching his successful bid for the presidency. Shortly after his inauguration in March 1913, the now-president came to the Capitol to deliver his first message to Congress, following the suggestion of a New Jersey newspaperman who thought it would be a "good opening trick" to revive this practice associated with George Washington, which Thomas Jefferson and subsequent presidents had abandoned.[72] Wilson wanted to give the impression that the president was a person, not a governmental department. Symbolically, if not constitutionally, he was prime minister at last.

Despite all that Wilson accomplished during the first two years of his presidency, he could not get over the Princeton rebuke. At dinner on December 22, 1913, after House had discussed some of Wilson's achievements, the president replied "that his Princeton experience hung over him sometimes like a nightmare; that he had wonderful success there, and all at once conditions changed and the troubles, of which everyone knows, were brought about. He seemed to fear that such a dénouement might occur again."[73]

This fear of recurring, uncontrolled, and painful events was for Freud a typical sign of neurosis. The Princeton discoveries excited Bullitt. Wasn't the case of Hibben, a dear friend who became for Wilson a traitor, reproduced a few years later by House? And what of West, with whom Wilson could not compromise even over minor differences, and the Princeton trustees, alumni, and friends whom Wilson antagonized until he destroyed his own project? Was the same situation not reproduced later with Lodge and the Senate?

7

Neurosis on the World Stage

IN MID-MARCH 1917, when Wilson was struggling with the decision to enter the war, he asked *News of the World* editor Frank Cobb to visit him at the White House. "You know what this means?" Wilson asked.

> It would mean that we should lose our heads along with the rest and stop weighing right and wrong. It would mean that a majority of people in this hemisphere would go war-mad, quit thinking, and devote their energy to destruction . . . they'll forget there ever was such a thing as tolerance. To fight, you must be brutal and ruthless, and the spirit of ruthless brutality will enter the very fiber of our national life, infecting Congress, the courts, the policeman on the beat, the man in the street.

Wilson worried that the Constitution would not survive, that free speech and the right to assembly would go. "If there is any alternative, for God's sake, let's take it."[1] Yet finally he did decide to go to war and to apply the very domestic measures he feared, such as whittling down freedom of speech by means of the Espionage Act of 1917 and the Sedition Act of 1918. How to explain these shifts?

The answer perhaps lies in Wilson's psyche: his personality was playing out on the world stage. Throughout the period of the war and during the Versailles negotiations, the conflict and distrust characteristic of his time at Princeton emerged again. But this time the consequences were far greater.

Lurching toward War

During a June 1914 trip to Europe, House met the German kaiser in Berlin, British foreign secretary Edward Grey in London, and many other German and British leaders. Though House and Wilson both were pro-British—House more so than Wilson—they had decided that the

United States should remain neutral and seek peace between the parties. Though House's mediation efforts failed, the experience gave him a sense of the issues and individuals that contoured European affairs.[2] "When I was in London for Wilson," House said, "I . . . saw the King often."[3] When war broke out on July 28, 1914, House communicated by code with Grey and his successor Arthur Balfour. On a few occasions, Wilson spoke to the British government through House, circumventing the State Department and the US ambassador in London.[4]

With the war underway, House remained Wilson's emissary. In early 1915, when the German ambassador in Washington gave signals that his country was ready for talks, House set on a mission to Europe. This mission, too, ended with little to show. In London, the British demanded that peace talks be delayed until the Allies were in a better military position. When House arrived in Berlin in March, the Germans were no longer disposed to negotiate: they had the feeling they could win the war and were preparing a submarine offensive in retaliation for Britain's blockade. On May 7, 1915, a U-boat sank RMS *Lusitania,* the pride of the Cunard Line, a graceful, four-funnel vessel; about 1,100 passengers died, among them 128 Americans. The news created an unforgettable shock comparable to that caused decades later by the bombing of Pearl Harbor and the Kennedy assassination. Years on, people still "remember[ed] the surroundings in which they read [about] it, the emotions they had, their actions the rest of the day." A few days later, after some hesitation, Wilson composed a note to the German government on his typewriter, requesting that it disavow the act, provide reparations, and take immediate steps to prevent any recurrence.[5] But William Jennings Bryan, Wilson's pacifist secretary of state, convinced him to send a secret note to the German government telling them he was ready to submit the *Lusitania* dispute to an investigative commission. Robert Lansing, then a legal adviser to the State Department, intercepted the note. Together, Lansing and Tumulty, Wilson's secretary, convinced the president not to send it. Wilson instead sent a second *Lusitania* note to the German government to underscore his first position, provoking Bryan's resignation.[6] He was replaced by Lansing.

Soon House was back in the United States, where he found Wilson in love. This was a major turn in Wilson's life. His wife Ellen had died on August 6, 1914, leaving Wilson in misery. His despair was so great that he told House he wished somebody would kill him.[7] Seeking companionship, Wilson asked Tumulty to come live in the White House. And Wilson grew even closer to House. Then in March 1915, through Admiral Grayson, Wilson met Edith Bolling Galt. A tall, elegant forty-three-year-old with gray eyes and dark hair, she was the widow of Norman Galt, a prosperous Washington jeweler. Wilson immediately began courting her. By June, he was dying to get House's opinion on whether they should marry. How, Wilson wondered, would the public react to a love affair that had started less than a year after Ellen's death? House heard the president's concerns and then gave his full support. In July, Edith Galt agreed to marry Wilson, and the ceremony was scheduled for December.

Not long after the couple were engaged, on August 19, a U-boat sank another civilian vessel, the British liner SS *Arabic*. Then came revelations of German spying in the United States. And in October, the British nurse Edith Cavell faced a German execution squad in Brussels for helping 200 Allied soldiers escape from German-occupied Belgium. Cavell's story impressed the American public and deepened US opposition to German militarism. For his part, House was anxious that Germany was winning the war. He feared that Germany would dominate the seas and drag the United States into a war for control of South America. When that day came, the country would be unprepared and would need allies on its side.

House believed it was time for Wilson to take steps to prevent German victory. He also thought the president might be persuaded. Wilson had recently told House—"much to my surprise," House wrote—that "he had never been sure that we ought not to take a part in the conflict, and if it seemed evident that Germany and her militaristic ideas were to win, the obligation upon us was greater than ever."[8] And House had something to offer Wilson: a grandiose vision of statesmanship, courtesy of Grey. To convince the United States to join the Allies, Grey suggested to House that the president "propose a League of Nations binding themselves to side against any power breaking a treaty or certain rules of warfare on land or sea. The government of the United States is the only government that could make it with effect," Grey added.[9]

Wilson did not immediately endorse the league idea, but he supported a plan whereby House would proceed to Berlin and "tell them it was the President's purpose to intervene and to stop this destructive war . . . If the Central Powers were still obdurate, it would *probably* be necessary for us to join the Allies and force the issue." It was Wilson who added that word—"probably."[10] On October 17, House shared the plan with Grey. The British responded with disappointment. After weeks of delay, Grey replied that he was not in a position to negotiate. The British war cabinet sought a vigorous Allied effort, with no hesitation.[11]

Still, in December, Wilson pushed House to go to Europe. There, he was to convey the message that the United States was to have nothing to do with local settlements. "The only guarantees for a lasting peace," the president insisted, "were a) military and naval disarmament and b) a league of nations to secure each nation against aggression and secure absolute freedom of the seas." This was Wilson's first statement in support of Grey's proposed League of Nations.[12] During House's trip to Europe, Wilson wrote to him only once, to reaffirm that he would "be willing and glad when the opportunity comes to cooperate in a policy seeking to bring about and maintain permanent peace among the civilized nations."[13] A league had become Wilson's mission. To succeed, he needed a way for the United States to intervene more actively in the conflict.

House, in contrast, was more focused on tying the United States to the British and the French. On February 22, 1916, in London, he and Grey agreed on a joint memorandum stating, "Colonel House told me that President Wilson was ready, upon hearing from France and England that the moment was opportune, to propose that a conference should be summoned to put an end to the war. Should the Allies accept this proposal, and should Germany refuse it, the United States would probably enter the war against Germany." The conference would secure peace "on terms not unfavorable to the Allies."[14] If the Germans were too demanding, "the United States would probably leave the conference as a belligerent on the side of the Allies." The second instance of the word "probably" was again the sole change Wilson made to the memorandum, but the addition left the British concerned that Wilson would not secure a declaration of war from Congress.[15] Germany was occupying Belgium, Serbia, Alsace-Lorraine, and Poland and was not about to abandon these territories simply because of an Allied request made with equivocal US backing. Only a declaration of war and active US participation on the Allies' side could sway Germany.

After a torpedo attack on the French steamer *Sussex,* on March 24, 1916, killing four Americans, Wilson was willing to go further. He wrote to Grey on his own typewriter, "Since it seems probable that this country must break with Germany on the submarine question unless the unexpected happens, and since, if this country should once become a belligerent, the war would undoubtedly be prolonged, I beg to suggest that if you have any thought of acting at an early date on the plan we agreed upon, you might wish now to consult with your allies with a view of acting immediately." The United States was ready to go to war—would the British agree to limit their postwar claims of German territories? Grey did not respond to Wilson's note. On May 5, 1916, the Germans accepted Wilson's demands and promised to cease attacks against passenger and freight vessels.

Frustrated by Britain's rejection, and annoyed by British seizures of mail on American ships as well as Westminster's brutal repression of Irish rebellion, Wilson wrote to House that it was time for the United States to insist on its rights toward Great Britain as firmly as it had vis-à-vis Germany.[16] The day after his reelection, Wilson told House he wanted to address a letter to all belligerents demanding that fighting cease. But House opposed any attempt to mediate without Allied approval. He also warned Wilson of the risk of war with England and France. This was a departure from House's approach to handling Wilson when they disagreed; usually House would keep quiet and drop the matter. Then, eventually, Wilson would come to House with an idea, forgetting that it was House who had first proposed it and that he, the president, had rejected it.

This time Wilson was not convinced, but his position assured him few allies. Feeling very much alone, he struggled to sleep. He had admitted before that he was not made of steel and was, more than any man he knew, dependent upon his friends' sympathy and belief in him for the strength to do his work.[17] He suffered intensely the disagreement with House. Lansing, it turned out, was on the colonel's side. What is more, Wilson had just asked Tumulty, his faithful secretary, to resign, leaving himself that much more isolated.[18]

Wilson delayed sending his letter to polish it. Too long, as it turned out, because on December 12, the German government sent its own letter offering peace to the belligerent governments before Wilson was able to dispatch his peace note on December 18. Wilson called for ending the war and for a public statement of terms asking if "each side was ready to consider the formation of a league of nations to ensure peace and justice throughout the world." Neither side welcomed the note. The British and their allies bristled because Wilson placed them on equal footing with the Germans by "calling attention to the fact that the objects, which the statesmen of the belligerents on both sides have in mind in this war, are virtually the same."[19] As for the Germans, those who favored negotiations could not be "forced to publicize and reveal their minimum position in advance to fulfill Wilson's request." Doing so would backfire domestically or force Germany into an untenable negotiating position.[20]

Wilson continued his efforts. In the Senate on January 22, 1917, he advocated peace without victory. "Victory would mean peace forced upon the loser," he said, "a victor's terms imposed upon the vanquished. It would be accepted in humiliation, under duress, at an intolerable sacrifice, and would leave a sting, a resentment, a bitter memory upon which terms of peace would rest, not permanently, but only as upon quicksand."[21] Bullitt called it the "greatest speech of [Wilson's] career." But it came too late. The German government had already decided that it would start unrestricted submarine warfare on February 1. On February 3, the president, aghast, decided to break diplomatic relations with Germany as a final means of applying pressure. Matters grew still worse a few weeks later, when the so-called Zimmermann telegram—promising New Mexico, Arizona, and Texas to Mexico as a reward if it joined the war on Germany's side—was revealed to Wilson and the US public. Arthur Zimmermann, the German secretary of state, confirmed the offer's authenticity: "I cannot deny it. It is true," he told an American journalist. The United States and its president were outraged.[22]

On March 19 three US ships were sunk. For Wilson, this was the last straw. "Our motive will not be revenge or the victorious assertion of the physical might of the nation, but only the vindication of right, of human right, of which we are only a single champion," he stated. "The present German submarine warfare against commerce is a warfare against mankind. It is a war against all nations." As he explained to Congress, "There is one choice we cannot make, we are incapable of making: we will not choose the path of submission . . . With a profound sense of the solemn and even tragical character of the step I am taking and of the grave responsibilities which it involves, but in unhesitating obedience to what I deem my constitutional duty, I advise that the Congress declare the recent course of the Imperial German government to be in fact nothing less than war against the government and people of the United States." After the speech, Wilson was shocked by the applause he received. Did the people's representatives not understand how many would die? He returned to the White House and exploded in tears.[23]

Wilson was slow in making up his mind, but once he did, it became "as hard as adamant."[24] Two days after requesting—and receiving—the war declaration, the president formed the Committee on Public Information to "sell the war" to Americans. The committee organized a system of "self-censorship" for newspapers; produced a stream of films, posters, and pamphlets; and recruited 75,000 volunteers to serve as "Four Minute Men" who presented patriotic information during the roughly four minutes it took to change film reels in movie theaters. June 5 was declared registration day; nearly 10 million American men between the ages of twenty-one and thirty-one were obligated to sign up for the draft. That same month, Congress passed the Espionage Act, which punished "false statements with intent to interfere with the operations of the military forces" and empowered the postmaster general to censor material "advocating or urging treason, insurrection, or forcible resistance to any law of the United States." Wilson also called on industry to put patriotism before profits and keep prices low. A newly established War Industries Board would coordinate between industrial and military leaders to ensure sufficient supplies for the Allied war effort.

Herbert Hoover, who spent the first two and a half years of the conflict directing US relief to Belgium, was placed in charge of a new government body, the Food Administration. Operating under the slogan

"Food Will Win the War," he used the agency's powers to freeze prices, organize farmers for greater productivity, and protect against profiteers. The Allied cause depended on food, and he was responsible for providing it—enough to feed 100 million Europeans.[25] Hoover called on Americans to tighten their belts and on proscribed days of the week go "meatless," "wheatless," or "porkless" to save food for shipment to Europe. "Hooverize" entered the lexicon, meaning to be sparing and economical. The results were phenomenal. In just a quarter of a year, reduction in sweets consumption alone enabled the United States to send 500,000 tons of sugar abroad.

Bullitt could not help but notice that the president was a poor strategic thinker. Wilson would rarely envision the consequences of actions on the global scale, nor did he realize that those consequences had consequences of their own—second-order effects. For instance, Bullitt was horrified when Wilson, on March 3, 1918, blessed French and British plans to support Japanese military intervention in Vladivostok, Siberia, to protect valuable military stock perceived as under threat from the new Bolshevik government.[26] Bullitt believed that Japanese intervention would push the Bolsheviks into Germany's arms. He urged Frank Polk, counselor of the State Department, not to communicate Wilson's approval, but the French ambassador was already waiting in a nearby room and Polk did not want to disobey Wilson. Bullitt telephoned House, who agreed with his position in toto. Bullitt asked House to write to Wilson that the moral position he had given the Triple Entente cause might be destroyed in one night.[27] On March 5, Wilson had Polk deliver a new note to the Triple Entente ambassadors opposing the intervention. The reversal was complete.[28] "His judgment was very bad," House would later say of Wilson. "It was necessary to call his attention to the results of certain lines of action."[29]

On October 6, 1918, with the war approaching its end, German chancellor Maximilian of Baden wrote to Wilson acceding to the Fourteen Points. Wilson was thrilled. Tumulty, whom the president had ultimately kept as his secretary, later testified, "Wilson wanted to accept . . . immediately. I struggled with him in New Jersey and all the way down on the train telling him he could not take the bloody paw of the Kaiser."[30] Wilson relented and sought counsel from House and Lansing. Collectively, they worked on a response that took the form of three questions: Were the Germans accepting all fourteen conditions? Would they evacuate all occupied territories? Was the chancellor speaking in the name of the "authorities of the Empire who have thus far conducted the war?" The German government responded affirmatively to each question, suggesting it was ready to negotiate. But on October 12, a German submarine sank the British steamer *Leinster.* Hundreds died at sea. Wilson's response on October 14 was harsh, saying that conditions of armistice could be decided only by the Allied military chiefs on the ground. That same day, Wilson appointed House his representative in the Supreme War Council, the central command that coordinated Allied military activities in Europe. House called that day "one of the most stirring . . . of my life."[31]

Then, with House in Paris, Wilson made one of the biggest political mistakes of his presidency. At a time when he would have been well served to set aside partisan concerns, he called on Americans to elect a Democratic Congress. Enraged Republicans united behind Theodore Roosevelt's banner and won the 1918 midterm elections. With the Senate now in Republican hands, Wilson's global leadership was crippled. In contrast, the British and French leaders enjoyed the backing of their parliaments. At Versailles, the US delegation was weakened by Wilson's electoral defeat and his refusal to include any prominent Republicans in the negotiating team, especially those who could have helped him obtain Senate approval for a treaty. "He felt strong enough to do the job alone," Bullitt wrote. "He intended to make the peace himself with the unobstructive assistance of House." Wilson wanted "to lay down the terms of peace in person, and to organize the League of Nations as he had organized the debating clubs at Princeton, Virginia, and Johns Hopkins."[32]

Losing the Peace

In Paris, Wilson lived in a magnificent *hotel particulier* on Rue de Monceau with his wife, his doctor, his chief usher, and two stenographers. The location was isolated—half a mile from House and the American delegation, who were at Hotel Crillon, Place de la Concorde, just beside the US Embassy. There was, at least, a direct telephone line installed between Wilson and House.[33] Tumulty, having stayed behind in the White House, kept Wilson abreast of public opinion in the United States and sent the president advice. In a clipped December 16 telegram, Tumulty suggested that Wilson visit American soldiers: "Stories that come over only show tribute to president as an official living in a palace and guarded by soldiers makes bad impression here."[34] One week later, Wilson spent Christmas with American troops.

Before the opening of the Paris conference, Wilson presented himself to the European people in a three-week tour, including trips to London and Rome. The president could feel it: a "Wilsonian" conception of peace had emerged, taking precedence over other forms of thinking and embarrassing the associated European powers. Self-determination, democracy, an alliance of nations, an end to war—a new regime of peace was on its way.[35] Wilson intended that the League of Nations be the beginning and center of the whole program, with everything else revolving around it. House agreed. The drawing of borders "had been the subject matter of peace conferences since time immemorial"; the treaty to come would be something new. Not a division of spoils but a foundation for a stable and nonviolent international system. Wilson had "a great opportunity to make himself the champion of peace and to change the order of things throughout the world."[36]

The peace conference opened solemnly on January 18, 1919, in the Clock Room at the Quai d'Orsay. A week later Wilson earned conference approval to make the league a full part of the treaty. Now he needed to negotiate the treaty's contents. He satisfied the British by turning over control of the German colonies. Lloyd George started by defending direct annexations claimed by British dominions, including the German colonies of New Guinea and Southwest Africa for Australia and South Africa, respectively. Wilson, however, wanted all colonies managed by the League of Nations. Appreciating Wilson's strict opposition to annexation, Smuts, the South African general, proposed placing German colonies under trusteeship after having divided them between different legal statuses: a) those near self-government; b) those where the mandatory power should be responsible for administering the colonies; and c) ex-German colonies bordering British dominions. Wilson, who was deeply taken with Smuts, ultimately agreed with this framework, which would see Britain assume all the powers it claimed in numerous former German domains.

For his part, Clemenceau was not interested in the colonies. "Clemenceau's horror for colonial policy bothers me," the French diplomat Paul Cambon wrote. "We need Cameroon, or at least the part that England is abandoning us. As for Togo, it would be good to share it with England for the security of our Dahomey"—a French protectorate in what is now Benin, in West Africa. Cambon wanted "to prevent Clemenceau from making declarations of abandonment that are difficult to revise afterwards."[37] Very early, in December 1918, Clemenceau had given Mosul, Iraq, which should have fallen under French authority per the Sykes-Picot Agreement, to Lloyd George. Nobody knows why. French diplomats fought to prevent Clemenceau from making further unilateral renunciations. They prevailed.[38]

On January 30, 1919, Orlando refused to put Tyrol, a disputed territory claimed by Austria-Hungary and Italy, under international control, leading to further delicate negotiations. "I cannot consent for Fiume to go to Italy," Wilson said, referring to another region under contention. "But you may count upon me for the Brenner line"—the new Italian border with Austria, established by one of the secret treaties. In exchange, Orlando supported the League of Nations.[39] For Wilson, this meant accepting certain clauses of the secret treaties between the Allies. In his eyes, the creation of the League of Nations was worth such concessions. With the terms of the league covenant now set, the public unveiling ceremony was held on February 14, after which Wilson immediately left for the United States. He was accompanied to the train station by France's president, Raymond Poincaré, as well as Clemenceau and House. Wilson left House in charge of the US delegation in his absence. This was the last time Wilson ever placed his arm around Colonel House. At the time, the president compared his aide favorably to Theodore Roosevelt.

It was at this point that House, working with aides to Lloyd George and Clemenceau, dealt with the main French territorial demands regarding the Saar and the Rhineland. Wilson had asked House to remain prudent and not decide anything before his return.[40] On March 13, when Wilson landed in the French port of Brest, House told him the French apparently wished to sidetrack the League of Nations by establishing a preliminary peace treaty with Germany that would include disarmament but not the league.[41] House indicated no position on the agreement, which Wilson took as his approval. But the president saw a trap: the Senate would ratify the preliminary treaty, but not the final treaty including the league. Wilson declared there would be only one treaty, including the league.

The following day an important procedural change occurred in the negotiations. Instead of ten representatives—two each from France, Great Britain, Italy, Japan, and the United States—the Allied group shrank to the Big Four: Clemenceau, Lloyd George, Orlando, and Wilson. In a sign of Wilson's loss of confidence in House, he insisted that no Americans join him for the talks. That Wilson might prefer to work alone was hardly unusual: "One of his most striking characteristics," Swem, the stenographer, wrote, "was the inability to delegate authority. From the typing of his own letters to the formulation of a foreign policy, he found it impossible to trust out of his own hands what he felt capable of doing himself."[42] But these were extraordinarily complex negotiations, and the other principals would have assistants with them. Yet Wilson refused even to share reports of the meetings—compiled by the British diplomat Maurice Hankey—with House.

Wilson was overwhelmed. He had never worked under such conditions. "The President was not in reality a hard worker," House wrote. "He did not know how to work for long hours, he needed a good deal of relaxation and exercise."[43] Wilson had thought that announcing the league would bring a sense of security and brotherhood to all nations, facilitating territorial negotiations. Yet he grew afraid that the Allies wanted to destroy the league. There was no basis for such anxieties, but Wilson's conference partners sensed them and were ready to take advantage.

On April 3, while Wilson was becoming violently ill, Clemenceau and Lloyd George rejected the idea that the treaty would account for Germany's capacity to pay reparations. Wilson faced a terrible dilemma: he could break the promises of the Fourteen Points and accept Lloyd George's and Clemenceau's demands, or he could break his relationships with them. But Wilson also feared that breaking with the Allied leaders would drive Europe deeper into Bolshevism. Hungary had just gone Bolshevik on March 21, and Bavaria would follow on April 7. "Europe is on fire," Wilson said, "and we must not add fuel to the flames."[44] He also did not want to lose the League of Nations, an instrument that he could use to revise the treaty's evil provisions. On April 6, while in bed, Wilson received his adviser Bernard Baruch. "He said he had come to the end of his tether in argument with the English, French, and Italians and had to put pressure on them somehow," Baruch told Bullitt. "I suggested that he squeeze them financially, give them absolutely not one more cent of credits. He sent a telegram to [Treasury Secretary Carter] Glass to stop all credits to them. [Wilson] then turned to Grayson and ordered Grayson to cable at once for the *George Washington*"—the president was so incensed that he was ready to leave the conference. Baruch did not buy it, though. "It was more or less of a bluff," he said. "We all felt that if he went home the French and the Germans would be fighting again within a week." The following day, Wilson was adamant about Baruch's recommended campaign of financial pressure, telling House that he was determined to reject Italy's claims to Fiume and France's to the Saar.

Neither of Wilson's ploys proved workable. Glass telegraphed back that he had already granted the credits until July 1.[45] And Tumulty, still in Washington, pointed out that leaving the negotiations would play poorly at home. On April 9, Tumulty cabled Wilson, "The ordering of the *George Washington* to return to France looked upon here as an act of impatience and petulance on the President's part and not accepted here in good grace either by friends or foes." Indeed, there was more at stake than Wilson's popularity: leaving would instigate the conference's failure. "A withdrawal at this time would be a desertion," Tumulty concluded. With House on the outs, Wilson needed Tumulty more than ever, Bullitt thought—and the president listened.[46] After receiving the cable, "it was Mr. Wilson and not the French or British who made concessions during the following four days on the Saar and Rhineland," House noted in his personal papers. On April 9 and 10, Wilson compromised on the Saar, and on April 15 on the Rhine occupation. At this point he also agreed to the transfer of Shantung from Germany to Japan. In doing so, Wilson hoped to placate the Japanese, who were angered when he rejected proposed league covenant language affirming the equality of all races. Wilson feared that if he opposed another Japanese claim, Japan would leave the conference, and the League of Nations would be without Asian members.[47]

Then the Fiume crisis exploded. It was a relic of maneuvering in the war's early days. In 1914 Italy had been allied with Germany and Austria-Hungary; to break Italy away and ensure her entry in the war on their own side, France and Britain had guaranteed her territorial conquests in the north (Tyrol and Trentino), islands on the Adriatic coast, and part of Dalmatia. The French and British also promised Italy the region of Istria, with the exception of Fiume.[48] Amid the postwar negotiations, Wilson immediately agreed that Tyrol would go to Italy. But, upon discovering that Tyrol was home to 250,000 Germans, he was horrified and confessed his mistake to his entourage.[49] Bullitt thought it possibly desirable to offer the Italians Fiume—a majority-Italian city—in return for giving up the promised Tyrol. But Wilson refused to withdraw his pledge and instead decided to resist Italian claims to Fiume while consenting to the transfer of Tyrol, the interests and likely grievances of its quarter-million Germans be damned. House tried to find a compromise, for he thought the poor treatment of the Italians would "throw them into the arms of Germany." In response, Wilson only became more distrustful of House.[50] For both the Italian government and Wilson, Fiume became a symbol. The crisis went from bad to worse. Orlando left the conference a few days before the treaty was to be revealed to the Germans. On April 23, Wilson made a dramatic and direct appeal to the Italian people. He called for their support of "the new order" and begged them not to ask for anything inconsistent with the principles that, on his own initiative, had become the basis of peace.[51] His appeal sank in indifference.

On May 7, the treaty was handed over to German foreign minister Ulrich von Brockdorff-Rantzau. Three weeks later, on May 29, Germany protested the loss of her colonies, the surrender of her merchant marine, and the prosecution of her former emperor. The Germans rejected the occupation of the west bank of the Rhine and the Saar regime. With respect to reparations, Germany rejected the so-called war-guilt clause and accepted responsibility for damage to civilians only in occupied portions of France and in Belgium—not in Britain, as Lloyd George had demanded, which had never been occupied. Germany also demanded plebiscites on the future of Alsace-Lorraine and Upper Silesia—which was to be split between Germany and Poland—and insisted on immediate admission into the League of Nations.[52] The day after the Allies received the German reply, the British prime minister met Bernard Baruch. "Lloyd George sent for me to have breakfast," Baruch wrote:

> He said to me that he had taken the opinion of his cabinet on the German reply and that unless the Conference agreed to modify the treaty in accordance with the German observations, neither the British fleet nor the British army will move to enforce the terms. I went down the Crillon where Wilson was with the American commissioners. He came out and together we went to Lloyd George's house. Lloyd George repeated what he had said to me. Wilson sat there twiddling his thumbs in his lap, as he so often did. His thumbs did not miss a twirl, but his jaw grew white and forehead grew red and he said, "Mr. Lloyd George, now, after months of making difficulties, you take the position that I have been taking all along. We have to have some treaty. The world needs it. Now when we are facing the enemy and need a united front you say this. I wish truly to you that you can persuade the French to agree with your new position, I will agree also."[53]

The British were willing to agree to concessions on Upper Silesia, the Saar, the occupation of Rhineland, and German admission to the league.[54] The French agreed to self-determination for Upper Silesia and that was all. The Fourteen Points had receded amid horse trading over territories, colonies, and reparations. Now more than ever, the league itself would have to compensate for the treaty's weaknesses.

The league was thus more important than ever. On June 28, the day the Treaty of Versailles was signed, House had his last conversation with Wilson—indeed, the two would never see each other again. From House's perspective, the discussion was not reassuring. House advised Wilson to compromise with Republicans in the Senate and thereby preserve the league. To negotiate, Wilson would need to acknowledge facts and deal with equals; he would need to admit that the Treaty of Versailles was not a perfect peace. But Wilson was not in a conciliatory mood. Lansing noted that the president was returning to the United States "with blood in his eyes and his loins girded for battle." The secretary of state had never seen his boss "more pugnacious or bellicose."[55]

With both facts and equals, Wilson was uncomfortable. Turning away from facts and reality because one finds them unbearable was, for Freud, a basic symptom of neurosis.[56] Unable to cope with the truth of the situation, Wilson decided to crush Lodge and his allies. The president's tools included bullying and lies. Thus, for instance, he told the Senate Foreign Affairs Committee that he never knew about the secret treaties. It was like Princeton all over again, when he was unable to remember having edited Andrew West's proposal for a graduate school. As with the Princeton board, so with the Senate: Wilson's deceit lost him credibility. In both cases, Wilson was unable to consent to reality and plowed his anger into resentment of individuals—West and Lodge. The costs were enormous, as Wilson triggered the rejection of the League of Nations because of his hatred of Lodge.

Wilson could not bear to take responsibility for his failure. Instead he blamed House, whose supposed treachery came when he tried to prize apart the League of Nations and the military, financial, and territorial dimensions of the treaty—despite Wilson having placed House in charge in his stead and despite House's clear understanding that Wilson had every right to overrule him. Nonetheless, House had become Judas Iscariot to Wilson, who had gone forth to be Jesus Christ.[57]

These were Bullitt's first conclusions after two months of thorough investigation. On September 29, 1930, he visited House at his home in New York and briefed the colonel on his discoveries. House turned over copies of some of Wilson's letters, and Bullitt left to join Freud in Vienna.[58]

8

Analyzing Wilson

WHEN FREUD AND BULLITT GATHERED in Vienna on October 17, 1930, Freud was suffering a "feverish sickness," an after-effect of surgery to treat another precancerous lesion in his mouth.[1] Their meeting was short. Bullitt updated Freud on his summer research, then traveled to Baden, where Kurt Hahn gave him full access to the papers of Prince Maximilian, the chancellor who had agreed to a framework of peace based on the Fourteen Points. The files filled the wall of a large room in Maximilian's castle. Bullitt had enough time to note what was available and read the most important pieces. He was seeking documents in German, Russian, and British archives with the passion of a historian.[2] On October 27, Bullitt returned to Vienna, and found Freud excitedly waiting for the latest discoveries. "Saw Freud this evening at 6," Bullitt wrote:

> He was seated in his study at his desk, dressed in pajamas & a dressing gown. He jumped up & seemed genuinely glad to see me. He looked well—eyes sparkling—but he told me that he was just recovering from an attack of pneumonia. "I think I recovered more quickly," he said, "because I wanted so much to see you and to see the material you have brought." I then showed him & left with him the material from Col. House's diary; and copies of a number of the more important letters from Wilson to House.[3]

During their first meeting about the book, Freud and Bullitt concluded that they had to devote a volume to Wilson—not just a chapter—if Bullitt collected information sufficient to support it. Evidently they decided that the facts were indeed sufficient. They laid out their plan. Bullitt would complete a statement of facts regarding Wilson's career, and then they would work on the analysis. They also agreed on how the book should be constructed: with an introduction signed by Freud, another introduction signed by Bullitt, the statement of facts signed by Bullitt, and an analysis of Wilson signed by both.

Major Facts Revealed

Freud first asked Bullitt for any facts related to Wilson's physical condition, on the grounds that "we must not attribute to psychological causes symptoms which may have a physical origin."[4] Bullitt had tallied Wilson's illnesses: on fourteen occasions, his nervousness, dyspepsia, and headaches were severe enough to seriously interfere with his work. Bullitt gave the list to Freud and read him the memos of his conversations with doctors who had treated Wilson.[5]

One of the physicians was Alfred Stengel, a Philadelphia internist. While at Princeton in 1906, Wilson came to him with a broken blood vessel behind his left eye. Stengel found a moderate arterial problem and recommended rest.[6] He told Bullitt that he thought Wilson "would have collapsed from a stroke long before he did if he had not had the luck to be elected governor of New Jersey and then president. That acted as a tonic to him. Success kept him going where failure would have killed him."[7]

The second physician was Dr. Dercum, the same famous neurologist Bullitt consulted after Louise was diagnosed with the disease that bore his name. In 1919 Dercum was called to Wilson's bedside after his stroke. Dercum diagnosed a "thrombosis . . . confined to the right side of the brain producing paralysis of the left limbs." Dercum added that "the left side of [Wilson's] brain was entirely unaffected, that controls the higher functions, and he still seemed to retain his judgment and good sense. He wrote several state papers after the thrombosis. We had many long conversations."[8]

Finally, on October 9, 1930, Bullitt spoke with Admiral Cary Grayson, Wilson's physician during his time in the White House and the last years of his life, who had become his intimate adviser and companion. Grayson spoke to Bullitt frankly and warmly. The two had met in 1917 but had deeper connections. Before joining the Navy in 1903, Grayson had done medical research at Johns Hopkins under the revered Professor William Osler, who was Bullitt's beloved great uncle.

As for Wilson, Grayson recounted that the president brought to the White House "a stomach pump which he used almost daily, and a quart can of some sort of coal-tar product—headache tablets." Grayson dissuaded Wilson from taking the tablets.[9] The admiral spoke with Bullitt about the break between Wilson and House but also recalled Wilson telling him, "My heart bleeds for Colonel House." Grayson had misgivings about Wilson's August 1919 US tour stumping for the league. "For three weeks I kept Wilson from taking his western trip," Grayson told Bullitt. "Finally, he said to me: 'I hope it won't have any bad effect but even if it does, I must go. The soldiers in the trenches did not turn back because of danger and I cannot turn back from my task of making the League of Nations an established fact.'"[10]

Bullitt also shared with Freud impressive insights provided by Wilson's official biographer, Ray Stannard Baker, who had been one of the president's advisers. Bullitt interviewed Baker at length three times and took notes on the conversations as they unfolded. The connections between different topics were not always evident. Sometimes Baker would repeat himself. But Bullitt wanted Freud to read what Baker said in the order he said it. Baker offered important information, but not just that. Bullitt was especially impressed and comforted by certain of Baker's psychological interpretations, which the biographer had not included in his published volumes. In a first draft of his preface, Bullitt mentioned his indebtedness to Baker, "evident on nearly every page of this work."[11]

"There are almost no records of Wilson's early life," Baker told Bullitt during their first conversation. But the biographer had learned much about his subject's early years.

> He was a sickly child who wore eyeglasses and suffered from indigestion (dyspepsia). His father absolutely dominated his life and the relation between them was one of the most intense affection. Their letters to each other can only be described as love letters. The father habitually wrote "my darling son" and Wilson wrote as affectionately. Until he was forty, Wilson never did anything without consulting his father. When he wrote *Congressional Government,* he was extremely nervous, absolutely on pins and needles till he heard what his father thought of it. The father who had been a professor of rhetoric as well as a preacher loved to talk and hear himself talk.
>
> Wilson was deeply religious from the start. Every day of his life he said his prayers, said grace before meals and read the Bible. His first wife, one time, began to have religious doubts. Wilson absolutely refused to think about religious matters. He believed absolutely that

> he was under guidance and formation of God who has chosen him as an instrument to carry His designs. He believed and would say of people he hated that if they were not punished in this life they would be in the next. He believed absolutely in the immortality of the soul. All his family were afraid of him and not on terms of close intimacy, although he would discuss his problems freely in the home circle.
>
> Wilson absolutely had to have the love of one man in his life. First it was his father, then [his adolescent friend] Chas Talcott, then Hibben, then House. House was his substitute for Hibben. At the end of his life, he felt even more bitterly about his defeat at Princeton and the loss of Hibben's friendship than about the League of Nations defeat. His eyes would blaze when he talked about Princeton. Wilson desperately wanted to have a son and so did Mrs. Wilson. They were both very much disappointed that they had a succession of daughters.
>
> Wilson's younger brother, "Joe," ten years younger, was a weak, boring, inferior person and Wilson had a lot of inferior relations, including two or three scapegrace cousins or nephews. He always helped them with gifts of money to pay debts, etc., even when he could not afford it. He was so poor after his election to the presidency that he had to borrow money at the bank to get proper clothes for his inauguration. He hated West, a Scotsman like himself, wanted to dominate him, and considered him insubordinate. He could not endure opposition. Wilson's break with House was due to several causes. One: Wilson felt that House wanted to compromise on everything in Paris . . . then the Wickham Steed interview finished matters.[12]

Bullitt explained to Freud the incident involving Wickham Steed, the British journalist who revealed that the Allies were planning to recognize the Bolshevik government in return for its accession to the new world order defined by the Versailles Treaty and the league. One morning amid the peace conference in April 1919, as House was regaling Mrs. Wilson with statements of devotion to her husband, she asked him who Steed was. The colonel replied, "He takes orders from me; he is one of the finest men in the newspaper business I have ever come in contact with. He is very strong for the president, and I can just by the turn of my hand tell him what to write and he does it." Then Mrs. Wilson picked up an issue of the *Public Ledger* containing an article in which Steed lauded Colonel House at the president's expense. According to Steed, during President Wilson's absence in the

United States, House "brought matters rapidly forward." Steed wrote that "any real improvement in the prospects of the conference" could be attributed to the "practical statesmanship of Colonel House, who, in view of President Wilson's indisposition, has once again placed his savoir faire and conciliatory temperament at the disposal of the topmost peacemakers." Mrs. Wilson then said, "If you have so much influence upon Mr. Steed, I wish you would please explain this article." House had nothing to say to that.[13]

Bullitt finished reading for Freud the notes he had taken during the first interview with Baker:

> Wilson absolutely seriously considered leaving the Paris conference. He sent for the *George Washington* seriously intending to go home. He discussed with me many times his alternatives. He could have gone home and continued his fight for a decent treaty. He even considered resigning in order to carry on that fight. He did not do it, he explained, because he had gone to Europe to work out a treaty in cooperation with other statesmen and he did not wish to give up cooperation as an idea, especially as he was convinced that however bad the treaty might be the League would grow in power and that eventually it would be able to change the bad things in the treaty. Wilson feared and hated socialists and communists. He was surely convinced that the Senate would ratify even the supplementary treaty with France. He was sure of the power of his own words. He had always been successful with an appeal to the people. He was convinced that he could arouse the country and compel ratification with a speaking tour. Grayson told him that such a tour would endanger his life. Nevertheless, he went. Religious communion was such a fact in his own life that he was convinced he could convert the U.S. and the world by his words.

In a second conversation, Baker added:

> Wilson after the break with Hibben said he would never have another friend in his life, but he could not do without one and took House. House's value to Wilson was that of a reporter. Wilson had to have a woman at home and one much loved friend and then could be hard as steel to any man outside that circle. Wilson hated to teach women and to work under a woman and only took the job at Bryn Mawr

> because he wanted to get married. He was absolutely dependent on having at least one man friend to love and some woman to be as he directed it . . . quiet for his life. He had a low idea of woman's value in life, a contempt for women. He was very much opposed to woman's suffrage. He was very lucky in his two marriages and had no sexual experience in his life except with his two wives. He liked to have women around whom he could dominate. His daughters were all afraid of him.
>
> Wilson used from time to time to have outbursts of high spirits when he would dance a hornpipe! He did that in college at Princeton and even once in the White House. He was always extremely intense. He once said to me, "I am too intense always. I wish I were not." He suffered all his life from minor ailments. Indigestion, sick headaches, later neuritis in his shoulder, high blood pressure resulting in the broken blood vessel his eye, cramp in his right hand so that he learnt to write with his left hand. Immediately after the 1906 stroke when he could not use his right hand he started writing with the left hand. He had enlarged prostate, bloody urine, flu at the peace conference.[14]

A few days later, Bullitt delivered to Freud 421 pages of factual material about Wilson's life.[15] On November 22, 1930, Freud complimented him, "I am just through your manuscript. It is glorious. I am sure you are a great writer . . . There is only one passage where you suddenly dive into deep analysis which I would like to see omitted." Bullitt asked for an appointment, but Freud thought he "ought to have a short respite." "Don't be impatient," the good doctor concluded.[16]

After their next meeting, on December 12, Freud started delivering to Bullitt the essential elements of psychoanalytic theory they would introduce in the book. The first axiom of psychoanalysis is that, present in all of us from birth, is an erotic force, the libido. Like electricity, this energy must be stored somewhere. Initially it is stored as love of the self, the stuff of narcissism. Later it is directed in large part to love for other persons, or "object-love." All of us face the challenge of moving beyond narcissism, and most succeed.

The second axiom is that every human being is fundamentally bisexual, in the sense of combining elements of masculinity and femininity. Bisexuality is physical, as, to a point, the same organs exist in male and female bodies. But bisexuality is also psychic. After the primary phase of pure narcissism, the libido finds additional release in both masculinity and femininity. Here, masculinity refers to desires for activity, in particular the desire to love and the desire to control other human beings and the external world generally, so as to alter it in accordance with one's wishes. Femininity reflects those desires characterized by passivity: above all the need to be loved and the inclination to submit to others, the apex of which is masochism—the desire to be hurt by others. Freud was sketching here a hydraulic model of the mind. The libido charges three "accumulators"—narcissism, masculinity, and femininity—and is discharged through five outlets: 1) passivity toward the father; 2) passivity toward the mother; 3) activity toward the father; 4) activity toward the mother; and 5) activity toward the self, a remnant of narcissism.

A key factor in Freud's system, closely related to the second axiom, is the Oedipus Complex. Freud held that all male children experience the Oedipus Complex, which constitutes the most difficult problem the boy must resolve. The complex arises in later stages of childhood, when the boy realizes that his imposing father possesses his mother, which means the boy's relationship with his mother is limited. This a blow to the child, whose attraction to his mother dates from a very young age, before the boy even recognizes that there are physical differences between the sexes. During this phallic phase, the boy believes that all human beings possess a penis as he does. When he discovers the penis is missing from the body of other human beings—for example, his sisters—he begins to suffer castration fear. Once the boy understands that he cannot have his mother, a struggle with his father ensues: hostility, hate, and submission spring from the fear that his father will castrate him for desiring his mother. In the throes of the Oedipus Complex, the boy desires at once to kill his father and to submit utterly to him even to the point of suffering castration and becoming a woman. He wishes to possess his mother as a lover and at the same time is repelled by her because in her very body she warns of abhorrent castration.[17] The conflict between these antithetical desires finally becomes so intolerable that the boy is compelled to invent some sort of escape from it. The solution is to regulate his aggressivity and passivity toward his father through identification—that is, he makes himself like his father. In doing so, he can express his love and admiration toward his father while also removing his father from the external world by incorporating him as in an act of cannibalism. "Thenceforth," Freud concluded, the boy "is himself the great admired father."[18]

The incorporated entity is not a true representation of the father, but a version magnified in power, virtue, and ability. Freud called this internal psychic being the superego. The superego commands, forbids, censors, and directs the wishes of the libido. The relationship between the libido and the superego depends on their relative strength. Between the demands of each, the ego—the conscious person—seeks an equilibrium, a reconciliation within the self. One possible solution is repression, which is the denial of a desire, as if it does not exist. Yet the repressed desire always breaks out. Another solution is sublimation, where the unattainable desire is successfully replaced with a substitute approved by the superego and society at large. A fruitful relation to the father starts with identification and shifts to sublimation. In the end, the individual must reconcile conflicting desires and face the reality of the world: he cannot kill his father, sleep with his mother, or become God. He must live with them and the rest of the world.

Freud's third axiom is the *Todes Trieb,* or death drive, an impulse to destruction and aggression and an antagonist to Eros—the impulse toward life, creation, and love. Freud considered *Wiederholungszwang,* the compulsion to repeat, a facet of the death drive and wished to analyze Wilson in these terms. Bullitt, however, disagreed. He recorded that, during their December 12 conversation, Freud

> told me that, until 1912, he had held exactly the same point of view that I hold now: that polarity in the Libido was sufficient to explain all the conflicts in the human being but that in 1912 he had first thought that there was something left unexplained by this theory & considered adding the theory of the Todes Trieb. He said that he had not made up his mind until 1928. That during the intervening 16 years he had accumulated data in support of both theories. That the pile of evidence in favor of the Todes Trieb had finally become overwhelming and to him at least absolutely convincing. He said that almost all cases in actual practice could be explained by both theories but that there were certain slight cases of Sadism & especially

> Masochism that could not be explained by the theory of the Polarity of the Libido and could be explained by the Todes Trieb. He said that this was the most uncertain thing in the whole of Psycho-Analytic Theory. That most of his pupils *rejected* the Todes Trieb but that to him it was as if he had made a chemical experiment & found that he had left an unexpected residue. He would have to work out a theory to explain that residue. He had done that for the residue he had found in cases of Masochism (particularly desire to be humiliated only) and a few of Sadism. Thus, the Todes Trieb theory developed. He was compelled to put it in the book because he believed in it. I suggested then that he rewrite his passage on the Todes Trieb & he agreed to do so.[19]

They finally wrote in their manuscript: "The Death Instinct displays itself to us as an impulse to attack and destroy. It is the opponent of the Eros, which strives always to produce larger and larger unities held together by the libido. Both instincts are from the beginning present together in the psychic life and seldom or never appear in pure form but are, as a rule, welded together in varying proportions."[20]

Having established the theory, Bullitt and Freud set about applying it to Wilson. Freud wrote in his introduction, "The elements of the psychic constitution are always the same. What changes in the mixture is the quantitative proportion of the elements and, we must add, their location in different fields of the psychic life and their attachment to different objects."[21] The man to whom the theory would be applied appeared as follows in Bullitt's notes: "Inheritance—a placid, quiet baby, bad eyes, nervous, indigestion, emotional intensity. Environment—absolute religious faith that he is the chosen of God. Sexual Life: chastity until he marries his wife at the age of 29." Was Wilson's libido "great, small, or *average*? Impossible to estimate. What about his Narcissism, excessive or average? Or *somewhat exaggerated*?"[22] Freud thought Wilson's "narcissism, preserved from childhood, contained perhaps a greater charge of libido than is usual, but not an abnormally great charge."[23] Bullitt, however, thought Wilson's narcissism was stronger, and they ended up writing as much: "He did in fact love himself always. We can find no evidence that he was ever deficient in admiration for himself or in attention for his own aggrandizement." On this view, even the part of Wilson's libido that discharged itself through the love object was in fact directed narcissistically: he was attracted to people in whom he could recognize some part of himself. "His abundant Narcissism," Freud and Bullitt wrote, "has always made him acutely sensitive to anything which might affect his career." Wilson's narcissism led to a concentration on himself that helped him preserve what small physical strength he possessed and apply it for his own advancement.[24]

Wilson's relationship with his mother occupied a much smaller portion of his emotional discharges, but he said it all, after her death, in a letter delivered posthumously to his wife, Ellen Axson:

> As the first shock and acute pain of the great, the irreparable blow passes off, my heart is filling up with tenderest memories of my sweet mother, memories that seem to hallow my whole life . . . I remember when I clung to her (a laughed-at "mamma's boy") till I was a great big fellow: but love of the best womanhood came to me and entered my heart through those apron-strings. If I had not lived with such a mother I could not have won and seemed to deserve—in part, perhaps, deserved, through transmitted virtues—such a wife.[25]

Wilson's attachment to his mother was sublimated through transfer of love from the mother to sisters and then other women. His deep attachment to his older sisters, particularly his sister Anne, provided a normal outlet for this emotion. Later, the few women he knew would be dear friends to him, like sisters. Ellen, his wife, was also a mother symbol. Like his own mother, she was a preacher's daughter.

Fixation on the Father

Freud and Bullitt saw fixation on the father as the primary feature of Wilson's psyche. Normally identification is a temporary stage in a boy's development, which occurs in adolescence and then recedes as the child incorporates his father and sublimates his feelings about him. But Wilson remained fixed on identification, constantly elevating his father's ideal ever higher. Consider two excerpts from Wilson's letters to his father, which Baker drew upon in his biographies and discussed with Bullitt:

My Precious Father,

My thoughts are full of you and dear "Dode" [Wilson's brother Joe] all the time. Tennessee seems so far away for a chap as hungry I am for a sight of the two men I love. As the Christmas recess approaches, I realize as I have so often before, the pain there is in a season of holiday and rejoicing away from you. As you know, one of the chief things about which I feel more warranted in rejoicing is that I am your son. I realize that benefit of being your son more and more as my talents and experience grow: I recognize the strength growing in me as of the nature of your strength: I become more and more conscious of the hereditary wealth I possess, the capital of principle, of literary force and skill, of capacity for first-hand thought and I feel daily more and more bent toward creating in my own children that combined respect and tender devotion for their father that you gave your children for you. Oh, how happy I should be, if I could make them think of me as I think of you! You have given me a love that grows, that is stronger in me now that I am a man than it was when I was a boy, and will be stronger in me when I am an old man than it is now, than it is now—a love, in brief, that is rooted and grounded in reason, and not in filial instinct merely—a love resting upon abiding foundations of service, recognizing as in a certain real sense the author of all I have to be grateful for. I bless God for my noble, strong, and saintly mother and for my incomparable father. Ask "Dode" if he does not subscribe? And tell him that I love my brother passionately . . . Ellie joins me in unbounded love to you both.

Your devoted son,
Woodrow[26]

And here is a second letter from Wilson, just after his appointment as professor at Princeton:

My Precious Father,

I find that everybody regards my election to P. as a sort of crowning success; congratulations pour in from all sides; I am "writ down" in the category of "successful men." I suppose I ought to feel an immense accession of personal satisfaction, of pride but somehow, I can't manage it . . . My *mind* can't give me gratification. I know it too well, and know it a poor thing. I have to rely on my heart as the sole source of contentment and happiness; and that craves, oh so fiercely, the companionship of those I love. It seems to me that the older I get the more I need you; for the older I get the more I appreciate the debt I owe you, and the more I long to increase it. It seems to me that my separation from you, instead of becoming a thing of wont, becomes more and more unendurable. Are you quite well, now? Please, sir, let me know as soon as possible your plans for the summer—how soon they include us. I suppose dear "Dode" will come north too this summer. I keep his picture on my desk all the time, and all the time long to see him. Dear Ellie is much better though her foot is still far from being well. She pretends to love you and "Dode" as much as I do; but that is impossible.

Your devoted son,
Woodrow[27]

This dominant trait of Wilson's—his intense, lifelong love for his father—led Freud and Bullitt to conclude that there was an element of absolute passivity in the relationship.

In these letters, Wilson also expressed unconditional love for Joe ("Dode"). Nevertheless, when he became president, Wilson distanced himself from his brother, a distance that would later yield to cold hostility, perhaps liberating repressed feelings on Wilson's part. Freud and Bullitt believed that Wilson repressed unconsciously an aggressiveness toward his father. Freud had noticed that many cases of neurosis involved such ambivalence: "a well-grounded love and a no less justifiable hatred towards one and the same person."[28] It was obvious that hostility was the reverse side of great affection, such as Wilson's for his father. Wilson's hostility to father figures—apart from his actual father—was enormous. This feeling broke out in unreasonable ways against West and later Lodge, both of whom Freud saw as paternal stand-ins.[29] On this reading, Wilson could have saved the substance of the treaty and the League of Nations by accepting Lodge's reservations, but this would have meant the triumph of his father. Wilson could not allow that symbolic triumph—he could not submit to his father.

Wilson's fixation had another consequence: he desired an exclusive relationship with his father. Wilson had to be, at least in his own mind, the only son. Indeed, in his mind he was the only son and therefore never experienced relationships of equality. He was always subordinate to his father while dominating others, whether through gentle protectiveness or by means of authority. Whichever avenue he adopted, Wilson could not endure the notion that any man near him possessed intellect or moral standing on par with his own. Whenever colleagues stepped out of his shadow to claim equality, they became traitors in his eyes. These traits were present in Wilson from a young age. As noted, he had a lifelong penchant for creating rules and institutions; these were ways to establish his authority and exercise superiority. Joe's birth marked the beginning of an inclination to establish friendships in which he played father to younger and smaller men, which persisted with Hibben, House, and Tumulty. Freud and Bullitt concluded that Joe's birth aroused in ten-year-old Wilson far stronger emotions than a child that age usually experiences. His hostility toward his younger brother outstripped the supplanted only child's normal run of feeling and proved durable.[30]

Wilson's sense of superiority was such that he could admit neither weakness nor error. Thus, when it became clear that the Senate could defeat him, he became hysterical. Over and over Wilson encountered obstacles like this and repeated the same pattern. He could not negotiate the people in his way because doing so would require acknowledging equality between himself and his rivals, or even their superiority. Instead Wilson believed and acted as though he could fail only due to betrayal by others. Here was Wilson's Christ complex in bold relief. His father being subordinate only to Jesus Christ, to supersede him, Wilson would have to become Christ by sacrificing himself for the highest causes and through betrayal by his friends. Thus when Grayson told Wilson that he might die if he went on the western trip, Wilson took the trip. He went because he could either defeat his father or die. He could earn victory on the trip or, absent that victory, submit in a way that was acceptable to his unconscious. He could perish for his cause and thereby become Jesus Christ.

This was to be the psychoanalytic frame of the book, applied to Bullitt's 421 pages of facts. Bullitt composed the text, and Freud read successive drafts. He had the habit of working into the small hours of the morning, after having an after-dinner walk accompanied by his wife, daughters, or sister-in-law.[31] From mid-February to the end of March 1931, work was interrupted because, Freud told a friend, Bullitt "has resumed his analysis at my place and is currently unfit." Bullitt was at the time recovering from his divorce with Louise Bryant.[32] The first weeks after the divorce were full of excitement and productivity, but then Bullitt's anxiety became overwhelming. At the same time, Freud was contending with his own illness. He had submitted to another mouth operation on February 7 and was suffering a great deal. In April, he wrote to a friend that since the operation he had not had a "single bearable day."[33] On April 26 he had yet another surgery.[34]

Despite these challenges, the pair continued talking through their discoveries and ideas. For instance, Bullitt and Freud debated interpretations of Wilson's autumn 1876 revelation, while reading "The Orator," that he "had a mind." They agreed that, by deciding to become a statesman on the model of Gladstone, Wilson withdrew, perhaps for the first time, from the influence of his father and achieved a degree of independence. He had, probably for a long time, worried about himself, doubted his intelligence, or feared that his mental ability had been impaired.[35] But Freud and Bullitt disagreed on the sources of the epiphany. Freud thought it was a reaction to a previous stage in life when Wilson was guiltily masturbating. Freud had noticed that adolescent male patients tended to follow this pattern. Such guilt could explain the numerous "breakdowns" Wilson suffered, especially as an adolescent. These breakdowns could be of purely physical origin. But "if any young man, seventeen or eighteen years of age, should call on a physician to complain about general nervousness, headaches, and dyspepsia," which could produce over time "complete inability to work and a feeling of being seriously ill," a physician would connect this condition "with the disturbances which puberty may produce." Masturbation helped Wilson's libido find a sexual expression before he married and had his first sexual encounter. Freud did not believe that masturbation provoked physical injuries, which was the common view at that time. But it did often foster a feeling of guilt and neurasthenia.[36]

Bullitt did not share Freud's view. On March 7, 1931, he wrote a long letter to Freud: he was revising their manuscript "and became convinced that the part about Wilson's decision to become a statesman was bosh." He reread the sources and had a new idea that connected to

Freud's "about his masturbation and also fits the facts."[37] Bullitt noted that, after his religious conversion, Wilson hung a picture of Gladstone over his desk and said, "That is Gladstone, the greatest statesman who ever lived. I intend to be a statesman too." However, when Wilson went to study at Davidson College, he still wanted to become a minister, which was his father's wish.[38] Bullitt's interpretation of the "Orator" episode therefore differed from Freud's:

> Thus, the matter rested until [Wilson] read the article on the Orator, which caused him to write to his father that he had discovered he had a mind. Thenceforth, his decision to become a statesman and not a minister was "unalterable" . . . it is the habit of the unconscious to identify even highly diverse objects if they may be called by a common name . . . Mr. Gladstone, "the Christian statesman" who used the House of Commons as a pulpit, resembled the Reverend Joseph Ruggles Wilson not only in his oratory and the religious cast of his thought but also somewhat in physique. And he was the Prime Minister. These words seem the key to the riddle. Both have double meanings of the sort in which the unconscious delights. The word minister means both minister of State and a minister of a church . . . It seems very probable that this was the mechanism by which Mr. Gladstone was installed as the object of . . . Wilson's newly awakened aggression.[39]

Wilson's father was a prime minister, the first and incomparable minister of the church. Wilson could try to be the first minister as well—the prime minister of the state, the chief of his country. In reaction to passivity toward his father, he developed a masculine activity, supported by his identification with the figure of Gladstone. Wilson could simultaneously fulfill and decline his father's wish by becoming a prime minister. He would be a minister like his father but greater than him—a Christian statesman, a preacher whose congregation was the United States.

Bullitt was proud of his interpretation. "If you accept it," he wrote to Freud, "I should say that Wilson's choice of statesmanship would be one of the most interesting features of our work instead of one of the least interesting."[40] They finally decided to include both interpretations in the book—the masturbation hypothesis and Bullitt's, which he referred to as his "language" hypothesis.

By early May they had made significant progress on the manuscript. But then Freud was back in the hospital, which "greatly delayed the job."[41] Bullitt went to the United States for the summer and a last round of fact-checking.[42] He had also held final interviews with Baker and Grayson.[43] This time, the more important contribution came from Grayson, who explained that "the break between Wilson and House began when House met him at Brest." Wilson "said to House, 'Is it true that you have agreed to make a preliminary treaty not including the League of Nations?'" Grayson added that Wilson's "conversation with House upset him greatly. He could not sleep afterwards. He said to me that House had consented to separating the League from the treaty. He could not get the idea out of his mind that 'House had let him down when he was in America.'" Grayson went on:

> Two days after our arrival, on March 16, 1919, he asked me if I did not feel that Colonel House had changed and was no longer the same man than before . . . One day, speaking of House, he began to weep and said, "To think that that man for whom I did everything should have betrayed me" . . . Wilson was a very fatigued man at that time, and when he was tired, he could not remember what he had said or done. He had no secretary and often said to me how much he needed me to stick close to him. That I was the only friend he had . . . Night after night Wilson talked to me about whether he should compromise or not. He hated to do it . . . [Before the western trip,] I appealed to him using the plea that my professional reputation would be ruined if I let him go on speaking and he died. He said: "I'd rather die for the future of the world."[44]

Grayson related another episode speaking to Wilson's duplicity and his fragility, this one from after his time in the White House. In April 1922, Tumulty had delivered to New York Democrats gathered at a Jefferson Day dinner a statement from Wilson to the effect that he was ready to support "any man who stands for the salvation of America." The press took this as an endorsement of Cox, who had been the party's 1920 presidential candidate. This infuriated Wilson, who publicly denied having sent the message or authorizing anybody to convey a message on his behalf.[45] Grayson, who was Tumulty's friend, complained to Wilson, "I am very sorry you did that. It will just give more ammunition to the people who say you cannot be loyal to any friend."

Wilson looked his doctor straight in the eyes and said, "Grayson, you know nothing about the matter, and it is none of your business." Grayson then left Wilson alone, only to hear from him in the early hours of the next morning. "That night at 3 A.M. I had a telephone call from him saying he had not slept at all and wanted to see me. I went up to his house at once and he said to me that he was sorry for what he had said to me and that I was the only friend he had left and he wept and I cried also."[46]

Grayson's testimony seemed to confirm Bullitt's and Freud's interpretations of Wilson's personality: obsessed, to the point of paranoia, with treason; an unwillingness to acknowledge facts; and a preference for Christlike sacrifice rather than compromise.

Before returning to Vienna to report to Freud and put the final revisions on their manuscript, Bullitt saw Louise and Anne. They all left for Europe in October 1931. Louise had decided to write a book on Jack Reed, her deceased husband.[47] At the end of the previous year, Gwen Le Gallienne had broken with her; Louise believed Le Gallienne was trying to poison her.[48] Her paranoia had deepened. But, back in Paris, she drifted from café to café in Montparnasse and was famous for parties that ran to the early morning hours in her studio adjoining a nunnery on Rue d'Assas. "With its candles, ikons, silken fans, bronze images and canvases, [the studio] was a day and night club for everybody," the journalist Wambly Bald wrote.[49] During this time, Louise learned to fly planes. She loved to fly and flew alone.

Though the divorce from Louise was more than a year old, Bullitt remained very distraught about the breakdown of their relationship and of her condition. He continued to see Freud for psychoanalytical sessions.[50] His grief over Louise was evident one Sunday in early 1932. That day he was having lunch at a rustic Viennese restaurant with two American journalists, John Gunther and William Shirer. The group began the meal in high spirits, with champagne, fine food, and much talk. The story of the day was the Democrats' impending nomination of a presidential candidate, and Bullitt hoped with "burning admiration" that it would be Franklin D. Roosevelt, the governor of New York. At one point, Shirer and Gunther left the table to call their offices and check the news. There was a wire reporting that Louise had died. When they told Bullitt, he "paled, lapsed into silence," and finally asked them to call his chauffeur to fetch him as soon as possible.[51] The report of Louise's death, it turns out, was false. The rumor had circulated in Montparnasse for a month, and Bald published it as fact in his weekly Paris chronicle for the *Chicago Tribune.*[52]

Amid his own self-work, Bullitt completed the manuscript that spring. On April 29 he informed Colonel House, "The book is at last finished." He thought it in sufficiently good form even then, writing, "It could be published if both F. & I were to die tonight." However, Bullitt wanted to undertake some revisions, explaining that the text would benefit from being "expurgated" and that he wished to check every reference. He decided to put the manuscript "in a vault and forget it for six months, so that I could finally judge it and cut it with the detachment that is impossible now." And there was a twist. With "a complete manuscript" at the ready, Bullitt was "beginning to think about politics again."[53] In fact, he had been for some time.

9

Signing On with FDR

IMMEDIATELY AFTER BULLITT joined Freud in Vienna to work on their book, Freud told him, "I hope one result of the publication of this work will be your reintroduction to politics." Freud had interpreted an unconscious and unspoken wish. "I told him I hoped it might be," Bullitt replied.[1]

One year later, Bullitt would indeed be preparing to return to US politics, but the work he and Freud were completing together would have nothing to do with it. What mattered most for Bullitt's career prospects was a change in the power dynamics of Washington: the Democrats were back. The Great Depression had put millions of Americans out of work, exhausted President Hoover's credit and popularity, and paved a path to the White House for Franklin D. Roosevelt.

Struggling for a Position

Bullitt's first partner in securing a post under Roosevelt was Colonel House. House endorsed Roosevelt for the Democratic nomination in June 1931 and then worked for the campaign.[2] In December, in the midst of the campaign, Bullitt sent him a detailed report on global affairs, based on meetings he had held in London and Paris with leading British, French, and Soviet politicians. House was impressed with the work, in which Bullitt analyzed the various factions and alliances in British politics, the Soviet desire to avoid war with Japan, and French concerns about Hitler's rise to power. Bullitt forecast the development in Europe of "dictatorships and state socialism, labeled Fascism or Communism, but essentially similar" and expressed regret that France and Germany were making little progress toward reconciliation.[3]

House wanted Roosevelt to read the report so that the Democratic nominee would "know what a valuable ally" Bullitt could be.[4] House also encouraged Bullitt to travel in Europe and reconnect with his contacts before coming back to the United States. On May 27, 1932, Bullitt left Vienna to meet Tomáš Masaryk, the Czech president, in Prague. Then Bullitt traveled to Berlin and Moscow, where he had dined with Maxim Litvinov, the Soviet foreign minister with whom he had negotiated during the secret 1919 talks.[5] Bullitt also visited John Reed's grave along the Kremlin's wall, where he placed a large wreath and stood with head bowed for many minutes. When he returned to his car, "tears were rolling down his cheeks and his features were drawn with sorrow."[6] Only Ernesta and Louise knew the reason for this emotional outpouring. Then he spent a few days in Paris.

Yet by the summer of 1932, there was no government position on the horizon. House had failed to win Texas for Roosevelt during the primaries; he also disagreed with Roosevelt on many issues, especially economic policy, on which House was quite conservative. For all these reasons, House lost his influence with the campaign.[7] As early as February, he was forced to admit of Roosevelt, "I seldom or never see him or hear from him."[8]

So Bullitt found another champion: Louis B. Wehle, an old acquaintance and a longtime friend of Roosevelt's. Wehle had been a Wilson administration hand and met Bullitt in 1917. They had a good rapport and connected over family history: both traced their roots to Louisville, Kentucky. Like House, Wehle thought Bullitt would be a fine addition to Roosevelt's foreign policy team, the sort of mature expert who could prevent a president from blundering around a global scene he did not understand or even think about with much conviction. For instance, recording notes from a lunch with Roosevelt on July 26, 1932, Wehle wrote, "Over the salad Roosevelt gravely suggested that the United States should join the League of Nations to help restore world order"—a position exactly opposed to one he had taken during an address in Albany a few months earlier. Wehle replied that joining the league was impracticable. The league scarcely resembled the organization contemplated by Wilson, he thought, and US participation would not prevent war or settle international hostilities. Indeed, Japan had just invaded Manchuria and made it into a puppet state, and the League of Nations had been helpless to confront this international crime.

Before connecting Bullitt with Roosevelt, Wehle wanted some guarantees. He had approved of Bullitt's 1919 Senate testimony and understood his admiration for Lenin but wanted to make sure that Bullitt had no Bolshevist sympathies.[9] Bullitt reassured Wehle that, even before Lenin's death in 1924, he had lost any sympathy for the Soviet regime. Louise Bryant had shared with Bullitt John Reed's confession, made a few weeks before his death, of his complete disillusionment with the Bolshevik regime, and Bullitt found himself of a similar mind.[10]

Through Wehle, Bullitt began working for the campaign. Then he met Roosevelt in Albany on October 5.[11] In fact, they were not strangers to each other. The two had met in 1909 and, during the First World War, both had offices in the State Department building adjacent to the White House—Roosevelt as assistant secretary of the Navy, Bullitt as an assistant in the State Department. They were on a friendly basis, addressing each other as Bill and Franklin.[12] Albany hosted a happy reunion. "In that first talk, the two men became warm friends," Wehle reported; Roosevelt "was pleased as Bullitt had been." It helped that the two were aligned in terms of their fundamental goals. Like Bullitt, Roosevelt had never abandoned Wilson's liberal internationalist vision of a world committed to American values. But Roosevelt was more realistic than Wilson, readily differentiating "between ideals and the methods of obtaining them." He wanted to effect change, just as Bullitt did.[13] Roosevelt and Bullitt also shared a common social background and similar temperaments: "both were brilliantly and boldly intuitional." Wehle also saw complementary differences between the two. "In the main, Roosevelt was apt to absorb only what he could grasp quickly," Wehle wrote, while "Bullitt had the capacity for prodigious sustained toil, for critically selecting relevant facts, and for resolving them into a plan for action." For Wehle, "they made an ideal team."[14]

After winning the election in November, Roosevelt considered visiting Europe before taking office the following March, as he wanted to build more amicable relations with Britain and France and throw the full weight of the United States behind a Franco-German rapprochement. Bullitt's influence was likely at work here, for he had convinced the president-elect that entente was urgently needed to prevent another world war.[15] However, with Hoover still in office until March, Roosevelt could not be seen usurping. So Roosevelt sent Bullitt in his place; there was, Roosevelt thought, no harm in him going over "purely on his own for a look-see."[16] Bullitt set out at once and on November 28 began sending coded reports from the Continent. In London and Paris, he met the British and French premiers. He visited Geneva and Moscow. At the end of the trip, he also stopped in Vienna, for two days of psychoanalysis with Freud. The doctor considered these productive sessions.[17]

Bullitt explained to Freud that if he were hired by Roosevelt, their book publication would be postponed. Bullitt felt that, if he published a book critical of Wilson, the most recent Democrat in the White House, he could say goodbye to his political aspirations.[18] Freud was ready to make the best of it. Bullitt was "the only American," he wrote to a friend, "who understands something about Europe and wants to do something for Europe. Therefore, I can't trust myself to hope that he will really be given a post in which he could be effective and have his own way."[19]

On December 27, back in Albany, Bullitt provided Roosevelt and Wehle a full account of his meetings. Europe was still saddled with debts from the First World War. At the Lausanne Conference of June-July 1932, the creditor powers (Great Britain, France, Belgium, and Italy) and Germany had secured a final reparations settlement under the condition—kept secret but agreed to by Hoover—of expunging war debts with the United States. Bullitt thought the Democratic platform sensible on the issue: the Democrats aimed to collect on foreign debts, but also to abolish the Smoot-Hawley Tariff Act of 1930, which would help Allied nations pay their debts with revenues from US sales.

Roosevelt was satisfied and asked Bullitt to return to Europe and prepare for the 1933 London Economic Conference, which had its origins in Hoover's earlier call for a global discussion about fighting deflation and reducing tariffs. However, before leaving for Europe, Bullitt made a mistake: he talked about his mission to the one person he could not imagine leaking it, Colonel House. Nevertheless, word got out. By January 26, US reporters were all over Bullitt in London, making headlines of his meetings. The prime minister doubted his credentials; in Washington, Senator Arthur Robinson of Indiana called for his arrest if it turned out that he was involved in debt negotiations.[20] Bullitt, then in Paris, denied being Roosevelt's envoy or carrying out any such negotiation. In Vienna, he reappeared at Freud's home as "a Meteor."[21]

When Bullitt returned to the United States, he discovered that many of the top foreign policy posts in the incoming administration had been taken. Roosevelt had just chosen Cordell Hull, one of his first supporters and campaigners, as secretary of state. Born in a log cabin in the foothills of the Cumberland Mountains of Tennessee, Hull had been elected to Congress three decades prior. In 1913, under Wilson, he wrote the first federal income tax law, and in 1916 he drafted inheritance and estate tax legislation. A senator since 1931, he was a classic conservative Southern Democrat, with the exception of his strong belief in "free trade."[22] For undersecretary of state, Roosevelt chose William Phillips, a career diplomat. An old Bullitt enemy, Phillips remembered too well the 1919 testimony. He twice opposed assistant secretary of state appointments for Bullitt. The situation became so desperate that Bullitt proposed serving as a financial attaché at the US Embassy in either Paris or London.[23]

Without news from him, Freud thought that the hope of seeing Bullitt called to high office had flown away.[24] But Raymond Moley, a key Roosevelt campaign speechwriter and the leading member of his Brain Trust, came to Bullitt's rescue. Moley gave Bullitt credit for having seen before many—and contrary to Wilson—that the Bolshevik regime would keep its grip on Russia. From Moley's perspective, loyalty to one's country superseded loyalty to a president. He decided to bring Bullitt's case directly to Roosevelt and did not stop until Bullitt was nominated special assistant to the secretary of state, an important role but also one not requiring Senate confirmation.[25] Bullitt would now be heading to the June 1933 London conference as the US delegation's executive officer.

Roosevelt's Bold First Steps

On the eve of his election, Roosevelt told the *New York Times:*

> No man can cross the continent in these times and remain the same. I find conditions different and worse than I expected. I have looked into the faces of thousands of Americans and they are faces of people

> in want. I don't mean the unemployed alone. Of course, they would take anything. I mean those who still have jobs and don't know how long they'll last. They have the frightened look of lost children. And I don't mean a physical want alone. There is something more. I was in Paris when Wilson first went over. I watched the crowds in the streets, and I noticed there, particularly in the faces of women, the same expression I see here today. A kind of yearning. There they were thinking of the war. Perhaps this man, their eyes were saying, can save our children from the horror and terror we have known. Now they are saying: We're caught in something we don't understand; perhaps the fellow can help us out.[26]

Roosevelt admired Wilson and Hoover but recognized that both had sunk for having locked themselves into dogmatic causes.[27] "He is certainly a wonder and I wish we could make him President of the United States," Roosevelt wrote of Hoover in early 1920. "There could not be a better one."[28] But, like Wilson, Hoover had an idée fixe. When the depression arrived, his unyielding opposition to federal intervention in the economy led to his downfall. The new president would not be prisoner of any one idea, associate, or group of associates.

On March 5, 1933, the day after his inauguration, Roosevelt proclaimed a bank holiday to prevent further financial collapse, then extended the closure another three days. He introduced an emergency banking bill in Congress, which became law on March 9. On the evening of March 12, a Sunday, he gave his first Fireside Chat. Over the radio, he explained the banking crisis in language all could understand and urged the 60 million Americans listening to put their savings back in the banks. The effect was electrifying. "In one week," Lippmann noted, "the nation, which had lost confidence in everything and everybody, has regained confidence in the government and in itself."[29]

Still, commodity prices were at 60 percent of 1926 levels and farm commodities were at 40 percent. Even those with jobs could barely earn enough to survive. It was Roosevelt's conviction that prosperity and recovery are built "from the bottom up, and not from the top down."[30] He resolved to invigorate the "forgotten man" through monetary manipulation.[31]

On March 6 Roosevelt announced that he was abandoning the gold standard, by prohibiting the hoarding and export of gold. The dollar's value tumbled until it reached a discount rate of 13 percent at the end of April, immediately reducing American production costs and giving US industries a competitive advantage vis-à-vis the rest of the world. But there was a risk. For Congress to authorize Roosevelt to devalue the dollar or print money without limit would be a bombshell, sending a devastating message to the world and potentially bringing about further economic catastrophe. In a meeting at the White House, James P. Warburg, a young New York banker brought on by Moley for his knowledge of financial and monetary issues, challenged the president and convinced him to seek changes to the money-printing legislation—an amendment to the Farm Bill—so that it would not be interpreted as opening the door to uncontrolled inflation.[32]

Bullitt took to Warburg on the spot, and for the next few months, leading up to the London conference, they were inseparable. Following their advice, Roosevelt said in mid-April, "One of the things we hope to do is to get the world as a whole back on some form of gold standard."[33] Roosevelt also encouraged Moley, who had become "the most determined advocate of economic nationalism in the Roosevelt entourage," to declare that "a good part of the ills of each country is domestic . . . There are relatively few remedies which might be called international remedies."[34] In appearance, Roosevelt was walking two contradictory paths. In fact, he hoped that his national emergency plan would have sufficient impact before the London conference because he knew that in the long run only reciprocal trade agreements would lead to an orderly international economy with foreign markets open to US agriculture and industry.[35]

Upon arriving in London, Hull found that negotiations for monetary stabilization had begun several days in advance of the conference and, indeed, reached an agreement: the British pound would be reconnected to the dollar at around $4 per pound, not at a fixed rate but a bracketed-ratio gold value. Immediately, in the United States, the ratio was perceived as disadvantageously high. Some commodity prices resumed their decline. On June 20, Roosevelt cabled Hull that "far too much influence is attached to exchange stability by banker-influenced cabinets."[36] The conference was suspended until Moley's arrival. Moley came to London by plane, dismissed Warburg, snubbed Hull, and soon agreed with the foreign delegations on a nonbinding and innocuous declaration reaffirming the commitment of gold bloc nations to remain part of the conference and acknowledging a collective interest in returning to the gold standard "under proper conditions."[37] Moley was expected to do Roosevelt's bidding, yet the president proved deeply dissatisfied. On July 3 he declared the conference "a catastrophe amounting to a world tragedy." As he saw it, "the great Conference of Nations" was allowing "itself to be diverted by the proposal of a purely artificial and temporary experiment affecting the monetary exchange of a few nations only." Instead, he warned, "the old fetishes of so-called international bankers are being replaced by efforts to plan national currencies with the objectives of giving those currencies a continuing purchasing power."[38]

Roosevelt's only priority was his domestic agenda; the outburst crushed the conference.[39] Warburg resigned on July 6 because he thought Roosevelt, by refusing to set an agreement with Britain, France, and the gold standard bloc, had committed a crime against world peace. Moley went, too; after he returned from London, Roosevelt eased him out of power. Bullitt's fate was different. Not only did he survive the conference, but he also earned his stripes in the administration. He had served as an effective informant for Roosevelt and had helped the president keep the support of the American delegation at the conference, especially Hull. Warburg felt Bullitt had real talent as a negotiator, calling him "the only man who had any finesse, or any sense of the kind of things that a Roosevelt was capable of doing."[40]

Bullitt's next challenge would be highly significant: helping to establish relations with the Soviet Union. The United States was the only major power having no diplomatic relations with the Soviet Union; during the London conference, Litvinov told Bullitt that the Soviet government wanted a thaw, which Bullitt reported to Roosevelt.[41] At the time, the State Department remained in its refusal to formally recognize the Soviet Union for three significant reasons. First, the Soviets did not recognize their international obligations—that is, their debts to other countries. Second, the Soviet Union did not respect the rights of citizens of other states—whether property or religious rights—within its jurisdiction. Third, the Soviets refused to refrain from interfering in the domestic affairs of other states via prolific and vitriolic propaganda. Thus the official position of the State Department in 1933 was that the Soviet conception of international relations was "entirely alien to its own . . . utterly repugnant to its moral sense."[42]

Since January, however, Hitler had come to power and was threatening the peace in Europe. By establishing relations with the Soviet Union, Roosevelt could outflank a seemingly emerging German-Japanese alliance—1933 saw both countries exit the League of Nations amid hardening militarism and right-wing ideological ascendance—without antagonizing the majority of Congress, which harbored antiwar and isolationist feelings. Roosevelt decided to approach the Soviets through Bullitt and Henry Morgenthau Jr., an economic adviser and future secretary of the Treasury. Morgenthau contacted Amtog, the Soviet trading company, and by August 1933 was able to report to Roosevelt that the Soviet Union was willing to purchase $75 million of raw material from the United States.[43] Bullitt then approached Boris Skvirsky, head of the Russian Immigration Bureau, who served as an unofficial ambassador to the United States.

The next step was a letter to Mikhail Kalinin, the Soviet president, which Bullitt drafted in consultation with Skvirsky. The letter suggested that the Soviets send a "suitable representative" to Washington to explore the possibility of establishing diplomatic relations. This representative turned out to be Litvinov. His boat, the *Berengaria,* reached New York Harbor on November 7, 1933, and Roosevelt received him at the White House that same evening. Negotiations began forthwith.

Initially Litvinov refused to guarantee that the Soviets would refrain from distributing propaganda in the United States, prompting Bullitt to hand him a schedule of steamships sailing for the Soviet Union.[44] Duly chastened, Litvinov continued negotiations, which were held directly with—and only with—Roosevelt and Bullitt. On November 16, the parties came to an accord, the so-called Roosevelt-Litvinov agreements. In exchange for diplomatic recognition, the Soviet government made three pledges: to cease Comintern activities and propaganda in the United States; allow complete freedom of worship for all Americans—tourists and residents—in Soviet territory; and pay tsarist debts and compensation for American-owned properties that had been nationalized. An additional gentleman's agreement committed the United States to a significant reduction of the Soviet debt to the US Treasury and American creditors, from $600 million to a figure between $75 million (the Soviet reckoning) and $150 million (the US number).[45] On November 17, Roosevelt announced diplomatic recognition of the Soviet Union and named the first American ambassador: William C. Bullitt.

This was of course a "brilliant political success" for Roosevelt.[46] And for Bullitt, it was also a personal victory. For one thing, his diplomatic skills had brought about a major change in global affairs.[47] For another, he had earned the recognition that in 1919 he was right to accept Lenin's proposal for diplomatic recognition, and Wilson was wrong for having killed the plan through inaction. Cissy Patterson cabled him, "So few people in this life get any just reward either way. In fact, right now, I can't think of any other case. Love and congratulations."[48] Steffens wrote him, "I do congratulate you and admire you, the second most persistent son-of-a-gun in my history."[49]

Bullitt was also happy to have the privilege of working with a president who mixed "audacity and common sense in perfect balance." He compared Roosevelt to Li Shimin, who became the Chinese T'ang emperor T'ai-Tsing the Great. "It is almost miraculous to have as president the very best man that we have in the country," Bullitt wrote to George Lansbury, the British Labour Party leader. "It is a good thing for us and will be, I think, a good thing for the whole world."[50]

10

Ambassador Bullitt Goes to Moscow

BULLITT ARRIVED IN MOSCOW on December 11, 1933, with his daughter Anne and with George Kennan as his aide. A young diplomat at the time, Kennan was borrowed from the US Embassy in Riga, Latvia, to supervise the establishment of the new mission in the Soviet Union. Bullitt recalled being "ushered into a suite" at Moscow's National Hotel upon arrival. "My daughter was with me and imagine my feelings when she and I entered the identical rooms in which [in July 1914] my mother and I heard he first outcries of the Great War."[1] Kennan accompanied Bullitt to his first meeting with the Soviet president, Kalinin; both diplomats were excited at the encounter and the warm welcome they received.

A Kremlin banquet combining initiation, seduction, and diplomacy was organized in the ambassador's honor on December 20 by Defense Minister Kliment Voroshilov. "Everyone . . . got into the mood of a college fraternity banquet, and discretion was conspicuous by its absence," Bullitt reported to Roosevelt. Joseph Stalin, the country's uncontested leader, attended the banquet dressed in a common soldier's uniform. He smoked a large pipe, which he held in his left hand throughout the dinner save when he needed to use both knife and fork. After the tenth vodka toast, Litvinov noticed that Bullitt was discreetly attempting to sip rather than drain his glass and told him the gentleman who proposed the toast would feel insulted if he noticed. So Bullitt resumed drinking bottoms-up until the last toast—the fiftieth or so. Before leaving, Stalin asked Bullitt whether there was "anything at all in the Soviet Union" that he wanted. Bullitt replied diplomatically that he wanted nothing. Upon Stalin's insistence, however, Bullitt described the embassy he could see in his mind's eye: modeled on Jefferson's home and located at Sparrow Hills, a bluff overlooking the Moscow River. There was a lake and a wooded area nearby, and the bluff offered an unparalleled view of the river and the city. "You shall have it," Stalin said. Bullitt recorded that, as Stalin was leaving, he "took my head in his two hands and gave me a large kiss! I swallowed my astonishment, and, when he turned up his face for a return kiss, I delivered it."[2]

A Brief Honeymoon

Litvinov offered Bullitt his choice of ambassadorial residence either at the Supreme Court building, which Bullitt felt "might do well for a jail," or Spaso House, the seat of the Central Committee. Constructed in 1914 by a merchant who traded vodka for furs, Spaso House was a fine home in the center of the Moscow. Bullitt found it cheerful, except for a colossal central hall. It remains today the US ambassadorial residence in the city.

Next Bullitt began assembling a staff. One of his first hires was Charles Thayer, a West Pointer who had decided against military life and came to Moscow to learn Russian.[3] Bullitt needed a secretary and an interpreter and thought Thayer could handle both tasks. He knew little about secretarial work—he barely typed and knew nothing of shorthand. He also had a lot of Russian to learn and spent his first weeks on the job cramming.[4] Bullitt also decided to keep Kennan. "I have rarely been so impressed by the ability and character of a man of his age," Bullitt wrote apologetically to the US ambassador in Riga, sure that Kennan would "be the wheel horse of the embassy." Kennan was thrilled. "The last few weeks took my breath away," he said of his introduction to Moscow. "Now that I think back on it, I can scarcely believe my own memory."[5]

Bullitt then returned to Washington to receive instructions, secure appropriations for construction of the Moscow embassy, and hire additional staff. On February 15, 1934, he set out for Moscow again with an impressive team: John Wiley, who would take the number-two post as counselor of the embassy, had spent eighteen years at embassies in Europe and Latin America; Loy Henderson, a disciple of the chief of the Russian Division at the State Department, would be economic adviser and third in command; Elbridge Durbrow, who had served in Poland, Romania, and elsewhere, was named vice consul; and Charles Bohlen, who had worked in Paris and Prague and spoke Russian, would be tasked with research, translation, and maintaining the library. Bullitt also brought along a detachment of Marine sergeants, a pilot, and a single-engine, two-seat Douglas plane in which he could fly freely throughout the country.[6] On the ship to Moscow, he told his men that he would observe no distinction between professional and nonprofessional staff and that, in spite of formal ranks, he would dispense with hierarchy for day-to-day purposes. He was more concerned with good management than with etiquette.

Amid the excitement, Bullitt had not forgotten Freud. It had been a difficult year for the father of psychoanalysis. After April 1933, Nazis persecuted Freud by blacklisting all his publications. May saw the burning of books—including Freud's—in public squares, an auto-da-fé of a century of German culture.[7] Bullitt recognized that Freud was in danger; in January 1934, speaking on the phone from Washington, Bullitt offered him his house in the Berkshires: "if things should become difficult," it was waiting for him.[8] Freud refused the offer, which did not surprise Bullitt, who was convinced that Freud would not leave Vienna except under the "pressure of actual violence."[9]

The situation in Austria was deteriorating rapidly. Engelbert Dollfuss, the right-wing chancellor and leader of the Christian Social Party, had suspended Parliament in March 1933 and banned the Communist and Nazi parties. In February 1934, Dollfuss provoked a civil war with Austria's Social Democrats. "Not much personal suffering," Freud noted at the time, "just one day without electric light, but the 'stimmung' [atmosphere] was awful and the feeling as of an earthquake."[10] Freud's friends, disciples, and family abroad began informally coordinating to protect him. Bullitt was very active in this group. At his instigation, George Earle, the US ambassador in Vienna, offered Freud sanctuary at the American embassy in case of personal threat from the Nazis. "Apparently, I am on top of the Nazi list," Freud replied. "I hope it will not come to a situation where I would have to accept this protection."[11] Earle urged Freud to leave, but he chose to stay in his Vienna home, which he would soon call "a very comfortable—prison."[12]

While starting up in Moscow, Bullitt also tried to stabilize his relationship with Louise. She was living in Paris at this time, growing sicker and sicker. Not often, but regularly, Bullitt set up telephone appointments between Anne and Louise, too.[13] Louise wrote Anne frequently; she missed her daughter and always wanted her to know she loved her.[14] At the end of 1933, Louise wrote Bullitt to wish him and Anne a happy Christmas and New Year. "I cannot expect much for myself—ça va," she wrote. "I do hope you will be generous enough to let me see Anne while you are here." Bullitt invited her to dine at Rue de Ponthieu on December 29. A month later, on January 25, 1934, she wanted to know when they would be back in Paris. "I want so to see Anne again . . . I *am* the little girl you fell in love with but just grown up. Much nicer if you only knew it and much kinder."[15] Money was a struggle for Louise. At the beginning of December 1933, Bullitt had received a letter from Clément Geslin, the manager of the Hotel Lutèce in the Montparnasse neighborhood of Paris. He explained that, by the sixth or seventh of the month, she had typically spent or given away her alimony check. "She was always generous."[16] "If you do not lend money to your friends who do you lend it to—to your enemies?" she wrote to a supposed friend. Geslin eventually ensured that she at least covered the cost of her lodging and small expenses. However, in the days after she learned of Bullitt's appointment as ambassador, Geslin wrote, she "has been overexcited, her bad habits have taken over." The hotelier asked if Bullitt might consider remitting the allowance directly to him, so that it could be disbursed to her in installments. Bullitt agreed to the request before returning to Moscow, where serious difficulties awaited him.[17]

The Soviets, it transpired, were disinclined to fulfill their promises.[18] The land Stalin had pledged for the embassy was not forthcoming, leading to friction.[19] On Easter 1934, Bullitt wrote Roosevelt that "the honeymoon atmosphere had evaporated completely."[20] Bullitt rightly attributed the change to improving Soviet relations with Japan. Fear of Japanese power was one factor that pushed Stalin to accept US conditions for diplomatic recognition.[21] But while the Soviets were negotiating with the Americans, they were also talking with the Japanese. When Stalin agreed to sell them Russian-owned railroads in China, tempers calmed in Tokyo, enabling accommodations with the Soviets.[22] No longer facing a Japanese threat—at least for the time being—the Soviets needed less from the Americans.

The United States also contributed to the deteriorating relations. The Johnson Act, which became law in April 1934, prohibited US loans to indebted countries—such as the Soviet Union. Consequently, the

Soviets were unable to obtain a line of credit at favorable rates, which would have permitted them to purchase American products. This left the Soviets unenthusiastic about paying off their US debt. "We have been unable to get anywhere in our negotiations with regard to debts and claims," Bullitt wrote to Colonel House, "and have considerable difficulty in working out other minor matters."[23]

In fact, those minor matters could be of great significance. One was scarcity of housing for US diplomats; Bullitt was allotted only a quarter of the rooms he requested. He was forced to recruit mostly bachelors, and married staff often had to leave their wives at home until they got their own apartments.[24] The seven-story Mokhovaya building, located near Red Square and the Kremlin, became the embassy's cramped home. The first three floors of the pretty but narrow structure provided offices for the US mission, while the upper floors were allocated to Americans for housing—except for three apartments, which were occupied by Soviet officials. In the course of purges, these Soviet neighbors were arrested and sent away, freeing up a few more apartments for US diplomats and their families. For example, a month after the embassy opened, Dmitry Florinsky, a resident of the building and director of Foreign Office protocol, suddenly disappeared. He was at a dinner at the British Embassy when one of the servants whispered in his ear. He excused himself, left the table, and went to the front door, where two men were waiting for him. He was never seen again. It turned out that Florinsky was charged with sodomy and received a five-year sentence; later he was executed for espionage. The US diplomats liked him, and they regretted his fate. But they immediately attempted to persuade the Soviet authorities to let them rent his apartment. By the end of 1934, such killings of Communist Party insiders were becoming more common. Stalin used the assassination of Sergei Kirov—first secretary of the Leningrad party organization since 1926, and a member of the Politburo who was considered Stalin's heir apparent—as a pretext to launch the Great Purge. About a million people perished, most labeled counterrevolutionaries and enemies of the people. In 1937, after the arrests of the remaining apartments' occupants, the US Embassy petitioned again, and by the spring of 1938, all the apartments of the Mokhovaya were available for its staff.[25]

Bullitt was anxious about spies among his ranks, and with good reason. The whole US diplomatic corps, numbering thirty to forty people, was under surveillance, and agents of the secret police followed Bullitt wherever he went.[26] During a 1935 reception, the influential Communist intellectual Karl Radek repeated to Bullitt verbatim a conversation he had recently had with Josef Beck, the Polish foreign minister. Radek's source, he said, was a Soviet spy within Poland's ruling clique.[27]

To boost security, Bullitt hired Roscoe Hillenkoetter, a naval intelligence officer who couriered the Paris-Moscow diplomatic pouch and impressed Bullitt with his exceptional knowledge of European politics. Hillenkoetter would go on to become the first director of the CIA in 1947. At the embassy in Moscow, he discovered wires with no obvious purpose entering the building; when they were cut, there was no disruption to lighting, power, or telephones.[28] At Spaso House, he found a microphone in the process of being installed in a ventilation duct separated from Bullitt's desk by only a thin layer of plaster. Hoping to surprise the culprit when he returned to finish the work, Kennan, Durbrow, and Thayer spent the next few nights taking turns on watch with a revolver in one hand and a flashlight in the other. One morning, when Durbrow awoke from an unfortunate watch-duty nap, the microphone had disappeared. In Washington, "no one believed us," Durbrow later recounted.[29] Bullitt also worked with David A. Salmon, the State Department's chief of communications and records and the nation's top cryptography expert, to ensure that transmissions to and from the Moscow embassy would be the most secure in the whole US network.[30]

Bullitt had his own informants, and the Soviets knew it. In October 1934, the top Soviet agent within the State Department—code name Willie—reported anxiously to his handlers that Bullitt had informed the State Department that his confidential telegrams were known in Moscow by the Soviet government. Ironically, Willie himself was ordered to investigate the leak—because Willie was David Salmon, the State Department's chief of communications and records.[31]

Bullitt faced the difficult obligation of behaving professionally with the cynical criminals of the Stalin regime. For instance, there was the night he sat between Defense Minister Voroshilov and Marshal Semyon

Budyonny at a dinner celebrating Red Army generals.[32] They had drunk a bit of vodka and were cheerfully reminiscing about their victories. At one point Voroshilov brought up "the most extraordinary thing we ever did together." Bullitt asked what happened, and Voroshilov went on to describe the capture of Kiev. "There were 11,000 Czarist officers with their wives and children in Kiev and they had more troops than we had, and we never could have captured the city by fighting," he explained. "So we used propaganda and we told them that they would be released and allowed to go to their homes with their families and treated as well as possible by our army, and they believed us and surrendered." "What did you do then?" Bullitt asked. "We shot all men and boys and we put all the women and the girls into brothels for our army . . . My army needed women," Voroshilov said. "I was concerned with my army's health and not with the health of those women; and it didn't make any difference anyhow, because they were all dead within three months."[33] Bullitt managed to keep his composure and turned to lighter matters, introducing Voroshilov and Budyonny to the game of polo.[34]

Life and Work in Stalin's Moscow

Amid the tense atmosphere, Bullitt took pleasure in art and artists. As soon as he arrived in Moscow, he requested a meeting with Natalia Sats, the founder in 1918 of the world's first professional children's theater, who had also commissioned Prokofiev's *Peter and the Wolf.* Before departing for Moscow, Bullitt had promised Louise that he would bring Anne to the theater. They did so many times.[35] Bullitt also befriended the writer Mikhail Bulgakov, whose work he adored. Bullitt found Bulgakov's play *The Days of the Turbins* so beautiful that he attended five performances. Bulgakov and his wife Elena became regular guests of the ambassador and his advisers. Bullitt also entertained Moscow ballet dancers, who gave private performances at the embassy. A prima ballerina, Lolya Lepishnikaya, fell in love with Bullitt, calling him "her sun, her moon, and her star." She amused him, and, in 1934, was a regular guest in the Spaso House.

Thanks in part to the ballerinas, who had permission to fraternize with the American diplomats, the embassy could be a raucous place.

"We knew they were agents, reporting to the secret police," Durbrow said of the ballerinas, "and they knew we knew."[36] The ballerina and avid Communist Irena Charnodskaya had taken "the trio of Bullitt, Bohlen, and myself by storm," Thayer wrote in his diary. "We simply cannot keep our hands off her. She has become an acquisition of the Embassy and . . . sleep[s] in some vacant room which the three of us carefully lock together and then fight violently as to who will keep the key . . . What an embassy!"[37] Some years later he would write to Kennan with reminders of "the madness of 1934."[38]

But life was not all parties—not even close. The embassy staff were often sick or depressed. Kennan fell ill in July 1934 and recovered in Norway, where he remained until mid-August. At the end of December, he was ill again. This time he also suffered depression. "I react so strongly to the confidence or mistrust of others," he wrote to Bullitt, while also thanking the ambassador for demonstrating that very confidence and thereby restoring to his aide a degree of "self-respect."[39] In April 1935 Kennan went to a Baden sanatorium with instructions to "rest and diet" in hopes of recovering and returning to work by September.[40] The State Department suggested bringing Kennan back to Washington, but Bullitt refused. "He is the best officer I have had here," Bullitt said, "and I could release *two* officers when he returns."[41]

To fight stress and help him manage the embassy, Bullitt needed a good secretary. Eventually he found an exceptional one, but he needed to kiss some frogs first. Thayer had charm and intelligence but no sense of how to manage the embassy or the ambassador.[42] Bullitt's next secretary left because his wife refused to live in Russia. Another then developed a nervous condition and collapsed. All this came in Bullitt's first year on the job. "For God's sake, send a secretary who can stand both Moscow and me," he telegraphed the State Department. That turned out to be Carmel Offie. Born in 1909, Offie grew up in a large, poor Italian family near the coalfields of Sharon, Pennsylvania. He was recruited by the State Department in 1931 as a clerk and assigned to the American mission in Tegucigalpa, Honduras. An excellent stenographer and typist—the best in Moscow, Bullitt said—Offie distinguished himself by his demonic concentration on clerical work, assuming responsibilities nobody else wanted.[43]

Offie understood how an embassy should function and served as a bridge between embassy staff and Spaso House, where Bullitt did much of his work when he was in Moscow. Bullitt normally got up in the morning between 5 and 7 o'clock, then took a walk with Offie. The workday ended at 7:30 in the evening.[44] If Bullitt had an idea during the night, or an urgent telegram to send, Offie would take down a draft. Offie's numerous talents made him indispensable. Bullitt relied so heavily on his secretary that Orville Horwitz, Bullitt's cousin, made fun of him for it. "I don't mind Mr. Offie answering this letter as long as—1 it gets answered! 2 he consults you as to what to say," Horwitz wrote.[45]

Bullitt's relationship with President Roosevelt was excellent. On the purchase of the embassy building, debts, and other subjects of tension with the Soviet government, the president supported Bullitt's decisions. Bullitt's 1934 Easter letter to the president was full of affection: "in this past year," he wrote, "you and Mrs. Roosevelt and Miss LeHand have made me feel that I was a member of the family."[46] Missy LeHand was Roosevelt's longtime secretary, a key member of his personal entourage, and the president's de facto chief of staff. She accompanied the president on most of his travels and had a private apartment in the White House. And it was she who was friendliest of all with Bullitt.

They had begun exchanging cordial letters in August 1933, then dined together in Washington during the September and October negotiations with the Soviets.[47] LeHand became infatuated with Bullitt, at one point writing, "I miss you most awfully Bill—I try hard to forget you—really—but it always ends in an overpowering surge of longing for you . . . I am indescribably happy (though *not* independent) when I am with you—even when I can talk to you from Philadelphia on the telephone. Please come home soon—I want to *know* that you are well, and I want to touch you, to make sure that you are real. Well, at any rate, please *write*." She waited on his every word, writing on another occasion, "I am so glad you called me. I think of you constantly." LeHand confided in Bullitt, relating details of her life, small as well as important, and reporting with pride Roosevelt's warm feelings for him. "The President, too, was delighted to hear from you," she told Bullitt in response to some of his letters. "When he read the last paragraph, he said: 'That's pretty sweet—let's drop him a note right off'—which he did! That, sir, is unprecedented . . . he really misses you."[48] For his part, Bullitt was enamored of LeHand, though perhaps not as much as she was of him.

Despite their feelings, they remained simply good friends and collaborators, as if they were always a little afraid of going further under Roosevelt's protective but dominant and possessive shadow. As Kathryn Smith, LeHand's biographer, put it, her "love affair" with Bullitt was "conducted mostly by letter and by phone, a secret to hold close in her bedroom at night, the secret that made her smile to herself as she worked at her desk outside FDR's office. Even FDR could not penetrate the place she kept that secret in her laboring, damaged heart."[49] She was perhaps the most powerful woman in the United States during Roosevelt's presidency. She was his gatekeeper. And she would open many gates for Bullitt.

Another means for fighting stress and resisting Soviet pressure was relentless travel. Bullitt flew all over the Soviet Union with his pilot Tommy White, guided by nothing "except incorrect maps and false weather reports."[50] They had tremendous fun until June 1934 when they landed upside down in a swamp near Leningrad Airport. The pair were unhurt, but the plane was badly damaged. The Soviets did not authorize the importation of another plane and so the aerial adventures ended. Of course, Bullitt traveled outside the country as well. Indeed, over the course of his ambassadorship, he spent more time outside the Soviet Union than within it. Sometimes he would be Roosevelt's visible representative, as when, in May 1935, he traveled to Warsaw for the funeral of Józef Piłsudski, the revered Polish head of state.[51] And sometimes he would be more discreet.

Such was the case during Bullitt's first trip to Asia, an unofficial visit in fall 1934. A few months earlier, in Moscow, he had had several informative conversations about conditions in Asia with Jean Monnet, a French diplomat, businessman, and old friend who had been deputy general secretary of the League of Nations, who would later work with Bullitt to secure US industrial support for the WWII Allies, and eventually become a founding figure of the European Union. After 1929, Monnet moved to Shanghai to work as a merchant banker. During the 1934 meetings with Bullitt—the contents of which the ambassador shared with Roosevelt—Monnet described a dangerous and unstable situation in East Asia, but one that he believed could be resolved peacefully. Roosevelt authorized Bullitt to spend a couple of weeks in China and Japan to verify Monnet's observations.[52] On Bullitt's behalf, Monnet reached out to officials he knew on the ground, especially Chiang Kai-shek.

On October 20, 1934, Bullitt sailed for Tokyo, where he met the Japanese emperor and numerous officials. Their polite conversations yielded little of interest.[53] In late November he met with Chiang and his wife Soon Meiling, who served as her husband's interpreter. Facing the risk of further Japanese aggression, Chiang swallowed his strong aversion to working with Communists and asked Bullitt to let the Soviet government know that if they would "play fair" in the province of Xinjiang, where they were deploying much propaganda, he wanted to work together. Chiang's priority, however, was to expand China's cooperation with the United States. Chiang praised the US fleet's Pacific presence, which he thought had prevented the Japanese from keeping Shantung. Chiang also asked Bullitt to convey a personal message to Roosevelt: he proposed that the United States and China open trade relations "on a barter basis," with Chinese silk exchanged for secondhand rail equipment, which China needed desperately.[54] Bullitt conveyed the message to Roosevelt upon his return to Washington in mid-December.

Bullitt was managing his Moscow team remotely via memo when, on January 2, 1935, he received a telegram from Wiley. Diplomats from all over the globe in Moscow were murmuring moodily about the US Embassy's failure to date to host them for a large evening party. Wiley felt that the embassy needed to host a party bringing together the staffs of the other embassies in Moscow. At first reluctant, Bullitt eventually warmed to the idea when he saw its political potential. He envisioned a party on a grand scale and instructed that invitations be sent to more than 500 people, including the entire foreign diplomatic corps, all of the Soviet ministers and their deputies, and many other official and nonofficial persons of importance, including, of course, Stalin. "I want you to arrange a party to show the Commissars what life was like under the Tsars," Bullitt wrote to Wiley. "Spare no expenses."[55] To Wiley's wife Irena, who would help to plan the party, Bullitt wrote, "The sky is the limit." Irena worked with Charles Thayer to recreate on a grander scale the memorable Christmas 1934 party they had organized for US Embassy staff. That time, three seals had opened the evening with a balancing-ball routine, ladder-climbing, and Christmas carols "performed" on the harmonica. They made a huge impression, even if they were unmanageable the rest of the evening after their trainer passed out from too much champagne.

For the April 1915 affair, Irena arranged a "Green, White and Gold Spring Festival" at Spaso. But spring came late in Moscow that year, making it difficult to obtain the desired flowers. A courier was dispatched to Holland and brought back a thousand blooming tulip bulbs. Embassy staff used a sun lamp to coax green leaves out of a dozen young birch trees that had been uprooted and stuck in Bullitt's bathtub the day of the party. Instead of a seal, the zoo provided half-a-dozen newborn goats in little pens and a flock of small, colorful birds. Irena came up with an idea for an aviary: nets were extended across the pillars of Spaso's great hall, and the birds flew above, singing and flitting merrily. White roosters were housed in spectacular glass cages. An orchestra was hired. The banquet table was covered in a carpet of emerald-green grass sprouted from a wet cheesecloth that staff had laid out in the embassy attic. As a coup de grâce, the director of the Moscow Zoo offered an appearance by a baby bear (and a trained attendant to keep an eye on him).

When the night of the party came, everyone who mattered in Moscow took part—with the notable exception of Stalin. Foreign Minister Litvinov's wife Ilvy immediately picked up a baby goat and held it throughout the evening. Radek played a prank on the baby bear, swapping his bottle of milk with champagne. The bear had two or three sips before hurling the bottle onto the floor. General Alexander Yegorov, noticing the little bear's distress, took it upon his shoulder as if he were rocking a baby. The bear immediately threw up all over the general's brand-new uniform, decked in medals. He left the party, apparently furious, only to reappear an hour later "gay as a lark" in another uniform. When the orchestra began playing, the birds grew excited, broke through the netting, and flew everywhere. Droppings rained down, but the guests loved it. Bullitt's party provided direct inspiration for Bulgakov's depiction of Satan's ball in *The Master and Margarita.* In fact, it was at the ball that Bulgakov met Baron Steiger, one of the Soviet Union's best-known informants, who commonly attached himself to foreigners in Moscow and who appears in Bulgakov's novel as Baron Meigel.[56]

At the White House, there was a lot of enthusiasm about the ball. Roosevelt asked Missy LeHand to send Bullitt a news clipping, "Moscow Goes High Hat," which noted that "the humble servants of the proletariat came in full evening clothes. There wore beautiful gowns . . . It was the swellest party Moscow has seen since the Revolution."[57]

In the long run, though, the party failed in establishing friendly personal relationships between US diplomats and Soviet officials.[58] The Soviets' deceptions, the collapse of debt negotiations in late 1934, the daily fear to which American staff were subjected, and the loss of Russian friends—the neighbors who disappeared from the diplomatic quarters, locals who helped staff the US Embassy for a time, vanished and censored artists—exhausted Bullitt. Despite going to bed early most evenings, he had to rest after lunch for two hours each day.[59]

The situation grew even worse in summer 1935 when delegates of the American Communist Party, led by Earl Browder, were invited to Moscow to attend the Seventh World Congress of the Comintern. The Comintern was determined to expand activities in the United States, a gross violation of the conditions of diplomatic recognition. Bullitt received the invitation of the US delegates to the Comintern as a personal offense and defeat. He gathered embassy staff to brainstorm a response.[60] Significantly, Bullitt ignored the Comintern congress's strategic shift toward alliances with European Social Democratic parties; in doing so, the Comintern was abandoning an earlier commitment to forcibly erect Communist governments in Europe, the threat of which had helped bring Hitler into power in Germany.[61] Instead, Bullitt focused on Soviet violations of the recognition agreement with the United States and recommended closing the Soviet consulate in San Francisco, curtailing visas, and having Roosevelt discuss the violations publicly. The president decided instead to issue a note of protest.[62]

Bullitt took matters further. When he was in Berlin in late 1935, he advised the French against signing the proposed Franco-Soviet Pact, a bilateral treaty pursued by France since 1934 with the aim of enveloping

Nazi Germany. It was ratified anyway in February 1936.[63] The bitterness Bullitt displayed toward the Soviets during the talks surprised Ambassador William Dodd, his Berlin counterpart. Dodd noted in his diary on November 25, "The President must know the man's mentality, but if so, how could he have appointed him Ambassador to Soviet Russia?"[64] Roosevelt was aware of the talks and of Bullitt's attitude and did not seem to mind. In fact, the president appreciated Bullitt's combination of passion and strategic thinking. Roosevelt liked "novel ideas, bold courses, and dramatic actions, and he liked the sort of men who could come with such suggestions."[65] Bullitt was that sort of man. As it turns out, the Soviets were also aware of Bullitt's talks. Dodd's daughter Martha, a newly recruited Soviet agent, reported to Moscow that Bullitt had "scolded" the USSR.[66]

On January 9, 1936, Louise died suddenly at her hotel in Paris, where she had been living after suffering a stroke. She had known for months that she was dying and wrote to her lawyer, Art Hays, to describe her will, which left everything to Bullitt. "There is no use in fooling myself into believing that I am not in failing health," she wrote Hays. "Don't think I am bitter or afraid to die." Quoting the nineteenth-century English poet Ernest Dowson, she added, "'I am not sad but only tired of everything that I ever desired.' I feel like that. To me death means peace. But I have . . . letters, books, paintings given to me by the most famous people of our time. I have my own books and manuscripts which I think Anne should have . . . so if I die here, or somewhere else, suddenly, someone will take charge of things here. Perhaps Bill will see that I get buried decently—also for the sake of Anne."[67]

Hays passed the letter to Bullitt after Louise's death. With Robert Murphy, the US consul in Paris, Bullitt organized her funeral and buried her at Versailles. Anne remembered happy times with her mother—"a lot of comings and goings" because her mum was traveling. Anne remembered the excitement of her mother's suddenly arriving from faraway places with exotic presents for everyone. Things had changed when Louise became ill and could no longer see Anne often. Even after Louise's death, Bullitt concealed the divorce from his daughter and the wider world, and Anne would not become aware of the split until she discovered it in her father's papers after his death.[68]

Bullitt was depressed in the wake of Louise's death. He talked constantly about her and expressed a desire to leave Moscow.[69] Roosevelt agreed, as he wanted a more optimistic approach to the Soviet Union.[70] LeHand suggested that Bullitt be reassigned as Roosevelt's budget director, but Roosevelt wouldn't hear of it. "He is all wrapped up in international diplomacy and knows nothing about [budgets]," the president replied.[71] Bullitt was too useful in the foreign service. There was talk of assigning him to Rome, which he did not want. He would serve wherever he was placed, of course, but he craved action and felt he could get it in Washington as part of Roosevelt's 1936 reelection campaign, after which he hoped to be assigned to Paris.[72] Roosevelt agreed and asked Bullitt back to Washington.

In a valedictory cable to the State Department upon completing his mission in Moscow, Bullitt shared compelling insights into the "labyrinth of the Soviet Union." It was "unique among the great powers," he wrote, because it was not only a state but "also the headquarters of an international faith . . . The mystical essence of the communist faith is the belief that when Communism had been established on earth, all cruelty, hatred, jealousy, avarice, and deceit will ipso facto be eliminated from human nature. But until Communism is established, all power and authority is concentrated in the state." He added, "The Soviet Union is a Godless theocracy if such a contradiction in terms may be permitted . . . Like Islam during its first centuries of expansion, Communism offers all men conversion on the sword. The works of Marx are its Koran. Lenin, the second great prophet. Stalin is the third. To preserve the purity of the faith the party is purged constantly." Relations with the Soviet Union would always be "a subordinate part of the problem presented by Communism as a militant faith determined to produce world revolution and the 'liquidation' (that is to say murder) of all non-believers." However, Bullitt warned that democracies must deal with Communists not as the Nazis did—that is, through repression—but "by preserving the liberties that have been gained so painfully by western peoples since the Middle Ages."[73]

Bullitt valued the colleagues he was leaving, and they did him. "William C. Bullitt was a fine ambassador," Kennan wrote in his memoirs. "I believe I reflect the views of others beside myself among those then stationed in Moscow when I say we took pride in him and never had occasion to be ashamed of him." Kennan described Bullitt as a "charming, brilliant, well-educated, man of the world capable of holding his own intellectually with anyone, including such great intellects of the Communist movement as Radek and [Nikolai] Bukharin, both of whom were then still around and had no objection to coming to the embassy to talk with him." It mattered to Kennan that Bullitt was not just a cog in the bureaucratic machine. "He resolutely refused to permit the life around him to degenerate into dullness and dreariness," Kennan wrote. "All of us who lived in his entourage were the beneficiaries of this blitheness of spirit, this insistence that life be at all times animated and interesting and moving ahead."[74]

Back in Washington, Bullitt invested his skills and charisma in the president's reelection campaign. Sometimes he stumped on the trail, as when he appeared at the Patrick Henry Bicentennial celebration in Hanover County, Virginia. With the European situation in mind, Bullitt declared, "Dictatorships, based on secret police and fire squads, have been set up in many lands. The noblest words that can issue from the mouths of man have been prostitute and the noblest sentiments of the hearts of men have been played upon by propaganda to conceal the simple truth: that dictatorships are tyrannies imposing their dogmas on enslaved people."[75]

On other occasions Bullitt was closely involved in developing Roosevelt's policy message. On the eve of the Democrats' nominating convention in late June 1936, Bullitt joined the president and others at the White House to work on the party's platform. Roosevelt wanted it short and simple. But as evening gave way to morning, the draft was still not moving forward. A little past midnight, Bullitt took charge. "We'll never get anywhere this way," he said. "My suggestion is that we have someone sit down and spend the rest of the night getting up a draft of the platform which we can look at tomorrow. My nomination for this job is Sam Rosenman." It was an intelligent and practical choice. Rosenman was Roosevelt's main speechwriter and a member of his brain trust. Rosenman was immediately assigned to the uncomfortable guest room opposite the president's study and given a few instructions. "I would like to have as short a platform as possible this year," Roosevelt said, and "I would like to have it based on the sentence of the Declaration of Independence 'We hold those truths to be self-evident.'" Rosenman worked through the night, and the president was satisfied with what he read at breakfast. After Bullitt drafted the foreign affairs plank—with a peroration added by Harry Hopkins, one of the president's closest advisers—the platform was set.[76] On June 27 Roosevelt made his acceptance speech at Philadelphia's Franklin Field; one sentence made the headlines: "This generation of Americans has a rendezvous with destiny."[77]

11

Diplomacy to the Rescue?

WITH ROOSEVELT'S STATUS as the Democratic candidate wrapped up, Bullitt's next job was in Paris. He was nominated ambassador to France on August 15, 1936, and took up his post in October. Bullitt found Paris in a state of anxiety. Earlier in the year, in March, the French had failed to react to Hitler's armed occupation of the Rhineland. Hitler knew his army was not yet strong enough to hold territory against the French, so he had ordered his generals to retreat from the Rhineland the moment the French moved. But, instead, the French stood pat. Under the terms of the Versailles Treaty, France had the right to respond with force, but the opportunity came and went. The government's hands were tied by budgetary concerns—mobilizing soldiers was expensive—by the public's aversion to a military draft, and by strategic challenges. At the time, no French government was willing to act without British support, which did not prove forthcoming.[1]

In early 1936, British liberals and Labor supporters still had considerable sympathy for postwar Germany. As British prime minister Neville Chamberlain put it, given "the way in which Germany was treated after the war . . . no foundation for peace in Europe would be laid until Germany had been given her full rights in the matter of her frontiers, the *Anschluss*"—unification with Austria—"and equal armaments." Chamberlain maintained that resolving German grievances should be the priority and "felt that the interior persecution in Germany was in great part the result of the denial to Germany of the rights every other sovereign nation claims."[2] Without the British, France was isolated militaryly. And few believed at the time that Roosevelt and the United States could be their savior.

Still, France was ready to receive Bullitt with open arms. He immediately got along well with Léon Blum, the new French premier. A socialist of the Popular Front, Blum was enthusiastic about Roosevelt's New Deal. Bullitt reported to Roosevelt, "He is attempting to do what you have done in America for the lower classes without disturbing any of the ancient liberties." Blum had "the sort of quicksilver intelligence and the little fluttery gestures of the hyper-intellectual queer ones."[3] Coming from Bullitt, this was a high compliment. Blum repaid it in his memoirs, writing of Bullitt, "I was then and still am with him in a relation of personal friendship. As soon as he arrived in Paris, a sympathy, and I can say an intimate affinity, had bound us to each other."[4]

The new US ambassador was speaking French for the first time in thirty years, but with his genuine appetite for social contact and political and strategic thinking, he was a natural interlocutor for everyone who mattered in Paris. From the standpoint of the French elite, Bullitt was the epitome of an ambassador, and the US Embassy became a center of Parisian life. At one ball for 600 guests, Bullitt served 490 bottles of Champagne Pommery 1928, his favorite; a worthy Pouilly-Fumé; and all the best whiskeys and brandies. The crowd danced to a jazz band into the early hours, until the party finally ended at 5:30 in the morning.

Bullitt and the embassy settled into a routine. Every day, he wore a dark-red carnation in the buttonhole of one of his well-made outfits sent from London. Offie, who stayed on with Bullitt in Paris, began most working days at 4 o'clock in the morning. He and the cook would show up at the Paris central market, Les Halles, to pick over the meat, fish, fruits, and vegetables for the ambassador's upcoming meals, parties, and events. Bullitt's food and drink became the stuff of acclaim in diplomatic circles; King Zog of Albania wrote asking to borrow Bullitt's cook for his wedding feast. A few months after Bullitt's arrival in Paris, Janet Flanner wrote in a *New Yorker* profile:

> He is eclectic, enthusiastic, adrenal—in conversation turns scarlet with displeasure or delight—is hospitable, sociable, hot-tempered, and overpunctual. He has an uproarious sense of humor and loves to laugh out loud at his or other people's jokes. He is an inveterate reader and a lively raconteur. Headstrong, spoiled, spectacular, something of a nabob, and a good showman, he has complicated ambitions.[5]

Bullitt rented the Château de Saint Firmin, which sat on 10,000 acres of woods threaded with beautiful streams, adjacent to the Château de Chantilly. The property had belonged to the Condé family, one of the oldest and most distinguished of the historic French nobility. Standing along the right bank of the Grand Canal, the château had not been occupied for many years and was in bad condition. The rent was low at $1,000 per year, though Bullitt spent $6,000 putting the building in order.[6] He was not exceptionally wealthy—his personal fortune was the subject of myths—but he did enjoy spending money to keep up his patrician lifestyle.[7] Saint Firmin became for Bullitt a quiet country getaway, as his farm in the Berkshires had been—a place where he could relax and welcome friends and important people. He and Anne would go to horse races at the beautiful Chantilly Racecourse, where "the stables backed up against the forest and the stands [looked] out over rolling green slopes toward the big chateau."[8] After a tennis tournament or round of golf at the adjoining Chantilly golf course, Bullitt enjoyed splashing around in spring-fed pools, icy even on warm summer afternoons.

In 1937 it was still possible to poke a bit of fun at Hitler, as when Bullitt shared with Roosevelt an anecdote from a dinner with the Duchess of Windsor. She had described to Bullitt Hitler's intense interest in architecture, reporting the Führer's claim that "our buildings will make more magnificent ruins than the Greeks." In a dispatch to Roosevelt, Bullitt wrote, "That seems to me to be about as revealing psychologically as anything I have ever heard."[9]

At the same time, there was no doubt that renewed German militarism posed a major concern. Bullitt thought that France's failure to retaliate in March 1936 held major implications for the United States. If France could not contain Hitler, then soon the whole continent "might be organized for attack on Great Britain and eventually on ourselves." In other words, the Atlantic Doctrine was at risk. This doctrine, which Bullitt saw as a key legacy of Wilson's, held that any power that might become hostile to the United States could not be allowed to control the Atlantic coast of Europe and Africa or the gateways to the Atlantic, North Sea, English Channel, and Strait of Gibraltar.[10] Since 1919 Bullitt had thought that French-German reconciliation would resolve the structural problem of peace in Europe and ensure preservation of the Atlantic Doctrine. By the time he was ambassador, he still hoped for this outcome despite Hitler's increasingly provocative actions and the reluctance of the British to respond. Hitler had promised that he "desired most ardently to reach agreement with France," and Bullitt wanted to take him at his word. Bullitt thought that the only way to stop the approaching deluge was through direct negotiations between Paris and Berlin.[11] Blum agreed that it was worth trying and welcomed the German minister and governor of the Reichsbank, Dr. Hjalmar Schacht, on August 28, 1936, for talks in Paris. Blum did not want to believe ideological barriers were insurmountable and offered Germany the possible recovery of colonial zones and raw materials in exchange for a lasting peace. But the Germans did not respond to his entreaties.[12]

Recognizing that it would not be easy to draw down tensions in Europe, Bullitt pressed for a more interventionist approach from the embassy.[13] He convinced Roosevelt to create an active network of American diplomats who could work with him in Paris. Soon the embassy became the center of a pan-European courier system, with a staff of 38 diplomatic personnel—4 more than London—and 320 additional local employees.[14] All diplomatic messages from the State Department to continental embassies and delegations—save those in Moscow—were funneled through the Paris embassy.[15] Heads of mission all over the continent presented Bullitt or his envoys with complete accountings of their local situations. And "Bullitt was closer than anyone in the diplomatic service to the president," said James Farley, the Democratic Party don.[16] They were in constant communication about France, Europe at large, and affairs from the rest of the world. At the time, heads of state generally did not talk to each other directly, as telephone conversations were not secure. Leaders still communicated through their respective ambassadors, and for serious matters Bullitt and Roosevelt conversed via code.[17]

Bullitt wanted to improve the professionalism of the whole American diplomatic effort. At the end of 1936, he secured support for Salmon's initiative to increase communications security across all embassies and State Department divisions.[18] At the time, there was no intelligence officer stationed at the embassy in Paris; instead, Offie coordinated intelligence-gathering. He would go through every telegram to make sure Bullitt didn't miss anything important. Only matters of the highest significance reached Bullitt; everything else ran through Offie. "When anything is to be done, Offie sees to it," Douglas MacArthur II, a diplomat and nephew of the famous general, remembered. "Each of us are born with a set of glands and had to operate accordingly on a twenty-four-hour shift. But [Offie] had three sets, and just shifted over every eight hours. He had a mind like a tape recorder." Another colleague testified, "You could feel the intelligence coming out of Offie in waves."[19]

Bullitt became Roosevelt's roving emissary, the informal inspector general of the diplomatic service and "Eminence Grise" who "pull[ed] all the wires from behind screens." Everyone in the State Department agreed that he was their number-one man at the White House.[20] Until 1940 Roosevelt worked directly with Bullitt on ambassadorial nominations, or at least confidentially sent him a list of nominations for comment.[21] Bullitt opposed Dodd remaining in Berlin. Bullitt had no objections to Dodd's strong anti-Nazi opinions; however, Bullitt thought Dodd's refusal to have professional contact with Nazis was unwise. Others at the State Department shared Bullitt's view. "What in the world is the use of having an ambassador who refuses to speak to the government to which he is accredited?" Undersecretary of State William Phillips wrote in his diary and said to Roosevelt.[22] At the end of 1937, when Dodd stepped down, Bullitt recommended his replacement, the long-standing diplomat Hugh Wilson.[23]

To Save Freud's Life

In 1938 Bullitt arranged for John Wiley's nomination as chargé d'affaires at the US Embassy in Vienna. Bullitt gave him a special assignment, namely keep a watchful eye and protective hand on Freud and his family. On the eve of the German invasion of Austria in March, Bullitt called Wiley and requested that he show "his presence."[24] On March 10, Freud received Wiley "in the most charming way." Wiley told Freud he would do everything in his power "to meet any situation which might affect him." All Freud had to do was have someone telephone him and he would appear at once. Freud was, Wiley noticed, obviously delighted. "He asked me to come again," Wiley told Bullitt. "I shall, and shall take Irene with me."

Bullitt had another job for Wiley, as well: to recover the Wilson manuscript, which had remained in Freud's home since 1932. Bullitt worried that if the officials found the manuscript, Freud's life, and possibly his own career, would be in danger. But Freud told Wiley he had nothing of a "dangerous" nature—the manuscript he and Bullitt had written together was not dangerous in his mind, so there was nothing for Wiley to collect. Freud claimed he feared nothing. "He was an 'old liberal' but not a member of any party. Nothing would happen to him," Wiley reported to Bullitt.[25] Two days later, on March 12, the German army invaded Austria. Vienna was occupied the following day.

Ernest Jones, Freud's disciple and one of the most influential psychoanalysts in the English-speaking world, immediately flew from London to Vienna to persuade Freud to leave. He arrived on March 15. The same day, a gang of Viennese hoodlums imitating Nazis broke into the office of Freud's son Martin and took all the money they could find. Wiley telegrammed Bullitt that he "fears Freud, despite age and illness, [is] in danger."[26] Bullitt asked him to do everything he could, including offering financial assistance for which Bullitt would be responsible, to help Freud and his family find refuge in Paris.[27] Bullitt also reached out to Roosevelt, who instructed Ambassador Wilson to take the matter up personally with German officials in Berlin.

On March 17 Nazi officers searched Freud's house and confiscated his passport and 6,000 shillings. Irena Wiley would always remember that day. Her husband called her, saying, "The SS are at Professor Freud's house. I am worried about him. Take the car with the [diplomatic] flag flying and go there at once. I'll see what can be done to protect him but hold the fort in the meantime." She arrived and pushed past two armed SS guards at the entrance of Freud's apartment, only to find six more men inside, some breaking furniture and others pulling books off the shelves, tearing out their pages, and throwing them on the floor.

With "a rude and commanding voice" Irena ordered them to stop immediately and asked to see the officer in charge. He was absent. She commanded the men to get out, and they did. She found Freud in his library at the far end of the apartment, sitting calmly behind his imposing desk, which was covered with his collection of Egyptian statuettes. He smiled at Irena and handed her a small sculpture of an Egyptian bird, asking, "Whom does this bird resemble?" He was overjoyed when she responded, "of course Queen Victoria." Freud started telling her about Egyptian myths and their influence on contemporary civilization. "There was not one word of what was going to happen to him," she wrote. "It was a most staggering show of philosophical detachment."[28] That same day, Ernest Jones returned to London to take care of visas for the Freud family.

On March 22, Freud's daughter Anna was taken to Gestapo headquarters, at the Hotel Metropole. At this point, she had already obtained barbiturate pills from the family doctor, Max Schur, and planned to commit suicide if she was to be tortured. Schur and other family intimates spent the whole of Anna's absence with Freud. He was very worried, pacing the floor and smoking incessantly. After Anna was released in the evening, Freud was highly emotional. It was then that he decided the time had come to leave.[29] Years later, Anna told Schur that she had asked her father, "Wouldn't it be better if we all kill ourselves?" to which he replied, "Why? Because they would like us to?" He still had a desire to live and to finish the book he was writing about the biblical Moses. He resisted out of what Schur called "sheer defiance" and wrote to his son Ernst, who was already in London, that he wanted to "die in freedom."[30]

The Nazis imposed in Austria the same policy that they were enforcing in Germany. Every "Jewish business" would have a Nazi commissar appointed to run it. While Freud and his family were still negotiating the emigration process—a highly onerous one under the Nazi regime—Anton Sauerwald, a chemist and fervent Nazi and antisemite, was assigned to oversee Freud's organization, Internationaler Pschoanalytischer Verlag. Sauerwald carried himself as a "tough brute." But, out of curiosity, he started reading Freud's works. They captured his interest and even impressed him. Soon he met Freud himself. Luckily, Sauerwald had studied with a Professor Herzog, one of Freud's lifelong friends and a man for whom Sauerwald had great respect and affection.[31] Ultimately Sauerwald protected Freud and his family. For instance, when Sauerwald learned that Freud had money abroad—which was illegal under Nazi rules—he kept the knowledge to himself, at great personal risk. When the Freud family was finally ready to depart, Sauerwald supervised the packing of Freud's belongings, including his books and art collection.[32]

Before that, on March 25, John Wiley visited Freud again. That day, to Bullitt's relief, Wiley was able to take the Wilson manuscript with him. At this point Freud had decided to leave, but he told Wiley he would not go without his family of twelve, nor without Schur and his wife and two children. Bullitt told Wiley he could personally provide $10,000, but supporting sixteen people was beyond his resources. Bullitt also recommended seeking assistance from Princess Marie Bonaparte, a patient and acolyte of Freud's, whose fortune came not from her great-granduncle Napoleon but from her grandfather François Blanc, a casino operator.[33] In case Bonaparte could not cover costs, Bullitt asked Bernard Baruch, the financier and former Wilson hand who was now a key Roosevelt adviser, to step in. Baruch immediately guaranteed his support.[34]

In the wake of the German occupation, the European democracies opened their doors to the Freuds. On March 15, the French announced that visas would be granted if exit permits were.[35] And soon enough, with support from the Royal Society and Sir Samuel Hoare, the British home secretary, Jones gathered sixteen residence permits.[36] At the same time, the United States was pressing the Germans to let Freud and his family leave. In Vienna, Wiley took the Freuds personally to Freiherr von Stein, a diplomat who had been attached to Germany's embassy in Austria, defunct since the *Anschluss*. Von Stein agreed to take up the matter of Freud's exit with SS chief Heinrich Himmler.[37] Bullitt also contacted the German ambassador in Paris, Count Johannes von Welczeck, pointing out in the strongest terms the consequences if something happened to Freud. By March 30, Bullitt was sure that the pressure had convinced the German government to release Freud, and the following day Wiley got the good news: the Freuds would be allowed to depart. There was one condition, though.[38] The Nazis had valued Freud's fortune at 125,000 Reichsmark, on which he would have to pay an exit tax of 25 percent in order to leave.[39] It would take time to assemble the necessary paperwork.

Bullitt spent April in the United States. On May 5, in London on his way back to Paris, he met Freud's son Ernst and told him that "he would do everything he possibly could" to hasten the family's departure from Vienna, even if it was necessary to "go to Berlin and there see [leading Nazis Konstantin von] Neurath and [Joseph] Goebbels."[40] Back in Paris on May 14, Bullitt convened Wiley and Hugh Wilson at the embassy to coordinate Freud's exit. The final days were stressful. On May 27, Bullitt telegraphed Wiley, "My advice is to hurry."[41] Freud, his wife and daughter, and two maids finally left Vienna on June 4 on the *Orient Express*. Wiley had confirmed to Bullitt that an American bodyguard, one Lieutenant Weaver, would be on the train.[42] Anna noticed his presence during their travels, later writing to Jones that "he came and looked in on us repeatedly."[43]

At 3 o'clock in the morning on June 5, they crossed the Rhine into France at Kehl and breathed a sigh of relief. Anna spent the rest of the night thinking about the people who had no chance of getting out of Austria and Germany.[44] She never forgot that "day of Liberation in Paris; but also the tiredness of her father after arrival. Eighty-two is no age for emigration."[45] Bullitt and Marie Bonaparte welcomed Freud and his family at Paris's Gare de l'Est in the early morning hours. Freud then rested half a day in Bonaparte's home garden on rue Adolphe Yvon before taking the train and then the ferry to London. Hovering in the background was Baruch, whose pledge of support gave Bullitt and his circle the confidence to move forward with the exit of Freud and his family. "I should not have dared to go ahead as I did in the matter," Bullitt wrote to Baruch, "if I had not known that I could have turned to you in case of need."[46]

The first letter Freud wrote from London was to Marie Bonaparte. "The one day in your home in Paris restored our dignity and morale," he wrote. "After having been wrapped in love for 12 hours, we left proud and rich, under the protection of Athena"—Bonaparte had smuggled out one of Freud's favorite antique Greek statues.[47] Later, on June 18, Freud wrote to Bullitt:

> Now that I am sitting here in tranquility, peace, and beauty, however in poor health after all the experiences of the past months, I feel compelled to thank you once again for the part you had in the liberation of myself and the members of my family. I cannot evaluate that part for sure, as everything went on behind the scenes, but it was probably very powerful. And if there was, behind you, someone else at work, about whom I should officially know nothing, I ask you to express my thanks, should the occasion arise. In the hope I can welcome you some day in London, yours faithfully, Freud.[48]

Bullitt visited Freud in London as soon as he could, on July 30, 1938. "Bullitt was here today," Freud wrote to Anna, "the same, very kind. Thinks there will be no war."[49]

If Bullitt was still convinced that war was avoidable, it was not because he was blind to German aggression. Rather he believed that, all the same, there might be a strategy to escape mass bloodshed. At this point he understood that Hitler could not be contained solely through traditional diplomacy. Instead, he would have to be made to understand that, in the case of war, he could not win. And that meant the United States would have to be involved in arming Britain and France.

France especially. After the Great War, France had enjoyed air superiority in Europe. But that changed after 1935, when Hitler, violating the Treaty of Versailles, ordered the rebuilding of German air power. Using new aluminum-based technologies, the Germans set about developing the world's most powerful air force. The French reacted by launching their own rearmament but proceeded cautiously, in light of budget constraints. The air force was not a priority.[50] French leadership seemed unaware of how far behind they had fallen. Thus, in late November 1937, Chamberlain startled French prime minister Camille Chautemps with his observations about the "lamentable" state of French aviation. "You have no modern planes," Chamberlain said. "You are not ready to produce any." In December Amaury de La Grange, a French senator and president of the Aéro-Club de France, confirmed the situation: Germany already possessed a thousand combat planes able to fly over French territory with impunity at more than 250 miles per hour. In contrast, France had only twenty-seven fighters of a similar type.[51] "The situation is grave, extremely grave," General Joseph Vuillemin, the chief of staff of the French Air Force, bemoaned in early 1938. "If war comes this year, the French air force will be wiped out within a few days."[52]

War Creeps In

La Grange was a friend of Roosevelt's, so Chautemps sent him as his unofficial envoy to the White House, seeking aid to build up France's air defenses. La Grange discovered that the US aeronautical industry, while ahead of the French in producing commercial planes, was no better when it came to manufacturing military planes. The Curtiss Wright P-36 was the only US fighter that approximated German combat standards.[53] Through Bullitt, Roosevelt authorized a skilled French test pilot, Michel Détroyat, to fly one of them. The test was successful, and the French decided to purchase the whole 1938 production of P-36 fighters, a hundred aircraft in total.

Georges Bonnet, France's finance minister, opposed the plane order as excessively costly. The order also faced opposition from those who wanted planes manufactured in French factories. Édouard Daladier, the defense minister and Chautemps's replacement as prime minister, finally pushed the order through in May 1938. He also ordered $940,000 be invested in another set of US-manufactured P-36s. This, too, provoked stiff opposition within the French administration, but Daladier feared that French factories would not be able to produce the needed aircraft in time to prevent a war.[54]

Bullitt had the idea to call on his friend Jean Monnet. During WWI, Monnet had been instrumental in forging a logistical partnership between France and Britain, which was key to feeding and equipping both countries and ultimately to their victory. Monnet had also led the Allied Maritime Transport Council, which had proven essential in redressing the Allied sea-power deficit. Bullitt thought Monnet could do something similar for the aircraft industry and introduced him to Daladier. Monnet agreed about the importance of building up French airpower and recommended the "establishment of an aeronautical industry abroad out of reach of enemy attack."[55] From that moment until June 1940, when France surrendered to Germany, Monnet dedicated his time to securing from the United States a supply of arms for those fighting in Europe.

It was no easy task. In 1938, there was serious disunity between the European nations threatened by Hitler and the Axis powers. On March 17, the day after Mussolini gave his consent to the *Anschluss,* the Soviet Union proposed a conference with Great Britain, France, and the United States to discuss a response. Chamberlain quickly rejected the idea. A month later, on April 16, Chamberlain signed an agreement with Mussolini recognizing him as "Emperor of Ethiopia" in return for "assurances" that Italy would refrain from involvement in the Spanish Civil War and from causing trouble elsewhere in the Mediterranean. And on September 13, Chamberlain met Hitler in the Bavarian town of Berchtesgaden. Chamberlain opposed Hitler's plan to take the so-called Sudeten territories from Czechoslovakia by force but agreed on the principle of self-determination whereby Hitler sought to justify annexation, for the Sudeten area was home to a majority of German speakers. On September 22, Chamberlain and Hitler met again in Bad Godesberg, near Bonn. Chamberlain proposed a British-French guarantee of Germany's new borders incorporating Austria, in exchange for a German-Czech nonaggression pact, preventing annexation of the Sudeten area. Hitler rejected the proposal.

Fearing imminent war in Europe, on September 26, Roosevelt sent a message to Hitler, Chamberlain, Daladier, and Prime Minister Edvard Beneš of Czechoslovakia, calling on the leaders not to break off negotiations. Two days later Hitler announced that he was inviting Daladier, Mussolini, and Chamberlain to meet him in Munich. Roosevelt was relieved and cautiously optimistic.[56] Bullitt's sentiments were even stronger; that day, he held an ecstatic telephone conversation with Undersecretary of State Sumner Welles.

Then came the pact itself. Signed on September 30, the Munich agreement recognized the Sudeten annexation, while Hitler promised to make no further territorial claims. Roosevelt congratulated Chamberlain on the agreement, and Welles declared that it would lead to lasting peace.[57] The return to reality was brutal. In an October 3 phone call, Bullitt relayed to Roosevelt what Daladier told him upon his return from Munich: Britain and France were humiliated, and Hitler's appetite for conquest would never be satisfied. There would be war. With catastrophe looming, Bullitt boarded the first available ship to the United States, the SS *Normandie.*[58]

12

After Munich

BULLITT REACHED THE PORT of New York on October 13, 1938, took the first train to Washington D.C., and in the evening briefed President Roosevelt on Daladier's report from Munich. The meeting ran late. The following day, Roosevelt convened a press conference and announced that he had "sat up last night hearing the European side of things from Ambassador Bullitt." What the president learned was deeply distressing. Far from assuring peace, the Munich agreement had only increased the likelihood of conflict. It was time, Roosevelt said, to "recheck defense preparedness carefully." In particular, the United States would need many more combatworthy aircraft: "If I had 3,000 or 4,000 aircraft, Munich would never have happened," Daladier had said, according to Bullitt. Roosevelt immediately began conversations with top aides about how to finance the arms race.[1]

Joseph Kennedy, who at the time was the US ambassador to the United Kingdom, would later accuse Bullitt—along with "the Jews"—of dragging Roosevelt into war. What Bullitt did was persuade Roosevelt of what he already suspected: the führer's total disregard for the political process and his absolute will to dominate. The president was left to conclude that Hitler posed a grave threat to US security. Already, Roosevelt had been terrified by Hitler's September 12 speech at Nuremberg, which had been broadcast in the United States. Now, Bullitt's account of Daladier's Munich report would be seared into Roosevelt's mind.[2]

Bullitt also shared with Roosevelt the French plan for an airpower buildup. On October 3 Monnet had submitted his proposal to Daladier and Guy La Chambre, the minister of air, who oversaw the French Air Force.[3] The proposal called for significant purchases of newly constructed, US-designed aircraft: 1,000 by July 1, 1939, and 4,500 more by the same date the following year. Due to constraints of the Neutrality Act, the planes could not be assembled in the United States and would instead be built in Canadian plants just across the US border from Niagara Falls. From Roosevelt's perspective, even this strategy did not go far enough. During dinner with Bullitt and Monnet few days after receiving Bullitt's report, Roosevelt stated that if the United States could produce 10,000 planes a year, Hitler would not continue his acts of aggression. "To win the war . . . 50,000 planes will be necessary," Roosevelt said. He jotted down how many planes he thought each of Britain, France, and the United States would need. Monnet kept the document as a souvenir. Before the dinner ended, Roosevelt called Treasury secretary Morgenthau and asked him to meet Bullitt and Monnet as soon as possible.[4]

The following day, Monnet, with Bullitt at his side, pitched Morgenthau the idea for building plane factories in Canada. The initial cost, Monnet estimated, would be $85 million.[5] "From what I know of it," Morgenthau replied, "there is absolutely no hope of your government's finding the necessary foreign currency in one year." So he proposed an alternative on the spot: $4 billion worth of gold had left France in the previous four years; surely some of it was in the United States illegally, and, as fugitive capital, could be requisitioned under the Tripartite Agreement the United States, France, and Britain had signed in 1936.[6] Bullitt found Morgenthau's scheme "an absolute stroke of genius."[7] But the French and British would have to do some of the dirty work, requisitioning funds from their own citizens. "Would Daladier have the guts to do it?" Morgenthau asked. Bullitt believed so, but it turned out there was another obstacle: Paul Reynaud, France's new finance minister, who had been brought into the government for his opposition to Munich and as a symbol of strength. Reynaud denounced the plan as offensive to his liberal principles. He also pointed out that the legal mechanism at play in the United States—where the government was empowered to fine citizens for failing to declare foreign property—did not exist in France. Finally, he worried that the proposal needed the British government's endorsement.[8]

Still, the principals moved ahead. Now Roosevelt wanted the planes to be manufactured and assembled in US plants, with Canada serving as "'insurance' used in case of necessity."[9] Daladier and La Chambre agreed and submitted orders for 700 bombers and 700 fighter planes, to be delivered by July 1939. Reynaud opposed the order, but Daladier eventually prevailed. On December 9, 1938, Reynaud approved an initial purchase of 1,000 planes. The cost would be borne by the French Department of War.[10]

The French order amounted to a tenth of the planes Roosevelt planned to build. In mid-November, Roosevelt met at the White House with Morgenthau, Assistant Secretary of War Louis Johnson, Deputy Chief of Staff of the Army George Marshall, and Chief of the Air Corps Hap Arnold to discuss his vision of an imposing air force. "A new regiment of field artillery, or new barracks in an Army post in Wyoming, or new machine tools in an ordnance arsenal . . . would not scare Hitler one blankety-blank bit!" Roosevelt announced, according to Arnold's recollection. "Airplanes were the war implements that would have an influence on Hitler's activities." The president sought to assemble 10,000 airplanes as soon as possible, while developing the capacity to produce 20,000 more in each following year.[11]

But Secretary of War Harry Woodring opposed planes for France, and Army Chief of Staff Malin Craig rejected outright the shift to airpower. During another White House meeting, on January 16, 1939, Craig and his deputy, Marshall, argued that the United States did not need to focus on air defense because it was protected by two oceans. Woodring, meanwhile, argued that the new Douglas bomber the French ordered contained secret technologies designed partly with federal funding; to give these planes to a foreign power ran contrary to War Department policy. Roosevelt looked Woodring in the eye and said, "Harry, have you never learned that there is no such thing as the policy of the War Department? Don't you know that, with regard to national defense, there is only the policy of the president of the United States? If you are not ready to follow my policy, you may resign now."[12] Woodring instantly relented and Roosevelt reaffirmed his decision "that every effort be made to expedite the procurement of any types of planes desired by the French government," including the newest models.[13]

Supplying arms under conditions of official neutrality—and while France was not technically at war with Germany—would be enormously controversial, so all parties hoped to keep it secret. But on January 27, a Douglas bomber crashed during a test mission in France, killing the chief test pilot. With the secret now in full view, Morgenthau was forced to testify in the Senate. For his part, Roosevelt went directly to the press in support of the sale of planes to France by a private company, which he noted would be beneficial to a US industry that was struggling to develop. The revelations ultimately proved no obstacle. In mid-February, the French signed contracts for airframes and engines with numerous American manufacturers, including Douglas, Martin, Pratt, Whitney, North American, Wright, and United. By Labor Day, the French received their first orders of Martin bombers, most of their basic trainers from North American, half of their dive bombers from United, half of their airframes, and one-third of their engines.[14]

Bullitt became the chief advocate for Roosevelt's new European strategy—a position that both reflected and reinforced the ambassador's unique access to the president. No one else so thoroughly commanded Roosevelt's attention when it came to foreign affairs. The two exchanged letters, telephone calls, and other communications in full confidence. For the most important communications, Bullitt visited the president in person. At the same time, Bullitt enjoyed a great deal of autonomy, making clear how completely Roosevelt trusted him. Both sought something short of formal alliance—which would put the United States at direct risk if war broke out—that would still enable deterrence. The objective was to prevent war by propping up European democracies with material and industrial support. Bullitt channeled all of his energies toward achieving this goal.

Bullitt also had an intimate relationship with Daladier.[15] Both were anti-Communists who believed that, in the event of war, there would be revolutions all over Europe—revolutions that might end with Communist victories.[16] But, for the moment, Bullitt and Daladier had become anti-Nazi above all else. Bullitt kept Roosevelt and Daladier in communication. On several occasions, Bullitt arranged for Daladier to speak with Roosevelt from his office at the Paris embassy. Roosevelt assured Daladier that, despite disagreement within his own administration, he was backing both the airpower agenda and the larger program of providing material aid. "Don't worry," Roosevelt told Daladier on one occasion. "The Johnson law, I will end up having it suspended," the president said, referring to the aforementioned 1934 Johnson Act, which made it illegal for US citizens to lend money to debtor states, such as France.[17] Roosevelt's support energized Daladier and galvanized his commitment to the aircraft procurement policy.

Roosevelt had no trouble speaking honestly about the once-secret aircraft program. Perhaps he wanted the world to know—after all, deterrence thrives on the open display of power, even if that display was not nearly enough in this instance. Such directness and willingness to engage in confrontation was starkly at odds with Wilson's caution and caginess, a comparison that was on Roosevelt's mind as the war set in. In February 1939, Roosevelt told a story about Wilson's state of mind in February 1917, after Germany proclaimed unlimited submarine warfare. Impatient for action, Roosevelt, as assistant secretary of the Navy, asked Wilson for permission to improve fleet readiness. Wilson refused. "I'm going to tell you something I cannot tell the public," he said to Roosevelt. "I do not want the United States to do anything . . . by way of war preparations that would allow the definitive historian in later days to say that the United States had committed an unfriendly act against the Central Powers." Roosevelt himself refused to go "faster than the great mass of our people would permit," but he was not worried by historical assessment.[18]

The War for Europe Begins

On March 15, 1939, the Wehrmacht seized what remained of Czechoslovakia. The Munich agreement was no more, and the floodgates were open.

Through intelligence sources, Bullitt learned just how wide. Speaking to Roosevelt a few days after the invasion—and, off the record, to *New York Times* editor-in-chief Arthur H. Sulzberger—Bullitt described a meeting that took place "on or about the 9th or 10th of March" in which "Hitler called on a group of some half dozen men" and reportedly told them, "On March 14th, I shall wipe the state of Czechoslovakia off the map. I shall swallow Poland, Hungary, Greece, Romania, and with the strength of their raw materials destroy the French army and reduce England to vassalage. Then with the combined fleet of Germany, Italy, France and England, I shall teach the US not to take sides against us." This was indeed a decisive meeting: on March 11, Germany's Supreme Command instructed the Foreign Ministry to dictate ultimatum terms to Prague, and, on March 12, orders were given to the German Army to prepare for invasion. More followed quickly. On March 22, Lithuania ceded the region of Memel in response to a new Nazi ultimatum; Memel had been one of several territories with substantial German-speaking populations placed under League of Nations control, and in 1923 was occupied and soon annexed by Lithuania without league objection. Hitler's allies were also on the march. In the first week of April 1939, Mussolini invaded Albania, and Francisco Franco triumphed in the Spanish Civil War.[19]

Bullitt still believed a wider war in Europe could be averted through an Anglo-French-Soviet alliance. The Soviets proposed such a plan in April and found a welcome reception from the French Ministry of Foreign Affairs. But the British stalled. Soon, Litvinov was out as Soviet foreign minister, replaced by Vyacheslav Molotov. The shakeup likely reflected Stalin's decreasing interest in working with Britain and France, which at this point seemed unreliable. By August the Soviets had made an about-face, embodied in the Molotov-Ribbentrop Pact, a nonaggression accord negotiated with German foreign minister Joachim von Ribbentrop. The pact took Daladier by surprise and "placed France in a most tragic and terrible situation," Bullitt wrote.[20]

On September 1, 1939, at about 3 o'clock in the morning in Washington, the telephone rang next to President Roosevelt's bed. He was awake in an instant. "Who is it?" he asked. "This is Bill Bullitt, Mr. President." Bullitt proceeded to explain that "several German divisions" had penetrated "deep in Polish territory." There were reports of heavy fighting and "bombers over the city" of Warsaw. "Well, Bill, it's come at last," Roosevelt replied. "God help us all." Roosevelt called Secretary of State Hull and Undersecretary of State Sumner Welles. Then he spoke again with Bullitt, who received word from Daladier that France would come to Poland's aid. A few minutes later, Kennedy called from London to report that the British would do the same.

In fact, neither did—even after September 17, when the Soviets joined the Germans in invading Poland; per the terms of the Molotov-Ribbentrop Pact, the two powers would share the spoils of their common neighbor. While France and Britain declared war in formal solidarity with Poland, they largely stayed on the sidelines. Although the conflict was at this point very real in Poland, Czechoslovakia, Finland, and elsewhere, its first eight months—preceding the invasion of France, Belgium, Luxembourg, and the Netherlands in May 1940—came to be known as the Phony War.

But if France and Britain did not initially fight, declaring war had legal consequences. Per the Neutrality Act, Americans could not sell arms to declared belligerents. So Roosevelt summoned Congress to amend the law, and not for the first time. Over the summer of 1939, he had tried and failed. On November 4, he finally succeeded in revising the law's Cash and Carry proviso, extending it to armaments. The constraints of the measure—weapons had to be sold for cash on the spot, not on credit, and they had to ship immediately—favored Britain, which had a strong navy and could transport and protect significant amounts of materiel on the open sea.[21]

Bullitt anticipated that Poland would be crushed within a matter of weeks and that the short-term prospects for Nazi domination were good.[22] But he was also prescient about Europe's long-term prospects. Writing to Alexander Kirk—who, as chargé d'affaires, replaced Ambassador Wilson as the highest-ranking US representative in Berlin in the wake of Kristallnacht—Bullitt predicted that "Mr. Hitler has already lost this war completely. I rather imagine that he thinks he can finish the French and British quickly enough to turn around and smash the Bolshies; but that isn't going to happen and in the end the Bolshies will gradually eat like a cancer to Berlin. Then the next stage will be of finishing off Stalin Khan . . . how?"[23]

Daladier responded to the invasion of Poland by ordering 1,000 additional combat planes from the United States and authorizing Monnet to negotiate an arrangement with Britain for joint armament orders.[24] Roosevelt supported the idea, but Chamberlain needed convincing. He finally came aboard on October 22.[25] On Bullitt's suggestion, Monnet was named head of the Anglo-French Coordinating Committee, based in London. Arthur Purvis, a Canadian businessman with experience supplying the British in WWI, would represent the committee in D.C.[26]

It was clear to Daladier that the Allies would need more than had been requested so far; he proposed that France and Great Britain purchase 10,000 planes from the United States, to enable dominance in the air and an Allied offensive by spring 1941. "I implore you to leave for the United States as soon as possible to work on this problem," Daladier told Bullitt. If the ambassador could not gain support for the order, Daladier would resign, he said, and turn over the government to rivals Georges

Bonnet or Pierre-Étienne Flandin, "either of whom would make an early compromise peace with Germany."[27] Again, Roosevelt needed little convincing. Bullitt dispatched René Pleven, Monnet's assistant, to discuss the idea with the president, who quickly approved a purchase of 8,000 US aircraft, to be delivered in October 1940. The $1 billion price tag would be shared between France and Britain. On December 1, 1939, Roosevelt appointed Morgenthau to represent the United States in dealings with the Anglo-French Coordinating Committee, which was responsible for overseeing the purchase. This way Roosevelt was able to circumvent Secretary of War Woodring, who was consistently sabotaging efforts to put US industrial resources at the disposal of the Allies.[28]

But once again, Reynaud, the French finance minister, was reluctant. A $500 million order was too much, he contended. How would the country rebuild after victory, if it had no gold reserves left? Other specious arguments came from the army, which asserted that, if the War Department's strategy of delaying the enemy's offensive until 1941 succeeded, US aircraft would be obsolete. To which Pleven replied, "There's nothing more obsolete than having no aircraft at all."[29] On January 9, 1940, Reynaud told Bullitt that there was no way he would authorize the expenditures necessary for additional aircraft purchases.[30] Daladier overrode Reynaud's opposition and on March 4, the Anglo-French Coordinating Committee committed to buying 4,600 planes from US factories—the largest such order since 1918.[31]

In the weeks that followed, battle lines continued to harden within the US government. Roosevelt, Morgenthau, and Bullitt—joined by other influentials such as Commerce Secretary Harry Hopkins, Interior Secretary and consummate New Dealer Harold Ickes, Supreme Court Justice and former presidential adviser Felix Frankfurter, and State Department economic adviser Harold Feis—constituted a "war party." They did not want to see American boys sent into another European battlefield, but the fate of Western civilization required the United States to support France and the United Kingdom.[32] Defenders of neutrality included State Department higher-ups such as Welles, Assistant Secretary of State Adolf Berle, Chief of the European Affairs Division Jay Pierrepont Moffat, and Special Assistant Secretary of State Breckinridge Long, who was closely involved in advising on matters arising from the war. Welles had for some time envisioned the United States leading a group of neutral powers in setting rules of international behavior, which would include concessions to Germany.[33]

Roosevelt sent Welles to Europe in February and March 1940. To the French leaders Reynaud, Daladier, Chautemps, and Blum, Welles gave the impression that the United States thought Germany was invincible and that France and Britain ought to pursue a peace of compromise through the intercession of the "great man"—Mussolini.[34] Welles's effort achieved exactly the opposite of what he had intended. Afraid that the United States might succeed in detaching Mussolini from him, Hitler sent Ribbentrop to Rome on March 10, in the middle of Welles's visit, with a personal message from the führer. Eight days later Mussolini, during a face-to-face meeting with Hitler, committed Italy to entering the war on Germany's side.[35] Bullitt "howled with rage," seeing Welles's mission as undue interference in his own domain. It was a sign that Bullitt's reign as head of US diplomacy in Europe was coming to an end.[36]

Only a few weeks later, Bullitt was again made uncomfortable, this time by the German Foreign Office's publication of documents purportedly seized from the Polish Ministry of Foreign Affairs. The documents revealed an isolationist Kennedy, who regarded the Nazi regime with a degree of sympathy, and, on the other side, Bullitt and Anthony Biddle, the US ambassador in Warsaw, encouraging Poland to take a firmer stand against Germany. The leaked documents also had Bullitt making controversial promises on behalf of President Roosevelt and affirming that "France and Britain have the moral assurance that the United States will leave the policy of isolation and be prepared to intervene on the side of Britain and France in case of war."[37] US representative Hamilton Fish of New York and Senator Robert Reynolds of North Carolina, both isolationists, demanded a congressional investigation into the purported conversations.[38] Bullitt denied these accounts, but to his foes they signaled a man who thought "he runs the country, and to some extent the world."[39] Embarrassed, Roosevelt denounced the document dump as a propaganda maneuver, and the State Department denied the materials' authenticity. A few days later, on April 9, the attention of the US public shifted to the invasions of

Denmark and Norway. Reynaud, who had replaced Daladier on March 22, responded by sending an expeditionary force to "make war."[40]

Daladier, who remained minister of defense, had wished to continue the Phony War. He didn't want "to contemplate effective action against Germany until France had a powerful air force."[41] But, as it turned out, the French did not have the luxury of waiting. On May 10, 1940, German forces brought the war to them, attacking not only France but also its neighbors Belgium, Luxembourg, and the Netherlands.

France Falls, Britain Rises, and America Pays

Bullitt was with Daladier at 8:40 on the evening of May 15 when they received news that the Belgian Army, which had been holding the line at the Meuse River, was collapsing. German divisions were now pouring into France through a large hole at Sedan, on the Belgian border. Daladier was incredulous. "It cannot be true," he kept exclaiming. "Impossible." He urged Maurice Gamelin, chief of staff of the French Army, to organize a counterattack. Gamelin responded that he did not have enough men. "So, this is the end of the French Army?" Daladier asked. "Yes," Gamelin replied. "This is the destruction of the French Army."[42]

On June 3, German aircraft bombed the dining room of the Ministry of Air, where Bullitt had just lunched. He was shocked. Obviously, Bullitt thought, Providence had protected him.[43] The attack was part of Operation Paula, a large-scale, deep-penetration assault by the Luftwaffe involving 500 aircraft, comparable to attacks carried out later during the Battle of Britain.[44] The historian Marc Bloch would later describe the effects of the bombing on people's nerves, writing of the overpowering sound of the aircraft and the terror experienced by all—not just the direct victims. The resulting panic broke down the will to resist.[45]

Bullitt, however, was not inclined to back down. On June 1, he had seen René de Chambrun, a French-American aristocrat and heir of Marquis de Lafayette, the Revolutionary War hero.[46] Chambrun had just arrived in Paris from London and told Bullitt an impressive story. When the war started, Chambrun was named liaison officer with the British Army. In the last days of May, amid France's debacle, he had been evacuated with British troops via Dunkirk. While crossing the channel for England, he saw three squadrons of German Heinkels, twenty-seven bombers in all, converge from three directions. At the precise moment when the Germans jettisoned their mines, six British fighters appeared in the sky at high altitude and dove toward them. In a few minutes, almost all the Heinkels had been hit and were falling into the sea, leaving long trails of smoke. The saviors in the air were piloting the first Boulton Paul Defiants, an innovative design with turret-mounted guns, built to carve up slow-moving bombers. The Defiants had been sent over the channel with full success. This extraordinary sight convinced Chambrun "that any German attempt at landing on British soil would be doomed to fail."[47]

Chambrun's testimony was crucial to Bullitt, who had thought the British would be crushed after a French defeat.[48] "They are very pessimistic in Washington," he told Chambrun. "Roosevelt, Cordell Hull, . . . and others, believe that the German air force is invincible and will crush the British." But perhaps Chambrun's experience would convince them otherwise. "Would you be ready to go to Washington at very short notice?" Bullitt asked. "It would be important." Chambrun replied he could go only by order of his military superiors. The next day Bullitt had an appointment with Reynaud. Immediately thereafter Maxime Weygand, who replaced Gamelin as the top commander of the French armed forces, named Chambrun assistant military attaché at the French Embassy in Washington, with orders to assume his post as soon as possible.[49] Chambrun took the first train to Lisbon, where he departed on a Clipper for New York. He arrived on June 12 with a letter from Bullitt asking President Roosevelt to listen to Chambrun and to "have him talk as soon as possible with the competent officials and officers of our War and Navy Department[s]."[50] Upon arrival in the United States, Chambrun called Missy LeHand at the White House, who told him that the president "wanted to see him as soon and as long as possible" and that he should share once more everything he had told Bullitt. Chambrun had his first meeting with Roosevelt the next morning and related his story to the president. The Luftwaffe was far more vulnerable than was generally believed, Chambrun explained. With sufficient support, Britain's Royal Air Force could beat them.

Roosevelt wanted Chambrun to meet with his advisers as soon as possible. Pessimism had taken hold among Roosevelt's cabinet and brain trust; just two days before, they had decided to withhold anti-aircraft guns, planes, and small arms ordered by the Allies and awaiting shipment from Baltimore and Norfolk, Virginia. Believing there was nothing the French and British could do, US leaders increasingly felt that military production should be kept at home for the national defense.[51] But Chambrun was changing minds. Alongside Roosevelt, he soon met with Hopkins and Averell Harriman, a key White House foreign policy aide, aboard the presidential yacht *Potomac*. There, Chambrun repeated his story of the downed Heinkels and the "miracle" of Dunkirk: the Germans massed a gigantic force on a single port for five days and nights but were still unable to prevent the evacuation of 355,000 men. The British pilots took down seventy-five to a hundred German bombers a day.[52] The morale of the British airmen was high, and the Royal Air Force had thousands of quick fighters in stock. True, they were of no use in the French campaign on account of their short range, but they could defend British coasts and ports.[53] Under these conditions, a successful defense was possible. How, then, could the United States hold back the thousands of rapid-firing anti-aircraft guns France had ordered? "It is madness to keep them here," Chambrun argued. Roosevelt grabbed the arm of his wheelchair and said, "René, you have convinced me." Turning to Harriman and Hopkins he asked, "What about you boys?" Harriman replied, "Chief, I think we feel as you do."

Roosevelt ended the *Potomac*'s cruise early, so that Chambrun could confer with other important Americans—twenty-three in all. When the cruise ended, Chambrun was welcomed at the pier by Hull and Welles. That night he had dinner with William Knudsen, director of war production. The following day, he met with Secretary of Labor Frances Perkins. He lunched with Vice President Garner, members of the Senate Committee on Foreign Relations—including its powerful chairman, Key Pittman—and the heads of the other Senate committees. Pittman called Roosevelt to report that "the French captain hit a home run." Chambrun also visited with the British and Australian ambassadors in Washington and boosted their morale. He shared his story with union leaders and with Morgenthau, Ickes, Frankfurter, Baruch, Senator Sam Rayburn, New York mayor Fiorello La Guardia, and Eleanor Roosevelt. Finally, he dined with two influential Republican Party figures, Senator Robert Taft and Chambrun's own aunt, Alice Roosevelt Longworth—wife of former House Speaker Nicholas Longworth, daughter of Theodore Roosevelt, and therefore a relative of the president's as well.[54] All were convinced. President Roosevelt ordered that available US materiel be sold to the British.

The British, after all, needed US support as well, and they were not shy in asking for it. "I am delighted to have that list of surplus materiel which is ready to roll," Roosevelt wrote Morgenthau on June 6. "Give it an extra push every morning and every night until it is on board ship."[55] But Secretary of War Woodring and his allies continued speaking out against the danger of aiding the Allies at the expense of the United States. General Marshall wrote to Roosevelt on June 22, "To release to Great Britain additional war materiel now in the hands of the armed forces will seriously weaken our present state of defense."[56] Roosevelt had had enough: he fired Woodring and instructed the US Army, through the US Steel Corporation, to sell Great Britain 500,000 Enfield rifles with 130 million rounds of ammunition, 895 pieces of artillery, 81,000 machine guns, 316 three-inch mortars, 20,000 revolvers, 25,000 Browning automatic rifles with a million rounds of ammunition, and new aircraft. The price would be ten cents on the dollar. There were yet more rifles on hand, and by February 1941, the United States had shipped more than 1.1 million to Britain. Later Churchill wrote that, after Dunkirk, "We had lost the whole equipment of the Army." At the time, US surplus could not replace everything, but it was nonetheless a vital resource.[57]

Protecting—and Escaping—Paris

On the morning of June 9, 1940, Bullitt motored out of Paris for Domrémy, the village where Joan of Arc heard the voice of God, to attend the consecration of an altar in the church adjoining her birthplace. The year before, when returning from a visit to the Maginot Line—the post-WWI defensive fortifications lining the French-German border, which proved useless when the Germans invaded via Belgium—Bullitt had taken a detour to visit Domrémy and found the place abandoned. He commissioned the French sculptor Maxime Real del Sarte to design the altar, with a statue of St. Joan of Arc, and raised $2,300 from American relatives and friends to fund the project. The altar was, he said, "offered to France and to God by young and old Americans." He added, "Americans know on which side stand right, justice, and Christian decency and on which side are wrong, cruelty, and bestiality." Bullitt returned to Paris through roads crowded with civilians fleeing at dusk, just a few hours before the Germans occupied Domrémy.[58]

On June 10 Mussolini, having pledged his support for Hitler, entered Italy into the fray by engaging French forces in the Alps. At the time, Roosevelt was about to deliver a commencement speech at a graduation ceremony at the University of Virginia. Upon hearing the news, he decided to change his script. "On this tenth day of June, 1940," he told the assembled students, "the hand that held the dagger has struck it into the back of its neighbor."[59] "Stabbed in the back" was Reynaud's phrase. Welles urged the president to remove the line from his final draft for fear of offending Mussolini, but Roosevelt delivered it anyway. It would be a long while before the United States committed troops, but already Roosevelt was convinced that peace could not be achieved without defeating the Axis dictators through force.[60]

The next day, Churchill met Reynaud's government in Briare, a hundred miles south of Paris. He pushed the French to go on fighting. This was, after all, the man who only a week earlier had electrified the British people with a speech that would become one of his most famous, pledging, "We shall fight on the beaches, we shall fight on the landing grounds, we shall fight on in the fields and in the streets, we shall never surrender." And Reynaud himself had proclaimed that the French would fight to defend Paris street by street and house by house. "If by misfortune we lost our armies," he declared on May 25, "we would have to save honor and fight to the death to defend Paris."[61] Charles de Gaulle, at the time a high-ranking officer making his entry into politics, also wanted to organize resistance there. Yet when Churchill posed his question—"Will not the mass of Paris and its suburbs present an obstacle dividing and delaying the enemy as in 1914?"—it was obvious that such an effort would be suicidal. Weygand agreed on the importance of a counterstroke but pleaded that he had inadequate forces to implement it.[62] From Churchill's perspective, this was not necessarily a problem. He felt that if Paris were destroyed, Americans, who loved the city so dearly, would move from neutrality to solidarity. Bullitt, however, opposed sacrificing the capital and its people.

On June 12, the French authorized Bullitt to inform the Germans that Paris was an open city.[63] With his own embassy now shuttered—the staff had been moved to Bordeaux, seat of the government in exile—he contacted German authorities through the US Embassy in Bern, at the request of the newly appointed military governor of Paris, General Henri Dentz. Dentz's mission was to hand the capital over to the enemy as peacefully as possible.[64] On June 13, Paris was empty and waiting for the Germans. They arrived after dark. A representative of Bullitt's met them in Saint-Denis, in the north of the city, and proposed that they delay their entrance until dawn. The Germans agreed. At 10 o'clock in the morning, the German commander, General Bogislav von Studnitz, called Bullitt to announce that his forces had entered Paris.[65]

Bullitt's decision to remain in Paris comforted the locals.[66] His only role, which he assigned himself, was to save Paris or die. "My deepest personal reason for staying in Paris is whatever I have as character, good or bad, is based on the fact that since the age of four I have run away from nothing however painful or dangerous when I thought it was my duty to take a stand," he wrote to Roosevelt. "If I should leave Paris now, I would be no longer myself."[67] Bullitt had no illusions about his own safety. The French government, he told Roosevelt, expected the Germans to bomb Paris with everything from high explosives and incendiary bombs to the newest gases. A radio channel under the name of the French Communist newspaper *Humanité*—in fact run by Nazi propagandists—began broadcasting in the first days of June 1940, and Bullitt was so regularly menaced that the French police were concerned for his life.[68] "An American Ambassador might be more useful dead than alive," Bullitt told Reynaud.[69]

On the night of June 14, Reynaud sent Roosevelt a private letter, cautioning that "France cannot continue the battle unless American intervention will reverse the situation by rendering the victory of the Allies certain."[70] On the radio, speaking to the French public but also to America, Reynaud appealed to Roosevelt for "clouds of planes from across the Atlantic to crush the evil force that dominates Europe." Given his earlier obstruction of US plane purchases, his "extraordinary, almost hysterical" entreaty, to quote Secretary of State Hull, struck the president as a domestic political appeal rather than a request of the United States.[71] At this point, it was too late anyway. Tens of thousands of French soldiers were killed attempting to block the German advance, and the battle of France was nearly over.[72] The French Army had collapsed in four cruel weeks, notwithstanding desperate acts of resistance and sacrifice.

In these last days before France's formal capitulation, Monnet was in London with a small group of French and British civil servants desperately trying to unify the forces of Britain and France before Hitler could intervene. They had an extraordinary idea: to immediately merge France, Britain, and their empires. Each French citizen would immediately become a British citizen and vice versa.[73] Monnet convinced de Gaulle to present the idea to Churchill and the British government, who approved the proposal. Churchill then transmitted it to Reynaud, who also approved. But time had run out. Most of Reynaud's government supported the armistice the Nazis were offering. Harrison Freeman Matthews, a US diplomat who was part of the embassy team in Bordeaux, reported, "Finally, Reynaud sent for us—the diplomatic corps—11 P.M. on June 16 and told us of his resignation and of the formation of the Pétain government."[74] In the few hours between Reynaud's resignation and the installation of the new government under Marshal Philippe Pétain—the WWI hero who agreed to lead France as a Nazi vassal—Monnet's purchasing commission in Washington negotiated the transfer to the British of the remaining $600 million in French aircraft purchases and ground contracts.[75]

On June 20 Bullitt had lunch at his Paris residence with Gaston Henry-Haye, a senator and mayor of Versailles, and the US journalist William Shirer. Bullitt was "still stunned of what has happened," Shirer wrote. He never expected Reynaud to collapse. Shirer shared with Bullitt what he had seen. He had followed the German troops from Berlin to Paris, where he found the city deserted. It was curious "to see the *Agents,* minus their pistols, directing traffic, which consists exclusively of German army vehicles." When Pétain offered to surrender and asked for an armistice, Parisians got the news via loudspeakers erected by the Germans in every square of the city. French citizens could scarcely believe it. It was clear that their army had to give up, but most expected their government to endure in exile, like the Belgian and Dutch. Reynaud had even boasted that the government would reconstitute in Africa. When the loudspeakers blared, the people looked at the ground, then at each other. Shirer mingled with them, heard their murmurs: "Pétain had offered to surrender. What does it mean? Why? How?"[76]

Bullitt left Paris on June 30 in a five-car caravan. That evening, the group reached La Bourboule, sixty miles from the coastal town of Vichy, where Pétain's government was constituting itself.[77] The following evening, Bullitt sent a long, confidential telegram to the president and secretary of state describing discussions with Pétain, Weygand, Chautemps, and other top French political and military figures.

> The impression which emerges from these conversations is the extraordinary one that the French leaders desire to cut loose from all that France has represented during the past two generations, that their physical and moral defeat has been so absolute that they have accepted completely for France the fate of becoming a province of Nazi Germany. Moreover, in order that they may have as many companions in misery as possible, they hope that England will be rapidly and completely defeated by Germany and that the Italians will suffer the same fate. Their hope is that France may become Germany's favorite province.[78]

He concluded his telegram by reporting on "a long letter from General [Édouard] Réquin who commended at the end the superb resistance at Rethel where his troops stood until they had not one cartridge left. It gives the same impression. I have talked with many soldiers who fought until they were totally without munitions and charged with the bayonet. The simple people of the country are as fine as they have ever been. The upper class have failed completely."[79]

Three days later Bullitt suddenly expressed a desire to return to D.C., but Roosevelt rejected the notion. On July 6 Hull informed Bullitt that the president "considers it extremely important" that he remain in Vichy. "No one could do so well," the president said, expressing his admiration for Bullitt's continuing reports.[80] At the time Bullitt was unable to communicate with the State Department except through oral messages transmitted by the US Embassy in Berlin, so he could not explain why he had decided to leave urgently, in spite of orders to the contrary. He took with him Minister of Air Guy La Chambre and his wife, to whom he provided false US passports. Bullitt thought La Chambre could be useful in helping the United States expand aeronautical construction—his plane orders had already boosted the US aviation industry, leading to improvements that would be decisive after Pearl Harbor.[81]

The departing group—which also included Offie and two friends of Bullitt's, a Mr. and Mrs. Gilroy, listed as Bullitt's butler and maid—planned to leave from Portugal, via Spain. They were extremely nervous at the border; after all, Franco's Spain was a German ally, and Franco himself was an old acquaintance of Pétain's. A Spanish border guard took a look at Mrs. Gilroy and proved incredulous. "She is not a maid," he said, judging by her clothing. "Of course not," the quick-witted Offie replied. "Don't you understand the ambassador has a mistress?" With these words, the whole group was authorized to cross the border. On July 13, they continued from Madrid. Bullitt telegrammed the White House to explain that he had felt compelled to leave and described France as a "new fascist state."[82]

After a short stop in Lisbon and a weeklong one in the Azores due to a broken-down plane, Bullitt arrived in New York on July 20 with confidential cargo in tow. Most important were secret plans, given to him by Reynaud, for manufacturing a 47-millimeter antitank gun, which during recent fighting had proven the best antitank gun on the European battlefields.[83] He also had a suitcase given to him by Blum, the former prime minister. The suitcase contained archives from the First International—the foundational leftist meetings of the 1860s and 1870s—and a letter of sympathy and friendship, handwritten by Churchill, after the last Blum government had fallen.[84] Blum passed the letter on to Bullitt, as he knew he would be arrested and his papers confiscated, and he did not want Hitler, who was campaigning against "agents of Jewish Internationalism and Bolshevism," to be able to expose Churchill's respect and friendship for a man who was both a Jew and a socialist, the leader of the French Popular Front.[85] Bullitt secured Churchill's letter in his diplomatic pouch, along with other sensitive documents. Finally, he was bringing back two pistols given to Marquis de Lafayette by George Washington, which Bullitt had received from the French parliamentarian Charles Baron.[86]

The previous two months—to say nothing of the preceding years—had been trying for Bullitt. Upon his arrival at New York Municipal Airport (now LaGuardia Airport), he was beset by reporters and stumbled when asked about Marshal Pétain, declaring him "universally respected in France." Contradicting his own statement to Roosevelt, he added, "I don't know if it is right to call [France] a fascist state. Marshall Petain has a tremendous reputation and is thoroughly honest and straightforward."[87] Perhaps, too, Bullitt was trying to be kind to René de Chambrun, who had come to welcome him: Chambrun's father-in-law, Pierre Laval, was a key figure in the new Vichy government. The press statements upset friends like Frankfurter, who wrote Bullitt about "his dubious remarks on arrival about the Pétain régime."[88] Was this really the same man who had telegrammed about France "becoming a province of Nazi Germany"? It was all, one suspects, too complicated for Bullitt to explain in public, in the moments after his escape from occupied France. He needed to talk to the president in person. They dined together at the White House that evening.

13

A Phony War

IMMEDIATELY UPON THEIR MEETING, Bullitt explained to Roosevelt why, despite the president's order, he had to leave Vichy urgently: his telegram stating that Vichy's ambition was for France to become the finest province of Nazi Europe was leaked to the Vichy government forty-eight hours after its delivery to Roosevelt. It had reached Paul Baudouin, the foreign minister, from Jules Henry, the French ambassador in Brazil, whose government had received the information from "the highest quarters of the State Department."

The French were deeply put out, and a few members of the cabinet demanded Bullitt's recall, as Henry and others thought the telegram damaging to France. Henry attributed Vichy's poor image in Brazil to Bullitt's assessment and asserted that the US press had backed the Royal Navy's destruction of a French fleet in Mers el Kébir, Algeria, on July 3, 1940, because of anti-French sentiment provoked by the telegram. In a meeting the following day with Pétain, Bullitt tried to reverse the terrible impression he had made. And Pétain managed to shift Bullitt's impression of Vichy. "Only a defeat of Hitler by some other power could restore independence to France," Pétain told Bullitt. "He is . . . sincerely desirous of a British victory," Bullitt wrote, no matter that Britain had attacked the French fleet just a day before. Pétain also expressed his hope that Bullitt would leavy Vichy soon—perhaps to get rid of him but also, and this the marshal said explicitly, to report to Roosevelt on what had happened in France.[1] The president was upset by the leak, but he was more interested in hearing Bullitt's up-to-date thoughts and recommendations. Bullitt spent three days with Roosevelt at his Hyde Park, New York, home, sharing news and perspective.

In and Out of Roosevelt's Circle

In the weeks after his return from France, Bullitt enjoyed close and constant access to the president. And no one had deeper insight into the situation in France. Even while stateside, Bullitt was developing critical intelligence.

Bullitt had come to believe that the geopolitical situation of France's African colonies could offer an opportunity. These territories were under Vichy's formal control but were perhaps not unfriendly to the Allies. What if Britain or the United States tried to land force there? Before leaving Lisbon to return to the United States, Bullitt dispatched his intelligence aide, Roscoe Hillenkoetter, to Casablanca, to assess local attitudes toward what remained there of the French Army. On July 25 Hillenkoetter reported that, among the many military and civilian figures he spoke with, all but two thought France should remain Britain's ally. The exceptions were the two highest officials Hillenkoetter visited: General Charles Noguès, the top colonial official in Morocco, and Rear Admiral Jean-Bernard d'Harcourt, the naval commander. Hillenkoetter was amazed by his interlocutors' near unanimity. The Mers El Kébir incident—an effort to keep French ships out of German hands—was seen as unfortunate, but Hitler remained the principal enemy. Meanwhile, France's surrender was perceived as an outrage. French officials in Morocco thought their country had enough firepower, fuel, and men to rise up and continue the war alongside the British. Noguès and Harcourt's own staffs told Hillenkoetter that if an Allied landing occurred, they would "head a revolutionary movement that would sweep those two persons into oblivion."[2] Confident in his North African strategy, Bullitt shared Hillenkoetter's secret report with Roosevelt and the State Department.

At this point, Bullitt was also preparing to deliver the most important speech of his life. On August 18, he was to give a high-profile address at Independence Square, in Philadelphia, which would be broadcast nationwide on the radio; he and Roosevelt intended to use the opportunity to impress upon the American people the hazards they faced if the Nazis were to win Europe. To think and write, Bullitt traveled to Camp Pasquaney, in New Hampshire, where he had spent the best summers of his youth. He telephoned President Roosevelt every morning right after breakfast. The president would talk at length, urging him to continue writing. Bullitt often responded, "Yes, it is coming along. I am working on it."[3] He submitted his draft on August 13, and after it was approved by the president himself, 2 million copies were printed for distribution.

The day of the speech arrived, the grounds prepared and seats erected. Choral singers and the Marine Reserve Band of Philadelphia were scheduled to perform. At 2:30 in the afternoon, Bullitt began his address. "America is in danger," he warned. "The United States is in as great peril today as was France a year ago. And I believe that unless we act now, decisively, to meet the threat, we shall be too late. It is as clear as anything on this earth that the United States will not go to war, but it is equally clear that war is coming to America." He called on the public to support Great Britain and urged conscription. "Write and telegraph to your senators and representatives," he concluded. "Write to your newspapers. Demand the privilege of being called into the service of the nation. Tell them that we want conscription. Tell them that we back up General Pershing," the heroic WWI general who had, two weeks earlier, urged selling surplus naval destroyers to Britain.[4] After the speech, Bullitt received 22,000 letters and telegrams, almost all of them favorable.

But on the floor of the House and Senate, demands were heard for Bullitt's impeachment. Who was this ambassador to dare break the custom of "discretion"? And even Roosevelt was hanging back, refusing to publicly throw his weight behind Bullitt's words. This despite an earlier promise to follow with a fireside chat on the topic, assuming the speech was well received.[5] Roosevelt, however, remained silent. Only weeks remained before the 1940 presidential election, an election in which Roosevelt was himself breaking custom by running for an unprecedented third term. Not only that, but the election was charged with antiwar sentiment. Public opinion was pro-Britain but against the war and for neutrality. Wendell Willkie, the surprisingly popular Republican nominee, was winning support by attacking Roosevelt as a warmonger. At the end of September, Wilkie claimed American boys were "already almost in the transports." With Willkie cutting into Roosevelt's lead, on October 4 Hoover predicted there would be a new president soon.[6]

However, if silence was the prudent course for Roosevelt, he was not inactive. Already in place by the end of August was a destroyers-for-bases deal according to which fifty US Navy destroyers would be transferred to the Royal Navy in exchange for land rights on British possessions. But the president knew this deal, which would be approved September 2, was not enough. The British desperately needed more support, lest their forces collapse, leaving the Atlantic a Nazi lake. Bullitt described a late August meeting with Roosevelt. "He cocked his cigarette holder, stared at the ceiling, then scratched his head and said: 'Bill, if my neighbor's house catches fire and I know the fire will spread to my house unless it is put out, and I am watering the grass in my back yard, and I don't pass my garden hose over the fence to my neighbor, I am a fool. How do you think the country and the Congress would react if I should put aid to the British in the form of lending them my garden hose?'" Bullitt thought this revealed Roosevelt's political genius—he was developing a message that could move even the most isolationist Americans by explaining how unstinting support for Britain was a necessity for US security.[7]

A few days later, in early September, Robert Murphy, Bullitt's number two at the US Embassy in France, arrived in Washington and was informed that Roosevelt wanted to see him at once. When he reached the White House, he found the president's desk covered in a large map showing French colonial possessions in North and West Africa. Roosevelt had read Hillenkoetter's report and "had given much thought about how to help French officers operating under the relatively independent conditions prevailing in Africa." Murphy shared with the president additional information provided by Hillenkoetter, who had just returned to Vichy. With 125,000 combat-trained men on active duty, 200,000 more in reserve, and fighting spirit far outstripping that in mainland France, the French military establishment in North Africa was stronger than many realized. "If France is going to fight again anywhere in this war, I believe North Africa would be the place," Murphy predicted. Roosevelt was also interested to learn that the Spanish had prevented ten German divisions from crossing Spain to reach Gibraltar, not by force but through diplomacy. "Hitler had a blind spot toward the Mediterranean," José Félix de Lequerica, Spain's ambassador at Vichy, reported to Murphy.[8]

Roosevelt ordered Murphy to obtain the required clearances from the French, proceed to North Africa, and travel the region for three months. Murphy would report to the president personally and bypass the State Department and the military. Soon he would become consul-general of the United States in Algiers, a de facto US ambassador to French North Africa, deploying a set of consular officers and informants and signing agreements with Maxime Weygand, who had become France's delegate-general in North Africa but was skeptical of the Nazis. Murphy's actions wound up being decisive in the development of Operation Torch, the Allied landing across Morocco and Algeria in November 1942. Encouraged by Bullitt, Roosevelt had recognized the strategic value of North Africa as early as August 1940.

By fall 1940 Bullitt could point to numerous victories: he had contributed greatly to the modernization of the US aircraft industry and had developed the North African strategy that the president had adopted. He had worked closely with Roosevelt to try to prevent the war and, when that was no longer possible, to prepare the United States to take part in it. Yet there were nagging issues. Why had Missy LeHand been so cold to him recently? Bullitt's relationship with LeHand was an important marker of his place in Roosevelt's inner circle.

Bullitt asked LeHand two or three times to attend his speech, but she declined. On August 14, he had written to her: "Dear Lady, do you know that you had a luncheon engagement with me today? Do you know that I have phoned you three times since luncheon yesterday?" In this letter alone, he said twice, "I am counting on you." After refusing all invitations, she sent only a polite telegram: "Heard the speech on the train it was grand, congratulations."[9] That future had been stalled for months. In March 1940 Roosevelt had told Bullitt that he wanted him to become secretary of the navy.[10] Bullitt was enthusiastic and counted his chickens early. On May 29, 1940, when he forecast German victory in France, he wrote to LeHand, "If I become useless here, I would like to try being useful at home. And after a couple of weeks of silence from me, the president, will, I hope, make that appointment."[11] But the appointment was not forthcoming. Instead, when Roosevelt had the chance to name top-ranking defense officials, he looked to Republicans. Perhaps he was taking a lesson from Wilson, whose failure to include prominent Republicans in his cabinet and the US delegation to the Paris Peace Conference cost him badly needed across-the-aisle support. As Roosevelt put it in a 1937 conversation with a friend, "Wilson made just one mistake: he failed to do things that were required to bring the Senate along."[12] Thus, when Roosevelt fired Woodring as secretary of war, he replaced him with Henry Stimson, who had served in the cabinets of Taft and Hoover. And for secretary of the navy, Roosevelt tapped Frank Knox, who had been the Republican vice-presidential candidate in 1936. Knox took the job on July 11, 1940, while Bullitt was making his escape from France. Then, too, Roosevelt had reservations about Bullitt. As the president told Harold Ickes, who suggested Bullitt for secretary of state, the ambassador "talked too much" and was "too quick on the trigger."[13]

The president told Bullitt to wait until after the election, and so he did. The situation took its toll. On September 25, George Biddle dined with him in D.C. and remarked, "Bill looked remarkably well, pink cheeks, and bursting with vitality. At the same time one is aware of his nervous laugh, and shouts of excitement, at times almost apoplectic." Offie told Ickes that Bullitt "is becoming sensitive about his anomalous position to the degree that he is not going around or seeing people. This means a good deal in Bill's case."[14]

Bullitt spent his time taking care of friends and refugees in Europe. He helped Heinrich Mann, the writer and brother of Thomas Mann, obtain visas and transportation to the United States for himself and his son.[15] On July 27, 1940, Bullitt ensured the departure, under US diplomatic protection, of Jean Monnet's mother and sister.[16] With Albert Einstein and the leading French scientist Henri Laugier, Bullitt worked to free the French physicist Paul Langevin from jail and bring him to the United States. Journalist Geneviève Tabouis and the families of high-ranking civil servants Georges Boris and René Pleven and banker and diplomat André Istel all found refuge in the United States or Britain thanks to Bullitt. In addition, he supported the rescue mission led by the US journalist and activist Varian Fry, who aided in the escape of thousands of refugees from occupied France.[17]

Bullitt also continued protecting Freud's family and others in psychoanalytic circles. Among these was Dorothy Burlingham, a friend of Anna Freud's. After Burlingham finally joined her in London, Anna wrote to Bullitt, "I know of course that it could not have happened without you. So, I am very grateful, and I wish I could do something for you in return some time."[18] Bullitt tried in vain to help Sigmund

Freud's young sister obtain an American visa.[19] He did help Harry, Freud's nephew, travel to the United States and Canada and secured visas for the Austrian psychoanalyst Ernst Kris and his family.[20]

At the end of October, Ernesta, Bullitt's first wife, asked to see him. It was not an easy request for her to make. Five years after their divorce, she had married Samuel L. M. Barlow, a classical composer, and put Bullitt behind her. But Bullitt's prominence as ambassador in Paris ensured that Ernesta's past was dragged out insistently, and she could not adjust. Her ex-husband's name in the headlines, his picture in the papers—they kept pulling her back, blocking her path with ramparts of yesterday. For the first time in her life, she found memories crowding in on her, pushing out the present, dominating her thoughts. She decided to give those memories free rein in handwritten memoirs, hoping this would allow her to be herself and leave room for other things.[21] After a year of work, she had written three hundred pages, but it was not enough. She needed to meet him. No, she was not looking to resume their relationship, even if he would have liked that. "For both of us," Ernesta wrote, "the page was turned, the book closed. With bitterness, with disillusion, and certainly for me with sorrow." She just wanted to speak to him; she was suffering, he was suffering, and she thought that if they "would talk the ghost might walk elsewhere."[22] They met on October 30, days before the presidential election, while Roosevelt was in Boston making a pledge that resembled Wilson's from 1916: "While I am talking to you mothers and fathers, I give you one more assurance . . . Your boys are not going to be sent into any foreign wars." Roosevelt knew that reality was probably different, but it was a tense moment politically, and he always believed that "before you could do anything, you had to be elected—or reelected."[23]

On November 5, Roosevelt received 55 percent of the popular vote to Willkie's 45 percent and won the Electoral College by a much larger margin. Two days later, Bullitt submitted his resignation from his post as ambassador to France, "in accordance with excellent custom."[24] On November 9, Roosevelt responded with a short note: "Dear Bill 1. Resignation not accepted 2. We will talk about that and the future later. 3. Hope to see you very soon? As ever FDR." But that same day, Bullitt heard that Summner Welles had told the French ambassador in D.C. that a new US ambassador, former Navy chief and Puerto Rico governor

William Leahy, was on his way to Paris. In the evening, Bullitt called Roosevelt. "Believe it or not, I forgot all about it," the president told him. "It's alright, though, Bill, because you remain as ambassador until the appointment is made."

Bullitt was furious: "Yes, but what on the earth am I going to do after you put me in that awful position? Leahy is now ambassador—after I told the press this afternoon, I was remaining ambassador to France . . . I don't hold anything against you for it. I never have held anything against you in my life . . . I had better tell the press simply I am returning to private life." Roosevelt replied, "Just for a short time." When Bullitt noted again how difficult his position was, Roosevelt added, "Sure Bill I understand. I must have knocked you cold. But let it go at that."[25] Roosevelt often left the announcement of news about appointments to subordinates. For instance, he never told Henry Wallace, the vice president, that he did not want him as a running mate in 1944, nor did he inform Harry Truman that he was next in line.[26]

The fact is that Roosevelt did not want Bullitt to remain ambassador to Vichy, and the Vichy government knew it even before election day.[27] The president had decided to pursue a new tactic, which garnered the label of the "Vichy gamble." It was strategically important for the United States to keep North Africa, the French fleet, and French possessions in the Western Hemisphere outside of direct Nazi control as long as possible, to buy time for developing US military strength. To this end, Roosevelt—with Welles's support—was looking for somebody who could impress Pétain and inspire confidence in him. This could not be Bullitt, who was perceived as hostile to the regime because of his July 1 telegram and continuing friendships with leaders of the former French Republic. Roosevelt and Welles decided they could do no better than a very high-ranking officer from the armed services, someone in whom the marshal could recognize a kindred spirit. On December 28, upon receiving Vichy's acceptance of Leahy's accreditation, Bullitt resigned.

There were probably other reasons as well for Roosevelt's sudden disfavor toward Bullitt. In the seven years Bullitt had been ambassador in the Soviet Union and then France, Roosevelt appreciated his creativity and tolerated his independence. During the preceding two years, when the president and ambassador tried to support France in preventing the coming deluge, they worked hand in hand in an extraordinary manner. But now war was underway, and Roosevelt wanted to centralize the handling of major foreign policy decisions. As George Kennan was later told, "In wartime, the State Department has only an advisory function on matters of high policy, and it gives advice only when it is requested to do so."[28] In this scheme, there was not much room for people speaking frankly to the president—and Bullitt was frank. As Ickes put it, there were only three men close to the president who dared disagree with him: Bullitt, Bernard Baruch, and himself. Others—led by Harry Hopkins, who, after the war began, became Roosevelt's top foreign policy aide—were yes-men.[29] Welles was charged with managing the professional diplomats for whom Roosevelt had cultivated a newfound dislike.

Perhaps Bullitt did not want the job of ambassador to Vichy after all. His Philadelphia speech was not that of a man preparing to return to Europe. Twice, in the days following his mishandling of Bullitt, Roosevelt offered him the London embassy—Joseph Kennedy had also resigned—but Bullitt declined. For one thing, he wanted to remain in D.C. because he and his daughter Anne missed each other. For another, "he could not go to London with [Welles] at his back with a knife."[30]

By this point, Bullitt and Welles were mortal enemies. In his July 1940 Casablanca memo, Hillenkoetter included a message from a State Department informant who wanted Bullitt to know, "Sumner Welles was preparing a coup against you."[31] And before Bullitt's departure from Vichy, two French cabinet members had informed him that it was Welles who leaked his confidential telegram.[32] At the end of July 1940, Welles himself called Bullitt and expressed regret about the leak. He explained that the telegram—which he claimed not to have read—had been transmitted automatically to the Brazilian government, according to State Department policy. Bullitt did not believe him. Later he checked the State Department file containing all telegrams transmitted automatically to the Brazilian authorities and discovered that his was not among them.[33]

At the time, the undersecretary of state was the second-ranking person in the State Department, and by 1940 Welles was essentially number one—managing the State Department and implementing the president's decisions while the old and ailing Secretary of State Hull was frequently absent. Welles was already responsible for postwar preparations. Roosevelt and Welles had known each other since childhood, and Welles had been a page at the Roosevelts' wedding. He enjoyed the support of Eleanor as much as Franklin. Often the president would turn to Welles for "fresh ideas and quick action."[34] One might have expected otherwise, given Welles's stiff, buttoned-up demeanor, which became a subject of teasing. Hugh Wilson, the former US ambassador in Berlin, once joked about his first meeting with Hitler thusly:

> Promptly, at twelve the doors were thrown open and I was led into the room where Hitler was standing, behind him, in a solemn row were [Field Marshal August] von Mackensen, [Foreign Minister Joachim] von Ribbentrop and [chief of the president's office Otto] Meissner . . . During the entire conversation, the faces of the last three gentlemen never changed in expression, and Hitler and I carried on a conversation carefully listened to by three totally irresponsive and non-participative presences. Their unbroken gravity was such that it occurred to me that the scene might be reproduced if you, Mr. President, should receive a foreign representative in the presence of three Sumner Welles.[35]

Welles and Bullitt's relationship had not always been bad. When Welles was named undersecretary of state, Bullitt wrote him a congratulatory letter: "I had hope that the post would go to [Assistant Secretary of State R. Walton] Moore who has been as kind to me as a father; but I am sure you know that you will have my fullest and heartiest cooperation and I shall do everything I can to assist you in your work."[36] While preparing for Munich, they had indeed cooperated fully and enjoyed their time together.[37] But things rapidly deteriorated from there. A few days after the conference, on October 3, 1938, they were strongly at odds: Welles claimed that there was now a greater opportunity to establish "a new world order based upon justice and upon law" than at any time in the last twenty years.[38] On his mission to Europe at the beginning of 1940, when he tried to make Mussolini the solution to the European crisis, Welles undermined Bullitt's authority in France and the United States, adding bitterness to what had previously been passionate but generally civil disagreement. Welles was also overbearing and "never neglected to punish those who had crossed him."[39] The Vichy telegram leak was a stab in Bullitt's back, jeopardizing his career.

On December 29, 1940, the day after Bullitt's resignation, the president held a fireside chat in which he shared the message he had tested with Bullitt in August. In the speech, considered one of the most successful Roosevelt ever made, he advocated for the Lend-Lease Act and America's role as "the great arsenal of democracy."[40] The legislation would give the president the authority to aid any nation whose defense he believed vital to the United States and to accept repayment in kind, in whatever form he deemed satisfactory. Some Republicans protested the bill as the harbinger of a quasi-dictatorship. In front of the House Foreign Affairs Committee, the heroic aviator, neutrality activist, and antisemite Charles Lindbergh argued that US aid would be ineffective and that Britain could not possibly win. Joseph Kennedy opposed aid as well, fearing it would lead the United States into war. But Willkie, who a few weeks earlier had been Roosevelt's Republican opponent, supported Lend-Lease. Bullitt joined the supporters, arguing that earth had been so shrunken by the airplane that, for the first time in history, Europe's war machines could reach the Western Hemisphere in a scant few hours. Supplying the British was vital to minimizing the danger the Axis posed: so long as the Royal Navy and Air Force continued holding the Germans on the other side of the Atlantic, the United States would be protected to its east, and the US fleet could defend the country's Pacific Coast.[41] Congress passed the bill on March 11, 1941. In April the president used his authority under the law to extend aid to China, which was waging war against Japan.

After Roosevelt's fireside chat in support of Lend-Lease, Bullitt returned to making speeches across the country. He prepared them carefully, with the support of friends in the State Department who provided him up-to-date information. Stanley Hornbeck—an adviser to Hull, former head of the Far Eastern Affairs Division, and one of Bullitt's best friends—edited all of his speeches before he delivered them. That included the August 1940 speech in Philadelphia. The same was true of a January 7, 1941, speech Bullitt delivered at the University of North Carolina, Chapel Hill.[42] In the evening address, broadcast nationwide by NBC Radio, Bullitt renewed his warning against stubborn neutrality, arguing that planes and radio propaganda had eliminated natural barriers. The way to avoid war was to provide Britain all the resources she needed for the struggle she was facing alone against the

Axis of Nazi Germany, fascist Italy, and imperial Japan. On February 18, at a Phi Beta Kappa Society dinner in New York, Bullitt pressed for doubling US warplane production to prevent Nazi control of the air. A week and a half later at the Overseas Press Club, he tried rousing the audience, saying, "We should at this hour be producing every element of defense that we need . . . with a great speed as though we were at war."[43]

Despite all his activity, Bullitt could not endlessly bury his frustration at being out of government. Yet he did not want just any job. On April 23, 1941, when Roosevelt finally offered a new position, Bullitt turned him down. Roosevelt had asked him to take charge of a new federal agency within the Office of Emergency Management aimed at raising public awareness of the imminent German threat, to which Bullitt replied that he did not want to work on home defense but on "licking Hitler."[44]

So April 23 did not become a new anniversary of Bullitt's public service. But it was nonetheless a day to remember, thanks to a secret Bullitt divulged to Roosevelt. He would have preferred not to be the bearer of news—he would rather have left the task to Moore, but Moore had died in February, leaving Bullitt a duty he could not evade, however unpleasant it was to carry out. At the end of November 1940, Moore had informed Bullitt that, on September 17, in the presidential train returning to Washington from the funeral for the late speaker of the house, Sumner Welles had drunk quite a bit in the dining car.[45] After returning to his compartment, Welles rang the porter and made "sexual proposals of the most indecent and immoral nature." Later, Welles propositioned a number of waiters in the dining car, offering money in exchange for sexual favors. Moore heard the story through his old friend and fellow Virginian Ernest Morris, the president of Southern Railway. Morris and Luther Thomas, head of the railway's secret police, told Bullitt the story.[46] Morris added that Welles acted in a similar manner during an overnight trip to Cleveland on the Pennsylvania Railroad in the first half of October. Bullitt was shocked. So was Secretary Hull, who heard the story from Moore. Just before he died at the age of eighty-two, Moore wrote that documents containing relevant testimonies should be delivered to Bullitt, one of the best friends he had in the world.[47]

LeHand exhorted Bullitt not to speak to the president about the train incident because Roosevelt already knew about it and wished to avoid the matter.[48] Nevertheless, on April 23, 1941, Bullitt handed the president a document he had prepared summarizing the testimonies of the porter and waiters. After reading the first page, Roosevelt told Bullitt what LeHand had said: "I know all about this already." The president had been informed by a Secret Service agent and ordered an FBI investigation. Welles acknowledged that he was drunk and had taken pills and drunk coffee but did not remember anything more. FBI director J. Edgar Hoover concluded that Welles had a mental condition, and that was that.[49]

Roosevelt's solution was to order Pa Watson, his appointments secretary, to ensure that Welles was never without a bodyguard. The president told Bullitt there was no risk any newspaper would publish such scandalous material or that the porters would initiate criminal proceedings. The main witness, the porter whom Welles initially propositioned, had since died. No affidavits or complaints were filed. Whether or not Welles was in the clear, the president wanted him close by: "He is useful to me," Roosevelt told Bullitt repeatedly. Bullitt hardly thought so; "he had been wrong on most subjects," after all. Now the country was about to undergo a test of character; the president should not have men without character around him. Roosevelt ended the meeting by ringing for Watson. "Pa, I don't feel well," he said. "Please cancel all my appointments for the rest of the day. I want to go over to the house."[50]

French Connection

Neither Roosevelt nor Bullitt knew it at first, but by keeping him out of the State Department the president had inadvertently offered Bullitt a gift. He was no longer the official ambassador to Vichy and so could become the de facto ambassador to French opponents of the new regime, especially political prisoners at home and refugees in North America. Through his former embassy staff now working in Vichy, Bullitt received letters from Daladier, Reynaud, Blum, La Chambre, and Georges Mandel, the former interior minister who had also been Clemenceau's top aide two decades earlier. He would cheer them with packages containing hams, chocolates, "remarkable" preserves, the "most delicious biscuits," and American cigarettes. He carefully followed Blum's situation and had the US Embassy intervene to improve the conditions of his imprisonment.[51]

Daladier was another of the prisoners. He had been among the twenty-seven French MPs who, on June 21, 1940, had refused to accept defeat and embarked on the ship SS *Massilia* from Bordeaux. They travelled to Casablanca with the goal of maintaining an independent French authority within the empire. All twenty-seven had been arrested and transferred to France except Daladier, who remained in Morocco under a sort of protective custody. When Hillenkoetter found him there, around July 20, Daladier had already tried on several occasions to join the British and help prosecute the war. Hillenkoetter arranged for Daladier to communicate with the British government. The Brits tried three times to get him out on a destroyer, but French authorities blocked each attempt. In one instance, he was on a Moroccan fishing boat two miles from a destroyer when a French tug carrying Admiral d'Harcourt himself forced him to row back to Casablanca.[52]

Daladier was then jailed near Vichy, ready to face the so-called Riom Trial, a legal proceeding in which the new government hoped to pin blame for France's defeat on its former political leaders. He was eager to explain his motives and actions at the trial, together with the former minister of air, La Chambre. Rather than see his loyalty to France questioned, La Chambre had returned from the United States after the Vichy government issued a warrant for his arrest.[53] Daladier, Reynaud, La Chambre—all these ministers were now in prison for having been opposed equally to Hitler and, in a sense, to collaboration with each other. Before the war, they had been unable to coordinate. They all rejected Hitler but failed, with dramatic consequences, to overcome their personal ambitions and political quarrels when their country's destiny and honor were at stake.

For their part, the Germans were not interested in pinning blame on French officials. They wanted to show that it was British and Americans—especially Bullitt—who were responsible for starting the war. On July 5, 1941, Ribbentrop asked the Vichy government to furnish all documents it possessed proving collusion among Bullitt, Reynaud, and Mandel to provoke war with Germany. A month and a half later, Ribbentrop was informed that no such documents could be found.[54] Earlier, Daladier was offered freedom if he testified that Bullitt had promised him US aid, which, alongside British pressure, would have been decisive for the declaration of war. Daladier, contemptuous of the demand that he lie, refused, knowing that he might be executed. "I don't know if I'll ever see you again," he wrote Bullitt in December 1940, "but I want to tell you that the memory of our friendship is one of the best of my life."[55]

Bullitt's ongoing communication with anti-Vichy French officials only deepened his conviction that the United States needed to do more. On June 6, 1941, he had lunch with the president at the White House. That day, he really felt that he was "one of the family." Roosevelt talked to him frankly, not holding back as Bullitt felt he usually did with others. To jolt the president out of what he perceived as inertia, Bullitt told him that if the United States did not join the war effort, Britain would soon fall, leaving America alone against unfavorable odds. At the time, Roosevelt wanted to continue waiting for Germany to give him a casus belli.[56]

However, two weeks later, on June 21, Hitler's attack on the Soviet Union changed the situation. Churchill immediately offered unconditional support to Stalin. "There was only one man to defeat, one philosophy of government to destroy. Russia was now fighting that man and that philosophy," Churchill told Harry Hopkins, who happened to be in London at the time. Roosevelt immediately sent Hopkins to Moscow to meet Stalin and assess the situation. Stalin was unequivocal: "Give us anti-aircraft guns and aluminum and we can fight for three or four years," Hopkins reported him saying. Hopkins returned to the United States with the impression that Hitler would not prevail if the Soviets were sufficiently empowered, and Roosevelt decided to extend Lend-Lease to Moscow.[57]

During the summer of 1941, Bullitt wavered as to what position the United States should take with respect to the embattled Soviet Union. Immediately after Hitler's invasion of the Soviet Union, Bullitt opposed extending Lend-Lease to Moscow, on the grounds that partnership with the USSR might help the Allies win the war but would destroy the peace. Roosevelt reacted strongly, arguing that "the Allies have to win the war if democracy is to survive." In response Bullitt advised Roosevelt to exploit the Soviets' desperate need for US support by predicating aid on Soviet security guarantees for its European neighbors and for China.[58] Later that summer, Bullitt's main concern became the Soviet Union's possible collapse, as the Red Army seemed to be on the verge of defeat. He warned Roosevelt against relying on the Soviets; they could not defeat the Nazis without the United States joining the fight, he predicted.[59] On July 1, Bullitt suggested that Roosevelt increase production of war materials to new highs in preparation for facing Germany alone.[60]

Bullitt visited with Roosevelt again in August, a few days after the president's first meeting with Churchill in Placentia Bay, Newfoundland. The president told Bullitt that he wanted to use him but had no position to offer that was commensurate with his standing and abilities. Bullitt thought he was out.[61] He began to speak in public more aggressively. In September he called for an immediate declaration of war on Germany. "We are caught in a conflict of emotions so deep we cannot resolve it," he said. "We want to defeat Hitler, but we don't want to go to war . . . It's a sad thing to say. But the only way we can defeat Hitler is by the United States putting all its resources into this fight and going to war now."[62] Roosevelt rejected this idea, figuring that the public would react badly. The United States would remain neutral—at least formally. Bullitt continued to campaign and convinced Knox, the secretary of the navy, who endorsed Bullitt's call for "an Expeditionary Force in Casablanca"—150,000 US troops.[63] But Stimson rejected the idea and turned Roosevelt against it.[64]

A month later, to Bullitt's surprise, Roosevelt appointed him as a roving ambassador reporting directly to the president. What Bullitt did not know was that he had a supporter in Churchill. When the UK prime minister heard of Knox's support for the Casablanca landing, he abandoned the existing British plan of defeating the Germans in Libya and instead supported Bullitt's.[65] On December 3, 1941, Bullitt left for North Africa and the Middle East.

On December 7, Bullitt was en route to Egypt via Trinidad when he learned of the attack on Pearl Harbor. "Now we are in it together," he quipped.[66] What came next was a whirlwind tour. Bullitt began in Cairo from December 13 to 20, then stayed three days in Beirut, three days in Jerusalem, and in Cairo again from December 26 through

January 5. This was followed by Baghdad, Tehran, Cairo again, Libya, Khartoum, and Accra.[67] Bullitt conferred with British minister of state for the Middle East Oliver Littleton and with General Georges Catroux, the Free French commandant, and their staffs. All agreed to send a common message to Roosevelt that it was crucial to get French North Africa to side with the Allies. Bullitt again recommended sending a US expeditionary force to Casablanca.[68] In March 1942, supported by US generals George Marshall and Dwight Eisenhower, Bullitt urged the president to send aircraft to Egypt under US command.[69]

The recommendations garnered no response from Roosevelt or anyone else in the administration. Bullitt was sidelined; he could feel it. His patience was exhausted. On June 18, 1942, Bullitt resigned as Roosevelt's roving ambassador, stating that he was "seeking another field of service."[70]

14

Liberating France, Confronting the "Red Amoeba"

AMONG THE FRENCH Bullitt had helped find refuge in the United States was Marie Cuttoli, an important patron of modernist textiles, credited with introducing such artists as Fernand Léger, Le Corbusier, Jean Lurçat, and Picasso to the art of tapestry. To provide her an escape, Bullitt reconnected with Albert Barnes, a Philadelphia inventor and industrialist. Barnes was also a collector of French impressionist works and had met Bullitt when he was ambassador in Paris. In October 1940, Barnes invited Marie Cuttoli to show her work at his foundation, which housed the largest private collection in the United States. With this invitation, she was able to obtain a visa.

Barnes was perceived as "terrible-tempered" and had a reputation as a lone wolf, but he did have a few friends, Bullitt among them. During a visit in May 1942, Bullitt and Barnes discussed politics and the future. If Roosevelt was to have nothing more to do with Bullitt, what about launching some sort of political movement on his own? Barnes thought Roosevelt's activities an "incongruous mélange" of "reality versus phantasy." "Declaration of Independence, Bill of Rights, Morality, Fair play, Decency, Honesty—all these cashed in by F.D.R.'s 'firesides,'" Barnes said, reflecting on Roosevelt's talent for public relations. But his popularity was not "reflected in actual doing." Bullitt, Barnes thought, would be the right person to tell the world. "The public will lap it up," he said. "The chief and his coterie have no defense if the argument is presented with force constructed of logic and sound psychology." Barnes and Bullitt agreed that a "4th of July radio address from coast to coast could start [their movement] right." Bullitt could say—"between the lines"—"my ancestors made this country and I've done my part to carry on; 'you can't do this to me' I stand on my record." The purpose would not be to attack Roosevelt but to foster a "new, well informed public opinion." As Barnes wrote to Bullitt, "Nobody has yet done it—

just said it": there had been plenty of talk about the United States taking a stronger role in the conflict, but "it remained wishful thinking." Would Bullitt be the one to turn fantasy into reality?[1]

Bullitt to Roosevelt: Defeat Hitler, but Block Stalin

Bullitt was not ready to confront the president, even if Roosevelt had been stringing him along since he resigned as ambassador to France.[2] "I am doing nothing in this war," Bullitt wrote to Roosevelt on June 17, 1942. "I do not care about anything except helping defeat Hitler and the Japanese. If there is anything I can do with you or for you, I want to do it. If there is nothing, I must try to serve in other ways." Roosevelt responded that he realized how Bullitt must feel, but that he did not want to put Bullitt "in as a Second Lieutenant."[3] This is effectively what Roosevelt proposed, however, offering Bullitt a post as special envoy to Australia. Bullitt refused and instead accepted a job as special assistant to the secretary of the navy, Knox, whom he liked. He moved back to D.C. and busied himself mainly with antisubmarine warfare. He also became, and would remain until 1944, a secret adviser to Hull.

In July 1942 Bullitt traveled to Britain. Officially, he was on a naval mission for Knox. Unofficially, at Hull's request, he was investigating the situation and ambitions of the Free French.[4] Bullitt at this point was closely involved with the Free French forces in the United States and Canada. At the invitation of Henri Laugier—one of their leaders and, incidentally, Marie Cuttoli's lover—Bullitt spoke in Montreal in July 1941.[5] Bullitt also wrote a preface for *L'Histoire Jugera*, a book published by Free French agents collecting Léon Blum's speeches and articles.[6] Just before his departure for London in July 1942, Bullitt visited General Pershing and convinced him to preside over a Free French celebration of Bastille Day in New York. The Vichy French Embassy managed to have Pershing's appearance canceled, but the resulting controversy generated favorable press for the Free French.[7] On July 15, Bullitt lunched at 10 Downing Street with Churchill.[8] On the twentieth, he dined with de Gaulle and his friend Pleven, who had worked with Monnet on aircraft purchases. The first time Bullitt had met de Gaulle was in early June 1940. Reynaud had just officially brought de Gaulle into the French government to run the Ministry of War. A few weeks earlier, de Gaulle had been a colonel in the tank corps and showed great initiative and courage stemming the German advance on Paris. "He is a young man who appears to be vigorous and intelligent," Bullitt wrote Roosevelt at the time.[9] Now, after spending time with the French general in London two years later, Bullitt thought, "There is something wrong about De Gaulle. I don't know what. His face looked as though it were constructed in various pieces badly but together with beauty."[10]

De Gaulle joined the British in opposing a US plan for an Allied landing in France in 1942 or 1943, which General George Marshall was in London advocating for in July 1942.[11] According to Bullitt, de Gaulle considered it

> absolute folly for the British or Americans or both to land on the soil of France with less than twenty tank divisions. He said that he felt sure that any lesser force would be hurled into the sea. He advised an attack on Norway by the British and on Portugal and Spain by the United States. When I said that the Spanish would certainly fight fiercely against us, he said that on the contrary Spain was still Red and that we would be supported by the Communists; then added, "If you are afraid of installing communist governments throughout Europe you will never win this war." He made a thoroughly bad impression on me, but Pleven looked at him throughout the dinner with eyes of adoration and as we walked away said, "Isn't it horrible that such a wonderful man is made no use of?"[12]

Roosevelt took note of the British opposition to a landing in Europe. On July 23, he ordered his military staff to plan for the landing of Anglo-American troops in Casablanca and Algiers—Operation Torch—that Bullitt had advocated for since July 1940.[13] Bullitt was not involved in military operations. The president had decided to use him for his capacity to think ahead. On November 19, 1942, Roosevelt asked Bullitt to work on "the machinery of preparation for civil administration in occupied territories."

Bullitt perceived the scope of his mission very widely.[14] For instance, he suggested bold moves to meet the country's growing oil needs. In 1941 the military had used 25 million barrels of oil; by the war's end, that number was 588 million. In early 1943 Bullitt helped persuade Roosevelt to create a government corporation that would be based on the model of the Anglo-Iranian Oil Company (British Petroleum): the US Petroleum Reserve Corporation would buy shares in Aramco, the Arabian-America Oil Company, and construct a refinery in the Persian Gulf. "We are forty years late in starting—but we are not yet too late," Bullitt wrote.[15]

For Bullitt the major challenge was policy toward the Soviet Union, and he feared that Roosevelt was making a fateful error there. Soon, the Red Army would be occupying the Baltic states and the moment for negotiating the future of these territories was gone. On January 24, when Roosevelt and Churchill informed Stalin of their plans for the coming year, they promised to open a second front, with the intention of making their assault in Western Europe. Roosevelt announced that his goal was Germany's unconditional surrender. This was an attempt to prevent the recurrence of what had happened after World War I, when Germany, in the absence of occupation or invasion, alleged that she had not been defeated militarily but had been "stabbed in the back" by liberals, pacifists, socialists, Communists, and Jews.[16] Forcing Germany's surrender was also a way to reassure a suspicious Stalin that neither the United States nor Great Britain would seek a separate peace with the Axis.[17]

On January 29, 1943, Bullitt sent a memorandum to Roosevelt, which Kennan later found to be a "remarkable" statement that "deserves a place among the major historical documents of the time." Bullitt "predicted with startling accuracy the situation to which the war would lead if existing policies continued to be pursued." In particular, he urged that relying on Russian goodwill would result in the effective division of Europe after the war. "This letter had no counterpart as a warning of that date to the American President," Kennan concluded.[18] Instead of fighting in Western Europe, Bullitt recommended that US and British forces make their second front in the Balkans, specifically Greece. Doing so would still fulfill their promise to the Soviet Union while potentially preventing Soviet conquest and occupation of a large part of Central and even Eastern Europe.

Bullitt's memo was hotly debated. One evening in March, Anthony Eden, the British foreign secretary, dined at the White House with

Roosevelt and Harry Hopkins. "The big question which rightly dominated Roosevelt's mind was whether it was possible to work with Russia now and after the war," Eden noted. Roosevelt asked Eden what he thought of the "Bullitt Thesis"—the predicted spread of Communism unless the United States and Britain blocked "the flow of the red amoeba into Europe."[19] Eden replied that "even if these fears were to prove correct, we should make the position no worse by trying to work with Russia." He hoped that "Stalin meant what he said" when he chose in the first place to ally with Britain—an alliance that required both parties to forswear "territorial aggrandizement" and commit to noninterference in the internal affairs of other states.

Roosevelt decided in favor of working with rather than against the Soviet Union.[20] The president gambled on reassurance over confrontation, as both a wartime strategy and the core element of postwar diplomacy, believing that Soviet goals would be determined partly by US intentions and capabilities. In April, he made his position public.[21] That same month, responding to Roosevelt's request, a Hollywood studio released *Mission to Moscow*, which favorably chronicled the experiences of Ambassador Joseph Davies in the Soviet Union, where he succeeded Bullitt. For Roosevelt, this was crucial propaganda; he himself met with Davies four times to discuss the project.[22] Bullitt's recommendations had fallen definitively on deaf ears.

Bullitt Launches His Cold War

Certain that nothing good would come of concessions to the Soviets, Bullitt decided to take action. His first order of business came in response to a purge underway at the State Department. The main target was Bullitt's good friend and respected colleague Loy Henderson.[23] Henderson had been third in line at the Moscow embassy under Bullitt and continued to work on Soviet affairs at the State department. He shared Bullitt's circumspection toward the Soviet Union and his discomfort with the popularity that Stalin enjoyed in D.C. circles, where some called him by the affectionate nickname Uncle Joe.

Like Bullitt, Henderson knew the Soviet leaders and how they operated. He, too, realized that no amount of concessions would divert them from their objective of conquest. Litvinov, now the Soviet ambassador in Washington, knew what Henderson thought. At the beginning of 1943, Litvinov told William H. Standley, then US ambassador in Moscow, that the Soviet Union would never have good relations with the United States if Henderson remained in charge of Soviet affairs at the Eastern Europe desk. Litvinov later repeated the same to Eleanor Roosevelt and Sumner Welles. Henderson accordingly offered Hull his resignation, which Hull rejected. A few months later, under pressure from the White House, Hull reversed course and accepted Henderson's departure from Moscow.[24] But Hull knew Henderson's value and realized that he was being forced out for political reasons. The secretary of state insisted on naming Henderson chief of a diplomatic mission, even though he lacked the rank required for such a promotion. He would become ambassador to Iraq.[25]

Henderson described to Bullitt the enigmatic atmosphere in which his removal had occurred, suggesting that Welles had something to do with it. "Welles was a man of great strength," Henderson said, but "he seemed to falter in March 1943. He had undergone a great change at that time . . . [was] under great personal strain . . . maybe blackmailed. He had always been very friendly to me. All at once he froze up."[26] Henderson was not alone in sensing a change in Welles. Adolf Berle and others in the State Department "were peeved by Welles' sudden courting of Russophiles."[27] Welles was leading a group at the State Department that pushed for gentler treatment of the Soviet Union—including concessions—on the theory that this would succeed "in breaking down Russian reserve and suspicion" and thereby foster conditions both for winning the war and establishing a lasting peace afterward.[28]

Roosevelt had ordered Welles to maintain contact with Communists, and three times in 1942 and 1943, Earl Browder, head of the US Communist Party, visited Welles at the State Department. At their first meeting, on October 12, 1942, Welles and Browder discussed US policy in China. *The Daily Worker* had accused the State Department of supporting the Chinese Nationalists in their attempt to withhold a million troops to be deployed against Japan, so that those troops could instead be saved for battle with the Chinese Communists. Welles gave Browder a prepared memorandum to correct *The Daily Worker*'s misstatements, which satisfied Browder. What mattered most was the meeting itself, which gave the US Communist Party a certificate of respectability. The FBI reported that, a few days later, in a meeting of Communist leaders, Browder told his comrades that "he could make a fool out of Welles, of whom he spoke disparagingly, at any time."[29] This did not mean that Welles was a blackmailed agent, but it helped create that perception, especially in Bullitt's mind.

From April 1941 forward, Bullitt had continued to circulate in D.C. the story of Welles propositioning men for sex. Now, in 1943, with the support of Secretary Hull, he decided to force the issue. Carmel Offie became very active in orchestrating Welles's fall, as he admitted in a May 1943 letter to Bullitt's cousin Thomas:

> Would you like to make me bet that the man who makes a nuisance of himself in railroad trains will soon not be where he is now? Please let me know how much you want to bet, and what odds, if any, you will care to give. And when I have an occasion to look upon your beaming mug (by that time I hope it will have been done) I will tell you how a combination of dago blood together with some Yankee stubbornness does wonders. I know I speak in parables but keep your shirt on.[30]

On April 27 and again on May 1, Ralph O. Brewster, a Republican senator from Maine who was a staunch opponent of the New Deal, called J. Edgar Hoover and Bullitt to get information on Welles. He was ready to raise the issue in the Senate Special Committee to Investigate the National Defense Program, known as the Truman Committee, which had gained popularity and recognition for exposing wrongdoing in wartime procurements contracts.[31] On June 2, Hull told Roosevelt that Welles should be dismissed because of the indecency of keeping a man of his personal habits in high office, which risked blackmail by foreign powers. Everyone in the Senate was aware of it. "The president sat back and looked miserably at the ceiling and said nothing."[32]

On July 27, Bullitt visited the president with the official purpose of discussing Bullitt's political ambitions: he had decided to run for mayor of Philadelphia as the Democratic candidate. But there was another purpose for the meeting as well—a conversation about Welles. Bullitt had circulated the affidavit concerning the train incident to Cissy Patterson at the *Chicago Tribune,* earning him Roosevelt's reproach. "You have ruined Welles' reputation and his life," the president told him. "You have always hated Welles." Bullitt replied that this was not true, that he had repeatedly tried to build a good relationship with Welles only to be repaid with treachery. In fact, he told Roosevelt, "You yourself on several occasions tried to stop him from knifing me in the back." According to Bullitt, the president nodded his head and said nothing. Then Roosevelt told Bullitt that "talking about Welles had been unchristian," adding, "I have never attacked anyone in an unchristian manner." Hadn't he called Cissy Patterson "a damned bitch," Bullitt asked? "I have known you all my life and I can say anything to you," the president replied. Bullitt rose and left. It was the last time he would see Roosevelt.[33]

On August 11, Hull told Roosevelt that the choice was between himself and Welles. For Roosevelt it was no choice at all; Welles would have to go.[34] He presented his resignation to the president on August 16. A few weeks later, on September 8, Offie was caught soliciting an undercover police officer at 12:40 in the morning near Lafayette Park in Washington.[35] Hull, for whom Bullitt was still working as an informal adviser, immediately covered for Offie, claiming he was on official business related to the Welles affair. Then Hull dove right back into diplomatic affairs. At the end of October, he led the US delegation in Moscow and obtained Stalin's commitment to fight Japan without a quid pro quo. Hull and Bullitt felt no guilt over what had happened to Welles. A few months later, Hull told Bullitt, "No matter how much either of us suffer, neither of us ever did a more righteous act or a greater public service than kicking that son of a bitch into the open spaces."[36]

On November 3, Bullitt lost the Philadelphia mayoral race. He had not expected to win.[37] The Communist Party campaigned against him, calling him an anti-Soviet appeaser for having supported French reconciliation with Hitler before Munich, while Blum was in government. Focusing on his July 1940 press comments upon escaping France, Bullitt's leftist opponents also painted him as pro-Pétain and pro-Vichy.[38] Roosevelt wrote an official letter of support on Bullitt's behalf, but behind the scenes Roosevelt undermined Bullitt's candidacy, instructing Pennsylvania political bosses to "cut his throat."[39]

After his break with Roosevelt, Bullitt was at loose ends. With an appetite for action, he was still organizing meetings and dinners in

Washington. When he wanted to escape, he visited Barnes or the Berkshires. He had reconnected with Republicans like William Castle, the former undersecretary of state for President Hoover. They shared lunches and dinners and spent afternoons at the swimming pool. Bullitt "is certainly in the middle of things and knows a lot," Castle thought. He neither liked nor trusted Bullitt but found him interesting, noting he is "really an extraordinary person because he is not first class in any way, probably has a rotten character, is not loyal to his friends, and yet has many ardent friends."[40]

In fact, Bullitt had remained loyal to some, such as Missy LeHand. In June 1941, LeHand collapsed at a White House dinner party and suffered a major stroke that left her partially paralyzed with little ability to speak. After first convalescing at the president's cottage in Warm Springs, Georgia, and then the White House, she was now living in her hometown of Somerville, Massachusetts, where her sister Anna cared for her. Bullitt sent presents and wrote her. Through Anna, LeHand told him again and again that she loved it when he wrote to her. In a September 1943 letter, Anna said, "Do write to her often she loves to hear from you and is so lonely. Love from Missy."[41]

Bullitt phoned LeHand and repeatedly invited her to come stay with him. "Washington is queer and strange without you," he said, "at least for me." He could arrange a suite and a nurse for her. In fact, in February 1944, LeHand was expecting an invitation for a brief stay at the White House and rejoiced at the idea.[42] But Eleanor Roosevelt rescheduled the visit.[43] On April 24, LeHand dictated a letter to Bullitt congratulating him for an article he published in *Life*. She even signed the letter—the first time she had put her signature to paper since her stroke. "I was delighted to see all the letters written concerning your piece," the letter read. "Thank you for your nice little notes. I look forward to their newsy contents."[44] A few weeks later, on July 31, she suffered another stroke and died.

Joining de Gaulle

Bullitt could not attend LeHand's funeral; he had left the United States for the battleground. Frustrated by inaction, he had tried to join the US Army, but was rejected as too old to enlist. After the November 1942 landing in North Africa, many of his French friends exiled in the United States or Britain had joined de Gaulle in Algiers, in particular the former socialist parliamentarian Vincent Auriol and also Henri Laugier. All testified that de Gaulle, now president of the Provisional Government of the French Republic, had become the representative of a democratic France about to be reborn. At the beginning of 1944, Bullitt visited Algiers, incognito. On May 19, he wrote de Gaulle:

> General:
>
> The battle for the resurrection of France is at hand and I am seeking my active part in it.
>
> France needs the service of the young; but also, I believe, of those who are no longer young. I am fifty-three years old. I offer you my services as a volunteer soldier in the French army.
>
> Many cities of France have done me the honor to enroll me as a citizen. Grant me, General, the supreme honor of these days of sacrifice—the right to military service. Permit me to enroll myself as a soldier of France.
>
> William C. Bullitt[45]

De Gaulle responded immediately from Algiers on May 25, in a handwritten letter:

> My dear Ambassador,
>
> There are some consolations. Your letter is such for me. It will be so for all the French. Come along! Good and dear American friend. Our ranks are open to you. With us, you will reenter wounded Paris. There, together, we will see your Star-spangled flags standing mingled with our tricolors.
>
> I send you, my dear Ambassador, my warmest regards.
>
> C. de Gaulle[46]

For de Gaulle, the letter was a pleasant surprise. He was struggling against Roosevelt's opposition to involving him and the Free French in the liberation and administration of France after D-Day.[47] Suddenly de Gaulle was getting the support and legitimation of one of the most well-known Americans in France. Bullitt was also facing opposition: the White House blocked the issuance of a regular passport. He finally got permission to travel as a journalist for *Life*. In the first article he wrote from Algiers, "The Future of France," he introduced de Gaulle to American readers.

To Bullitt, de Gaulle was the best rampart against Stalin taking control of Western Europe. A severe Catholic and courageous general, de Gaulle had developed as a political leader during his years of exile and resistance. Bullitt predicted that the United States eventually would have to accept him.[48] In the *Life* article, he sought to explain the mysterious and emotional hold de Gaulle had on the French people by describing their guilt: by becoming a Gaullist and, indeed, by convincing himself that at heart he had always been a Gaullist, the individual Frenchman was able to assuage a conscience marred by the capitulations to Germany and Vichy. General de Gaulle personified France's emotional absolution.[49]

On Labor Day 1944, Bullitt—who was by then hoping for Roosevelt's defeat in that year's presidential election—published "The World from Rome," a direct and public attack on Roosevelt's Russia policy.[50] At this point, Bullitt was focused on what would come after the war. The Germans were about to receive just punishment for their crimes, and the prestige of Great Britain was enormous, but Britain could not lead Europe. It was emerging from the war a tired victor. Throughout Italy, the question was whether the war's result would be the subjugation of Europe by Moscow instead of Berlin. Bullitt anticipated just this: the Soviet Union would dominate Finland, Latvia, Lithuania, Estonia, Poland, Bulgaria, Romania, Hungary, and Czechoslovakia. He expected the Russians would also annex East Prussia to give the "so-called independent Poland all eastern Germany as far as the river Oder."[51] Bullitt suspected that the Soviet Union might be in a position to set up some sort of German state between the Oder and the Elbe. He feared for Austria and Yugoslavia's fate but was optimistic about Italy, for there was a factor in Italian life that the Soviets would find difficult to overcome: the lasting authority of the Vatican and the pope, whom Bullitt interviewed for his story. The article infuriated both the Soviets and pro-Roosevelt liberals. *Pravda*, the official propaganda organ of the Soviet Communist Party, attacked Bullitt as "a bankrupt spy" who sympathized with Hitler, staked his career on a German victory over the Soviet Union, and carried on "dirty anti-Soviet work" in the columns of *Life*.[52]

Next Bullitt joined the First French Army, commanded by General Jean de Lattre de Tassigny. He left Italy in an infantry landing craft and joined de Lattre at his headquarters at Pierrefeu, in southeastern France. Bullitt participated in de Lattre's military cabinet, followed the general into combat, and served as his translator and adviser. Soon, Bullitt created a division of psychological warfare—the French had never had such an organization—and became its chief.[53]

Comprising veterans from campaigns in Tunisia and Italy, the First French Army disembarked at Saint-Tropez, then captured the ports of Marseilles and Toulon with such tactical skill and reckless courage that they were sixty days ahead of schedule. They were progressively joined by thousands of *maquisards*—French and foreign guerillas—and swept up the valley of the Rhone, through Lyons to Dijon. At the beginning of October 1944, Bullitt escaped for two days to liberated Paris. He found the Château de Saint Firmin and his tiny Paris apartment intact. Then he went to the US Embassy and unlocked the gates, which had been bolted since his departure on June 30, 1940. When he appeared in the garden, the people of Paris cheered and applauded from the Champs-Elysées, confusing him with Eisenhower.

Bullitt took advantage of his stay in the capital to go to the Lycée Janson de Sailly. Since the liberation of Paris in August, the high school had been transformed into a large military barracks, welcoming young volunteers who trained to become protective units of the city. Their confinement to the capital frustrated many of them. Encouraged by Bullitt—and disobeying orders—hundreds left Paris on the night of September 25 to join the First French Army clandestinely, with de Lattre's support. They formed a shock battalion; Bullitt provided some of their equipment and became the regiment's godfather. The battalion's pennant depicted the Arc de Triomphe and, next to it, Philadelphia's Liberty Bell and the initials W.B., both in tribute to Bullitt.[54] "Nothing since 1919 had given me so much satisfaction as the job I am doing now and I haven't felt so well in twenty years," Bullitt wrote his brother. "I have spent about twenty hours a day with [de Lattre]—as he does not care for sleep and I go along wherever he goes . . . He is a great fellow with many of General MacArthur's characteristics, plus the dash of a French cavalry leader. He goes into the frontline constantly with your humble brother along—so I have a chance to be in the scrap both at the planning end and at the execution."[55]

Later, after the war, Bullitt frequently acknowledged de Lattre. At the end of 1949, de Lattre sent Bullitt an issue of *Revue Militaire d'Information,* containing de Lattre's account of their exploits in the Vosges Mountains and of the liberation of Strasbourg. Bullitt thanked him for bringing back good memories and for his army's superb achievements. But Bullitt also had one reproach for de Lattre:

> If I may say so, you do not do justice to your own brilliance. You were a far greater military leader than you would admit. I remember so many vivid moments when your ingenuity and determination were decisive factors that I should like to write something about you and the First French Army . . . [whose] role in the war has never been set before the people of the United States.[56]

From Bullitt's perspective, de Lattre lived for the art of war as a poet lives for verse. He was a genius as a strategist and tactician. For instance, in November 1944, he had broken through the Rhine even as he knew that the Germans were informed of his most secret plans. When he became aware that his information channels had been compromised, he continued to use them—he just started issuing false orders. The new orders referred to his army's exhaustion after fighting day and night for two months and directed commanders to send as many men as possible to rest camps until the spring. Meanwhile, de Lattre wrote his real orders by hand and had his chief of staff carry them personally to all commanders. In these orders, the general mapped an intricate plan in which divisions from the north of the Vosges would be requisitioned for a surprise offensive in the south near the Swiss border. Munitions and supplies were moved at night and concealed in the woods. In daylight, units from the north were moved slowly to the northwest; then at night, the same units were transported southward as quickly as possible. The day before the offensive, Churchill inspected the remaining troops of the north, found them tired, and advised de Lattre not to attack before spring. De Lattre bowed and made no reply. Early the next morning, he launched the offensive successfully. The commander in chief of the German Army was killed by artillery fire during the battle. In his briefcase was a report to the German general staff stating that his front was in no danger whatsoever because de Lattre had put his army in winter quarters until spring.

As 1944 drew to a close, Eisenhower—following a German counteroffensive that had begun on December 16—ordered US troops to evacuate from Strasbourg and the Vosges Mountains. The First French Army was also ordered to withdraw from the Vosges.[57] De Lattre protested to de Gaulle. De Lattre was then summoned to the Allied headquarters, where he was to receive detailed instructions from General Devers to withdraw alongside the Americans.[58] For an hour, de Lattre argued with Devers, who begged and then again ordered de Lattre to withdraw. De Lattre responded, "La question ne se pose pas," which Bullitt translated as, "The question does not arise." A few days later, at 4 o'clock in the morning, the US Army departed Strasbourg, leaving the city without a single defender and practically surrounded by German forces who were situated twenty miles to the south, fifteen miles to the north, and across the Rhine to the east. De Lattre immediately ordered General Augustin Guillaume to bring up the Goumiers—Moroccan troops—as soon as possible. De Lattre scared up a few artillery batteries and some tanks and brought in reinforcements from his troops in the Vosges. Fortunately, the Germans suspected that the US withdrawal was a trap. They stayed put in the east and south and advanced cautiously toward Strasbourg from the north. When they emerged from a forest, they were decimated by de Lattre's artillery. When the Germans attempted to mount a larger attack twenty-four hours later, de Lattre had gathered enough troops to fend off the assault and hold Strasbourg. "This direct disobedience to orders, although successful, did not endear General de Lattre to General Eisenhower," Bullitt concluded.[59]

In early January 1945, Bullitt was hit by a car in Montbéliard, injuring his left leg, hip, back, and ribs.[60] After his convalescence, he was fitted with an orthopedic corset and rejoined de Lattre. De Lattre was so fond of Bullitt that when the press published false rumors that the general had named Bullitt military governor of Baden-Baden, de Gaulle almost believed it. He asked de Lattre if the tales were true and told him it would be ill-advised for an American citizen, even one who was an officer in the French military, to hold such a position in a French-occupied territory.[61] A few weeks later, after de Gaulle's forces captured Stuttgart, he decorated Bullitt with the Legion of Honor and the Croix de Guerre.[62]

On July 14, for the Bastille Day celebration, General de Lattre and his troops led the military parade from Place de la Bastille to the Arc de Triomphe, passing by Place de la République, the Grands Boulevards, Place de la Concorde, and the Champs-Elysées. A few meters behind his vehicle, three other command cars carried officers he had personally chosen for the honor. In one of the cars were Commandant Bullitt and Commandant André Chamson. Chamson, a writer who had been in the resistance since 1940, later reported that, for the "former Ambassador of the United States in France, this passage across Paris, in all the intoxication of a victory which wiped out four years of servitude, was a thrilling adventure."[63]

Bullitt returned to Washington in August 1945 with a blessing from the pope, whom he had seen again in June; two French medals; and a signed Picasso lithograph, a gift from the painter.[64] Upon Bullitt's arrival in D.C., he found his daughter Anne nearly dead. Her appendix had abscessed a year earlier and the problem had grown dire. Nearly two years earlier, in October 1943, Bullitt had announced Anne's engagement to Daniel Brewster, the well-to-do scion of a political family and a future member of Congress and senator from Maryland. The media covered the engagement with great fanfare, including photos in both the *New York Times* and *Washington Post*. Since then, however, Anne had broken off the engagement and, on February 18, 1944, secretly married one Caspar Townsend without Bullitt's knowledge. He was shocked.[65] A year later, Anne went to Haiti to get a divorce. Now back in D.C., Bullitt could see and take care of her. At the end of September, she had an operation and was on her way to a complete recovery. Bullitt resumed his social life, accompanying friends to receptions and organizing dinners.[66]

Roosevelt had died in April 1945. "In the invention of political mechanisms and expedients, President Roosevelt was in a class by himself," Bullitt wrote. "In ability to handle American public opinion, he was unrivalled. At his best he was a political genius. This was a great asset to our country when the policy the President wanted to follow was in our national interest. But his very ability enabled him to lead our country toward disaster when he was wrong." In particular,

Roosevelt had erred by supplying Stalin with arms while demanding nothing in return. "In order to survive, Stalin needed all the aid we could give him," Bullitt wrote. "And in the summer of 1941," after the passage of Lend-Lease, "we could have laid down the terms on which we were prepared to give aid to the Soviet Union, and Stalin would have been obliged to accept our terms." Instead, Roosevelt imposed no conditions. It was, Bullitt wrote, "the great mistake of his life."[67] Kennan agreed with Bullitt's approach.[68]

Kennan was one of Bullitt's few friends in the new Truman administration. Another was Defense Secretary James Forrestal, with whom Bullitt shared a passion for reading and exchanged book recommendations. Conversations with Forrestal and Kennan furnished Bullitt with inspiration for a new book on foreign affairs: *The Great Globe Itself*, published in June 1946.[69] The essential problem of World War II, according to Bullitt, was that the democracies—the United States, United Kingdom, and France—had to ally with a Communist totalitarian state to defeat a fascist totalitarian state. The alliance did not temper the ambitions of the Communist state which, by nature hostile to democracy, remained committed to world conquest. The United States had entered the war with the goal of preventing Germany from dominating Europe and Japan from dominating China. Now that the war was over, both Europe and China were in danger of being dominated by the Soviet Union. In Bullitt's view, Roosevelt was responsible for the situation.

As a case in point, Bullitt looked back to the Tehran Conference of December 1, 1943, where Roosevelt met with Stalin and Churchill to discuss war strategy. As Roosevelt told the *Saturday Evening Post* in the wake of the talks, he believed in the efficacy of across-the-table conversation.[70] Throughout the conference sessions, he made every endeavor to understand Stalin's point of view and assure the Soviets of his own good faith and of the benefits of the "good neighbor" policy that the United States pursued in inter-American relations. After the conference, Roosevelt exchanged personal letters with the Soviet leader on a regular basis. Stalin assured Roosevelt that the Soviet Union had no desire to dominate Europe, and Roosevelt chose to believe him.[71] Bullitt thought that, like Wilson after WWI, Roosevelt failed to use the power he had attained. He should have used Lend-Lease as a bargaining chip to extract commitments from Stalin and should not have abandoned China at the 1945 Yalta Conference, where Roosevelt agreed to Soviet demands for official recognition of the Mongolian People's Republic, a Soviet satellite state of long standing.

Despite these errors, Bullitt wrote, he was convinced that the worst future outcomes could be averted by supporting the United Nations as much as possible while also creating a security alliance with the democracies of Europe and Latin America and with China, which was still under Nationalist control at the time. Additionally, Bullitt felt that the United States should back the founding of a democratic federation of the non-Communist European states. To master atomic bombs and forces of destruction at the world level, Bullitt suggested transferring their control to a government of representatives from democratic states. All of this was a precursor to an eventual world federal government, which could emerge after the totalitarian dictatorships had disappeared.

The Great Globe Itself was ambitious in scope but had limited impact. It thrilled hardliners in what was soon to be called the Cold War—General Albert Coady Wedemeyer sent it as a gift to General Marshall, who read it in one day in August 1946.[72] But inside the establishment, it was Kennan's famous 5,000-word "long telegram" that made the biggest impression. Sent on February 22, 1946, from Moscow, where he was chargé d'affaires at the US Embassy, and published the following year in *Foreign Affairs* under the cover name of Mr. X, Kennan's telegram came at the key moment when the foundation for a new US policy toward the Soviet Union was being laid. Since the end of 1945, US policymakers had viewed the Soviet Union as the most serious threat to the United States and its Western allies. These policymakers were ready to hear Kennan's suggestion: containment.[73] Bullitt did not disagree; containment was a break with appeasement, which he and Kennan both associated with the policy of Roosevelt and which they both condemned. But this left open the question of means. What should be done to contain Soviet expansion?

If Bullitt's book was largely ignored by policymakers, it also made few waves among the broader public. As far as the typical American was concerned it was not Bullitt but John Foster Dulles, the future secretary of state, who made headlines. In June 1946 Dulles published a two-part article in *Life* enjoining Americans "to maintain a strong military establishment" and stand up to the Soviets on every point. "Soviet leaders assume that peace and security . . . depend upon eradicating the non-Soviet type of society," Dulles warned.[74]

But Henry Luce, *Life's* publisher, knew that it was Bullitt who had prepared the ground for arguments like Dulles's. He wrote Bullitt to tell him how proud he was of his commentary and the role it had played in reorienting US public opinion "towards the truth about Russia. By that I mean that your *Life* article opened the battle for truth when it took great courage (as well as insight) to do so." Luce saw Dulles's piece as the successful conclusion of a twenty-month "Bullitt to Dulles" campaign. "When everyone was speaking of the Dulles articles, I was thinking of the Bullitt article—a long, long twenty months ago," Luce wrote. "You are a very gallant knight, Sir. God bless you."[75]

15

America's Freelance Secretary of State

AS A DIPLOMAT, Bullitt was unafraid to act beyond the limits of his office. A good illustration of the practices he advocated can be found in a 1946 anecdote from John Wiley, Bullitt's longtime staffer who had become US ambassador to Colombia. "Oh yes! I have done something here that was almost Bullitt-like," Wiley wrote.

> On our arrival to Cartagena, I heard that the old government buildings on the plaza de la Aduana were to be sold to private interests . . . I also learned that the lovely convent of San Francisco and its church (municipal property) had been sold to a Syrian gentleman who would construct a textile factory on the site. I announced loudly and firmly that if it was not stopped, I would close the Consulate immediately. The Cartageneros could go to their hated, rival city [Bogota] for their consular services. It worked! All is well. Just another case of foreign intervention.[1]

Now a private citizen, Bullitt was no less ready to act. In particular, he was prepared to use all the resources he had accumulated over his years as a journalist and diplomat to realize his preferred approach to the Soviet problem. One of these resources was Henry Luce, the publisher, who assured Bullitt financial support and press outlets in which to relate his stories of the global battle against Communism. Luce was interested in selling magazines, but he was also interested in sharing Bullitt's observations, hammering home the threat of the Soviet Union, and convincing readers that the situation in China was of enormous importance for the United States. Bullitt and Luce became partners in a project of both educating and arguably indoctrinating the public.

Bullitt had little time to lose, for two reasons. One was personal: his health was failing. Bullitt's back and spine caused him such pain that, by September 1946, he was on an operating table getting dislocated vertebra fused. On that occasion, an intern asked Bullitt how long he had suffered from leukemia. The question must have come as a shock. His cousin, Doctor Orville Horwitz, had examined him and diagnosed early-stage chronic lymphatic leukemia but hadn't told him for fear of causing needless alarm—at the time, Bullitt exhibited no symptoms and required no treatment.[2] Now, to fight the pain in his back and the anxiety of the leukemia revelation, there was no better medication than action.

The second reason Bullitt had to move fast was the increasing danger of a third world war. To prevent it, he believed that Communism had to be fought domestically and internationally. In March 1947, before the House Un-American Activities Committee (HUAC), Bullitt proposed strengthening the FBI, better informing Americans of the Communist danger, and, for naturalized citizens, making membership in the Communist Party prima facie evidence of fraudulent naturalization.[3] To fight Communism abroad, he argued that the United States should support the non-Communist left, including Socialists like his friend Léon Blum in France and the Labour Party in England, because these forces could make progressive appeals even as they respected democracy and individual rights.

After the hearing, Bullitt traveled to Paris to meet with the Socialist Prime Minister Paul Ramadier; Edouard Herriot, the president of the National Assembly; Vincent Auriol, the president of the republic; Georges Bidault, former prime minister; de Gaulle; and Blum. A few days later, the Communist Party was expelled from the government. With one-third of the MPs, the Communists had the largest bloc in the Assembly and seemed on the precipice of power. They accused Bullitt of inciting their removal, and massive strikes paralyzed the country.[4] But Bullitt believed that France's true postwar political crisis lay less in partisan alignments than in constitutional structure. No stable majority was possible in the all-powerful Assembly under existing arrangements. France would drift toward chaos, he believed, unless it got a new constitution. The political question was whether the "threat of chaos would bring in de Gaulle or whether chaos itself would come before he took power." Bullitt predicted that "none can stop the return to power of de Gaulle" and believed that it was in the US national interest to establish a close, friendly relationship with him.[5]

Success in Vietnam, Failure in China

In Paris, Bullitt also met with General de Lattre, his battlefield commander. De Lattre, who had greatly admired Bullitt even before approvingly reading *The Globe Itself,* encouraged Bullitt to visit Vietnam, which de Lattre thought would soon become a frontier in the Cold War. Luce, meanwhile, needed Bullitt to travel to China, so Bullitt decided to take a multistop trip to Asia.

In 1945 Chiang Kai-shek, haloed by triumph over Japan and the assurance of US support, had, against the advice of the Americans, ordered massive numbers of his best troops to Manchuria in a winner-take-all gamble far from his bases. "Without Manchuria, China is like Italy; with Manchuria, it is like India," Chiang said.[6] However, his Nationalist (Kuomintang) forces were losing.[7] The Sino-Soviet pact of August 1945 had recognized the Nationalists as the only legitimate Chinese government, but the agreement did not prevent the Soviets from offering support to Chinese Communists. Massive inflation, meager socioeconomic reforms, and corruption also weakened Chiang's position. On orders from President Truman, George Marshall spent much of 1946 in China on a mission to broker compromise between the Communists and the Nationalists. The negotiations failed, and Marshall blamed Chiang's Nationalists for the outcome. Truman recalled Marshall in January 1947 and sent in his place General Albert C. Wedemeyer, a hardline anti-Communist who was more favorable to the Nationalists. Yet Wedemeyer's report, like Marshall's assessment, was harshly critical of Chiang, whom Wedemeyer accused of leading a corrupt and incompetent government. However, Wedemeyer did recommend providing 10,000 US military "advisors" to shore up the Nationalist Chinese army and proposed UN guardianship of northeastern China, a Communist stronghold. For Luce, implementing Wedemeyer's recommendations represented the last chance to save China from Communism.[8] But release of the Wedemeyer report was blocked by Marshall and the State Department.

On October 13, a few weeks after the Wedemeyer report was put under wraps, Bullitt published an explosive article in *Life,* which was also excerpted in *Time,* another Luce publication.[9] "Can China be kept out of the hands of Stalin?" Bullitt asked. "Certainly—and at a cost to ourselves which will be small compared to the magnitude of our vital interest in the independence of China." In the article Bullitt launched a blistering attack on the agreements reached at Yalta, the February 1945 conference where Churchill, Stalin, and Roosevelt had developed plans for the remainder of the war and for the postwar situation in Europe and the Far East. "No more unnecessary, disgraceful and potentially disastrous document has ever been signed by a President of the U.S.," Bullitt thundered in print. For Bullitt, the most critical failure at Yalta was a secret agreement offering Manchurian bases to the Soviets in exchange for Stalin's promise to join the fight against Japan shortly after Germany's defeat. Established behind Chiang's back, the agreement violated a pledge Churchill and Roosevelt had made to him in Cairo in November 1943. The Yalta capitulation was also unnecessary, as former Secretary of State Hull had already received a pledge from Stalin in October 1943 to support the United States against Japan without any quid pro quo.[10] In addition to attacking the previous administration's choices, Bullitt outlined a reform program for China, along with a plan for military aid, credit, and a monetary fund totaling $1.35 billion.[11] He also suggested sending into the fray General Douglas MacArthur, the only American whom he believed could prevent China's subjugation to the Soviet Union.[12]

Bullitt's writing was controversial but had an impressive impact, especially among fellow anti-Communist hardliners. Wedemeyer wrote to MacArthur that Bullitt's *Life* article "has had a good effect."[13] The piece "has caused considerable discussion," Wedemeyer wrote to another friend. "It was pungent and almost dramatic. Many of the premises established were sound." Wedemeyer could not agree with Bullitt's expansive aid plan; even Alfred Kohlberg, head of the pro-Chiang "China Lobby," suggested scaling down the proposal. But Wedemeyer was happy that Bullitt had helped arouse Americans' interest in China. Bullitt also encouraged Congress to focus attention on his suppressed report, which was classified as secret. Asked during a Senate Appropriations Committee hearing whether he thought the United States had kept its promises to Nationalist China over the years, Wedemeyer answered, "No, sir, I do not."[14]

Bullitt also had considered views on Vietnam. As far as he was concerned, Ho Chi Minh, the Communist leader, was rallying millions not because he was a Communist but because he was a Nationalist fighting for his country's independence. To prevent the "replacement of the yoke of France by the yoke of Stalin," Bullitt advocated in *Life* for cooperation between France and the Vietnamese nationalists, with US backing.[15] Beyond putting his opinions on paper, Bullitt traveled to Hong Kong to meet with and personally endorse Emperor Bao Dai as leader of an independent Vietnam supported by the nationalists. Bao Dai agreed to talk to the French but had conditions. "I will neither be the puppet of France nor a lemon for the Americans to squeeze," he said.[16]

Bullitt flew to France in October 1947, to sell the idea of a Bao Dai regime to his friend President Auriol. Bullitt suggested that American support would be forthcoming if the French could separate Ho's Communists from the Nationalists.[17] Both the French and Bao Dai believed Bullitt's was the official US position, which it was not.[18] Bullitt was probably acting more on behalf of certain French personalities—for example, de Lattre—and trying to sell their Indochina policies to the US and French governments, as well as the Vietnamese. A first meeting between the French and Bao Dai occurred in December 1947 aboard a French naval ship in Ha Long Bay, but no agreement materialized. Bullitt then saw Bao Dai again in Geneva in 1948 and encouraged the emperor to moderate his claims.[19] This new approach was more successful. The French offered Bao Dai an independent state—albeit within the Union Française—that would have the right to levy taxes, maintain a national army (trained by the French), and enjoy a degree of autonomy in diplomacy. France would maintain its bases and military presence. Bullitt encouraged Bao Dai to accept, and he did, acceding to the Elysée Agreement, signed on March 8, 1949. Bullitt deserved some credit for this accord.[20]

In 1948 Bullitt was considered a possible secretary of state by Thomas Dewey, Truman's Republican opponent for the presidency. Earlier in the year, Bullitt had reconnected with John Foster Dulles, whom he had known since the Paris conference in 1919, and suggested mobilizing "Democrats for Dewey."[21] In September Bullitt published a *Life* article on Roosevelt's and Truman's failures to face down Communists.[22] Bullitt reported that Roosevelt once told him of Stalin, "I think that if I give him everything I possibly can and ask from him in return, *noblesse oblige*, he won't try to annex anything and will work with me for a world of democracy and peace." Bullitt reminded the president that "when he talked of *noblesse oblige*, he was not speaking of the Duke of Norfolk but of a Caucasian bandit whose only thought when he got something for nothing was that the other fellow was an ass."[23] The article had a terrific effect. Bullitt was riding a cresting wave, campaigning for Dewey, who looked like he had every chance of winning.[24] On October 30, Bullitt wrote Dewey that on the evening of election day he would be at the Yale Club in New York and could be called there.[25] The telephone never rang, as Dewey famously lost to Truman in an upset after the press had already announced Dewey's victory.

Bullitt already had plans to travel to China the week of the election on a mission for the Congressional Watchdog Committee on Foreign Aid, a joint House and Senate committee. At this point the situation in China was front-page news in the United States, as Communist forces under Mao Tse-tung were pressing every advantage.[26] Ultimately Truman refused to renew US aid to the unpopular Nationalist regime, and the Chinese Communists triumphed over the Kuomintang in November 1949. After a year of lingering anxiety, Chiang's fall was a final shock. It forced Bullitt to pause and reflect on his accomplishments and failures.

Far from centers of power and in a melancholy mood, Bullitt was preoccupied with bittersweet reminiscences. Eugene Boissevain, Inez Milholland's widower, had just died; Bullitt wrote to his second wife, the poet Edna St. Vincent Millay:

> If I had known he was ill, I would have gone anywhere to see him. I loved him—not as everyone loved him because he was lovable—but because he had shown me an enormously great spirit and had risen to a height to which I could and can never rise . . . I cannot think of Eugene as dead, any more than I could or can think of Inez as dead. And I am sure they are not.[27]

He also wrote "They Died Young," a nostalgic poem referencing Inez, Jack Reed, and Bullitt's old friend and fellow journalist Charles Sweeny, as well as Louise Bryant:

> They are all gone
> Inez, Charley, Jack
> Louise—the bravest of the brave
> Insane, trailing a dusty cape

In Paris gutters.
They are all gone.

We loved each other once
Loved and were sure of life
And of ourselves
Sure we could conquer

They are all gone
And I who remain am nothing

Ten years hence who will remember them
There will be no one even to remember
Inez Milholland's voice
Little Charley Sweeney's smile
Jack Reed's gaiety
Or Louise's courage

They are all gone

I remain and hope

Soon to be with them[28]

Another reminiscence came courtesy of Sam Rosenman, Roosevelt's main speechwriter. On February 21, 1949, Rosenman contacted Bullitt to ask if he remembered writing the "quarantine speech" delivered in Chicago on October 5, 1937, which had called for an international "quarantine" against the "epidemic of world lawlessness" by aggressive nations.[29] In fact, Bullitt had not written the quarantine speech, but he told Rosenman about other speeches he had worked on. The strangest experience concerned a September 1936 fireside chat discussing the Dust Bowl.[30] The draft of the speech had been written by Agriculture Secretary Henry Wallace; when Roosevelt started reading it to Bullitt a few hours before he was to deliver it, "It was so extraordinarily bad that Franklin started to gag it in his reading making long gestures and talking like Senator Claghorn," Bullitt said, alluding to the fictional Senator Beauregard Claghorn from the *Fred Allen Show,* a caricature of a blustery Southern politician. Roosevelt and Bullitt then went to work rewriting the speech. Its last page was dictated just before Roosevelt had to begin delivering the address—half a dozen pages had not yet been typed when he began speaking. They came straight from the stenographers, were corrected by Bullitt, and slipped under the papers from which the President was reading. "The speech was of course, a bad one," Bullitt said.

Most of the speeches Bullitt wrote for Roosevelt underwent significant changes before the president delivered them. Sometimes only a few paragraphs survived, "imbedded in a conglomerate composed by shears and paste and polished by these long discussions that you know so well," Bullitt told Rosenman.[31] By contrast, Bullitt explained that he wrote the 1936 "I hate war" speech that Roosevelt delivered in Chautauqua "from the first word to the last. Franklin asked me to prepare it and I used the phrase 'I hate war' because I remembered how deeply impressed I had been when Woodrow Wilson had said to me, handling my hand and with tears in his eyes, 'I hate war. I hate all wars. And the only thing I care about on earth is the peace I am going to make at the end of it.'"[32]

"I have seen war," Bullitt wrote for Roosevelt. "I have seen war on land and sea. I have seen blood running from the wounded. I have seen men coughing out their gassed lungs. I have seen the dead in the mud. I have seen cities destroyed. I have seen 200 limping, exhausted men come out of line—the survivors of a regiment of 1,000 that went forward forty-eight hours before. I have seen children starving. I have seen the agony of mothers and wives. I hate war."[33] Roosevelt understood that this was brilliant oratory. "That is the only speech I ever prepared for Franklin which he delivered exactly how I wrote it," Bullitt told Rosenman. "When I gave him my draft, he read it at once, and at the end said: 'It's all right, it's good, it's very good. Not a word in it needs to be changed.' So far as I know he consulted no one about it."[34]

Recollections like these were the stuff of memoir, and Bullitt had started writing one, which he planned to call *The Shining Adventure*. "Defeat has been the common lot of all men in my generation who have tried to bring sanity into the affairs of this disordered world," the manuscript began. "But adventure still shines."[35] He eventually stopped writing, though. He could not suppress his desire to return to the fray.

A Confrontational Alternative to Containment

For Bullitt, by 1950, the risk of a world dominated by Communism was real. China had fallen and France and Italy were both in fragile condition, each facing the prospect of a Communist Party takeover, if by initially democratic means. The Soviet Union had tested its first atomic bomb in August 1949. Bullitt thought there was no longer a question of whether there would be war between the Soviet Union and United States "but whether or not the war will be engaged at a time and in a manner which will give the United States a fair chance to win."[36] With this in mind, what strategy was required?

At the time, strategists and policymakers in D.C. discussed using the atomic bomb. Its power was obvious: Japan's surrender in the immediate aftermath of Hiroshima and Nagasaki had proven the coercive potential of nuclear weapons. And the need for drastic measures also seemed clear; until 1950, the Soviet Union was thought capable of mobilizing 10 million men in a month, and in September 1945 the Joint Chiefs of Staff had recommended that if deterrence did not work, the United States should be ready to strike the first blow using its nuclear capabilities. Both Truman and Eisenhower envisioned using the bomb during their presidencies, but neither agreed that the United States could launch a preventive nuclear attack, concluding that a nuclear first strike lacked moral justification. Bullitt felt similarly.

At the same time, he had a robust confidence in the utility of nuclear deterrence. "The Soviet government will refrain from starting any war," Bullitt averred in *The Great Globe Itself,* "if it knows that, when it commits an act of aggression, it will receive swift retribution in the form of atomic bombs."[37] In 1950 Bullitt added that US threats to use the bomb were intended to deter not only the slightest expansionary move from the USSR but also any aggressive behavior by Soviet satellite states.[38] But nuclear deterrence was not enough by itself. In preparation for a potential conflict, Bullitt thought the United States should develop a guerrilla warfare strategy aimed at countering Communist cells that threatened to spring up in the overly tolerant democracies.

This sort of flexible thinking reflected a widespread sense that the way of battle had changed. "There are not many of us who realize what new kind of fighting will be imposed on us by Russian strategy if war starts," wrote General Pierre de Bénouville—that was, "the revolutionary strategy of internal aggression combined with the normal strategy of airborne armies."[39] De Bénouville was charged with foreign affairs and defense issues in the Rally of the French People, the postwar party founded by de Gaulle, with whom Bullitt remained in close contact. Bullitt was also in touch with David Galula, the counterinsurgency theorist who would go on to apply his ideas during the Battle of Algiers.[40] In the late 1940s, Galula's argument that support from the population was crucial in defeating insurgents informed Bullitt's own advice to Chiang Kai-shek.

Bullitt saw Truman as insufficiently aggressive in confronting the Communist threat. In March 1950, he wrote to Secretary of State Dean Acheson to protest the administration's foreign policy position. "No war, hot or cold, has ever been won by remaining on the defensive," Bullitt asserted. "We have remained on the defensive since 1945. It would have been easy to take the offensive from 1945 to 1950, since we held annihilating power. But today the balance of military power is swinging rapidly in Stalin's favor. Unless we now build up our military power and the strength of our allies faster than Stalin is building up his power and the strength of his satellites, any possibility of taking the offensive will disappear." Bullitt accused Truman of disarming the country and argued that the United States and its allies needed to commit more money to defense. Between 1946 and 1947, the percentage of GDP dedicated to defense fell from 21.4 to 5.7. That number further decreased to 4.6 percent in 1950.[41] The European democracies were also weak and divided. Bullitt's solution was a federation of European democracies, built in alliance with the United States. The idea was not outlandish: at the time, Jean Monnet was promoting gradual European unification through economic cooperation.[42] Bullitt, however, thought nothing could substitute for immediate political union. He also pushed Acheson to embrace the French under de Gaulle. "If progress is to be made, it will have to be made through France," he wrote. "If we attempt to handle the question ourselves by direct negotiations with the Germans and others, the French, in suspicion and fear, will hold back." Bullitt concluded, "Fear of General de Gaulle is silly. Indeed, he may turn out to be the only French leader with sufficient personal integrity to carry through the necessary measures, some of which will be unpopular with large groups of Frenchmen."[43]

The letter fell on mostly deaf ears, as US attention had by this point shifted to Asia. In January 1950, Acheson had defined a defense perimeter in the western Pacific, specifying the security of Japan, the Philippines, and other regions as central to American interests.[44] On June 27, two days after Mao gave his support to the northern Korean Communists' massive invasion of the south, Truman announced that the United States would resist Communist aggression in Korea and—in an abrupt reversal of prior policy—Taiwan. The president sought and received UN approval to use force in Korea. This shift also implicated Vietnam, where Truman sent Ambassador Donald Heath in July to evaluate the Franco-Indochinese forces.

At the time, the French military situation in Vietnam seemed to be improving. For several years, the French and their local allies had been at war with the Viet Minh, the nationalist forces under the leadership of Ho Chi Minh. After early setbacks, General de Lattre took over as high commander and reestablished French military control, scoring victory after victory. Emperor Bao Dai, who had been very reserved since retaking the throne, finally engaged in the process of turning over the armed forces to Vietnamese control, which de Lattre advocated.[45] In August 1951 Bullitt arranged an official invitation for de Lattre to visit Washington and address US policymakers.[46] The speech—organized by Henry Luce, who saw de Lattre as the MacArthur of Vietnam—would reinforce the new US position of support for France's fight in Indochina.[47] The French had previously been perceived as fighting to maintain an old colonial order, but in his address, de Lattre emphasized that the French purpose in Vietnam was not to achieve imperial interests but to shore up the last barrier to Communist conquest of Southeast Asia. De Lattre also met with and impressed Acheson; military authorities, including Eisenhower; and reporters. They did not know that de Lattre was suffering from cancer and would not be around long to lead the anti-Communist ally in Southeast Asia. He would die in Paris the following January.

Meanwhile, primaries for the 1952 presidential election were underway. Bullitt had broken with the Democrats and now joined influentials such as former president Hoover, Wedemeyer, and MacArthur in supporting Robert Taft for the Republican nomination against Eisenhower. Bullitt helped Hoover revise and edit his speech to the Republican National Convention—Hoover's last convention speech—and poured his soul into it.[48] Eisenhower was a good soldier, but he lost support from some hardline anti-Communists because he had trusted Stalin and acceded to the policy of handing over Central and Eastern Europe to the Soviets.[49] He had also been chief of staff in the Pentagon when the Communists took over China, damaging his anti-Communist credentials. Taft, meanwhile, had opposed the agreements at Yalta and Potsdam—the latter a summer 1945 meeting among Truman, Stalin, and Churchill to establish various postwar conditions—and was ready to take action to prevent China from falling into Communist hands. Bullitt was left disappointed by his narrow defeat on the convention floor.[50]

Bullitt could take consolation in the selection of Richard Nixon as Eisenhower's running mate. The two had become friends during one of the key moments of the early Cold War: the congressional investigation of Alger Hiss, a former US government official. A graduate of Johns Hopkins and Harvard Law School, Hiss had had a distinguished career in the State Department before becoming president of the Carnegie Endowment for International Peace. He attended the Yalta Conference and led the US secretariat at the San Francisco Conference, which had set up the UN. But on August 3, 1948, Whittaker Chambers, a journalist and reformed Soviet spy, testified before HUAC that Hiss, among others, was a Soviet agent pursuing "Communist infiltration of the American government."[51]

During his HUAC hearing, Hiss flatly denied membership in the Communist Party or participation in espionage and claimed he had never heard of Chambers. His confidence earned him a warm reception in the press and political circles, and Truman dismissed the investigation as a "red herring" concocted by the Republican Congress. However, Nixon, then a young freshman representative from California, urged a thorough investigation of Chambers's story and was appointed head of a subcommittee to determine which of the two men—Chambers or Hiss—was lying. In a closed session, Chambers testified that in fact he and Hiss had been close friends and demonstrated intimate knowledge of Hiss's life. In a second HUAC appearance, Hiss appeared far less composed. He admitted to possibly knowing Chambers under a different name but also, rejecting testimony by Chambers, claimed that the two had not seen each other since January 1, 1937. A week later, on August 25, 1948, Hiss and Chambers testified again at a congressional hearing, this time in front of television cameras. The tide of public opinion began to turn against Hiss. After Chambers made his accusation again on *Meet the Press,* Hiss filed a libel suit.

In a deposition for the suit, Chambers produced documents strongly suggesting that he and Hiss had known each other long after Hiss claimed to have last seen him and that Hiss had engaged in espionage. The materials included four handwritten notes from Hiss and sixty-five copies of retyped State Department documents. Then, on December 2, Chambers led two HUAC investigators to a hollowed-out pumpkin on his farm containing five film strips of photographs of State Department and Navy documents, which came to be known in the press as "the pumpkin papers." The films included several messages sent by Bullitt to the State Department during his tenure as ambassador to the Soviet Union and France, including one with the most secret codes in use at that time. Questioned by the FBI in 1949, Bullitt explained that Prime Minister Daladier had told him in 1939 that two brothers named Hiss, both in the State Department, were "Soviet agents." Stanley Hornbeck, Hiss's superior, confirmed in court that Bullitt had warned him that Hiss was a "rumored fellow traveler."[52] On January 21, 1950, a jury found Hiss guilty on two charges of perjury: first, for lying when he testified that he had never given documents to Chambers; second, for lying when he claimed not to have seen Chambers after January 1, 1937. Hiss served three years and eight months in prison before being released for good behavior.

The Hiss case had repercussions far beyond the trial. As Chambers wrote in *Witness* (1952), "It was the 'best people' who were for Alger Hiss . . . the enlightened and the powerful, the clamorous proponents of the open mind and the common man, who snapped their minds shut in a pro-Hiss psychosis."[53] Senator Joseph McCarthy took advantage of the Hiss conviction to justify his "witch hunts" for Communists in the State Department. The case also launched Nixon into the national spotlight. Two years after the case, Nixon was elected to the US Senate, and two years after that, he was Eisenhower's running mate.

Bullitt appreciated Nixon's tenacity in pursuing Hiss. Beyond that, Nixon fought for the anti-Communist values and policies that Bullitt advocated. The vice-presidential nominee sounded alarms about Communists infiltrating the very highest councils of the Truman administration, attacked Truman for firing MacArthur, and upbraided the White House for not "unleashing" Chiang against the Chinese Communists. In doing so, Nixon forged a link between McCarthyites and more centrist Republicans who preferred to keep their distance from the Wisconsin senator.[54]

One month after his nomination, Nixon defended himself against corruption allegations in his famous "Checkers" speech. After the speech, Bullitt was the first to send Nixon financial support for his vice-presidential campaign. It was a gesture Nixon never forgot. Bullitt had become one of his best friends in D.C.[55]

A Nixon Man

After the election, Bullitt helped Vice President Nixon organize a trip to Asia, with visits to Vietnam, Thailand, India, Japan, Afghanistan, and the Philippines. Bullitt welcomed Nixon and his wife Pat in Taiwan, where Bullitt had taken up residence in winter 1952. Bullitt's relocation had come about thanks to his strong relationship with Chiang. "Chiang Kai-shek developed an apparent great liking for Mr. Bullitt" when he visited in 1934, Hornbeck wrote, "such that he, Chiang, later on several occasions asked Mr. Bullitt to come out to him as an adviser."[56] At the end of 1951—when both were exiled, Bullitt from the US government and Chiang from mainland China—the occasion was finally at hand. With Chiang's support, Bullitt had an apartment in Taipei and a small but beautiful home in Kaohsiung that he was quite proud of. It was at the south end of the presidential garden, about a hundred yards from Chiang's house, on land belonging to the government. The Nixons met with Bullitt on November 8, 1953, for "a relaxing and stimulating evening"—an "unusual and happy combination," the vice president wrote.[57]

A few days after their departure, Bullitt sent Nixon his ideas about US strategy for fighting Communism. Bullitt suggested a simultaneous attack by US allies in Korea, Indochina, and China—a three-front war in Asia—with support from American troops. It was an adventurous proposal, but Bullitt thought it the only real option. The alternatives were to drop an atomic bomb on the Soviet Union "in order to prevent a later Soviet attack on us"—at the risk of "reduc[ing] ourselves to the level of Communist morality" and forfeiting "the support of the world opinion"—or else "waiting without action" and thereby condemning mankind to Communist dictatorship. If successful, however, his strategy would mean that "450 million Chinese would be subtracted from Soviet strength and added to the strength of the free world." He supported assertions by Galula, the French counterinsurgency expert, that Asians were genuinely behind the United States, even as the United States was not fighting for Asians.[58]

Bullitt also had a strong relationship with Syngman Rhee, the South Korean dictator, who in 1954 proposed that Bullitt lead a society of anti-communist Asian states to be created on the initiative of the presidents of Taiwan, the Philippines, and South Korea and the prime minister of Thailand.[59] Bullitt and Rhee had first met in 1919, at the Paris Peace Conference, where Rhee pleaded in vain for Korean independence from Japan. At the end of June 1953, at a crisis point in negotiations to end the Korean War, Bullitt mediated between Rhee and Secretary of State Dulles at the request of both. The United States was offering a treaty of assistance to South Korea based on a truce along the 38th parallel; Rhee wanted to continue the war until the Communists were expelled from the whole of Korea. Dulles strongly opposed this demand. If Rhee insisted on absolute victory, Dulles told Bullitt, the United States would withdraw its troops and leave him to fight alone, which would surely leave the entire Korean peninsula in Communist hands. Bullitt broke the impasse, writing to Rhee—with Dulles's approval—that he approved the strategy to drive the Communists from North Korea but noted, "I am not the president of the United States." With "heavy heart and grim forebodings," he advised his friend to accept the US government's conditions.[60]

A few months later, Nixon sent Bullitt to Vietnam. Bullitt reported his findings to Eisenhower and Nixon at a White House lunch on March 19, 1954. Bullitt thought Bao Dai, a man of high intelligence and genuine courage, should continue to receive US support, since there was no other plausible candidate to lead an anti-Communist Vietnam. Bullitt argued that if Vietnam were lost, Cambodia and Laos would surely follow. Eisenhower agreed but affirmed that "he would positively not put American troops in Indo-China." Bullitt shared this position. He had told Nixon as much during a 1952 conversation at Georgetown University, and he made clear to Eisenhower and Nixon over lunch that "the terrain and climate were much too tough for American soldiers."[61]

At the end of the visit, Bullitt lobbied for an additional $40 million in appropriations for Taiwan, whose economic aid had been subject to severe cuts. At the time, Bullitt was still advising Chiang, but not for much longer. In 1954, Bullitt fell down a cliff, breaking his spine for a second time and paralyzing both of his legs. He could only travel in a prone position. A general assigned to the Chinese Embassy in D.C. had died, and a coffin had been sent to return his body; that coffin was used to transport Bullitt home. Bullitt would visit Taiwan for the last time in December 1955.[62]

Shortly after Bullitt returned to the United States, his leukemia became active. He was also plagued with skin cancer and needed to have lesions removed on a routine basis. And while chemotherapy was effective in combating the leukemia, he still suffered from the spinal injury, experiencing intermittent paralysis. He needed an aide to lift him into bed.[63] He swam every day and had spinal massages regularly. Travel beyond Europe was now out of the question. He spent the winter in Paris, spring in Ireland, and summer in the Berkshires.

Despite his health challenges, Bullitt remained involved in US politics, policy, and strategy. In 1956, he broke with Kennan. Together, they had fought the "idealists," who imagined friendship and alliance with the Soviet Union. But now, Bullitt thought that "realists" of Kennan's ilk—fans of the containment strategy—had succumbed to a static conception of the conflict. The occasion for the split was a June 29 article in which Kennan argued that nothing would change in the Soviet Union after Stalin was replaced by Nikita Khrushchev. Recent changes in Soviet attitudes and policies would not lead to lifting the "Iron curtain, in considerable degree," he asserted. "One should not ignore the real differences of historical experience and tradition," Kennan wrote. Russia was a "non-Western other. And where regimes of the nature of Communism have been in power for more than a decade, there can be no question of restoring the *status quo ante*."[64] Since the Soviet Union could not change, it had to be contained—still. Kennan therefore favored a steady course in which the United States supported neutral buffers between the two great world systems. Kennan thought Japan should be neutral in the Cold War and that US troops should not remain there. He also believed that East and West Germany could unify under a condition of neutrality. Kennan did not favor US recognition of Communist China but allowed that it might have a place at the United Nations.

Bullitt published a harsh critique, casting Kennan as defeatist. "In the past 11 years, the Soviet Union has seized control of more than 700 million persons," Bullitt wrote. "The communists will not stop their attacks—they can only be stopped." The last two centuries were marked by oppressed peoples' successful struggle for liberation from their oppressors; freedom was a universal aspiration, shared by Russians or Chinese as well as Americans. If Kennan was interested in neutrality, why didn't he suggest it for Soviet satellites in Eastern Europe, the Balkans, China, or North Korea instead of Japan and Germany? At a time of supreme peril, Bullitt thought that the essential factor for US survival was the "maintenance of its power to deliver, at any moment, on the Soviet Union a weight of nuclear explosive far heavier than the Soviet Union can deliver on us."[65]

Kennan replied privately in a nine-page letter. Mao's China, Kennan wrote, was autonomous; it was not a Soviet satellite. He did not find it advisable for a democracy like the United States to launch a war against a country that had not initiated at least some overt military action against it. He also thought that current Western policies toward Germany would eventually turn public opinion in the Federal Republic against the United States. Further, Kennan was alarmed by Bullitt's conclusion that "if we were to have war with the Soviet Union tomorrow, we would probably win." This was wild and dangerous nonsense coming from a person of unquestioned intellectual stature, rich experience, and exceptional qualifications, Kennan thought. Perhaps Bullitt might better devote his talents to "the difficult quest for real paths of exit from our present difficulties and dangers," Kennan concluded.[66]

For his part, Nixon was delighted by the way Bullitt "laid Kennan low."[67] Nixon remained one of Bullitt's best friends, and the two, along with Pat, spent a great deal of time together. "We look forward to hearing some interesting stories . . . told in the inimitable Bullitt style!"[68] they wrote him in January 1958. The group shared many meals that year. On August 5, 1959, Bullitt welcomed the vice president and his family to his home in the Berkshires.[69] Bullitt supported Nixon in the Republican primaries that year against Nelson Rockefeller and then in the 1960 presidential election against John F. Kennedy, campaigning for Nixon in New Hampshire and Pennsylvania.[70] In fall 1960, at Nixon's request, Bullitt spoke for him at meetings in San Francisco and Los Angeles. He railed against the Democratic Party, "out there taking the line of the recognition of Red China."[71] Bullitt suggested using information on Kennedy's bad health to derail his candidacy, but Nixon rejected that approach.[72]

After Nixon's 1960 defeat, Bullitt sent him several notes of comfort. On November 15 he wrote, "There is no point to tell you how sorry I am. For the United States, it is a disaster. For you, Pat and the children, I hope that it will be just one race lost by a whisker."[73] In January 1961, Nixon thanked Bullitt in a long letter. "As Pat and I look back to our fourteen years in DC," Nixon wrote, "there is nothing we will cherish more than the memories of those occasions when we have been together." He added that Bullitt's "loyal friendship through the years has meant more to us than I can adequately describe in a letter."[74]

Bullitt was an inveterate opponent of Kennedy. In August 1961, after Nixon wrote a courteous article on his erstwhile opponent, Bullitt chastised his friend: "You make the same mistake you made at the start of your campaign for the Presidency," Bullitt wrote. "You attribute to Kennedy 'high intelligence, great energy, the ability to inspire by his eloquence.'" Bullitt thought Kennedy was not distinguished by his intellectual gifts. "He is a synthetic product of great wealth," Bullitt wrote. "His 'high intelligence' is high-priced intelligence in the minds of his high-paid advisers. His 'great energy' comes out of a hypodermic syringe or a pill which supplies the products essential to life and action which his own adrenal glands do not produce. 'His eloquence' is produced by one or another slick ghost writer."

In the same letter, Bullitt also accused Kennedy of plagiarizing what would become the most famous works he had ever spoken. "The phrase you admire 'not what the country could do for them but what they could do for the country' is from my speech at Independence Hall in August 1940," Bullitt said.[75] Bullitt was exaggerating, but he was perhaps not entirely wrong to suspect that his words had inspired Kennedy's. At the end of Bullitt's 1940 speech, he challenged his audience to be prepared for war: "When are we going to tell [our legislators] that we want to know what are our duties, not what are our privileges?" he asked. "When are we going to say to them that we don't want to hear any longer about what we can get from our country, but we do want to hear what we can give to our country?"[76]

In Paris, in Retreat

It was no longer true of Kennan, but for many veterans of the State Department, especially of Bullitt's staffs in Moscow and Paris, Bullitt was still "the boss." In the early 1960s, his suffering back made him bitter and irascible, but he maintained warm contact with Robert Murphy, John Wiley, and Stanley Hornbeck, all of whom were by then ambassadors. Loy Henderson, after serving as ambassador in Baghdad, New Delhi, and Tehran, was ending his diplomatic career as deputy undersecretary of state for administration. Hillenkoetter was now CIA director.[77] Bullitt's supporters could be found in the highest ranks of the foreign policy and intelligence establishments.

Carmel Offie remained a liaison for all of them. He worked for Murphy in Algiers in 1943–1944, in Rome from 1944 to 1946, and then in Frankfurt.[78] In 1947, he left the State Department and, through his Moscow embassy friends, found a job at the CIA. By that time, Offie had come out as gay. He was soon under investigation by McCarthy and had to leave the CIA. He went on to work with the Free Trade Union Committee, a CIA-backed, anti-Communist international union effort.[79] For years he sent long handwritten letters to Bullitt and Murphy, apprising them of what he gleaned from his globetrotting and the dinner-party circuit.[80]

Bullitt still whiled away his summers in the Berkshires, but he no longer had a house in D.C.[81] Since 1954 he had lived in Paris. After spending time with de Gaulle in March 1958, Bullitt felt that the French leader's return to power was approaching. Bullitt reported to Dulles that the French government was "rotten from top to bottom and it would continue to be this way until 'some strong action' was taken." He thought "the Army ought not to initiate any coup but that the Communists should do it and then the Army could come in to restore constitutional order."[82] The coup arrived six weeks later, in May 1958, organized by the army to facilitate de Gaulle's return to power.

Alongside his trips to the Berkshires, Bullitt also made regular visits to Ireland, to see his daughter. Anne had been living in Ireland since the mid-1950s, where she became the country's first known woman breeder and trainer of thoroughbred horses. She owned a 700-acre farm with extensive horse stables and 100 acres of lakes in County Kildare, forty minutes west of Dublin. Her animals won the most prestigious horse races of Ireland and England.[83] There was nothing Anne did not know about horses, as far as her father was concerned. "She reads their minds," he said in an interview:

> She went to her first horse race with me in Paris when she was about three. We went down to the stalls to have a look at the horses, all twenty-one of them. She looked at each one with great care. At last, she said "Daddy, I have thirty-five Francs at home. Please bet them for me on this one." I asked her why she chose that horse which by no means been given good odds. "He has told me he is going to win," Anne said, "and the other horses say that he is right!" I thought I should teach her some lessons about betting, and I did as she asked me. She went home with 38,000 francs.[84]

Bullitt's brother Orville thought he had a miserable life in Paris. As far as Orville was concerned, William was just wasting time swimming at the American Club. Then he would have lunch and go home. He would fight with his acquaintances but otherwise do little. "If he had only written his memoirs or another book of fiction," Orville said.[85] Orville misunderstood his brother, though; Bullitt remained in Paris because he loved it.[86] Over the course of decades, his opinion of Paris had not changed. As he wrote to Ernesta once:

> I don't know if it is primarily due to happy childhood memories but each time I get home [in Paris] I feel much more at home than I do in New York, where my ancestors have played more or a less of a ruling

> part since 1630. Here I have no ancestors and very few friends. I miss my friends at home tremendously and with few exceptions I dislike the French nobles and upper class. But here, on the whole, I get on much better with the average person I meet. I think the French are more practical and more intelligent than any other people in the world and both their good and bad qualities added together produce a working philosophy under which life is pretty well worthwhile. If I am definitely blue, I don't know any cure in the world quite up to going to the Place de la Concorde and looking around.[87]

Orville was also mistaken about his brother's absence from the book-publishing scene. Bullitt still had something in the works, as Ernest Jones, the British psychoanalyst and Freud biographer, realized. In 1955 he wrote Bullitt searching for information on "the book on President Wilson which you and Freud composed together some quarter of a century ago."[88] In a flattering reply, Bullitt told Jones that he retained the only copy of the manuscript and was prepared to show it to him. The manuscript "was the result of much combat," Bullitt told Jones. "Both Freud and I were extremely pig-headed: somewhat convinced that each one of us was God. In consequence, each chapter: indeed, each sentence was a subject of an intense debate."[89]

Bullitt and Jones met in New York on April 16, 1956.[90] Bullitt brought the manuscript in its "formidable case with a letter lock," the code of which he gave to Jones under a solemn oath. Jones found Bullitt manic, secretive, and obstinate; Bullitt arranged for the manuscript's return as soon as Jones had read it. On April 20, after finishing, Jones wrote to Anna Freud that "the book is very interesting."[91] But it could not be published, Bullitt told Jones, until the death of Mrs. Wilson.[92]

16

The Wilson Book, at Last

EDITH WILSON DIED ON DECEMBER 28, 1961. With her passing, Bullitt wondered if the time to publish had finally come. Henry Laughlin, head of Houghton Mifflin, suggested as much.[1] Bullitt toyed with the idea. He had high hopes: a $500,000 advance; royalties; magazine, radio, and television coverage; movie rights.[2] But he hesitated.

At the time, Bullitt was looking forward to the 1964 presidential elections, in which he hoped President Kennedy would be defeated. However, after Kennedy's tragic assassination in November 1963 and the impressive achievements of Lyndon Johnson's first months in office—fulfilling many promises of the civil rights revolution—Bullitt understood that the Republicans would lose the 1964 presidential election. It had been more than twenty years since Bullitt reached the height of his influence under the Roosevelt administration, and he was still addicted to power. He had not abandoned hope of being dealt a new hand by a president who embodied his vision: one who was ready to impose liberal-internationalist ideas on the world by force, if necessary. His preferred candidates—Dewey in 1948, Taft in 1952, Nixon in 1960—kept losing elections, though not by much. However, Barry Goldwater—whom Bullitt supported in 1964, albeit less enthusiastically than he had the others—was beaten in a landslide. And so Bullitt was confronted with a hard truth: his career was over.[3] Not only that, but he was seventy-three years old and suffered numerous physical ailments. Politics took a back seat to white blood cell counts. Yet there was an opportunity here: publishing the Wilson manuscript could not harm a career that was finished. The publication itself could be seen as Bullitt's final act of service to his country.

In October 1964 Bullitt shared the manuscript with Max Schur, Freud's last physician. The doctor had initiated contact, out of interest in the writing Bullitt and Freud had done together; Schur also told Bullitt that Freud had spoken of him frequently with great appreciation, as had Marie Bonaparte.[4] Schur was fascinated by Bullitt's stories of working with Freud and strongly suggested that a university press publish the manuscript. Princeton would be inappropriate, as they would be reluctant to "publish controversial documents about Wilson." Schur suggested instead Rutgers University Press, which had published the collected works of Abraham Lincoln and some of John Dewey's philosophical work.[5] Two and a half years after his last estimate, Bullitt had lowered his expectations and now hoped for a $15,000 advance.[6]

Rutgers offered to publish the book as a historical document with notes from a Wilson scholar who would provide additional insights unavailable to Freud and Bullitt at the time of writing.[7] Bullitt refused. He insisted on publishing only the work that he and Freud had created. Likewise, when Ernest Jones had suggested revisions in 1956, Bullitt had demurred. He acknowledged at the time that the manuscript contained "a good deal of repetition," but he felt it unfair to make any changes as he could not get "the consent of my collaborator." And, substantively, the manuscript required no adjustment as far as Bullitt was concerned. He told Jones that, since completing the manuscript with Freud in 1932, he had not read any new publication that contradicted or cast doubt on the views it expressed on Versailles and on Wilson's personality.[8] Bullitt reiterated this opinion in 1964.

Bullitt was not merely being defensive: he had kept informed during the preceding three decades, reading about Wilson, Versailles, and psychoanalysis. What he read confirmed his and Freud's analysis of Wilson's personality. For instance, there were the memoirs of Irwin Hoover, the chief usher of the White House who served under ten presidents. Hoover was well-positioned to comment on Wilson, as the president and his family "spoke frankly [in front of Hoover] as they would do before a piece of furniture."[9] Hoover confirmed the intensity of Wilson's and House's relationship—one of deep appreciation, intimacy, and love, followed by obsession and hate.

> In the matter of Wilson and Colonel House, there were no others. No one else seems to count. There was nothing too big, too important, too secret, or too sacred to discuss with Colonel House. He was simply the President's one confidant, the one outlet he gave to his innermost thoughts, plans, and purposes. He was a constant visitor to the White House . . . He was constantly asked to come and always

> urged to stay on, and when he was at the White House the President would so arrange his time that he could be with him constantly . . . Hours and hours they would sit and talk, and the President always seemed much benefited by his visits. His deference and consideration for the Colonel were pronounced. . . . As time went on, House's position became stronger and stronger. During the War, he seemed indispensable to the President. He was sent for and consulted about everything. His visits became more frequent, and the two men corresponded almost daily . . . The President generally wrote his letters to Colonel House on his own typewriter, and no carbon copies were made. The most intimate and personal affairs of the President were shared by Colonel House. His second marriage was one of these.

According to Hoover, tensions first arose on the *George Washington* as Wilson sailed to the Paris conference in December 1918. Wilson resented House's nepotistic streak, which the president discovered when he saw that the list of the passengers included several of House's relatives and friends. Wilson hinted that House was getting all that he could out of negotiating the peace treaty. In February 1919, after Wilson became convinced that House had been ready to postpone the adoption of the league, their relationship rapidly deteriorated. "Once," Hoover recalled, "when the colonel called [the president] on the telephone asking for an appointment, I heard him say, 'I wish he would leave me alone,' at the same time as granting the request." After Wilson returned to Washington and had his stroke, "his feeling about Colonel House became an obsession. He could see no good in him at all," Hoover wrote. "Encouraged by those around him, his obsession turned to hatred. Yet he talked of [House] incessantly. Letters were coming from Colonel House pertaining to the closing up of the affairs of the Peace Conference, but they were never opened. They accumulated for months."[10]

Lloyd George, in his memoirs, remembered an extraordinary outburst of Wilson's. On one occasion, when holding forth about some idea connected with the League of Nations, Wilson compared himself favorably with Jesus Christ:

> "Why," he said, "has Jesus Christ so far not succeeded in inducing the world to follow His teaching in these matters? It is because he taught the ideal without devising any practical means of attaining it. That is the reason why I am proposing a practical scheme to carry

> out His aims." Clemenceau slowly opened his dark eyes to their widest dimensions and swept them round the Assembly to see how the Christians gathered around the table enjoyed this exposure of the futility of their Master.[11]

In this comparison, Wilson was God the Father judging His Son. Freud had thought about this phenomenon: "If the influence of the father was so great that he could generate such a powerful super-ego in the ego and such a scrupulously accurate identification with the father, this deification of the father had another consequence still," he wrote of Wilson. "If the father was God, then oneself would be Christ, God's beloved single son. Therefore, [Wilson] became Christ and in his unconscious a space for the two persons opened up, he was Christ and God the Father at the same time."[12]

Another work that augmented Bullitt's confidence in his and Freud's conclusions was Alexander and Juliette George's *Woodrow Wilson and Colonel House: A Personality Study*. This 1956 psychological portrait also recognized Wilson's father fixation and argued that Wilson's father represented a superego whom Wilson could never satisfy: no matter his accomplishments, he would always turn immediately to the next task, attempting to reach still higher toward his unattainable father. Thus Wilson could be subtle and open to compromise in the journey toward obtaining power, but once in power, he was authoritarian. He was also reluctant to take any advice that did not echo his views or intuitions. He therefore reproduced a common scenario over the years, building strong bonds with select individuals—Hibben, House—before breaking with them and rejecting them as traitors. Meanwhile those who challenged Wilson's authority, like Senator Lodge and Dean West at Princeton, were perceived as unbearably threatening representatives of the father whom he could never surmount. Wilson had to dominate and defeat them, even if doing so meant sacrificing his goals and suffering repeated defeats.[13] It was less painful to sacrifice even the Versailles Treaty and the League of Nations than to make concessions to intractable enemies. For the Georges, Wilson's whole life was an attempt to compensate for a complex created by an authoritarian father.[14]

Bullitt felt secure in the verdict of history. None of these publications had supplanted his own manuscript. Uniquely among the former president's psychobiographers, Bullitt had access to Wilson's intimate friends and collaborators—Baker, Baruch, Grayson, Tumulty, House, and others. And, of course, none of these others was Sigmund Freud. Bullitt would continue his search for a publisher.

Fighting with Freud's Heirs

By late 1964 Houghton Mifflin remained interested and offered Bullitt a contract, which he accepted. Philip Rich, an editor there, was attuned to Bullitt's interests. He proposed starting the book with Bullitt's foreword instead of Freud's introduction because the foreword was written more recently and because Bullitt, being the only living author, could use the space to explain the book's background. Rich found many repetitive sections within the text and suggested that some be deleted or changed.[15] Bullitt liked most of his proposals and accepted them.[16]

Bullitt then found Anna Freud's address in *Who's Who in England* and wrote to her. She responded immediately. She had often wondered, she told Bullitt, when the time would be right for publishing the book. In 1939 she had written him, "I still remember the pleasure it gave my father to do that work with you."[17] Now she was looking forward to reading their shared project.[18] Anna directed Bullitt to her brother Ernst, who managed their father's copyrights. Ernst's first impression was that the manuscript was excellent. He was "fascinated by the historical as well as the psychoanalytical content" and wanted it to be published quickly. He predicted an "American sensation."[19] But Anna did not like what she read. She shared her impressions with Alick Bartholomew, another Houghton Mifflin editor. Anna had met Bullitt in the 1930s and found him "tremendously personal and charming" but "also frightfully arrogant." She remembered her father thinking the book was essentially Bullitt's and that Bullitt had turned his own contribution into a kind of parody by thoughtlessly repeating phrases like "little Tommy Wilson," "one-track mind," or "identification with the Christ." Anna knew her father was a "stickler for precision of thought and economy of words," and she worried that publishing the manuscript would undermine his scientific contributions. In light of these concerns, Anna requested substantial changes to the manuscript. If Bullitt refused, she would insist on delaying publication until after his death on the assumption that such decisions would then fall to his daughter Anne, who, though "formidable," would be less aggressive than her father.[20]

On December 28, 1965, Ernst Freud sent Bullitt a copy of the manuscript incorporating Anna's revisions.[21] He asked Bullitt to "look through them with indulgence, especially as they concerned the psychological part of the work only, which means our father's part." In fact, Anna's changes did not concern psychological language and reasoning. Her suggested changes were numerous—often replacement of full sentences or paragraphs—but minor. She eliminated heavy-handed and recurring expressions. For example, she replaced "outlets for his reaction formation against his passivity to his father" with "precarious inner equilibrium"[22] and "his activity and his reaction formation against his passivity" with "masculinity was assured."[23] Her revisions included an amusing Freudian slip. Freud and Bullitt had written that, "to handle the conflict between his powerful passivity" toward his father "and his relatively feeble activity," Wilson's ego employed the method of "repression."[24] In the sentence she suggested in replacement, Anna substituted "repression" with "regression," perhaps expressing a transference of her own relation to her father.[25] Bullitt rejected all of Anna's revisions except one, which concerned an excessively dismissive characterization of Wilson's 1902 publication *A History of the American People*.[26] Perhaps Bullitt resented her teacherly intervention—Anna was a trained and highly adept schoolmaster. In any case, Bullitt allowed that "Miss Freud had some bright ideas about the manuscript." But, as he told Paul Roazen, a political scientist and preeminent historian of psychoanalysis, "it was not a book by her."[27]

Houghton Mifflin informed Bullitt that the Freuds were entitled to block the publication if Anna's changes were not accepted. Bullitt decided to break the contract and on January 20, 1966, requested immediate return of the manuscript.[28] Ultimately Houghton Mifflin's lawyers relented, though, and on March 14 agreed to go ahead with publication without Anna's revisions. Eventually, Ernst Freud, too, signed off. On July 26, Benjamin Tilghman, an editor at Houghton Mifflin, announced to Bullitt that Ernst had agreed to publish the manuscript without changes. "All gods, small and large, be praised," Tilghman wrote.[29]

But this was a short respite. On September 11, Tilghman drove to the Berkshires to meet with Bullitt. Bullitt showed him the original signed manuscript—the manuscript, Bullitt explained, "in which Freud introduced changes and additions after it had been signed."[30] Bullitt did not agree with the changes. In 1938 or 1939, when Bullitt visited Freud in London, they rolled back Freud's changes and agreed to additional corrections. Then Bullitt took the revised manuscript to Paris and had his secretary retype it. He brought the updated text back to Freud, who approved it in London.[31] This was Bullitt's official history of the manuscript that was to be published. He repeated it until he died.

A few weeks after the meeting with Tilghman, Houghton Mifflin was contacted by Erik Erikson, the leading American psychoanalyst. The *New York Review of Books* had asked him to review the publication and sent him galley proofs. Erikson asked Houghton Mifflin to cease publication or, at a minimum, to designate Bullitt principal author and cut the claim that Freud had signed each book chapter, which would have indicated coauthorship.[32] Erikson was outraged by the mechanical repetitiveness of the analytical language, which did not sound like Freud at all. He also thought that Bullitt had done a poor job of integrating Freud's interpretations, which extended, Erikson believed, far beyond Bullitt's understanding.[33]

By the end of October, more would-be reviewers were contacting Houghton Mifflin with objections. "Obviously, some people are going to go at you," Tilghman wrote Bullitt. "I do not mind their going after a foot or an arm, but I do not want them to have a chance at your throat."[34] Tilghman, who had seen a few pages of the original manuscript, now insisted on reading the whole thing side-by-side with the 1939 corrections. But Bullitt made excuses and begged off, while noting that he and Freud did not make "any changes in psychiatric terminology" in 1939.[35]

In the first days of November 1966, Erikson sent Bullitt, Anna Freud, and Max Schur a questionnaire he described as "deliberately impartial" and with which he sought to inform his review. What portions of the book were written by Freud, he wondered. In which language? Had the original draft been preserved? With Freud's signatures? Did Freud sign the unpublishable original manuscript or the one to be published? Were there disagreements between Freud and Bullitt? How did the text slated for publication differ from the original?[36]

Anna replied that she was certain her father wrote an introduction but none of the chapters, even in part. He probably suggested analytical interpretations to Bullitt, "never imagining that they would be used in this clumsy way."[37] Schur thought Bullitt did not understand the intricacies of analytical interpretations, their proper formulation. Schur believed that most of Freud's contributions were made orally and that any of Freud's prose appearing in the manuscript had originated in handwritten letters that Bullitt had, by his own admission, burned during WWII.[38] Bullitt never replied to Erikson.

Look magazine, with its circulation of 7.5 million, published an excerpt from the book just before its full release in December.[39] This provoked a tremendous amount of commentary, characterized by Tilghman as "outrage." He again asked to see the original manuscript. Houghton Mifflin could not afford to take matters lightly, not when there was so much at stake: "the book's reputation, yours, and ours as well."[40]

When the book was published at last, around New Year's of 1967, Bullitt was not in a position to pay much attention. "Bill was too sick to read the reviews," his brother Orville later told an interviewer.[41] At the beginning of February, Bullitt took a taxi from his home on Rue de Ponthieu, a narrow street along the Champs-Elysées, to the American Hospital of Paris, in Neuilly.[42] This time, he knew he was going to die. The US press reported his hospitalization. Nixon cabled immediately. "Terribly distressed to read of your illness," he wrote. "All the Nixons are confident that your fighting spirit will see you through."[43] A few days later, on his deathbed, Bullitt received a note from the Jesuit priest Hunter Guthrie, the former president of Georgetown University. Father Guthrie hoped that Bullitt would convert to Catholicism. "Bill, you are the most interesting person it has been my good fortune to meet in this life," Guthrie wrote. "So, naturally, I want to spend eternity in your company. I know you are High Church and just half-a-step from where I think you ought to be. Can I twist your arm and get you to take that half-a-step?" Then he added, "Apart from all this, I think you are one of the truly great men of history. I go back to Plato and Pico Della Mirandola. You will certainly enjoy their company."[44]

Bullitt was headstrong to the end. On February 15, Anne, his brother Orville, his cousin Orville Horwitz, and the ever-faithful Carmel Offie were at Bullitt's bedside when he died an Episcopalian. All the US newspapers reported the news, and Bullitt's body was flown back home.[45] A few hundred people attended the traditional Episcopal funeral service at the Church of the Holy Trinity at Rittenhouse Square in

Philadelphia; the Nixons were among the attendees, but few other luminaries or officials joined them. As he had wished, Bullitt was buried at Woodland Cemetery, next to the rest of his family.[46] From Paris, President de Gaulle sent a handwritten letter to Anne. "From M. William Bullitt, I will keep, like many French, the memory of a man of the highest quality," he wrote, "of a great Ambassador of the United States in the gravest days of History, of a sincere and dedicated friend of France."[47] A March 1 memorial service at the American Cathedral in Paris was better attended. Jean Monnet was there, as were Léon Blum and General de Lattre's widows, and Chip Bohlen, who had served with Bullitt in Moscow and was at the time US ambassador to France.[48] In Tel Aviv, the newspaper *Ma'ariv* praised Bullitt as a longtime supporter of the Zionist cause and friend of Israel.[49]

A few days after his funeral, Alden Whitman—the chief obituary writer of the *New York Times,* who considered every obit a "form of biography"—wrote a eulogy for an "Energetic Diplomat," at the center of three major events of his nation's history: the Versailles peace negotiations, the recognition of the Soviet Union, and preparation for the Second World War. "Few American diplomats of Mr. Bullitt's era had such a wide acquaintance," Whitman wrote. "Few diplomats moreover possessed his dynamic energy and endless flair for living . . . He was often described as President Roosevelt's Colonel House . . . In human relations he never tasted the peace of indifference. Some of the harshest things are said about him by his friends. Some of the kindest by his enemies."[50] Nixon thanked Whitman for the obituary. "As one who had the privilege to know William Bullitt as a personal friend, your story had the rare quality of recounting the usually dry facts of his distinguished public career in a way which vividly portrayed the man himself." Bullitt was, according to Nixon, "one of the most exciting personalities of our time."[51]

The excitement did not end with Bullitt's death. Nixon had concluded his last cable to Bullitt, "Congratulations incidentally on driving the liberal establishment out of their minds with your Wilson." Nixon got it right. Though his body was buried, Bullitt's presence would endure through the book he had written with Freud. From beyond the grave, Bullitt would do much as he had in his lifetime: he would stir controversy.

17

The Return of the Father

THE PUBLICATION OF BULLITT AND FREUD'S *Thomas Woodrow Wilson: A Psychological Study* created an immediate firestorm, with coverage in the *New York Times, Washington Post,* and other major papers; multiple articles in the *New York Review of Books;* and extensive comment in the specialty press. For weeks after its release, the book was the talk of the psychoanalytical community.

Anna Freud said she disliked it as soon as she read it, reflecting an apparent change in her views. When Paul Roazen interviewed her in June 1965, she mentioned the forthcoming publication and called the manuscript, which she had read, "very disturbing." It was astounding that a president could be so "ill," having experienced a "delusion" over what he had done in Paris. She also seemed to recognize the work's psychoanalytic contributions, telling Roazen that the core of the book was its theory of Wilson's passivity toward his father and "the role of 'psychotic' denial of reality connected with Versailles."[1]

Anna Freud rejected the book only after Bullitt opposed her corrections and upon witnessing its bad reception among her colleagues. She decided that Freud had overestimated Bullitt—something she never did—and wished that "the whole cooperation had never happened." She told Roazen that it seemed improbable her father had signed each chapter. This "was so very unlike my father who usually did not even sign his own manuscripts," she said. Yet, even with the oddity of the signatures, she did not doubt that her father had in fact worked with Bullitt and that he had taken initiative in the process. "In matters of this kind, my father was not guided by anybody," she said. "There was . . . no doubt," she acknowledged, "that he was interested and pleased and expected a worthwhile outcome."[2]

Amid the torrent of criticism, Anna wanted as little publicity as possible. She rejected her cousin Edward Bernays's suggestion that the American Psychoanalytic Association dissociate itself from the book—

such a stance would just prolong the controversy and draw more public attention, she said, "both the opposite of what one wishes." And the association's condemnation could be misinterpreted as a disavowal of Freud himself.[3] Instead, Anna cooperated discreetly with leading reviewers to ensure that the book was attributed to Bullitt alone and that its credibility was destroyed.

One of the reviews Anna read and amended before publication was Robert Sussman Stewart's in the *New York Times*. Like Anna, Stewart challenged the idea that Freud had actively participated in drafting the book. He found it uncharacteristic of Freud's work in the 1920s and 1930s. "Since 1920," he wrote, "the emergence of the so called 'ego psychology' shifted the center of interest away from the unconscious and repressed infantile libidinal strivings toward investigation of the mental 'structures'—the ego, the super-ego and the id—their relationship to one another, and the outside world." It was hard to imagine that Freud had abandoned the direction he "had been taking psychoanalysis."[4]

Erikson probably experienced the greatest outrage of all. With his Wilson biography, a long-dead Freud had stepped into Erikson's realm of scholarship. Psychological biographies of ideological innovators—Luther and Gandhi—had made Erikson a celebrity. Erikson had sanctified heroes, concentrating on the young Luther as an ethical preacher and neglecting his controversial career as a political leader and portraying Gandhi as a reconciler of religion and politics. In the case of Wilson, Freud had torn down a statue. More importantly, in doing so Freud had used the classical tools of psychoanalysis, assigning primacy to Eros and destructiveness as sources of psychic energy. This was far from the ego psychology Erikson had developed with colleagues like Heinz Hartmann—a development that Anna Freud had encouraged.[5] Focused on achievements and adaptation rather than pathology and freedom, Erikson put the external reality to which the ego adjusts at the center of psychoanalytical theory. This stood in contrast to Freud's first theories, which put inner drives and the unconscious at the core. Freud never disavowed the unconscious frame. For Erikson and his followers, the Wilson biography was a painful reminder of an intellectual conflict from which they wished to move on.[6]

Amid the indignation, dismissal, and suspicion, Theodor Reik, at least, was enthusiastic. One of Freud's most respected living disciples,

Reik was asked by Houghton Mifflin to author a preface for a new edition of the Wilson biography. He wrote in his draft:

> Considered from a purely stylistic point of view, some pages of this book belong to the best and clearest Freud wrote. This is valid not only for his presentation of psychoanalytical theories, but also in other parts of the book where Freud finds felicitous words and startlingly compressed phrases . . . His psychoanalytical study of Wilson's character is excellent. There is only one word to describe Freud's analytical penetration of Woodrow Wilson, the boy, the man, and the President, it is superb.[7]

Anna Freud was furious. Could Reik, who knew Sigmund Freud's style so well, "really believe that what Bullitt has written has been written by my father?" she asked in a letter to Schur. She remained certain of one thing: other than the preface and the exposition of psychoanalytical theory, which might have been partly inspired by Freud, not one sentence—not even a word—concerning Wilson could have come from her father. Schur, who had been instrumental in persuading Bullitt to publish the book, now reversed course. He and the Freuds blocked publication of Reik's preface.[8]

By the middle of 1967, public attention around the book ebbed, but questions about the manuscript remained. Was Freud really its coauthor? How much had he written? The book provoked the curiosity of scholars and treasure hunters. Among them was Roazen. He had been searching for the original manuscript for years and interviewed Bullitt at the end of 1966. "Did Freud regard [the book] as in any sense autobiographical, or did Bullitt regard it as a biography of Freud?" Roazen asked. "Oh no," Bullitt replied. Roazen suggested "certain similarities between Wilson and Freud," but "Bullitt could not see this at all." He told Roazen, "We tried to be as objective as possible. Worked a long time at it before we started to write it. First, I wrote some, then we discussed it together. We just did the job that's all."[9] After Bullitt's death, Roazen continued to hunt for information on the manuscript.

One source was Bullitt's papers, which Anne Bullitt kept in Ireland. She contemplated writing her father's biography but never did. Nonetheless, she was vigilant, bordering on obsessive, about protecting her father's memory. When her uncle Orville decided to publish Bullitt's correspondence with Roosevelt, she thoroughly revised successive drafts of the manuscript together with Carmel Offie. She remembered everything and had a sense of what her father went through at each stage of his political career. Over time, she distanced herself from Orville, who wanted to include in the manuscript criticisms of her father from Ambassador William Dodd.[10] Orville said he wanted to be objective, but Anne was aghast. Were other volumes or correspondence published that way?

Offie remained beside her to help preserve Bullitt's memory until 1972, when he died tragically in a plane accident at age sixty-three. Offie's friends and colleagues from his time at the Bullitt embassies in Moscow and Paris attended his funeral. So did Jay Lovestone, his boss of twenty-five years at the Free Trade Union Committee, where Offie worked as a liaison with the CIA. Louise Page Morris, Lovestone's lover, said that the news of Offie's death marked the only time she had seen Lovestone cry. She remembered Offie's drollness and his intellectual agility—"he had more lines out than the phone company."[11]

Anne Bullitt continued shielding her father's reputation for many years to come, while living alone in Ireland without contact with friends and family. When the first biography of Bullitt was about to be published in 1988, she worked with the lawyer Robert Pennoyer to have a variety of assertions about her father removed. The effort succeeded. In late 1990, she planned to sell her farm in Ireland and move back to the United States, but she developed dementia, retreating to her bedroom and refusing to see anybody except her housekeeper and a real estate developer. In early 2000, she was committed by the High Court of Dublin to a private nursing home where she spent the rest of her life. She left instructions that she wanted an Episcopalian funeral, as her father had, despite having converted to Catholicism in 1953. She died on August 18, 2007, and was buried beside her father in the Bullitt family tomb in Philadelphia. As directed by her will, Pennoyer, who had become a friend, created a foundation named for her father, which inherited the proceeds of her estate.

A few years earlier, in the basement of Anne's home, her court-appointed guardian found 400 boxes containing her parents' papers. Pennoyer paid for their cataloging and donated them to Yale's Sterling Library. Roazen was finally able to access Bullitt's papers in 2004, before they were made available to the general public. There he found clear evidence of Freud's active participation in the book. Of particular interest was a twenty-four-page, handwritten essay by Freud, focused on libido but also touching on narcissism, castration anxiety, repression, sublimation, homosexuality, and Christianity. After Roazen died in November 2005, his friend, psychoanalyst Mark Solms, carried the torch and published an English translation of the previously unknown Freud manuscript. Solms opined that the work "summarizes some of Freud's most fundamental ideas on the working of the mind."[12]

Did this discovery solve the mystery of who wrote the Wilson biography? Roazen and Solms believed the handwritten manuscript was a Freud "addition" that Bullitt had radically condensed and revised to create the first chapter of the published book. It was not. The material Roazen discovered was in fact Freud's own German translation of the first chapter of the original Wilson manuscript that he and Bullitt had written.

18

The Secret

PAUL ROAZEN ALSO BELIEVED the original manuscript of the Wilson book, signed by Bullitt and Freud at the end of each chapter, no longer existed. In fact, the original manuscript did exist. In 2014, after weeks in the archives at Yale Sterling Library, I found it by chance in a box whose markings made no mention of what was preserved within.

With the manuscript in hand—alongside additional pieces of the puzzle, drawn from dozens of archives in the United States, France, and the United Kingdom—all of Erikson's questions about the book can now be answered. Has the original draft been preserved? Yes. Does each chapter bear Freud's signature? Yes. To answer the remaining questions—which portions of the book were written by Freud? in which language? were there disagreements between Freud and Bullitt? how does the published text differ from the original?—we must return to Bullitt and Freud's working process.

After Bullitt finished compiling his 421 pages of notes on Wilson's life in the fall of 1930, he and Freud worked on a "general" chapter, introducing the main theories of psychoanalysis. This became the first chapter of their book. In the second chapter, they applied these theories to Wilson's personality in order to illuminate its main features. Most often, Bullitt would take notes from Freud's explanations and then write drafts that Freud would read and edit after further discussion, inserting words, sentences, or short paragraphs. In one of the final drafts of the first chapter, one can see Freud's corrections: a word here and there in English and more substantial changes or additions in German.

Freud alluded to these changes in a September 1931 letter to Bullitt. "I have been able to complete my task earlier than expected," he wrote. "I have changed some things in the general part, and written down everything in German." What he wrote in German is the "unknown" manuscript Roazen discovered—Freud translated the chapter into

German after it had been completed in English.[1] Roazen and Solms both suggested that the manuscript was Freud's doing alone, Roazen noting that it reminded him of one of the essays in Freud's 1932 *New Introductory Lectures on Psychoanalysis*. Solms wrote that the text was "confidently attributable to Freud" and published it under Freud's name only.[2] Yet the work was coauthored by Bullitt and Freud. Freud translated the text himself to ensure the accuracy of the manuscript in his own language. He also thoroughly revised the English version of chapter 2, though he did not translate it. He read the whole manuscript and suggested a number of changes, inserting brief psychoanalytic interpretations of biographical details about Wilson. Otherwise, he found the chapters "executed in an excellent fashion" giving "the strong impression as if . . . correct in all regards. Except for the comment that certain analytical formulas are being used too often, and my aversion to a paragraph . . . whose statements appear too 'sweeping' for me, I have nothing to object."[3]

When Bullitt joined Freud in Vienna in November 1931, he discovered Freud's handwritten text, composed in gothic German. Bullitt had it transcribed and typed in modern German; he then read the modern German version, compared it to the English version, and discovered that a paragraph had been forgotten. He restored the paragraph while also revising, adding, and deleting a few words here and there.[4] Freud, too, had tweaked the text during translation, changing a few words in the process in order to maintain the sense of the original in its new language, as a good translation often will. For instance, he did not translate literally an English metaphor that evoked the significant difference in human experiences of libido. The English version Freud approved says, "The libido of some may be compared to the electrical energy produced by the huge dynamo of a central power station, while the libido of others may resemble the feeble current generated by the magneto of an automobile."[5] In Freud's German translation, this language would become, "in some the reservoir on a mountain is a large lake, in others a small pool."[6] Freud considered the German version of the general chapter ready for publication.

Freud contemplated translating the "whole text into German" but told Bullitt he did not have time. Freud suggested that they engage a translator so that by the end of the year the whole manuscript would be ready, in German. They never did it.[7] Bullitt worked for a few months to complete the book in English. Both he and Freud read the next draft, introduced another round of slight revisions, and then approved a final version.[8] Then came April 29, 1932, when Bullitt informed Colonel House that the book was finished—that "it could be published if both F. & I were to die tonight," though he also wished to revisit it in six months' time.[9] In May Bullitt retyped the manuscript, he and Freud signed it at the end of each chapter, and it was ready to be published.[10] However, this text would not see the light of day. By the time of publication in 1966, Bullitt had introduced around 300 cuts and changes across the original 389-page manuscript.

How and why does the published text differ from the original? To answer this, we need to reflect on the changing status of the signed manuscript from both Freud's and Bullitt's perspectives. At the beginning, Freud did not think of himself as coauthor. In a December 1930 letter to a friend, the novelist Arnold Zweig, he claimed he knew too little about the human drive for power, for he had lived his life as a theorist. "I am . . . writing an introduction for something someone is doing," he wrote to Zweig, admitting that the subject was "political."[11] Freud wrote his introduction only when the book was nearly finished, and in early versions, he described the book as "the William C. Bullitt psychological portrait of Thomas Woodrow Wilson." It was Bullitt who changed "the William C. Bullitt" to "this," but Freud approved the edit.[12] Additional draft language from Freud, struck or altered in the final 1932 manuscript, suggests hesitation about claiming authorship. "From the analytical perspective," he wrote, "the groundwork and most of the conclusions are his, but I added so many corrections and supplements that I can claim responsibility for the result as well."[13] Finally, the sentence reading, "For the analytic part we are both equally responsible; it has been written by us working together" was crossed out in some versions but was approved by Freud in the final version.[14]

Bullitt's archive includes a contract signed with Freud on January 20, 1932, confirming their shared ownership of the book.[15] After signing, Freud became impatient to publish. In a letter to his disciple Abraham Brill, dated the 31st, he indicated that the book would be released in 1933.[16] By this point, Freud had fully embraced the manuscript as his own. On November 20, 1932, he wrote to a friend, "On the

1st of December, I am expecting my collaborator after the elections in the U.S.A. and will be hearing from him when the Wilson-book can be sent to the public." But then came a pause. A year later, on December 7, 1933, he wrote in frustration to Marie Bonaparte: "From Bullitt, no direct news. *Our* book will never see the light of the day."[17] In 1934 Freud was contacted by a researcher collecting opinions on Wilson from scholars, diplomats, civil servants, and politicians and explained that he had "written an estimate of Wilson which is anything but favorable but was not able to publish it because of a special personal complication." Freud added that he was "now safekeeping [the manuscript] with the possibility in mind that it may emerge from my literary estate."[18]

From the end of 1932, both Freud and Bullitt stuck to the same explanation for the book's delayed publication: it could not appear in print while Bullitt was working in politics and government. This is what Bullitt told Anna Freud in 1939, after her father died, when she asked him for a copy of the piece Freud "wrote as an addition to a MS of yours." Bullitt responded right away that he not only had Freud's introduction "but also the entire fat volume that your father and I worked on together . . . We worked over all the chapters of the book so many times together, and your father wrote so many portions of each of them, that in the end we both signed each chapter." But, for the moment, that coauthored work could not be made public. He hoped that as soon he "escape[d] from public life it may be possible to publish the entire work."[19]

In 1946, after Bullitt was no longer in government, Carmel Offie suggested publishing the book.[20] But Bullitt's cousin, Dr. Orville Horwitz, apparently expressed "grave doubts." Bullitt's daughter Anne, after reading it, is said to have "taken violent exception to it and had stated to her father that it should not be published and all in all expressed great displeasure that her father's name should be connected with it." Their reservations reflected the changed context of the time. In the 1920s, Wilson had been widely seen as a disappointment. But by the mid-1930s, his popularity surged in the wider public and in intellectual discourse. Amid Hitler's rapid rise and aggressive destabilization of Europe, the League of Nations came to be seen as the panacea that could have prevented another war that, at this stage, seemed inevitable. In 1940 Ray Stannard Baker won the Pulitzer Prize for the final two volumes of his Wilson biography, *War Leader* and *Armistice.* That year also saw the New York premiere of the stage play *In Time to Come.* Written by Howard Koch and John Huston and directed by Otto Preminger, the play chronicled its hero Woodrow Wilson's involvement in the League of Nations.[21] Wilson's birthplace was declared a national memorial in May 1941, with Roosevelt himself playing an instrumental role in securing the designation.[22] When Churchill addressed Congress just after the attack on Pearl Harbor, he asserted that "if we had kept together after the last war"—that is, if the United States had ratified the Treaty of Versailles—"this renewal of the curse need never have fallen upon us."[23] Then the 1944 film *Wilson,* which shows the former president striving for justice and the League of Nations against recalcitrant senators, won multiple Oscars.[24]

Amid adulation of Wilson, Bullitt needed a new reason to explain the lack of publication: the book could not see daylight while Mrs. Wilson was still alive. Bullitt probably felt uneasy that he had played a role in Wilson's collapse and the cost it imposed on his wife Edith. The diplomat William Castle, a friend of Edith's, told Bullitt that, according to her, "'Bullitt's treachery' was one of the most potent causes of her husband's breakdown."[25] Grayson had told Bullitt that his testimony before the Senate had "no effect whatever in producing Wilson's breakdown" and that the president "never mentioned it."[26] But there was space enough for guilt.

In 1953 Bullitt wrote a will giving his daughter the right to publish the manuscript after his and Edith Wilson's deaths, but only with the inclusion of the changes "made in the manuscript in the course of two conversations when [Freud] was a refugee in London."[27] After Edith Wilson died, this became the official story of the original manuscript—that Freud made some personal additions to the text after they had signed it, but after Bullitt visited twice in 1939, Freud agreed to restore the original. "I was delighted when he admitted that the additions he had made at the last minute were unwise," Bullitt recorded.[28] Yet, in truth, there were no such additions. Orville Bullitt had read the 1932 manuscript, with each chapter signed by Freud and Bullitt. Around 1950, the manuscript was in his possession once more and he "perused it again," finding "no new editing had been performed during the intervening years."[29] Freud had not added anything to the original manuscript, and Bullitt did not have his secretary type a new version of the manuscript after paying a final visit to Freud in London in August 1939, mere weeks before his death.[30]

The archival evidence shows that Bullitt brought the original manuscript to the United States in 1939 and gave it to his brother Orville in November 1941. A note included with the manuscript read, "This book on Woodrow Wilson by Freud and myself is positively *not* to be published in its present form."[31] For more than ten years, it remained in Orville Bullitt's possession until he returned it to his brother. In 1953 Bullitt made the first important revision to the manuscript, in his cousin Orville Horwitz's office.[32] On November 1, 1956, Bullitt wrote, "This manuscript, so far as I am concerned, is in its final form and may be published at any time by my daughter Anne Moen Bullitt to whom it belongs."[33] Bullitt revised the manuscript again in 1962 when he was thinking about publishing it, writing to Anne, "I am about at the end of corrections."[34] When Bullitt finally decided to publish the revised text in 1964, those who both have seen the original signed manuscript and noticed the changes were either dead—Freud, of course, but also Ernest Jones—or were members of Bullitt's family, namely his daughter Anne and his cousin Orville, who had advised him to amend the original.

What did Bullitt change in the manuscript? First, he removed a long passage on Wilson's handling of the Mexican revolution, probably because he thought it would not interest American readers fifty years after the events in question. He also made some significant changes to the psychological terminology. At many points in the original manuscript, Freud and Bullitt had used "instinct" to translate the term "trieb," as in Strachey's *Standard Edition* of Freud's work. But, as Bullitt knew, this translation had been challenged and criticized by some psychoanalysts, including the influential writer Otto Fenichel.[35] Freud himself drew a stark distinction between trieb and *instinkt*. The latter, in Freud's usage, is hereditarian and intrinsic to the animal organism. Trieb is the human sexual drive. It has a physical and heritable dimension but is essentially imaginative and therefore in its very nature open to variation in activity and object.[36] In the original manuscript, Freud and Bullitt wrote, "We believe that the sexual instinct expresses itself in all the manifestations which men describe by that word of many meanings: love. It embraces nearly the same field as Plato's Eros." For various reasons, they added that it seemed desirable in the early days of psychoanalysis to employ "sexual instinct" rather than "Eros." Bullitt decided to replace this original explanation with: "We begin with the axiom that in the psychic life of man, from birth, a force is active which we call libido, and define as the energy of the Eros."[37] In the rest of the manuscript, Bullitt frequently replaced "sexual instinct" with "Eros." And in many instances, Bullitt added the word "unconscious" to qualify Wilson's identification with Christ.[38]

Bullitt also removed references to psychoanalytic concepts he found objectionable, including some about which he had argued with Freud. For instance, Bullitt deleted all mentions of the castration complex, most notably three pages in the introductory chapter.[39] Bullitt also suppressed every mention of masturbation. Later, in his second set of 1962 corrections, he even removed his own thoughtful interpretation of Wilson's letter informing his father that he "had a mind." Bullitt preserved Wilson's identification with Gladstone, but gone was the insightful observation that both Wilson's father and Gladstone were ministers, allowing Wilson, by identifying with the latter, to obey his father while at the same time escaping his father's domination by becoming "prime minister" of his country instead of minister of a church.

But the most important features Bullitt deleted were ones that he and Freud had never disagreed about, including even those they knew would be most controversial.

Homosexuality and Christianity

While working with Freud in fall 1930, Bullitt would return to his hotel in the evenings and jot down notes that captured some of their conversations. On November 1 Bullitt recorded the following dialogue, opening with Freud:

> "You and I know that Wilson was a passive homosexual but we won't dare say it."
>
> I said: "Certainly we'll say it but subtly."
>
> Freud answered: "That's the equivalent of not saying it at all."[40]

Bullitt agreed with Freud. In his 1927 play on Wilson, he had created a role for a young secretary to the president, who is considering going to war in the summer of 1918:

"I'll have to enlist, Sir."

"Oh no, Tommy," responds Wilson, "I can't let you go. I need you."

"I have to go. If I didn't I'd never respect myself again. You've made us all see it's a kind of crusade."

"Yes. It's a crusade. But you, Tommy; well, I just don't want you to go. I need you."

"You've got Charley, Sir, and there are thousands of old men, stenographers who—

"But I want you, yourself. You help me, Tommy, in a way none of the others do."

"How, sir?"

Wilson (smiling very deeply): "Well, perhaps you're a sort of a son to me: the son I never had."[41]

Bullitt was alluding to the real story of Charles Swem, the stenographer hired by Wilson during his 1912 presidential campaign who soon entered his close circle. The scene described by Bullitt is reported by Swem in his unpublished memoirs. The July 1918 victory in the Battle of Chateau-Thierry had inflamed American patriotism, Swem's included. But when he told Wilson of his wish to join an aviation camp and take part in the battles to come, the president replied,

Look at it from this angle. This is a big war, and we are playing a leading part in it—the leading part of all matters, on counsel and decision. Whatever happens on land and sea seems to be submitted first to us for decision and, by the nature of the Constitution that means it is up to me. Everything which has a tangle in it is given to the President of the United States to unravel. If you go, at the least, it will be an inconvenience to me and, in the circumstances, I think I should be spared that inconvenience. Furthermore, I think you are more valuable here than you would be anywhere in the field—but you know my feelings and I leave the choice with you.[42]

Freud probably did not find this story sufficiently relevant, and it did not make it into the 1932 manuscript. Other material suggestive of Wilson's homosexuality did, however. In his interview with Bullitt, Dudley Malone reported having "slept in the same bed with [Wilson] on speaking trips." Malone hastened to add that "there was never a homosexual move on his part—no hugging, kissing, or caressing. He would occasionally take my arm but always with a strong masculine grip. A few times he put his arm over my shoulders."[43] But one day Wilson told him, "When I feel badly, sour, and gloomy and everything seems wrong, then I know that my mother's character is uppermost in me. But when life seems gay and fine and splendid then I know the part of my father which is in me is in the ascendance."[44] To one possessing a shrewd psychoanalytic sensibility, the equation of happiness—"when life seems gay and fine"—with the father's "ascendance" bears unmistakable meaning. Freud and Bullitt introduced this quotation "as somewhat illuminative" of Wilson's "mother identification" and believed that, through it, "a portion of his passivity to his father found outlet." They also mentioned that Wilson was "so fond" of a particular "handsome young blond man"—Malone—that "they shared a bed while on a speaking tour."[45] Bullitt excised this and related material from the published version.[46]

Another clue concerning homosexuality was Wilson's "ideal of purity." Wilson often spoke of his own intensity, restrained only by an ideal of purity. "Such [pure] men do not exist," Freud and Bullitt argued, for Wilson's ideal could never have been strong enough to restrain the direct expression of sexual desire, if his libido was powerful. Instead, Freud and Bullitt contended, the ideal of purity is usually "a screen behind which hide two forces: the castration fear (which makes a man impotent with women) and homosexual desire for men. By maintaining his 'ideal of purity' he is able to avoid facing the forces which are behind the screen."[47]

Perhaps most important was Wilson's recurrent overreaction to intimate friends such as Hibben and then House, who, simply by disagreeing with him, provoked his obsessive and inextinguishable hatred. At Princeton, the English professor Henry Van Dyke disagreed with Wilson's residential-colleges project more vociferously than did Hibben; it was Van Dyke who introduced the faculty motion against his plan, and then he "ran around the country saying everything under the sun against Wilson."[48] But Wilson harbored no resentment against Van Dyke, who later recalled that "this disagreement and opposition on his part never produced a personal break."[49] Van Dyke even served as Wilson's ambassador to the Netherlands in the key years of 1914–1917.[50] Yet Hibben bore the brunt of Wilson's fury: his persecution mania arose only in relation to a person most intensely loved. Freud saw a classic defense mechanism against passive—that is, unconscious—homosexual attachment.[51]

But would Freud and Bullitt have the guts to write that Wilson was a passive homosexual—and then publish it? Bullitt did not hesitate. Following his conversation with Freud in the last weeks of 1930, he included this conclusion eleven times throughout the manuscript.[52] Passive homosexuality first appears in chapter 1 as a general concept, then in chapter 3 it is explored as a feature of Wilson's personality. "Wilson, being a human being, had, like every other human being, a homosexual component in his nature," Freud and Bullitt wrote. "His pleasure in passivity to his father was indeed so much more intense than his other youthful emotions that we are compelled to note that he was predominantly a passive homosexual." As far as Freud and Bullitt were aware, Wilson "never gave overt expression to this element in his nature; but it played a vital role in his career, creating dominant sublimations and identifications, inhibiting his activity in his youth and, by a reaction formation, spoiling the latter years of his life."[53] Bullitt and Freud believed Wilson's femininity was stronger than his masculinity, but he could "easily find his way to normal heterosexual life" because "he was fortunate in the accidents of his childhood, especially in the love of his sisters and cousins, and as a result of this good luck he achieved normal heterosexual expression."[54]

For Freud, the assessment of passive homosexuality was no mark against Wilson. Freud observed a homosexual component in himself as well. In his case, acknowledgment and analysis enabled an overcoming of homosexuality that fostered greater independence.[55] Yet, to be actively and overtly homosexual was also not a concern. As he wrote to a woman who had corresponded with him about her son:

> I gather from your letter that your son is a homosexual. I am most impressed by the fact that you do not mention this term yourself in

> your information about him. May I question you, why do you avoid it? Homosexuality is assuredly no advantage, but it is nothing to be ashamed of, no vice, no degradation, it cannot be classified as an illness; we consider it to be a variation of the sexual function produced by certain arrest of sexual development. Many highly respectable individuals of ancient and modern times have been homosexuals, several of the greatest among them (Plato, Michelangelo, Leonardo da Vinci, etc.). It is a great injustice to persecute homosexuality as a crime, and cruelty too.

If her son was "unhappy, neurotic, torn by conflicts, inhibited in his social life," Freud continued, psychoanalysis "may bring him harmony, peace of mind, full efficiency, whether he remains a homosexual or gets changed."[56]

Likewise Freud and Bullitt did not suggest that Wilson was in any way at fault for being who he was. Rather, they aimed to suggest that, had he recognized this dimension of his inner life, he might have been able to sublimate it and thereby avoid the damage he inflicted on himself and the world by repressing it. For Bullitt and Freud, the presence and sublimation of homosexuality was in fact essential to humanity: "It is homosexuality, not indeed in its manifest form but in its sublimations, which assures the continuance of human society and will perhaps some day unite in a great brotherhood all the races of man."[57]

All of this was removed from the published book. Why would Bullitt cut these interpretations, which he had never forsworn? It is unlikely that in 1966, after Edith Wilson's death and with his own looming, Bullitt would have decided that analyzing Wilson's homosexuality was too controversial or somehow beyond the pale. No, the answer probably lies elsewhere. The problem was not suggesting that Wilson was a passive homosexual but that his homosexuality was associated with Christ and Christianity. As Bullitt wrote in 1927, introducing his play on the tragedy of Wilson:

> He had in his personality a violent conflict. He wished at the same time to be the supreme male, all powerful, all commanding, all inflicting, and the complete female, all loving, all submissive, all suffering. Only one individual in history has successfully resolved that conflict. Jesus Christ by being all submissive became all powerful:

God himself. But no miracle aided poor Mr. Wilson . . . He could not face his cross. He signed the Treaty of Versailles.[58]

Was this idea—of absolute submission leading to divinity—Bullitt's creation or was it inspired by Freud during the months when Bullitt lay on his couch at the end of 1926? It is impossible to say. What we do know is that the original manuscript contains language similar to that above:

> Identification with Christ accomplishes, (as if by a miracle), [*sic*] the feat of reconciling with each other two exceptionally powerful and absolutely hostile desires, while at the same time satisfying them both. The two wishes are: On the one hand to be entirely passive and submissive to the father, utterly feminine; on the other hand, to be as completely masculine, almighty and all commanding as the father himself. Christ was able by humbly submitting to the will of His Father God, to become God himself: By giving Himself up to the most complete femininity, He reached the goal of masculinity. Christ, thus, is the complete reconciliation of masculinity and femininity. Belief in his divinity includes the belief that one may by external passivity make real the most daring dreams of activity; by submitting utterly to the father one may overcome him and become God. It is, therefore, easy to understand any identification with Christ should be so frequently employed by men to settle the major problem of the Oedipus Complex, the relationship to the father.

When, like Wilson, "the believer identifies himself with Jesus Christ, he becomes convinced that by behaving with complete passivity towards his father, . . . he will overcome, by passivity he will conquer the world."[59] But the individual who identifies himself with Jesus Christ is not Jesus Christ. "The miracle by which Christ's passivity led to achievements of the dreams of activity is unlikely to follow for a mere mortal." Submission does not ordinarily lead to triumph.[60] Such was the case for Wilson.

This interpretation of Christianity, postulating a link between identification with Christ and bisexuality while also permitting sublimation of the homosexual dimension of every human being, was both original and revolutionary. It was not anti-Christian—to the contrary.

The quiet identification of the normal human with a God of peace and love was, for the fate of humanity, an ideal sublimation. It also demonstrated the deep value of Christianity. "So satisfactory is this method of reconciling the conflicting masculinity and femininity of the fundamentally bisexual human being that it assures a long life for the Christian religion," Freud and Bullitt wrote. "Men will not soon give up a belief which allows them to escape from the most difficult conflict they have to face. They will continue to employ identification with Christ for many years to come."[61] In addition, and perhaps without noticing, Bullitt and Freud contributed to theorizing the structure of religious or ideological fanaticism. Their analysis suggests that where absolute submission to a god or leader results in radicalism and destructiveness, this too may be a sublimation of passive homosexuality.

But Bullitt was afraid to put forward this interpretation of submission to God and of Christianity's power. He had been afraid from the very beginning of the project. The original plan had been merely to publish a piece on Wilson, signed by Freud, in a book of Bullitt's on the subject of diplomacy. When, in May 1930, Freud told Bullitt he could not write on Wilson without him, Bullitt was happy and proud; he couldn't refuse. He probably had some of the earliest and most important ideas that found their way into the work. But Bullitt soon grew fearful of his own psychological inventiveness—he worried that the backlash sure to greet his interpretations would harm his career and his reputation. Thus he kept the project a secret. When he started working with Freud, he asked his family to keep quiet about it. Freud's entourage knew all this very well. As Anna Freud wrote to Erikson in 1966, "This occupation had to be treated with the utmost discretion, since Bullitt was engaged in political life still" and "his career might be harmed if the fact became known."[62] When Freud told Bullitt, "You and I know that Wilson was a passive homosexual but we won't dare say it," it was a way to challenge Bullitt—his guts, his courage.

Bullitt would surely have realized that the public was not always open to or knowledgeable about matters of psychology and psychoanalysis. To derive an interpretation of Christianity from a psychoanalysis concluding that Wilson was a passive homosexual would have attracted considerable dispute, if not alarm. And one wonders if Bullitt did not experience a certain inner conflict of his own, given how Christianity lent coherence to his life. In Bullitt's unpublished memoirs, he wrote of his faith in God, "The happiness of our home was based on Christian faith. I cannot remember a time when I did not say my prayers at my mother's knees. I have felt always the imminence of God, and I am profoundly grateful to my parents for giving me a faith which has enabled me to face hard experience."[63] Unlike Wilson, who feared that fighting for Christ's doctrines of beneficence and generosity might give aid to Communists, Bullitt fought for Christian doctrine without reservation. For instance, after his 1919 Senate testimony, he indicated that he was willing to sacrifice his career if doing so could shift the US stance toward Russia and lead Americans to support the people struggling there through famine.[64] The next year Bullitt backed Keynes's proposals for revising the Treaty of Versailles, which Bullitt saw as "moderate, practical and Christian."[65]

In 1943, after Welles's resignation, Roosevelt received Bullitt at the White House and told him a story in which he appointed himself St. Peter. "Two men came up. The first was Sumner Welles—and after chiding him for getting drunk, Roosevelt let him into heaven. The second was Bullitt. After paying due tribute to what Bullitt had done, St. Peter accused him of having destroyed a fellow human being and dispatched him to hell."[66] But Bullitt was probably not impressed by Roosevelt's words and the prediction they implied. Bullitt felt he was fighting for the lives of millions of Eastern European Christians about to fall under the domination of Stalin thanks to Roosevelt's willingness to appease him, a position encouraged by Welles. Bullitt had faced off with Wilson to save millions of Russians from famine, and he would take down Welles—and ruin his own career by alienating Roosevelt—in hopes of protecting millions more.

The experience of Stalin's dictatorship during his ambassadorship in Moscow left Bullitt that much more committed to defending not only Christians but Christianity itself. He came to see the Church as the only institution that could stand up to totalitarian ideologies, whether Communism or Nazism. When, on September 28, 1939, Bullitt made the visionary prediction that "Hitler had already lost the war completely" and that "the Bolshies will gradually eat like a cancer to Berlin," he wondered how "Stalin Khan" could be defeated. Bullitt's answer: "God only knows. My own conviction is that you will have left in the world enough of the spirit that is represented by Jeanne d'Arc to bring the human race through. Hitler and Stalin are twin representatives of Satanism, and I do not believe that they will prevail against the cohorts of the Lord."[67] He would assert in 1949, "To combat world Communism, only one force is great enough: the belief that salvation flows from the grace of God and the love of our Lord Jesus Christ and the ever-living presence of the Holy Spirit. If we can find the way to make that belief the controlling power in our lives, we shall act effectively to defeat the attack of the totalitarian state against man-kind."[68]

By the end of WWII, Bullitt had abandoned the view that rationality and free-thinking liberalism could save humanity. He now believed that the intensity of the religious bond was a stronger dike against totalitarianism.[69] He was returning to what Tocqueville thought of as America's founding creed. "Although religion in the United States never intervenes in government, it must be considered as the first of America's political institutions," Tocqueville wrote, "for even if religion does not give their taste for liberty, it does notably facilitate their use of that liberty."[70]

What then, of Freud? When he told Bullitt, "You and I know that Wilson was a passive homosexual but *we* won't dare say it," was Freud only goading Bullitt, or did he also lack the will to make an audacious claim about Christianity? Freud had shied away from analyzing Christianity. Unlike Bullitt, Freud had not been raised in religion.[71] Freud's father would simply say, "Religion means right thinking and right doing."[72] Then, too, as a Jew in Austria, Freud faced harsh scrutiny. And what is more, officials were cracking down on psychoanalytic publications. On September 30, 1934, Freud shelved his Moses manuscript after the Vatican—following the recommendation of Father Wilhelm Schmidt, a German-Austrian confidant of the pope who was highly influential in Austria—ordered that psychoanalytic works no longer be published in Italy. Reflecting on the moment, Freud wrote, "It is not the proper occasion for martyrdom."[73] As for writing about Christianity, in a 1935 letter to fellow psychoanalyst Lou Andreas-Salomé, Freud observed that he could not publicly express the truth about religion in Austria "without bringing down upon us a state prohibition of analysis on the part of the ruling Catholic authority." To do so would not only make an enemy of Catholic leaders but also expose psychoanalysts to further danger. "It is only this Catholicism which protects us from Nazism," Freud wrote.[74]

Indeed, were a prominent Jewish intellectual like Freud to theorize a relationship among Christianity, homosexuality, and bisexuality, he might risk not only the lives of psychoanalysts but also Jews under Nazism. This is probably why, in 1938, Bullitt considered the manuscript to be "dangerous" if it remained in Freud's hands.[75] True, one year later, in *Moses and Monotheism*, Freud would challenge and reinterpret the posture of Christ sacrificing himself for a sinful mankind.[76] But this was a theoretical and indirect challenge, not perceived as provocative and harmful by common Christians and their churches. It could well have been concerns about offending Christians that could have led Bullitt and Freud to decide together to redact some parts of the book or to postpone its publication.

But after the war, when the danger was gone, why not publish the whole manuscript? Why the continued torment? In the context of the Cold War, publishing the book might not have been destructive to Jews, but it could have been perceived as providing succor to Communists. Bullitt became highly protective of the manuscript, lest it become a Communist weapon against Christianity. In 1956, responding to Ernest Jones's interest in obtaining the manuscript, Bullitt told his cousin Orville Horwitz, "I'll tear the demon thing up before I give it away." Horwitz replied that Bullitt had no right to destroy the book, for it belonged to posterity: "Something written by Sigmund Freud should not be the property of one person. It would be as if one person owned the 'Mona Lisa.'" Bullitt responded, "No, it belongs to me."[77]

Knowledge could be sacrificed to avoid harming Christianity in its resistance to atheistic Communism—Bullitt effectively said as much through his cuts to the manuscript for publication. Consider that the original, Freud-and-Bullitt-signed conclusion ends with the phrase, "Facts are more useful than faiths. Truth is a better ally than any deity." Reflecting their collaboration, the first sentence was added by Bullitt, the last by Freud.[78] But Bullitt later cut these lines and the paragraph of which they were a part, having decided that—to protect religion and serve the fight against Communism—faith was, at least for the time being, more useful than facts.

Yet Bullitt did not destroy the original manuscript or the sources that would one day permit the reconstruction of its existence and the story of how it came to be. The truth could not arrive in 1966—that would have been premature. The battle between Christianity and Communism was still being waged. But Bullitt knew that one day the original manuscript he signed with Freud would be discovered and revealed. One day the public would be able to read and comment on a work that belongs to history. And now that day has come.

19

Wilson in Retrospect

WHEN WILSON PRESENTED the Treaty of Versailles to the Senate on July 10, 1919, he knew what was at stake. He needed support from two-thirds of the senators to ratify the treaty and thereby secure his legacy and his contribution to humanity: the League of Nations. "Dare we reject it and break the heart of the world?" Wilson asked.[1]

He was satisfied with the treaty. Contrary to what many said at the time, he did not equivocate on the provisions that mattered to him. Even if idealists like Bullitt did not like the treaty because it did not declare war illegal or entirely fulfill the promise of self-determination, Wilson thought it embodied his vision. What he sought was less a league that would enforce peace than one that would ensure it through moral appeals and nonmilitary coercion.[2] The treaty created just such an institution, equipped not with law enforcement capacity but with mechanisms for the prevention of war through dialogue, mediation, and a novel form of economic sanctions, which Wilson believed "were more tremendous than war."[3]

Before the Senate that day in July 1919, Wilson could have defended the treaty rhetorically, without making concessions on substance. He could, with no sacrifice of honesty, have told his leading Republican opponents that he had taken into account their desire to restrict security guarantees to the victorious Allies. Many Republican leaders—including Henry Cabot Lodge, Elihu Root, and Philander Knox—alongside a majority of the irreconcilables favored maintaining the wartime coalition during the postwar years.[4] All understood France and Britain as America's shield against further German aggression. Many Republicans also thought that if Germany had won, the United States would have faced an aggressive new empire on the Atlantic, forcing the country to spend heavily on armaments to defend the Western Hemisphere. These politicians were ready to involve the United States in the Allies' security guarantees and to approve the Treaty of

Guarantee ensuring France's security.[5] What they did not want was a universal League of Nations that would permanently involve the United States everywhere in the world.[6]

Wilson could have told Senate Republicans that the treaty was theirs as much as his, that it incorporated their ideas: the guarantee of the Monroe Doctrine, the right to leave the league, the pact with France. Regarding the pact, Wilson publicly acknowledged that it was the sole US collective-security commitment. "We will not wait for the concerted action of other countries under the League of Nations, but will come immediately to France's assistance if Germany makes any unprovoked movement of military aggression against her," he said at one point.[7]

But Wilson did not speak those words to the senators. He did not allay their fears by explaining—truthfully—that the terms of the Versailles Treaty gave the United States veto power in the League of Nations Council, leaving Congress to assert its constitutional prerogatives unencumbered. He also postponed presentation of the Treaty of Guarantee to July 29. Instead, when he addressed the Senate on the 19th, he entrenched himself in religious vocabulary. The old system of international relations was satanic and needed to be defeated: "The monster that has resorted to arms must be put in chains that could not be broken," he averred. And in bringing to the world a new and better covenant, he was the vessel of divine will: "The stage is set, the destiny is disclosed. It has come about by no plan of our conceiving, but by the hand of God who has led us into this way. We cannot turn back."[8]

Why, when he could have won over opponents with firm legal facts, did Wilson preach? "Only impaired political judgment could explain this misstep," biographer John M. Cooper Jr. argued.[9] I believe Wilson simply could not speak the right message. To do so risked the disapproval of his superego and resulting personal collapse because it would have meant acceding to an imperfection of which his father Joseph would not have approved. Wilson did not have free choice as to the words he used; his father was always hovering nearby. On occasion, this was literally true. At one point, Wilson confided to Grayson that the most difficult speech of his career came during a Brooklyn address "when he happened to see, sitting on the back seat of the room, a little crouched down as though he did not wish to have his presence known, his father. Mr. Wilson said that he felt exactly like a boy again, and as if he would have to answer to his father afterwards for what he said."[10]

As Grayson told Bullitt, Wilson "worshipped his father as I have never seen any man worship any other." When he "got on his knees each night to pray to God, he felt sure that if his father approved of what he had done that day, everything would be all right with God."[11] Wilson tried to never do or say anything that his father would disagree with, and, in Wilson's mind, that included giving an inch on the treaty, even rhetorically.

From this worshipful behavior, Freud and Bullitt deduced that Wilson's love for his father took the form of total submission. At the same time, Wilson was also extremely competitive with him. That competitive spirit led him from the presidency of Princeton and to the White House. But Wilson would never claim to have attained superiority over his father, nor did he tolerate suggestions to that effect. On the night of his arrival in Paris in December 1918, Grayson said something that made Wilson believe "I thought he was a greater man than his father. He caught me up at once and said: 'I cannot compare to my father. I operate on a larger stage that is all. I am not the equal of my father in any way at all.'"[12]

In detailing Wilson's personality, Freud and Bullitt missed a key detail that Alex and Juliette George discovered in Ray Baker's archives. Joseph Wilson was not only a strong and imposing father, he was also a humiliating one.[13] Baker had interviewed Jessie Bones Brower, Woodrow Wilson's cousin, who recalled a scene from their childhood when "the family was assembled at a wedding breakfast. Tommy arrived at the table late. His father apologized on behalf of his son and explained that Tommy had been so greatly excited at the discovery of another hair in his mustache that morning that it had taken him longer to wash and dress. I remember very distinctly the painful flush that came over the boy's face."[14] Another cousin, Helen Woodrow Bones, told Baker, "Uncle Joseph was a cruel tease, with a caustic wit, and a sharp tongue, and I remember hearing my family tell indignantly of how Cousin Woodrow suffered under his teasing." She said the same thing to Arthur Walworth, another Wilson biographer, describing Joseph Wilson as a "cruel tease, whom only a man such as Woodrow Wilson could have stood."[15] In a letter she used firmer language, calling

Joseph Wilson "a horrid, selfish old man" and declaring, "I resented . . . his higher place in Woodrow's estimation than was given Auntie, Woodrow's mother."[16]

Stockton Axson, the younger brother of Wilson's first wife, knew well the effect Joseph Wilson had on his son. Axson met the future president in 1884 and remained his close friend for the rest of his life; "Brother Woodrow" was both a mentor and a confidant.[17] In his memoirs, Axson described Joseph Wilson as a "very genial but also ruthless sort of man with a distinct streak of perversity in him." He had "a sporadic tendency to treat at times some of those near to him with that aloofness, which, without consciousness on his part, almost amounted to cruelty."[18] On perhaps the only occasion when Wilson himself acknowledged his father's faults, he told Axson that Joseph's teasing "did sometimes hurt."[19]

The adult Wilson had repressed the truth of who his father had been, reinventing him as a figure worthy of not just respect but perpetual obedience. Freud had a knack for uncovering and interpreting such self-deception. Abram Kardiner, one of Freud's disciples, documented his own similar case. Kardiner had a dream that Freud understood as a wish to not examine Kardiner's relationship with his father—specifically, Kardiner did not want to see Freud mar the good image he had of the man who had raised him. "You evidently were terrified of him in your early childhood," Freud told Kardiner. However, after Kardiner's mother died, his father remarried, and his character changed for the better. Freud told Kardiner that it was this revised sense of his father that Kardiner wished to keep "and thereby to forget the angry father of your earliest years. But you remain submissive and obedient to him in order not to arouse the sleeping dragon, the angry father."[20] Wilson, too, remained "submissive and obedient" for fear of waking the sleeping dragon. No matter that he was operating at higher and higher levels of public importance: Wilson ceaselessly sought to protect himself by speaking in ways that would meet his father's standard of linguistic perfection.[21]

Wilson's perennial effort to tailor his language for paternal approval explains his sense that he was a slow thinker, as when he wrote to House, "Every day I am confirmed in the judgment that my mind is a one-track road and can run only one train of thought at a time!"[22]

Others did not necessary see it this way. Senator Hiram Johnson, Wilson's staunch opponent in the treaty fight, characterized the president as "alert and fairly quick thinking."[23] House agreed that the president could sometimes get stuck on an idea, but he also told Seymour that "Wilson was the quickest man that he had ever known or worked with at catching a point."[24] So why did Wilson think differently of himself? Because before speaking publicly, the words he used had first to be validated in his mind through a process that took him time. Wilson would not talk without first clearing his words with a divine paternal superego.

This was a matter of survival. To stick to his selected words was a way of being able to live with his father, of keeping his father with him—keeping a link alive. In the process of revising the general chapter, Freud wrote, "Wilson's libido found outlet through attachment to his father."[25] This is the appropriate phrasing. Wilson was still attached to his father—attached by love and fear and by the impossibility of living without him. He maintained that connection through the language he used until the end.

Joseph's cruelty helps us understand, as I believe Freud and Bullitt did not, why Wilson suddenly and recurrently broke with people for whom he had previously felt great respect or even love. Freud and Bullitt's thesis—as well as that of Alexander and Juliette George—was that the feeling of betrayal he harbored toward Hibben and House, and his stubbornness toward Lodge, arose in reaction to disagreements he could not bear to face. I do not share this view; Wilson could endure disagreements. What he could not tolerate was public humiliation. If one takes successively the cases of Hibben, House, and Lodge, a pattern emerges. Wilson transformed respected figures and dear friends into sudden, unforgivable enemies when they submitted him to public correction that he perceived as humiliation—the sort of humiliation to which his father subjected him.

The most painful and traumatizing break was with Hibben. It is difficult to overestimate the affection that Wilson once had for Hibben. In January 1907 Wilson wrote him, "It would be hard for me to tell you . . . how your thoughtfulness and love touch and delight me." Hibben's friendship gave Wilson "the feeling, just the feeling, that makes me happiest, that I was *needed,* needed for pleasure, as well as for business."[26] Wilson even promised Hibben that his opposition to the Princeton quadrangle reform would not harm their relationship. A few weeks before the matter came to a vote, the two discussed their disagreement, and Wilson assured Hibben, "A struggle is ahead of me—it may be a heartbreaking struggle—and you cannot stand with me in it; but we can see past all that to the essence of things and shall at every step know each other's love. Will not that suffice?"[27]

The cause of Wilson's change of heart toward Hibben is clear. It was not simply "a difference of opinion," as Bullitt and Freud put it.[28] It was Hibben's decision to stand publicly against Wilson, not merely voting against his plan—which, after all, passed the faculty plebiscite by a significant margin—but seconding Van Dyke's motion. This is what hurt Wilson beyond anything he had ever been through with a friend. Ellen Wilson's sister Madge seemed to understand this. She burst into tears when she heard what happened and lamented, "Oh, he *might* have let someone else second the motion."[29]

By contrast, when Dudley Malone broke with Wilson, the matter remained private, and the results were different. In July 1917, Malone confronted Wilson about the unfairness of the D.C. police imprisoning picketing suffragists. After the meeting, Wilson wrote to House of his "unmistakable sadness" in light of Malone's "tragic" attitude. "I was stricken by it as I have been by few things in my life." House reported to Malone that "the President did not sleep at all after your conversation with him."[30] But while Wilson was hurt, he continued corresponding with Malone.[31]

Then came House. It was not only that the preliminary treaty envisioned by House would not include the League of Nations. House, after all, followed the president's instructions to work on preliminary territorial arrangements, and when Wilson rejected the proposal, House obeyed the president's instructions. And the whole episode played out behind closed doors. The incident, however, came to seem a great betrayal in light of public humiliations. On the boat back to D.C. in mid-February 1919, Wilson was told a piece of gossip. Gordon Auchincloss, House's son-in-law, had said publicly, "My father-in-law is well again, so now Woody's batting average will begin to improve."[32] And during Wilson's absence from Paris, House had shared with journalists what Walworth called "not discreet remarks for the head of the government mission to make about his chief to newsmen."[33] For example, House said that Wilson was always doing things "in the hardest way," and "it slows up the preliminary work very much to have the big men here now so we are glad to have them out of the way." House was giving "such an enthusiastic and glowing account of his own prowess as a negotiator that it was very easy—especially after embellishment by Auchincloss—to transmute the statements into gossip that must have hurt when it reached the Wilsons," Walworth wrote.[34] Then, too, House trapped himself by boasting to Mrs. Wilson that he could control everything Wickham Steed wrote in the *Times*—just after Steed had written his piece praising House and diminishing Wilson.

House knew that he had overstepped. During all the years he had worked with Wilson, his influence was clearly conditioned by his absolute discretion. At the beginning of Wilson's administration, House refused a cabinet position, later saying, "Had I gone into the Cabinet I could not have lasted eight weeks." But the Paris conference thrust House into the spotlight. Basking in the attention afforded by the visible merit of his work, he created opportunities for Wilson's public humiliation and thereby contributed to his own fall from grace.

Wilson's relationship with Lodge offers yet another example of this behavioral pattern. Wilson once had the highest respect for Lodge, a fellow scholar. Lodge had written Wilson a letter of recommendation when he sought entry at Johns Hopkins and had published Wilson's first article in an academic journal.[35] Wilson quoted Lodge three times in *Congressional Government*.[36]

It was during the 1916 presidential campaign that respect was transformed into inextinguishable hatred. Lodge "created a sensation" and "brought a heavy storm" by revealing Wilson's dithering in the wake of the sinking of the *Lusitania*. Recall that Wilson sent a strong public note to the Germans, then, at the behest of Secretary of State Bryan, secretly intimated that the United States was willing to submit the issue to an international commission of inquiry. Robert Lansing, then the legal adviser to the State Department, saw the secret note before it was sent and reached out to Joe Tumulty, who convinced Wilson that the note "might cause Germany to feel that the United States was weakening and would not fight for her rights."[37] Wilson then ordered the note retracted. When Lodge brought the affair to light, Wilson could deny it on the grounds that the secret note was never sent. But privately he could neither forget nor forgive the wound Lodge had caused him. In the published version of their book, Freud and Bullitt noticed, "It was at this moment Wilson began to hate Senator Lodge with a violent hatred."[38] But they attributed this to Wilson's inability to face the truth, especially coming from a father figure like Lodge. They did not consider that Lodge, by demonstrating Wilson's indecisiveness, had caused precisely the kind of public humiliation Wilson could not bear.

Lodge understood that he had earned the president's permanent disdain. Thus, when Senator James Watson approached Lodge in fall 1919 with optimistic suggestions for passing the treaty with reservations, he could only reply ruefully that the outcome was impossible. "Suppose that the President accepts the treaty with your reservations," Watson told Lodge. "Then we are in the League, and once in, our reservations become purely fiction." Watson would never forget the smile "that betokened Lodge's full confidence in the assertion he was about to make. 'But, my dear James, you do not take into consideration the hatred that Woodrow Wilson has for me personally. Never under any set of circumstances in this world could he be induced to accept a treaty with Lodge reservations appended to it.'"[39] Lodge had already grasped how petty Wilson could be, in the wake of the *Lusitania* revelations. For example, in January 1917, Wilson declined to attend a ceremony celebrating the hundredth anniversary of St. John's Episcopal Church in Washington, D.C., because Lodge had also been invited. Wilson also demanded that none of his cabinet attend.[40] Lodge would not have been surprised that Wilson rejected his reservations in personal terms, as when Watson urged Wilson to accept the Lodge reservations, only to receive Wilson's angry rejoinder that he would "never consent to adopt any policy with which that impossible name is so prominently identified."[41]

Wilson himself felt that he was replaying with Lodge a painful and destructive situation. Speaking to his friend Mary Hulbert in September 1919, he said, "Oddly enough, I do not feel well. I feel as if all the things which I have succeeded in escaping have fallen upon me."[42] What was Wilson repeating? Through his reaction, Wilson was implicitly telling Lodge: I will never tolerate public humiliation at your hands again. But Lodge was not the true target here; unconsciously, Wilson's outburst was directed at his father—father whom he never confronted out of love, fear, or both.

During analysis, Freud would say, "A thing that has not been understood inevitably reappears; like an unlaid ghost, it cannot rest until the mystery has been solved and the spell broken."[43] Wilson had a strong wish to confront his father, but he never understood it. That wish remained unconscious. Had Wilson undergone psychoanalysis, he may have recovered the memory of his childhood humiliations and given voice to his anger at the man who inflicted them upon him. This might have helped Wilson free himself from the repetitive overreaction that tended to subvert his accomplishments at key moments in his professional and political life. With the aid of analysis, Wilson could have been freer to choose his words, speak his mind, and rationally think through his political tactics and objectives.

There was in Wilson another type of repetitive behavior. When in a position of power, at Princeton or in the White House, Wilson needed the support and affection of a dear friend to face his political and social obligations. As Baker told Bullitt, "Wilson had to have a woman at home and one much loved friend and then could be hard as steel to any man outside that circle."[44] After Wilson transformed one friend into a bitter enemy, he would seek out the love and support of another.

However, the replacements he found for House fell short of the task. Freud and Bullitt, in their signed manuscript, noted that, after Wilson's break with House, "a passionate desire to submit to a strong man may have played a great part in determining his actions. Those were the months in which he submitted to Clemenceau." The language is softened somewhat in the published text, though the meaning is similar, as Bullitt and Freud described Wilson having "submitted to the leaders of the allies."[45] Ever since the contents of the treaty were revealed, it has been conventionally understood that, after initially taking a firm stand against Lloyd George and Clemenceau, Wilson made many concessions to the French and British premiers in the first days of April 1919. Freud and Bullitt attributed these capitulations to Wilson's inability to face Clemenceau and Lloyd George, both of whom they saw as representatives of Joseph Wilson.

Many scholars have explored Wilson's sudden willingness to follow Lloyd George's and Clemenceau's lead, and some have ascribed it to Wilson's state of mind, suggesting that he was struggling after suffering a stroke on April 6. After studying the available data, the psychiatrist and author Edwin Weinstein concluded that Wilson did not have a stroke but did have a severe flu, which could have weakened him and affected his judgment.[46] But this, too, is an unsatisfying explanation. After all, Wilson's most significant concession came before he fell ill, at the request of the man at the conference who impressed him most: General Smuts.

Seduced by Smuts

In March 1919, Lloyd George suffered significant setbacks at the hands of Conservatives in the British House of Commons. Given the state of play at Westminster, he would be forced to resign unless he could secure a large German indemnity. But if the indemnity was to be calculated on the basis of material damages inflicted upon the Allies, most of the money would go to Belgium and France, whose territory had been ravaged. The British dominions—Australia, Canada, Ireland, New Zealand, South Africa—were unscathed and would get nothing, while claims on behalf of the island of Great Britain itself would be limited to merchant shipping losses and relatively minor damage sustained during air raids and raids by the German fleet on coastal towns.[47] An "arch-maximalist on reparations" since the December 1918 electoral campaign, Lloyd George reaffirmed his objective: "The British Empire must get as large an indemnity out of Germany as possible."[48] On March 23, Lloyd George explained the situation to Wilson, who urged that the prime minister fall on his sword: what mattered was not to stay in office but to do what was right. "I could not wish a more magnificent place in history," Wilson replied.[49]

But Lloyd George had discerned a vulnerability in Wilson. "He lighted with shrewd alacrity on the instrument to bring him down and win him to his own purposes," historian Antony Lentin wrote. "From his capacious bag of tricks, with an insight amounting to genius," Lloyd George "pulled out—General Smuts."[50] Wilson thought most highly of Jan Smuts, the South African soldier and statesman. Like Wilson,

Smuts aspired to a global role, beyond South Africa and the British Empire. He even contemplated, in June 1918, offering himself as chief of the US Army in Europe, which he described as "a first-class instrument of action" but "without a reliable High Command."[51] When Wilson first met Smuts in London in 1918, he immediately liked him. Wilson could identify with him. Smuts was a fellow scholar, firm Christian, and idealist—he was also a little pompous and pretentious. Smuts had made his name as an Afrikaner General Lee: the best general defeated in the Boer War. He continued as a South African Wilson, rising in politics and ultimately serving as his country's prime minister. Smuts's lofty purpose was to unify white Christian "civilization." Like Wilson, who moralized like a pastor while rejecting racial and gender equality, Smuts spoke a language of universal rights that applied in practice only to whites.

Smuts immediately adopted Wilson's vision of the League of Nations Covenant and became its coauthor. Early in the conference, Smuts proved to Lloyd George that he could sway Wilson like no other foreign negotiator when he convinced Wilson to support the British position demanding that Germany be stripped of its colonies. On January 29, 1919, Wilson penciled a message to House stating, "I could agree to this if the interpretation in practice were to come from General Smuts."[52] During the weeks that followed at the Paris conference, "numerous were the occasions when Grayson called on Smuts" with a message from Wilson "asking for his advice and suggestions."[53]

Lloyd George took note, and when he was fighting for the hefty indemnity and the political survival it would earn him back home, he called on Smuts—in the interest of the Empire and of South Africa, of course. What he wanted from Smuts was a legal opinion to the effect that the British were entitled to reparations for costs of soldiers' pensions, bereavement pay, and disbursements to families while their husbands, fathers, and sons were off to war. Though a trained lawyer, Smuts had not written legal opinions "for more than twelve years." But he agreed in the instance because, he was told, "Wilson will not listen to the English lawyer but will pay attention to what I say! It is a farcical world."[54]

The question was whether the armistice of November 1918 allowed Britain to collect reparations for damage done to civilians. The relevant line of the first draft of the armistice reads as follows: "Compensation will be made by Germany for all damage caused to the civilian population of the Allies and their property by the invasion by Germany." Edgar Abraham, a member of the UK war cabinet, noted that the word "invasion" could be interpreted as excluding his country from compensatory payments because its territory, unlike France and Belgium, had not been invaded. On Abraham's suggestion, Lloyd George proposed replacing "invasion" with "aggression." It was this language that the Allies, including Wilson, agreed to on November 4 and that Germany accepted on November 11.[55]

The change in language offered Smuts the wiggle room he needed to persuade the starstruck Wilson, who had previously been adamant in his opposition to Lloyd George's reparations positions. On March 31, 1919, Smuts easily convinced Wilson that demanding German reparations to cover British pensions and other payments to civilians conformed with the "Allied declaration of November 4th." Smuts raised the example of a shopkeeper whose store was destroyed by a German bombardment. Clearly he was entitled to compensation for his loss. But what if he then joined the army and was wounded? The cost of caring for him would be borne by the state—should not the Germans reimburse that cost? And what about the costs borne by his wife, deprived of the family breadwinner during his time in the army? Should she not be entitled to an allowance for her and their children during the entire period of their separation from husband and father?[56]

As Walworth put it, "Wilson clutched at the sanctifying support of General Smuts" and endorsed his tortuous reasoning, which would permit all UK dominions to claim a significant portion of German reparations.[57] Wilson's advisers were aghast. John Foster Dulles pointed out that including pensions and separation payments under the reparations clause would mean imposing all war costs on the vanquished enemy, thereby violating what had been Wilson's own interpretation of the armistice agreement. "We are bound in honor to decline to agree to the inclusion of war costs in the reparation demanded," Wilson had written to Lansing just a few weeks earlier.[58] But when Dulles objected, Wilson replied cheerfully that he was continually "finding new meanings" in "loose terminology" and that "he did not feel bound by considerations of logic."[59] Bernard Baruch, too, pressed for removal of the pensions and separations allowances until Wilson finally shut him down. "Don't ever speak to me about that again," the president told him.[60] Lentin concluded that Smuts had acted as "the devil's advocate in abetting Lloyd George's ploy to seduce Wilson from his integrity."[61] As biographer Arthur Link put it, accepting the Smuts memorandum was Wilson's "most important concession at the conference."[62]

It was after surrendering to Smuts on reparations that Wilson suffered his collapse. Ike Hoover, his loyal chief usher, wrote that "when he got on his feet again" after his flu "he was a different man." Wilson already had "his peculiar ideas," but now they became more pronounced.[63] He was gripped by paranoia and came to suspect that every French employee at his Paris residence was a spy for their government. Some evidence suggests that House gave him the idea, but even if it had not originated with Wilson, nothing could disabuse him of it. He insisted that all of the two-dozen or so French employees understood English, even as in fact only one did.[64] About this time Wilson also acquired the peculiar notion that he was personally responsible for all the property in the furnished palace he was occupying. He raised quite a fuss on two occasions when he noticed articles of furniture had been removed. "Coming from the President, whom we all knew so well, these were very funny things," wrote Gilbert Close, one of Wilson's secretaries. "I never saw the President to be in such a difficult frame of mind as he is now. He has jumped all over [Ike] Hoover several times and is sore at Swem." Close saw clearly that "something queer was happening in his mind. One thing was certain: he was never the same after this little spell of sickness."[65]

The obsession with lost objects—in fact, they had only been rearranged—could reflect anxiety over loss of status as the just and divine arbiter of the Paris Peace Conference. Smuts had trapped Wilson with his own carefully selected words—excerpted from the November 4 pledge—and Wilson readily caved. But in doing so, Wilson betrayed a higher language of justice and perpetual peace for the world, thereby displeasing his superego and dismissing his own principles just to satisfy a loved friend. Wilson himself was lost. Nobody protected him from his human desire. And Smuts was not House. Smuts seduced Wilson in the interests of the South African state and the British Empire before abandoning him.

House was convinced that he knew the answers better than the president did, but he was also fundamentally loyal to Wilson.[66] He was certain that, had he been in close touch with Wilson in fall 1919, he could have secured Wilson's acceptance of Lodge's reservations. "All that was necessary was to show the President that the U.S. must enter the League, or the effects of Wilson's whole career would be vitiated," House told Seymour. Agreeing with Lodge's reservations would have been the best "coup" Wilson could have carried out against the despised senator, so certain was he that Wilson would never accept them. But Wilson chose to break with House and to stubbornly face Lodge, with no remaining intimate who possessed sufficient judgment to show Wilson the effects of his obstinacy.[67] His will to dominate absolutely a father figure who had humiliated him led Wilson to choose the stillbirth of the League of Nations, of the institution in which he had invested his hopes for peace, rather than deign to make a minor concession.

Smuts remained beloved by Wilson until the end. After taking Wilson's final interview in October 1923, the journalist James Kerney noted that "the only world liberal he deemed worthy of singling out by name was Jan Smuts."[68] Smuts was more cynical. In 1948, he said that John Maynard Keynes's "portrait of Wilson was absolutely truthful; but Keynes should not have written it; after all Wilson was our friend."[69]

Conclusion

Personality in History

THE US REJECTION of the Treaty of Versailles and the Treaty of Guarantee was a tragedy for the world. And while Wilson was one of the authors of this tragedy, he was not the only one.

In the short term, Lloyd George and the British Empire were the winners of the peace negotiations. Great Britain took possession of Germany's major colonies and secured the destruction of her navy. And Lloyd George got exactly what he wanted with respect to the most significant issue: reparations. "By persuading Wilson to include pensions in reparations, he increased Britain's share," Margaret MacMillan wrote. "By not mentioning a fixed sum he managed to keep public opinion at home and the empire happy. He also took out insurance of another sort when he privately urged a prominent European socialist"—Emile Vandervelde, a Belgian politician and president of the Second International—"to whip up a public outcry against treating Germany too harshly. Finally, he managed to cast the French as the greedy ones."[1]

John Maynard Keynes played a key role in forming this persistent belief—that the Germans were treated unfairly and that the culprits were the greedy French and the inept Wilson. *The Economic Consequences of the Peace* encouraged German grievances and contributed to a guilt complex around the treaty in England—a loss of faith that paralyzed the Allies and fostered diplomatic distance between the United Kingdom and France.[2] Keynes's portrayal of the negotiations deliberately omitted much that he knew, seemingly to protect the British position. He drafted, then excluded, a devastating portrait of Lloyd George, which was published only in 1932. He also neglected to tell his English-speaking readers what he wrote about Britain in the preface to his French edition: "It is she who, above all, must be blamed for the form of the Reparations chapter. She took the colonies, the German navy and a larger share of the compensation than the one to which she was entitled."[3] To the contrary, Keynes's English edition opined that, in economic and financial matters, it was generally the French who made "the most extreme proposals."[4] He described Clemenceau as preoccupied with destroying Germany, even as the French premier agreed to allowing Germany the left bank of the Rhine and accepted a referendum on Upper Silesia that he reasonably and correctly predicted would lead to its attachment to Germany. Clemenceau even developed confidential contacts with the German government, to the point that he was ready to meet Hindenburg for talks in 1922.[5] Still, in Keynes's telling—at least for the English-speaking world—the Germans were justified in their complaints and the French were to blame.

The French and Wilson. Recall that Keynes castigated Wilson for having "capitulated" on reparations "before a masterpiece of the sophist's art."[6] What Keynes did not mention was that the sophist in question was Smuts—his friend and mentor at the Paris conference—working on behalf of the British. After reading Keynes's book, and following the defeat of the treaty, Bernard Baruch decided to set the record straight by making public the Smuts memo that had such a decisive impact on Wilson.[7] "The Americans certainly have very free and easy ideas about secret documents," Keynes wrote, accusing Baruch of using the Smuts memo "in a quite shameless way to suit his purpose."[8] But Baruch understood what was going on. The British had led "the French into the belief that Germany could . . . pay the costs of the war."[9] But their main achievement came when, through Smuts, they led Wilson to the same belief. For months Keynes tried to protect Smuts from the revelation of his role. Keynes privately acknowledged to fellow scholar and peace conference delegate Howard Temperley that Baruch was right. "It was indeed this argument which, to the dismay of many persons, finally carried the day."[10]

Yet Keynes's book remains the most widely accepted account today of what happened in Paris. His interpretation of the treaty as a Carthaginian peace—a diktat fashioned by Clemenceau, before whom Wilson collapsed—was widely shared. And this version of the story has only gained esteem, as it seems to have been accurate. Yet Keynes's interpretation was not merely predictive. It was a self-fulfilling prophecy. Keynes's book contributed to the failure of US ratification; as we saw, treaty opponents in the Senate quoted Keynes widely, using his words to persuade fellow senators and citizens. Thus did Baruch call it a "pernicious book . . . which did so much to bring about the very consequences [Keynes] claimed to fear."[11] Baruch never forgave Keynes.[12]

If the United States had ratified the Treaty of Versailles, history would likely have taken a different course. Postwar European-American cooperation would have swiftly come to life. Most significantly, the Allied representatives on the reparations commission were ready to make adjustments to Germany's indemnities "when the public opinion in the victorious countries . . . settled down to reason."[13] Soon enough, German reparations would have been lowered and debts reduced, while France would have been assured of security. The treaty could have quickly revealed its adaptability. This was the intention of the Allies.

Adjusting reparations would have reduced the prospects of Hitler's coming to power, but had he still done so, he could not have launched an aggressive war without facing the US security obligation toward France, which would have enabled Roosevelt to overcome the Neutrality Acts, arm his country, and intervene in Europe earlier. Instead, the consequences of US nonratification were immediately felt—and they were catastrophic. Panicked by the loss of the US security guarantee, the French government, under the leadership of Raymond Poincaré, pivoted away from leniency on reparations. In the absence of the US defensive umbrella, the French assumed a major role in the reparations commission, where they took a hard line. Reparations became a false substitute for lost security, making their effective scaling down—the original purpose of the reparations commission contemplated by the Big Four after signing the treaty—impossible until it was too late.

Clemenceau also deserves a portion of the blame. In January 1920 he ran for the French presidency "because," he told a friend, "I believed I could, in this situation, help better than anyone else in France to enforce the treaties I had concluded." Yet he undercut his chance of victory by playing hardball with the Catholic Church, thereby keeping him out of a position of influence from which he could have contributed to US adoption of the treaty. In 1904 France had broken off diplomatic relations with the Vatican, in the context of concerns over the separation of church and state. Just before the 1920 election, parliamentarians from the right and center—the French president was then elected by the Parliament—urged Clemenceau to declare himself in favor of "la reprise"—resumption of diplomatic relations with the Vatican—in exchange for their votes. But

Clemenceau, an avowed atheist and free thinker, refused to compromise, lost the election, and bowed out of politics.[14]

Had he been elected president of France in January 1920, Clemenceau could have made an official trip to Washington just in time for the last votes in the Senate. The US press had been eagerly discussing just such a possibility a month earlier, to the delight of Wilsonians still keen to have the treaty ratified. The fact was that Clemenceau enjoyed a strong reputation in the United States, across political boundaries. Wilson had left Paris in June 1919 on excellent terms with Clemenceau. Lodge, too, had been impressed with the French leader. He noted that, when moviegoers viewed newsreels showing Wilson and Lloyd George, they would applaud politely; in contrast, footage of Clemenceau "creates the greatest possible enthusiasm."[15] This public prestige was on display when Clemenceau visited the United States in fall 1922, to a fervent welcome.[16] Perhaps a visit from President Clemenceau could have contributed to a compromise between Lodge and Wilson leading to ratification of the treaty.[17] Stubbornly, however, both the Catholic right and Clemenceau sacrificed France's greater interest on the altar of petty differences.

So there was much blame to spread around. Yet, for most peace conference participants, including most of the Americans present, there was no question that Wilson bore primary responsibility for the failure of treaty ratification and its consequences for the world. Such has been the verdict of scholars as well. In *Woodrow Wilson and the Great Betrayal* (1945), historian Thomas A. Bailey summed up Wilson as "the supreme paradox": "he who had forced the Allies to write the League into the Treaty, unwrote it. He who had done more than any other man to make the covenant, unmade it—at least so far as America was concerned. And by his action, he contributed powerfully to the ultimate undoing of the League, and with it the high hopes of himself and mankind for an organization to prevent World War II."[18]

The cause of Wilson's fatal stubbornness in autumn 1919 will forever remain a matter for interpretation. Senator Gilbert Hitchcock thought Wilson's stroke on October 2 led to his obstinacy and the treaty's failure. "I shall always believe ratification would have been possible if Wilson's health would not have given way," Hitchcock said.[19] But this view was in the minority. Many were those who attributed

Wilson's behavior to psychological causes: Keynes, Lodge, House, Churchill, Lansing. Bullitt and Freud.

Their book was the first attempt to apply psychoanalytic theory to a political leader and, as such, brought about interpretive innovations. The book was not one of Freud's archetypal works, with his incomparable mix of insight, precision, and literary elegance. Instead, the Wilson book was sometimes monotonous, mechanical, and quite repetitive. Often it was vindictive. And I believe their interpretation goes too far: Freud and Bullitt saw Wilson's neurosis as ever-present, explaining everything in his life. My own view is that Wilson's neurosis limited his rational judgment at key moments, with profound reverberations in world history, but he was not a constant slave to his phobias and fixations. Even so, Bullitt and Wilson accomplished something highly original in drawing a psychological portrait of a world leader on the basis of inner-circle interviews and archival documents.

The authors were insisting on Wilson's responsibility for the tragedy that was unfolding in real time. He had created the illusion of a just and perpetual peace and then nurtured disappointment by being unable to realize it. When the treaty he negotiated came to contain a system of collective security, he was the man responsible for its nonratification. He armed the peoples of the defeated states with anger before disarming his allies. As Freud wrote in his introduction, "When, like Wilson, a man achieves almost the exact opposite of that which he wished to accomplish . . . when a pretension to free the world from evil ends only in a new proof of the danger of a fanatic to the commonweal, then it is not to be marveled at that a distrust is aroused in the observer which makes sympathy impossible."[20]

Alongside its pioneering contributions, the book represented a rare overt political gesture on Freud's part. From 1930 to 1932, as Bullitt and Freud were making progress, the Nazis were rising to power; Hitler would be chancellor within months of the manuscript's completion. Had the book been published in 1932, Freud and Bullitt would have been attacked for it. But at least Freud—old and sick, yet still the father of psychoanalysis—would have been able to write, speak, and give interviews. He had the scientific authority to explain how and why Wilson's neurosis had been responsible for the failure of the treaty. And he would have been seconded by a courageous American with the knowledge and access to speak candidly about the former president, what he had done in Paris, and the impact he had had on world peace.

But that is not what happened, and in 1966 there was no hope of political impact. By this point Wilson had been sanctified as the martyr of Versailles, whose ardent wish to foster peace through the League of Nations had been undone by isolationists. The failure of ratification was considered a product of ideological difference alone. Thus in a December 1966 *Look* article, former CIA director Allen Dulles denounced the Freud-Bullitt book as a study "bred in bitterness." He added, "I would hope that this book would not initiate a series of biographies based on posthumous psychiatric studies of our departed great idealists."[21]

But Frank C. Waldrop, at least, was not so sure. A noted author and newspaper editor, Waldrop thought Freud and Bullitt's book demonstrated

> how pallid and incomplete historical and biographical writing must be in avoidance of the evidence which counts in the measure of a public personage . . . State Papers, however elegant, are no final measure of a President's influence on the lives of others. There are also his secrets laid on his soul long before he thought he could call it his own, and which he, like all other men, must seek to endure without acknowledging them to exist. They matter. The Freud-Bullitt study . . . is an attempt to get at those secrets in the case of one man, insofar as evidence is available . . . It was not Wilson's idealism, but those springs in his nature which drove his pursuits, that weighted most in the world while he lived, and which weighted most, even yet. Not protestations, but acts, are what we must consider in choosing among those who would lead us, whether a Wilson, a Hitler, a Stalin, or a Mao.[22]

Freud and Bullitt wanted to warn their readers and all people that history and the fate of humanity are not only the products of ideas or structures or the hard material facts. Rather, they are also the consequences of individual action. Dictators are easy to read. Democratic leaders are more difficult to decipher. However, they can be just as unbalanced as dictators and can play a truly destructive role in our history. Today the question posed by Freud and Bullitt is as acute as it has ever been. By what means shall democracies prevent those who cannot be trusted with power from obtaining it—and using it to the detriment of their constituents, the wider world order, and democracy itself? The time has come to reopen this conversation.

Notes

Introduction

1. Camille Barrère, note on Foch's fears about the future of the French army, April 25, 1920, article 2, 10 notes de Camille Barrère, note H, Papiers François Charles-Roux, Papiers d'agents–Archives privées (PA-AP) 37, Ministère de L'Europe et des Affaires Étrangères, France.
2. John Maynard Keynes, *The Economic Consequences of the Peace* (London: Macmillan, 1919), 54; John Maynard Keynes to Norman Davis, April 15, 1920, box 32, folder "Keynes, J. M., 1920," Norman H. Davis Papers, MSS 17962, Library of Congress.
3. Arthur M. Schlesinger Jr., *The Crisis of the Old Order, 1919–1933* (Boston: Houghton Mifflin, 1957), 12.
4. William Bullitt to Alexander Kirk, American Chargé d'Affaires in Berlin, September 28, 1939, Bullitt Papers, box 45, folder 1076.
5. Richard Nixon, conversation with Henry Kissinger, June 24, 1971, between 11:23 AM and 11:35 AM, Oval Office, Conversation 529–16, White House Tapes, Richard Nixon Presidential Library and Museum, Yorba Linda, CA.
6. Adam Tooze, *Deluge: The Great War, America and the Remaking of the Global Order, 1916–1931* (New York: Viking Adult, 2014), 335.

1. The American Collapse of the Treaty of Versailles

1. Georges-Henri Soutou, *La Grande Illusion, Comment la France a perdu la paix: 1914–1920* (Paris: Tallandier, 2015), 73.
2. Henry Cabot Lodge to Henry White, April 8, 1919, Paris Peace Conference File, box 41, Henry White Papers, MSS 45328, Library of Congress.
3. "Statement of Mr. William C. Bullitt," September 12, 1919, in "Treaty of Peace with Germany: Hearings before the Committee on Foreign Relations," United States Senate, Sixty-sixth Congress, First Session, Senate Document 106 (Washington, DC: Government Printing Office, 1919), 1161–1297 (hereafter Bullitt Statement, "Treaty of Peace with Germany" Senate Hearings).
4. "A Conversation with Members of the Senate Foreign Relations Committee," August 19, 1919, Woodrow Wilson, *The Papers of Woodrow Wilson*, ed. Arthur S. Link et al., 69 vols. (Princeton, NJ: Princeton University Press, 1966–1993), 62: 343, 361.
5. Ray Stannard Baker, memo of conversation with Thomas Gregory, March 14 and 15, 1927, box 106, folder "Gregory, Thomas W.," Ray Stannard Baker Papers, MSS 11593, Library of Congress; Jeffrey K. Tulis, *The Rhetorical Presidency* (Princeton, NJ: Princeton University Press, 1988), 117–118.

6. William Bullitt, letter of resignation, *Papers Relating to the Foreign Relations of the United States: The Paris Peace Conference* (Washington, DC: US Government Publishing Office, 1942–1947), 11: 570–574.

7. Ernesta Drinker interview, December 27, 1954, in Beatrice Farnsworth, *William C. Bullitt and the Soviet Union* (Bloomington: Indiana University Press, 1967), 67.

8. In addition to Henry Cabot Lodge (MA), others in the meeting were Frank Brandegee (CT), Albert Fall (NM), Warren Harding (OH), Philander Knox (PA), and Harry New (IN).

9. See John M. Cooper, *Breaking the Heart of the World: Woodrow Wilson and the Fight for the League of Nations* (Cambridge: Cambridge University Press, 2001), 170; Chandler P. Anderson diary, September 21, 1919, box 2, Chandler P. Anderson Papers, MSS 10918, Library of Congress.

10. Anne Bullitt, comments on Edward Gulick, *Ambassador Bullitt and Ashfield,* galleys of an unpublished manuscript, 1992, 4, box 212, folder 248, William C. Bullitt Papers, MS 112, Manuscripts and Archives, Yale University Library (hereafter Bullitt Papers).

11. Lloyd C. Gardner, *Safe for Democracy: The Anglo-American Response to Revolution, 1913–1923* (Oxford: Oxford University Press, 1984), 239.

12. John Silverlight, *The Victor's Dilemma: Allied Intervention in the Russian Civil War* (New York: Weybright and Talley, 1970), 32–42; Nicholas Mulder, *The Economic Weapon: The Rise of Sanctions as a Tool of Modern War* (New Haven, CT: Yale University Press, 2022), 94.

13. Philip Kerr, memo to William Bullitt, February 21, 1919, Bullitt Papers, box 110, folder 381.

14. William Bullitt, cable to Edward House, March 16, 1919, box 21, folder 682, Edward Mandell House Papers, MS 466, Manuscripts and Archives, Yale University Library (hereafter House Papers).

15. Henry Wickham Steed, *Through Thirty Years, 1892–1922: A Personal Narrative* (Garden City, NY: Doubleday Page, 1925), 303.

16. Philip Kerr, Lord Lothian, to David Lloyd George, April 20, 1937, LG/G/12/5/60, Lloyd George Papers, Parliamentary Archives, ARCHON 61, National Archives, London.

17. Bullitt Statement, "Treaty of Peace with Germany" Senate Hearings, 1165, 1233.

18. Bullitt Statement, "Treaty of Peace with Germany" Senate Hearings, 1276.

19. Robert Lansing to Frank Polk, October 1, 1919, box 9, folder 315, Frank Lyon Polk Papers, MS 656, Manuscripts and Archives, Yale University Library (hereafter Polk Papers).

20. William Phillips to Robert Lansing, September 13, 1919, box 46, Robert Lansing Papers, MSS 29454, Library of Congress.

21. Bullitt Statement, "Treaty of Peace with Germany" Senate Hearings, 1280.

22. The Treaty of Saint-Germain-en-Laye established the Republic of Austria on September 10, 1919. The Treaty of Trianon was signed with Hungary on June 4, 1920. On August 10, 1920, the Treaty of Sèvres marked the dismemberment of the Ottoman Empire, igniting the Turkish War of Independence.
23. Frank Polk to Robert Lansing, September 22, 1919, Polk Papers, box 9, folder 314; "Lloyd George Sees 'Tissue of Lies' in Bullitt Version," *New York Times*, September 16, 1919.
24. Henry White to Henry Cabot Lodge, November 13, 1919, Henry Cabot Lodge Papers, box 19, Massachusetts Historical Society, Boston.
25. "Mr. Bullitt Disclosures," *New York Times*, September 15, 1919, 10.
26. Robert Lansing to Frank Polk, October 1, 1919, Polk Papers, box 9, folder 315.
27. "From Robert Lansing," Robert Lansing, cable to Woodrow Wilson, September 17, 1919, *Papers of Woodrow Wilson*, 63: 337.
28. Joseph P. Tumulty, *Wilson as I Know Him* (Garden City, NY: Doubleday Page, 1921), 441–443.
29. "From Robert Lansing," Robert Lansing, cable to Woodrow Wilson, September 17, 1919, *Papers of Woodrow Wilson*, 63: 338.
30. Woodrow Wilson, "An Address in Reno," September 22, 1919, *Papers of Woodrow Wilson*, 63: 433.
31. Woodrow Wilson, "A Luncheon Address in San Francisco," September 18, 1919, *Papers of Woodrow Wilson*, 63: 345–346.
32. Woodrow Wilson, "An Address in the San Francisco Civic Auditorium," September 17, 1919, *Papers of Woodrow Wilson*, 63: 329.
33. Cooper, *Breaking the Heart of the World*, 194.
34. Woodrow Wilson, "An Address in the Tabernacle in Salt Lake City," September 23, 1919, *Papers of Woodrow Wilson*, 63: 451, 453.
35. John Milton Cooper, "Disability in the White House: The Case of Woodrow Wilson," in *The White House: The First Two Hundred Years*, ed. Frank Freidel and William Pencak (Boston: Northeastern University Press, 1994), 78.
36. Ryan D. Jacobson, "President Wilson's Brain Trust: Woodrow Wilson, Francis X. Dercum, and American Neurology," *Journal of the History of the Neurosciences* 18, no. 1 (2009): 59–75.
37. John Milton Cooper, *Woodrow Wilson: A Biography* (New York: Alfred A. Knopf, 2009), 536–538.
38. Frank Polk to Robert Lansing, October 18, 1919, Polk Papers, box 9, folder 315.
39. Edith Bolling Galt Wilson, *My Memoir* (New York: Bobbs-Merrill, 1938), 288.
40. Cooper, *Wilson: A Biography*, 534.
41. Irwin H. Hoover, "The Facts about President Wilson's Illness," n.d., *Papers of Woodrow Wilson*, 63: 635–636.

42. Cary T. Grayson diary, various typed diary entries and notes, series: Grayson Diaries, box 1, Cary T. Grayson Papers, MS 000465, Woodrow Wilson Presidential Library and Museum, Staunton, VA.

43. Cooper, *Wilson: A Biography,* 542. The limerick, which Wilson did not quite recite perfectly, is Anthony Euwer, "The Face," in *The Limeratomy: A Compendium of Universal Knowledge for the More Perfect Understanding of the Human Machine* (New York: J. B. Pond, 1917).

44. Cooper, *Breaking the Heart of the World,* 166.

45. Richard Coke Lower, *A Bloc of One: The Political Career of Hiram W. Johnson* (Stanford, CA: Stanford University Press, 1993), 139.

46. *New York Times,* November 18, 1919. Wilson purposely used the term "nullification," a pejorative evoking South Carolina's efforts to nullify federal laws before the Civil War, a red flag for Republicans. See Cooper, *Wilson: A Biography,* 543.

47. Henry White to Henry Cabot Lodge, September 19, 1919, and Henry Cabot Lodge to Henry White, October 2, 1919, Henry Cabot Lodge Papers, box 19, Massachusetts Historical Society.

48. Ralph A. Stone, *The Irreconcilables: The Fight against the League of Nations* (Lexington: University Press of Kentucky, 1970), 138.

49. *Congressional Record,* November 5, 1919, United States Senate, Sixty-sixth Congress, 1st Session, 7959.

50. *Congressional Record,* November 19, 1919, United States Senate, Sixty-sixth Congress, 1st Session, 8776.

51. Arthur Walworth, *Woodrow Wilson,* 3rd ed., vol. 2 (New York: Norton, 1978), 378.

52. Woodrow Wilson, "A Draft of a Public Letter," c. December 17, 1919, *Papers of Woodrow Wilson,* 64: 199–202.

53. Cooper, *Wilson: A Biography,* 549.

54. Woodrow Wilson, "A Jackson Day Message," January 8, 1920, *Papers of Woodrow Wilson,* 64: 257–259.

55. Stone, *The Irreconcilables,* 155.

56. See Aaron Chandler, "Senator Lawrence Sherman's Role in the Defeat of the Treaty of Versailles," *Journal of the Illinois State Historical Society* 94, no. 3 (Autumn 2001): 279–303, 285.

57. Stone, *The Irreconcilables,* 161; and Leon E. Boothe, "A Fettered Envoy: Lord Grey's Mission to the United States, 1919–1920," *Review of Politics* 33, no. 1 (1971): 78–94.

58. John A. Thompson, *Woodrow Wilson* (Harlow, UK: Pearson Education, 2002), 237–238.

59. Raymond Clapper, diary entry for February 14, 1920, quoted in Stone, *The Irreconcilables,* 162–163.

60. John Maynard Keynes, *The Economic Consequences of the Peace* (London: Macmillan, 1919), 52–53.

61. Senator William Borah also read relevant passages aloud in the Senate chamber: Testimony of Senator William Borah, "Treaty of Peace with Germany," February 10, 1920, United States Senate, Sixty-sixth Congress, Second Session, 2699. Senator Charles S. Thomas was "strongly impressed with some features of [Keynes's] book." C. S. Thomas to Bernard Baruch, February 1920, correspondence with Thomas, C. S, 1919–1932, subseries 1B, box 45, Bernard M. Baruch Papers, MC006, Public Policy Papers, Special Collections, Princeton University Library.

62. Paul D. Cravath to John Maynard Keynes, December 18, 1919, (copy), Herbert Hoover Papers, Pre-Commerce Papers, box 4, folder "Cravath, Paul (1918–1920)," Herbert Hoover Presidential Library and Museum, West Branch, IA. See also Priscilla Roberts, "Paul D. Cravath, the First World War, and the Anglophile Internationalist Tradition," *Australian Journal of Politics and History* 51, no. 2 (2005): 194–215.

63. Lincoln Colcord to William Bullitt, February 20, 1920, Bullitt Papers, box 20, folder 439.

64. Cooper, *Wilson: A Biography*, 557–558.

65. James E. Watson, *As I Knew Them: Memoirs of James E. Watson* (Indianapolis, IN: Bobbs-Merrill, 1936), 202. Among the dissenting newspapers were the *Cleveland Plain Dealer, Brooklyn Eagle, Louisville Courier-Journal,* and the powerful *New York World*. Thomas A. Bailey, *Woodrow Wilson and the Great Betrayal* (New York: Macmillan, 1945), 266.

66. Denna Frank Fleming, "Lodge, The Republican Partisan," in Ralph A. Stone, ed., *Wilson and the League of Nations: Why America's Rejection?* (New York: Holt, Rinehart, and Winston, 1967), 83; Cooper, *Breaking the Heart of the World*, 366–367.

67. Gilbert Hitchcock to Bainbridge Colby, March 29, 1920, and Woodrow Wilson to Bainbridge Colby, April 2, 1920; both in box 2, Bainbridge Colby Papers, MSS 16360, Library of Congress.

68. Georges Clemenceau, *Grandeur and Misery of Victory* (London: George G. Harrap, 1930), 232.

69. Stockton Axson to Ray Stannard Baker, August 29, 1928, box 99, Ray Stannard Baker Papers, MSS 11593, Library of Congress; Robert Lansing to Edward House, November 13, 1920, box 69, folder 2279, House Papers; Robert H. Ferrell, *Woodrow Wilson and World War I, 1917–1921* (New York: Harper and Row, 1985), 229, quoted in Thomas J. Knock, *To End All Wars: Woodrow Wilson and the Quest for a New World Order* (New York: Oxford University Press, 1992), 269.

70. *Public Ledger* (Philadelphia), January 12, 1921; "The Bamboozlement," Associated Press, March 21, 1921.

71. "Wilson versus Lansing," *Public Ledger* (Philadelphia), March 25, 1921.

72. Philip Kerr to Nancy Astor, December 3, 1922, Nancy Astor Papers, MS 1416/1/4/51, Special Collections, University of Reading, UK.

73. Stephen Bonsal to Edward House, January 5, 1923, box 17, folder 533, House Papers; James Kerney, *The Political Education of Woodrow Wilson* (New York: Century, 1926), 466.

74. Gene Smith, *When the Cheering Stopped* (New York: William Morrow, 1964), 237–238.

75. Margaret Axson Elliott interview, June 1949, box 1, folder 15, Arthur Clarence Walworth Papers, MS 532, Manuscripts and Archives, Yale University Library.

76. Ernesta Drinker, autograph manuscript memoir, July 15, 1939–1940, Ernesta Drinker Barlow Papers, series 4, box 5, folder 1, GTM-081118, Georgetown University Libraries, 319 (hereafter Ernesta Drinker memoir).

77. William Bullitt, "The Shining Adventure" [memoir], 1950, Bullitt Papers, box 141, folder 101.

78. William Bullitt, telegram to George Lansbury, undated, Bullitt Papers, box 48, folder 1170; Ernesta Drinker memoir, 315–318; William Bullitt to Nancy Astor, January 17, 1920, Bullitt Papers, box 106, folder 312.

79. Harold Laski to William Bullitt, August 10, 1920, Bullitt Papers, box 46, folder 1117.

2. The Making of William C. Bullitt

1. Anne Bullitt, comments on Edward Gulick, *Ambassador Bullitt and Ashfield,* galleys of an unpublished manuscript, 1992, 4, box 212, folder 248, William C. Bullitt Papers, MS 112, Manuscripts and Archives, Yale University Library (hereafter Bullitt Papers).

2. Will Brownell and Richard N. Billings, *So Close to Greatness: A Biography of William C. Bullitt* (New York: Macmillan, 1987), 29–33.

3. William Bullitt, "The Shining Adventure" [memoir], 1950, Bullitt Papers, box 141, folder 101, 17–18.

4. William Bullitt to Ernesta Drinker, September 15, 1914, Ernesta Drinker Barlow Papers, series 1, box 1, folder 3, GTM-081118, Georgetown University Libraries.

5. Jake Alexander, "Ambassador Bullitt—He Rose from the Rich," *Saturday Evening Post,* March 11, 1939.

6. Michael Kazin, *War against War: The American Fight for Peace, 1914–1918* (New York: Simon and Schuster, 2017), 69.

7. Linda J. Lumsden, *Inez: The Life and Times of Inez Milholland* (Bloomington: Indiana University Press, 2004), 132–135.

8. Barbara S. Kraft, *The Peace Ship: Henry Ford's Pacifist Adventure in the First World War* (New York: Macmillan, 1978), 112–113.

9. William Bullitt, "Pilgrims Spring 'Revolution' on Peace Ship," *Public Ledger* (Philadelphia), December 13, 1915; William Bullitt, "Ford, Peace Apostle, Muzzles Insurgents," *Public Ledger* (Philadelphia), December 14, 1915; Kraft, *The Peace Ship*, 130.

10. William Bullitt, "Autocratic Leader Split Ford Parties," *New York Times*, January 31, 1916.

11. Burnet Hershey, *The Odyssey of Henry Ford and the Great Peace Ship* (New York: Taplinger, 1967), 120.

12. William Bullitt, "Delegates Depressed by the Departure of Ford," *Public Ledger* (Philadelphia), December 24, 1915.

13. Ernesta Drinker, autograph manuscript memoir, July 15, 1939–1940, Ernesta Drinker Barlow Papers, series 4, box 5, folder 1, GTM-081118, Georgetown University Libraries (hereafter Ernesta Drinker memoir), 23, 97, 134, 139–140; Ernesta Drinker Bullitt, *An Uncensored Diary from the Central Empires* (Garden City, NY: Doubleday, 1917).

14. For examples, see Meghan Menard McCune and John Maxwell Hamilton, "'My Object Is to Be of Service to You': Carl Ackerman and the Wilson Administration during World War I," *Intelligence and National Security* 32, no. 6 (2017): 743–757.

15. William Bullitt to Frank Polk, September 20, 1916, box 3, folder 89, Frank Lyon Polk Papers, MS 656, Manuscripts and Archives, Yale University Library.

16. James Kerney, *The Political Education of Woodrow Wilson* (New York: Century, 1926), 384.

17. Ray Baker, memorandum of conversations with Walter Lippmann, December 9 and 10, 1927, box 110, Ray Stannard Baker Papers, MSS 11593, Library of Congress.

18. Anne Bullitt, comments on Gulick, *Ambassador Bullitt and Ashfield* galleys, 4.

19. See John Snell to William Bullitt, January 5, 1951, Bullitt Papers, box 78, folder 1992.

20. Bertrand Favreau, *Georges Mandel ou la passion de la République* (Paris: Fayard, 1996), 113–114.

21. William Bullitt, memo to Colonel House, January 31, 1918, box 21, folder 676, Edward Mandell House Papers, MS 466, Manuscripts and Archives, Yale University Library (hereafter House Papers).

22. Charles E. Neu, *Colonel House: A Biography of Woodrow Wilson's Silent Partner* (New York: Oxford University Press, 2015), 369.

23. Harold Nicolson, *Peacemaking 1919* (Boston: Houghton Mifflin, 1933; repr. New York: Grosset and Dunlap, 1965), 24.

24. Meeting of the Superior Council of War, Versailles, November 2, 1918, transcript, Paul Mantoux Papers, box 9, folder F delta res 0858/01/12, Paul Mantoux Archives, La Contemporaine, Nanterre, France.

25. William Bullitt, USS *George Washington* diary, 1918–1919, entry for December 7, 1918, Bullitt Papers, box 104, folder 257.

26. *Petit Parisien,* December 15, 1918.

27. Cary T. Grayson, memo of conversation with General Jan Christian Smuts, January 14, 1930, Cary T. Grayson diary, various typed diary entries and notes, series: Grayson Diaries, box 1, Cary T. Grayson Papers, MS 000465, Woodrow Wilson Presidential Library and Museum, Staunton, VA.

28. "A Memorandum" [a copy of Jan Smuts' proposals on the League of Nations, typed by Woodrow Wilson], December 26, 1918, *The Papers of Woodrow Wilson,* ed. Arthur S. Link et al., 69 vols. (Princeton, NJ: Princeton University Press, 1966–1993), 53: 515–517; Mark Mazower, *Governing the World: The History of an Idea* (New York: Penguin Press, 2012), 118–119.

29. Mazower, *Governing the World,* 132–133.

30. William Bullitt to Ernesta Drinker Bullitt, January 1, 1919, Bullitt Papers, box 109, folder 371; Hugh R. Wilson, *Diplomat between Wars* (New York: Longmans, Green, 1941), 75.

31. William Bullitt, instruction of June 14, 1918, House Papers, box 21, folder 677.

32. William Bullitt to Robert Lansing, November 2, 1918, in *Papers of Woodrow Wilson,* 51: 567.

33. Joseph Grew to William Bullitt, January 29, 1919, Bullitt Papers, box 103, folder 250.

34. Marcel Cachin diary, February 4, 1919, in Marcel Cachin, *Carnets 1906–1947,* ed. Denis Peschanski, 4 vols. (Paris: CNRS Editions, 1993–1998), 2: 356.

35. Hugh Wilson, *Diplomat between Wars,* 74.

36. The two amendments drafted by Bullitt appear in David Hunter Miller, *My Diary at the Conference of Paris, with Documents* (New York: Appeal Printing Company, 1924), docs. 374–376, 238–241.

37. Alan Sharp, *The Versailles Settlement: Peacemaking after the First World War, 1919–1923,* 3rd ed. (London: Palgrave Macmillan, 2018), 59.

38. Aaron Aaronsohn diary, 60–61, Bullitt Papers, box 175, folder 6.

39. Arthur M. Schlesinger Jr., *The Crisis of the Old Order, 1919–1933* (Boston: Houghton Mifflin, 1957), 13.

40. George B. Noble, *Policies and Opinions at Paris, Wilsonian Diplomacy, the Versailles Peace, and French Public Opinion* (New York: Macmillan, 1935), 288–289; "Reminiscences of Adolf Augustus Berle, Jr.," 1969, transcript, 39, Columbia Center for Oral History, Columbia University.

41. Joseph Tumulty to Woodrow Wilson, April 2, 1919, quoted in Arno J. Mayer, *Politics and Diplomacy of Peacemaking: Containment and Counterrevolution at Versailles, 1918–1919* (New York: Knopf, 1967), 478.

42. Georgy Chicherin to Fridtjof Nansen, May 14, 1919, Russian Relief file, Pre-Commerce Papers, Herbert Hoover Presidential Library and Museum, West Branch, IA.
43. Stephen Bonsal, *Unfinished Business* (Garden City, NY: Doubleday, Doran, 1944), 147–150.
44. "Reminiscences of Adolf Augustus Berle, Jr.," 1969, transcript, 66.
45. Ernesta Drinker Bullitt to William Bullitt, January 1919, Bullitt Papers, box 109, folder 362; William Bullitt to Marshall Bullitt, January 22, 1919, Bullitt Family Papers, William Bullitt correspondence, box 111, folder 1381, Filson Historical Society, Louisville, KY.
46. Ernesta Drinker memoir, 226–236.
47. Felix Frankfurter to Marion Denman, quoted in Brad Snyder, *The House of Truth: A Washington Political Salon and the Foundations of American Liberalism* (New York: Oxford University Press, 2017), 252n106.
48. Chaim Weizmann to Aaron Aaronsohn, January 19, 1919, doc. ID: 2-487, Papers of Chaim Weizmann, Yad Chaim Weizmann, Weizmann Institute of Science, Israel; Aaron Aaronsohn diary, January 21, 1919, 38, Bullitt Papers, box 175, folder 5.
49. Ray S. Baker, *American Chronicle: The Autobiography of Ray Stannard Baker* (New York: Scribner, 1945), 404.
50. Jean Longuet, "William Bullitt, ambassadeur des Etats-Unis à Moscou," November 1933, Jean Longuet Collection, 671AP, Box 8A, Archives Nationales, Pierrefitte-sur-Seine, France.
51. Adolf Berle diary, May 10, 1919, Papers of Adolf A. Berle, Franklin D. Roosevelt Presidential Library and Museum, Hyde Park, NY.
52. Robert Struckman and John Shepardson, "And Do Silently: A Biography of Whitney Hart Shepardson," unpublished manuscript, MSS 08-16, 126, box 13, Papers of Whitney Hart Shepardson, Franklin D. Roosevelt Presidential Library and Museum, Hyde Park, NY.
53. Arthur Sweetser, "Criticism of the Versailles Treaty," May 18–21, 1919, unpublished manuscript, p. 6, box 1, folder 19, Arthur Sweetser Papers, MSS 42085, Library of Congress.
54. Manley O. Hudson to William Bullitt, September 7, 1936, Bullitt Papers, box 40, folder 941. The assembled signed a "present list" on the back of Bullitt's restaurant menu, Bullitt Papers, box 110, folder 396.
55. Oswald Villard to William Bullitt, May 27, 1919, box 9, folder 433, Oswald Garrison Villard Papers, MS Am 1323, Houghton Library, Harvard Library; Oswald Villard, "Broken Faith," *The Nation*, May 25, 1919.
56. Herbert Croly to William Bullitt, August 1, 1919, Bullitt Papers, box 21, folder 466.
57. Lincoln Colcord to William Bullitt, May 29, 1919, Bullitt Papers, box 61, folder 1482; Thomas J. Knock, *To End All Wars: Woodrow Wilson and the Quest for a New World Order* (New York: Oxford University Press, 1992), 257.

58. Lincoln Colcord to William Bullitt, November 17, 1933, Bullitt Papers, box 20, folder 439.

59. Walter Lippmann to Bernard Berenson, September 15, 1919, box 3, folder 138, Walter Lippmann Papers, MS 326, Manuscripts and Archives, Yale University Library; Francis Hackett, "Books and Things," *New Republic,* October 8, 1919, 295–296; Lincoln Colcord to William Bullitt, September 17, 1919, Bullitt Papers, box 20, folder 438.

60. Ernesta Drinker memoir, 322.

61. Max Eastman, "The Chicago Conventions," *The Liberator,* October 17, 1919; Benjamin Gitlow, *The Whole of Their Lives: Communism in America—A Personal History and Intimate Portrayal of its Leaders* (New York: Charles Scriber's Sons, 1948), 53–57.

62. Ernesta Drinker memoir, 158, 189, 332, 340–345.

63. Benjamin Huebsch to William Bullitt, January 19, 1920, Bullitt Papers, box 36, folder 424.

64. William C. Bullitt, "The Tragedy of Paris," *The Freeman,* March 17, 1920, 18.

65. Draft materials for *Economic Consequences of Peace,* Papers of John Maynard Keynes, GBR/0272/JMK/EC, box 10, folder 2, doc. 6, Archive Centre, King's College, University of Cambridge; John Maynard Keynes, *The Economic Consequences of the Peace* (London: Macmillan, 1919), 37, 39, 43–44, 45. Many Americans believed that certain passages had been omitted from Keynes's published book at the request of the British government. Keynes wrote to Felix Frankfurter that the allegation was "entirely without foundation" and that he had, on his own judgment, made "little more than verbal changes." John Maynard Keynes to Felix Frankfurter, January 25, 1921, box 72, Felix Frankfurter Papers, MSS 47571, Library of Congress.

66. "An Unchristian Peace," *New York Times,* March 14, 1920.

67. Charles Sweeney to William Bullitt, July 25, 1920, Bullitt Papers, box 80, folder 2049.

68. Ernesta Drinker memoir, 347, 353, 357–359, 364–365, 368–369.

69. William C. Bullitt, "An Open Letter to Mr. Lansing," *New Republic,* April 6, 1921.

70. Oswald Villard to William Bullitt, March 16, 1921, Bullitt Papers, box 84, folder 2170.

71. Ernesta Drinker memoir, 362.

3. An American in Paris and Vienna

1. Samuel Putnam, *Paris Was Our Mistress* (Paris: Viking, 1947), 87.

2. John Reed, *Ten Days That Shook the World* (New York: Boni and Liveright, 1922). Lenin's statement appears on p. 10.

3. William Bullitt to Louise Bryant, June–July 1922, box 11, folder 231, William C. Bullitt Papers, MS 112, Manuscripts and Archives, Yale University Library (hereafter Bullitt Papers).

4. William Bullitt to Louise Bryant, July 20, 1922, and January 1923, both in Bullitt Papers, box 11, folder 232; Amanda Smith, *Newspaper Titan: The Infamous Life and Monumental Times of Cissy Patterson* (New York: Knopf, 2011), 281–283.

5. Mary V. Dearborn, *Queen of Bohemia: The Life of Louise Bryant* (Boston: Houghton Mifflin, 1996), 212; William Bullitt to Ernesta Drinker, April 3, 1923, Ernesta Drinker Barlow Papers, series 1, box 1, folder 5, GTM-081118, Georgetown University Libraries (hereafter Drinker Papers).

6. Louise Bryant to Scofield Thayer, March 15, 1923, series IV, box28, folder 751, Dial / Scofield Thayer Papers, YCAL MSS 34, Beinecke Rare Book and Manuscript Library, Yale University Library.

7. Henri Gad to William Bullitt, April 24, 1923, Bullitt Papers, box 31, folder 691. Gad was Bullitt's lawyer. On divorces of American couples in Paris in the 1920s, see Nancy L. Green, "When Paris Was Reno: American Divorce Tourism in the City of Light, 1920–1927," *Arcade,* n.d., https://arcade.stanford.edu/content/when-paris-was-reno-american-divorce-tourism-city-light-1920-1927.

8. Louise Bryant diary, June 6, 1923, box 16, folder 108, Louise Bryant Papers, MS 1840, Manuscripts and Archives, Yale University Library (hereafter Bryant Papers).

9. William Bullitt, handwritten note, February 27, 1924, Bullitt Papers, box 206, folder 157.

10. Justin Kaplan, *Lincoln Steffens: A Biography* (New York: Simon and Schuster, 1988), 265.

11. Louise Bryant to William Bullitt, undated [probably 1923–1924], Bullitt Papers, box 11, folder 242.

12. William Bullitt to Ernesta Drinker, February 6, 1924, Drinker Papers, series 1, box 1, folder 5. On the envelope, Bullitt addresses Ernesta as "Mrs. Bullitt."

13. William Bullitt to Ernesta Drinker, February 8 and 14, 1924, Drinker Papers, series 1, box 1, folder 6.

14. William Bullitt to Harold Ickes, October 5, 1939, Bullitt Papers, box 41, folder 960; William Bullitt, handwritten note, February 27, 1924, Bullitt Papers, box 206, folder 157.

15. Louise Bryant, "A Turkish Divorce," *Nation,* August 26, 1925; Louise Bryant to Waldo Frank, August 15, 1924, box 5, folder 229, Waldo Frank Papers, Ms. Coll. 823, Kislak Center for Special Collections, University of Pennsylvania; Robert McAlmon, with supplementary chapters by Kay Boyle, *Being Geniuses Together 1920–1930* (Garden City, NY: Doubleday, 1968), 37; Dearborn, *Queen of Bohemia,* 226, 232.

16. Edward Gulick, *Ambassador Bullitt and Ashfield,* galleys of an unpublished manuscript, 1992, 14, Bullitt Papers, box 212, folder 248.

17. William C. Bullitt, *It's Not Done* (New York: Brentano, 1926), 262–264.

18. Louise Bryant to Claude McKay, October 5, 1926, box 1, folder 26, Claude McKay Collection, JWJ MSS 27, Beinecke Rare Book and Manuscript Library, Yale University Library (hereafter McKay Collection).

19. Oswald Villard to William Bullitt, June 9, 1926, Bullitt Papers, box 84, folder 2170.

20. Louise Bryant to Marguerite or John Storrs, October 12, 1926, John Henry Bradley Storrs Papers, series 2.1: Correspondence, box 3, folder 36, Archives of American Art, Smithsonian Institution, Washington, DC; Virginia Gardner, *Friend and Lover: The Life of Louise Bryant* (New York: Horizon Press, 1982), 248; George Biddle, interview with Virginia Gardner, February 23, 1971, box 4, folder 47, Virginia Gardner Papers, TAM.100, Tamiment Library, New York University (hereafter Gardner Papers). Emphasis in original.

21. William Bullitt, "The Shining Adventure" [memoir], 1950, 18, Bullitt Papers, box 141, folder 101.

22. Quoted in Gardner, *Friend and Lover,* 248.

23. George Biddle to Virginia Gardner, Gardner Papers, box 4, folder 47.

24. *Ostdeutsche Rundschau* quoted and translated in Edwin James, "Saw Lenin's Hands in Bullitt's Plan," *New York Times,* September 23, 1919.

25. Orville Bullitt to William Bullitt, 1926, Bullitt Papers, box 14, folder 299.

26. "Reminiscences of Heinz Hartmann," 1963, transcript, 14, Psychoanalytic Movement Project, Columbia Center for Oral History, Columbia University.

27. Abram Kardiner, *My Analysis with Freud* (New York: Norton, 1977).

28. James Strachey to Lytton Strachey, November 6, 1920, *Bloomsbury / Freud: The Letters of James and Alix Strachey 1924–1925,* ed. Perry Meisel and Walter Kendrich (New York: Basic Books, 1985), 29–30.

29. William Bullitt to Louise Bryant, undated, Bullitt Papers, box 11, folder 241.

30. Mark Brunswick to Marie Bonaparte, May 16, 1926, Marie Bonaparte Papers, correspondence, box 1926 A-L, folder 53, NAF 28230, Bibliothèque Nationale de France.

31. Ernesta Drinker, autograph manuscript memoir, 99–108, 165–166, Drinker Papers, series 4, box 5, folder 1 (hereafter Ernesta Drinker memoir).

32. *The Herald,* October 26, 1916; *Public Ledger* (Philadelphia), November 27, 1916; Max Eastman, memorial address for Inez Milholland Boissivain, Cooper Union, December 21, 1916, "Other Family Papers, 1832–1992," box 28, "Milholland Inez, Death and Memorial," Edna St. Vincent Millay Papers, MSS 32920, Library of Congress; William Bullitt to Jean Milholland, September 26, 1919, Bullitt Papers, box 57, folder 1406.

33. William Bullitt, *Introduction to Diplomacy,* unpublished manuscript, Bullitt Papers, box 148, folder 231.

34. Lincoln Steffens to William Bullitt, May 3, 1924, Bullitt Papers, box 78, folder 2009.

35. Ernesta Drinker memoir, 54. The practice of routine postnatal "health" circumcision originated in the nineteenth century. The rate of male circumcision in the United States was around 10 percent in 1880. See E. Wallerstein, "Circumcision: The Uniquely American Medical Enigma," *Urologic Clinics of North America* 12, no. 1 (1985): 123–132.

36. Bullitt, "The Shining Adventure," [memoir], 1950, 13, Bullitt Papers, box 141, folder 101; Will Brownell and Richard N. Billings, *So Close to Greatness: A Biography of William C. Bullitt* (New York: Macmillan, 1987), 104–105.

37. Ernesta Drinker memoir, 36; Ernest Hemingway, *Selected Letters, 1917–1961,* ed. Carlos Baker (New York: Charles Scribner's, 1981), 268.

38. Hugh Gibson diary, December 27, 1919, series: Diaries and Notes, box 3, folder October 1–December 31, 1919, Hugh Gibson Collection, Herbert Hoover Presidential Library and Museum, West Branch, IA. Felix Frankfurter wrote that Gibson "had done more mischief to the Jewish race than anyone who have lived in the last century" and had the habit of putting little "Jewish squibs" in his letters or notes. See Martin Weil, *A Pretty Good Club: The Founding Fathers of the U.S. Foreign Service* (New York: Norton, 1978), 39–42.

39. William Bullitt, "For My daughter Anne Moen Bullitt: A Preface to Life" (1928), Bullitt Papers, box 163, folder 519; Todd M. Endelman, "Jewish Self-hatred in Britain and Germany," in *Two Nations: British and German Jews in Comparative Perspective,* ed. Michael Brenner et al. (Tübingen: Mohr Siebeck, 1999), 333.

40. Sigmund Freud to William Bullitt, April 17, 1927, Bullitt Papers, box 30, folder 681; William Bullitt, *The Tragedy of Woodrow Wilson,* unpublished manuscript of a stage play, registered at the Library of Congress on March 1, 1927, Bullitt Papers, box 163, folder 509.

41. Bullitt, *The Tragedy of Woodrow Wilson,* Act 1, 34, 37, Bullitt Papers, box 163, folder 509.

42. Oswald Villard to William Bullitt, April 5, 1927, Bullitt Papers, box 84, folder 2170; Courtenay Lemon, report on Bullitt, *The Tragedy of Woodrow Wilson,* March 24, 1927, box 682, folder 10062, Theatre Guild Archive, YCAL MSS 46, Beinecke Rare Book and Manuscript Library, Yale University Library (hereafter Theatre Guild Archive).

43. Dearborn, *Queen of Bohemia,* 244; Wayne F. Cooper, *Claude McKay, Rebel Sojourner in the Harlem Renaissance: A Biography* (Baton Rouge: Louisiana State University Press, 1987), 210.

44. William Bullitt, draft of testimony to the divorce court, undated, 5, Bullitt Papers, box 207, folder 155.
45. Robert McAlmon to Louise Bryant, undated, Bryant Papers, box 5, folder 67.
46. William Bullitt, draft of testimony to the divorce court, undated, 5, Bullitt Papers, box 207, folder 155.
47. Dearborn, *Queen of Bohemia,* 265–266.
48. Gardner, *Friend and Lover,* 269.
49. Anne Bullitt, interview with Mary Dearborn, October 5, 1994, in Dearborn, *Queen of Bohemia,* 249.
50. William Bullitt, telegram to Louise Bryant, May 28, 1928, Bullitt Papers, box 11, folder 235.
51. Louise Bryant to Claude McKay, September 15, 1928, McKay Collection, box 1, folder 27.
52. William Bullitt to Louise Bryant, October 1928, and April 6, 10, 11, and 18, 1929, Bullitt Papers, box 11, folder 236.
53. William Bullitt to Louise Bryant, December 7 and 8, 1929, Bullitt Papers, box 11, folder 237.
54. William Bullitt to Louise Bryant, March 29, 1929, Bullitt Papers, box 11, folder 238.
55. Sigmund Freud to Louise Bryant, April 15, 1929, Bryant Papers, box 3, folder 35.
56. William Bullitt to Louise Bryant, April 17, 1929, Bullitt Papers, box 11, folder 238.
57. Louise Bryant, handwritten note to self, n.d., Bryant Papers, box 3, folder 35.
58. Lincoln Steffens, *Letters of Lincoln Steffens,* ed. and with introductory notes by Ella Winter and Granville Hicks, 2 vols. (New York: Harcourt, Brace, 1938), 2: 745; Sigmund Freud to Louise Bryant, April 23, 1929, Bryant Papers, box 3, folder 35.
59. Anne Bullitt, comments on Edward Gulick, *Ambassador Bullitt and Ashfield,* galleys of an unpublished manuscript, 1992, 16, Bullitt Papers, box 212, folder 248.
60. William Bullitt to Lawrence Langner, July 4, 1929, Theatre Guild Archive, box 38, folder 824.
61. Sigmund Freud to William Bullitt, August 1, 1929, copy in Theatre Guild Archive, box 38, folder 824.
62. Courtenay Lemon, report on William Bullitt, *Gobi,* September 30, 1929, Theatre Guild Archive, box 685, folder 10085.
63. Gardner, *Friend and Lover,* 254.
64. Art Hays to Louise Bryant, November 4 and 13, 1929, Bryant Papers, box 4, folder 45.

65. Louise Bryant to Frank Walsh, April 22, 1930, box 25, Frank P. Walsh Papers, MssCol 3211, Manuscripts and Archives Division, New York Public Library (hereafter Walsh Papers).

66. William Bullitt to Marsden Hartley, December 1, 1929, box 11, folder "Bullitt," Marsden Hartley Collection, YCAL MSS 578, Beinecke Rare Book and Manuscript Library, Yale University Library.

67. Leslie R. Naftzger to Louise Bryant, February 28, 1930, Bryant Papers, box 5, folder 75; Naftzger to Bryant, December 23, 1929, Bullitt Papers, box 207, folder 154.

68. William Bullitt, telegrams to Louise Bryant, October 13 and 15, 1929, Bullitt Papers, box 11, folder 239.

69. Art Hays to Louise Bryant, November 4 and 13, 1929, Bryant Papers, box 4, folder 45.

70. Frank Walsh to Margaret G. Reed, April 14, 1931, Walsh Papers, box 25.

71. William Bullitt to Louise Bryant, March 24, 1930, Bullitt Papers, box 11, folder 240.

72. William Bullitt to Ernesta Drinker, February 24, 1930, Drinker Papers, series 1, box 1, folder 6.

4. Sigmund Freud, Coauthor

1. William Bayard Hale, *The Story of a Style* (New York: Huebsch, 1920), 2.

2. Sigmund Freud to William Bayard Hale, January 15, 1922, box 1, folder 12, William Bayard Hale Papers, MS 814, Manuscripts and Archives, Yale University Library (hereafter Hale Papers).

3. Hale, *Story of a Style*, 6–8, 36, 87–88, 133, 229.

4. Freud to Hale, January 15, 1922, Hale Papers, box 1, folder 12.

5. Freud to Hale, Hale Papers, January 3, 1922, and January 15, 1922, Hale Papers, box 1 folder 12; see Freud's signed statement accompanying William Bayard Hale to Benjamin W. Huebsch, February 4, 1922, box 12, B. W. Huebsch Papers, MSS 50013, Library of Congress.

6. Sigmund Freud to Sándor Ferenczi, December 22, 1916, Sigmund Freud and Sándor Ferenczi, *Correspondence*, vol. 2: *1914–1919* (Cambridge, MA: Harvard University Press, 1996), no. 634, 156.

7. Ernest Jones, *The Life and Work of Sigmund Freud*, vol. 2: *Years of Maturity, 1902–1919* (London: Hogarth Press, 1955), 190.

8. Sigmund Freud to Sándor Ferenczi, October 16, 1918, Freud and Ferenczi, *Correspondence*, no. 764, 2: 301.

9. Sigmund Freud to Karl Abraham, February 3, 1919, *The Complete Correspondence of Sigmund Freud and Karl Abraham 1907–1925*, ed. Ernst Falzeder, trans. Caroline Schwarzacher (London: H. Karnac, 2002), 391–392.

10. John Maynard Keynes, *The Economic Consequences of the Peace* (London: Macmillan, 1919), 54.

11. James Strachey to Lytton Strachey, February 16, 1921, Giles Lytton Strachey Papers, corresp. MSS 60712, 64–65, Manuscript Collections, British Library, London.

12. Theodor Reik, preface to *Thomas Woodrow Wilson,* undated, box 1, folder "Anna Freud, 1966–69," Max Schur Papers, MSS 62040, Library of Congress.

13. Edward House to Charles Seymour, April 13, 1930, box 101, folder 3492, Edward Mandell House Papers, MS 466, Manuscripts and Archives, Yale University Library.

14. Sigmund Freud to George Viereck, July 20, 1928, *Letters of Sigmund Freud 1873–1939,* selected and ed. Ernst L. Freud, trans. Tania Stern and James Stern (London: Hogarth Press, 1961), 381–382.

15. Charles Seymour, "Re-fighting the War on Paper," *Yale Review* 18, no. 4 (1929): 625–645.

16. Seymour, "Re-fighting the War on Paper," 633.

17. On House's mandate to negotiate, see Edward Mandell House and Charles Seymour, *The Intimate Papers of Colonel House, Arranged as a Narrative by Charles Seymour,* 4 vols. (Boston: Houghton Mifflin, 1926), 4: 328–329.

18. Winston S. Churchill, *The World Crisis,* vol. 4: *1918–1928: The Aftermath* (New York: Scribner, 1929), 125, 488.

19. Anders Stephanson, *Manifest Destiny: American Expansionism and the Empire of Right* (New York: Hill and Wang, 1995), 129.

20. William Bullitt, *Introduction to Diplomacy,* unpublished manuscript, box 148, folder 231, William C. Bullitt Papers, MS 112, Manuscripts and Archives, Yale University Library (hereafter Bullitt Papers).

21. *Diary of Sigmund Freud, 1929–1939: A Record of the Final Decade,* trans. and annotated by Michael Molnar (New York: Scribner's, 1992), 71.

22. Sigmund Freud to Lytton Strachey, Vienna, December 25, 1928, in Michael Holroyd, *Lytton Strachey: A Critical Biography,* 2 vols. (New York: Holt, 1967–1968), 2: 615–616. Strachey's book was *Elizabeth and Essex: A Tragic History* (London: Chatto and Windus, 1928).

23. Edward House, interview by William Bullitt, May 7, 1930, notes on conversations about Woodrow Wilson, Bullitt Papers, box 148, folder 232.

5. The Failure of the First Atlantic Alliance

1. Edward Mandell House and Charles Seymour, *The Intimate Papers of Colonel House, Arranged as a Narrative by Charles Seymour,* 4 vols. (Boston: Houghton Mifflin, 1926), 1, 3.

2. Charles Seymour, memorandum of conversation with Edward House, March 17, 1920, box 52, folder 252, Charles Seymour Papers, MS 441,

Manuscripts and Archives, Yale University Library (hereafter Seymour Papers).

3. Christopher Lasch, *The New Radicalism in America, 1889–1963: The Intellectual as a Social Type* (New York: Knopf, 1965), 236.

4. Lincoln Colcord diary, June 17, 1917, excerpts, quoted in Lasch, *The New Radicalism,* 242–243.

5. William Bullitt to Anne Bullitt, undated, Accession 2008-M-037, box 1, folder 6, William C. Bullitt Papers, MS 112, Manuscripts and Archives, Yale University Library (hereafter Bullitt Papers).

6. Charles E. Neu, *Colonel House: A Biography of Woodrow Wilson's Silent Partner* (New York: Oxford University Press, 2014), 20–23.

7. Edward House, interview by William Bullitt, June 1, 1930, notes on conversations about Woodrow Wilson, Bullitt Papers, box 148, folder 232; Edward House to Sidney Edward Mezes, November 24, 1911, box 80, folder 2699, Edward Mandell House Papers, MS 466, Manuscripts and Archives, Yale University Library (hereafter House Papers).

8. Neu, *Colonel House,* 80–81.

9. House, interview by Bullitt, June 1, 1930.

10. Edward House, interview by William Bullitt, June [n.d.] 1930, notes on conversations about Woodrow Wilson, Bullitt Papers, box 148, folder 232

11. Norman Gordon Levin Jr., *Woodrow Wilson and World Politics: America's Response to War and Revolution* (Oxford: Oxford University Press, 1968), 216.

12. Edward House to Charles Seymour, July 3, 1922, House Papers, box 99, folder 3446.

13. Charles Seymour, memorandum of conversation with Edward House, March 17, 1922, Seymour Papers, box 52, folder 254.

14. George S. Viereck, *The Strangest Friendship in History: Woodrow Wilson and Colonel House* (New York: Liveright, 1932), 214.

15. *Centenaire Woodrow Wilson, 1856–1956: Discours tenus à deux séances commémoratives à Genève les 21 et 22 juin 1956* [*Centennial of Woodrow Wilson, 1856–1956: Speeches Given at Two Commemorative Sessions in Geneva on June 21 and 22, 1956*] (Geneva: Centre Européen de la Dotation Carnegie, 1956), 23.

16. Cary Grayson, diary entry for December 8, 1918, Peace Conference, first trip, original copy, 12, series Grayson Diaries, box 2, Cary T. Grayson Papers, MS 000465, Woodrow Wilson Presidential Library and Museum, Staunton, VA. On French responsibility for preventing the unification of Germany and Austria, see Margaret MacMillan, *Paris 1919: Six Months That Changed the World* (New York: Random House, 2001), 252–253.

17. Charles Seymour, "Woodrow Wilson in Perspective," *Foreign Affairs* 34, no. 2 (1956): 175–186.

18. Woodrow Wilson quoted in Ray S. Baker, *American Chronicle: The Autobiography of Ray Stannard Baker* (New York: Scribner, 1945), entry for May 30, 1919, 402.
19. Cary T. Grayson, "The Colonel's Folly and the President's Distress," *American Heritage* 15, no. 6 (October 1964).
20. Georges Clemenceau to Edward House, May 29, 1929, House Papers, box 27, folder 878.
21. See Georges Wormser, *Clemenceau vu de près* (Paris: Hachette, 1979), 180, referring to Clemenceau, in a November 28, 1922, speech in Chicago, thanking House for ensuring France reliable conditions of armistice.
22. See MacMillan, *Paris 1919*, 92.
23. Thomas J. Knock, *To End All Wars: Woodrow Wilson and the Quest for a New World Order* (New York: Oxford University Press, 1992), 220.
24. Antony Lentin, *Lloyd George and the Lost Peace* (London: Palgrave Macmillan, 2001), 52–53.
25. Georges Clemenceau to Woodrow Wilson and David Lloyd George, March 17, 1919, House Papers, box 27, folder 870.
26. Alan Sharp, *David Lloyd George* (London: Haus, 2008), 124–125.
27. Edward House, record of conversation with Georges Clemenceau, April 15, 1926, House Diaries, vol. 9, 228, House Papers, box 298, folder 1.
28. Edward House, interview by William Bullitt, May 31, 1930, notes on conversations about Woodrow Wilson, Bullitt Papers, box 148, folder 232.
29. Edward House to Charles Seymour, September 12, 1922, House Papers, box 99, folder 3447.

6. Princeton Nightmares

1. Victor Rosewater to Paul A. Hill, 1933, Paul A. Hill Collection (69075), box 14, folder Victor Rosewater, Hoover Institution Library and Archives, Stanford University.
2. Woodrow Wilson to Ellen Axson, March 18, 1884, December 18, 1884, and November 25, 1884, Woodrow Wilson, *The Papers of Woodrow Wilson*, ed. Arthur S. Link et al., 69 vols. (Princeton, NJ: Princeton University Press, 1966–1993), 3: 89, 553, and 484, quoted in Robert Alexander Kraig, *Woodrow Wilson and the Lost World of the Oratorical Statesman* (College Station: Texas A&M University Press, 2004), 54. Emphasis in original.
3. Charles Swem, "I Want to Be a Success in Life," unpublished ms., "Writings," box 87, folder 19, "Charles L. Swem (personal)," series 10: Papers of Others about Wilson, "Swem, Charles L.," Woodrow Wilson Collection, MC 168, Public Policy Papers, Special Collections, Princeton University Library.
4. Sigmund Freud, *The Complete Introductory Lectures in Psychoanalysis*, trans. and ed. James Strachey (New York: Norton, 1966), 19.

5. Sigmund Freud, "On Beginning the Treatment," in *The Standard Edition of the Complete Works of Sigmund Freud,* ed. James Strachey with Anna Freud, 24 vols. (London: Hogarth Press, 1953–1974), 12: 135 (hereafter Freud, *Standard Edition*).

6. See Sigmund Freud, *New Introductory Lectures in Psycho-Analysis* (1933), in Freud, *Standard Edition,* 22: 8; Jonathan Lear, *Freud,* 2nd ed. (London: Routledge, 2015), 107.

7. Freud, *New Introductory Lectures,* 22: 13–14.

8. Sigmund Freud, *The Interpretation of Dreams,* in Freud, *Standard Edition,* 4: 216.

9. Sigmund Freud, "From the History of an Infantile Neurosis" (1918), 18, quoted in Paul Roazen, *Freud and His Followers* (New York: Alfred Knopf, 1975), 114.

10. In Freud's case, the traumatic dream continued to return. Why? Perhaps because, as Jonathan Lear suggested, the dream reflected additional meanings with which Freud never reckoned. He reestablished conscious memory of the childhood scene but did not recognize that he had come to act like his father: Freud discarded multiple disciples in whom he had once invested great hope but who, in his opinion, "had come to nothing." Lear, *Freud,* 106.

11. Lear, *Freud,* 5.

12. Edith Gittings Reid, *Woodrow Wilson: The Caricature, the Myth, and the Man* (New York: Oxford University Press, 1934), viii.

13. William Bullitt, draft of Foreword, n.d., "Thomas Woodrow Wilson" manuscript drafts, box 146, folder 201, William C. Bullitt Papers, MS 112, Manuscripts and Archives, Yale University Library (hereafter Bullitt Papers).

14. Charles Seymour to Edward House, June 20 and 26, 1930, Edward Mandell House Papers, MS 466, box 101, folder 3492, Manuscripts and Archives, Yale University Library (hereafter House Papers).

15. Charles Seymour to William Bullitt, June 25, 1930, Charles Seymour Papers, MSS 441, box 3, folder 127, Manuscripts and Archives, Yale University Library (hereafter Seymour Papers).

16. Edward House to Helen Reynolds, August 7, 1930, House Papers, box 94, folder 3230.

17. William Bullitt to Edward House, July 29, 1930, House Papers, box 21, folder 684.

18. Edward House, diary entry for December 22, 1913, House Diary, vol. 1, 404, box 296, folders 1–2, House Papers; Edward House, diary entry for March 6, 1916, House Diary, vol. 4, 100, box 296, folders 7–8, House Papers; Edward House to Helen Reynolds, July 27, 1930, House Papers, box 94, folder 3230.

19. Woodrow Wilson to Colonel House, December 21, 1911, quoted in Ray Stannard Baker, *Woodrow Wilson: Life and Letters,* 8 vols. (Garden City, NY: Doubleday, 1927–1939), 3: 250.

20. Edward House, diary entry for October 16, 1913, Edward Mandell House and Charles Seymour, *The Intimate Papers of Colonel House, Arranged as a Narrative by Charles Seymour,* 4 vols. (Boston: Houghton Mifflin, 1926), 1: 119.
21. Arthur S. Link, *Wilson: The Road to the White House* (Princeton, NJ: Princeton University Press, 1947), 355, 394, 523.
22. Dudley Malone to Woodrow Wilson, September 7, 1917, *Papers of Woodrow Wilson,* 44: 167–169.
23. Dudley Malone, interview by William Bullitt, notes on conversations about Woodrow Wilson, July 9, 1930, Bullitt Papers, box 148, folder 233.
24. William Allen White, *Woodrow Wilson: The Man, His Times and His Task* (Boston: Houghton Mifflin, 1924), 46, 31.
25. Woodrow Wilson, "Abraham Lincoln: A Man of the People" address, Chicago, February 12, 1909, *Papers of Woodrow Wilson,* 19: 33–47, 33.
26. Woodrow Wilson, "Address on Robert E. Lee at the University of North Carolina," January 19, 1909, *Papers of Woodrow Wilson,* 18:631, 635.
27. Baker, *Wilson: Life and Letters,* 1: 42, 45.
28. Baker, *Wilson: Life and Letters,* 1: 66–68.
29. See William Hale, *Woodrow Wilson, The Story of His Life* (Garden City, NY: Doubleday, 1912), 63–65, reporting the moment.
30. Baker, *Wilson: Life and Letters,* 1: 89.
31. Hale, *Wilson, The Story of His Life,* 69–70; Baker, *Wilson: Life and Letters,* 1: 105; Woodrow Wilson to Ellen Axson, October 30, 1883, Baker, *Wilson: Life and Letters,* 1: 103–104.
32. Baker, *Wilson: Life and Letters,* 1: 89.
33. Baker, *Wilson: Life and Letters,* 1: 123; and Joseph Wilson to Woodrow Wilson, March 20, 1879, *Papers of Woodrow Wilson,* 1: 466.
34. Woodrow Wilson to Ellen Axson, October 23, 1883, Baker, *Wilson: Life and Letters,* 1: 46; Harriet Woodrow Welles to Ray Stannard Baker, n.d., Baker, *Wilson: Life and Letters,* 1: 31.
35. Baker, *Wilson: Life and Letters,* 1: 129–130.
36. See George C. Osborn, "Woodrow Wilson: The Evolution of a Name," *North Carolina Historical Review* 34, no. 4 (1957): 507–516.
37. Quoted in Baker, *Wilson: Life and Letters,* 1: 155.
38. Woodrow Wilson, *Congressional Government: A Study in American Politics* (Boston: Houghton, Mifflin, 1885).
39. See Marvin Rintala, Review of *Wilson and Congressional Government,* by Woodrow Wilson, edited by Arthur S. Link, *Review of Politics* 30, no. 4 (1968): 502–506.
40. Baker, *Wilson: Life and Letters,* 1: 166–167. Emphasis in original.

41. Woodrow Wilson to Robert Bridges, August 26, 1888, Baker, *Wilson: Life and Letters,* 1: 295.

42. Edward House, diary entry for December 12, 1913, House Diary, vol. 1, 393, box 296, folders 1–2, House Papers; Edward House, diary entry for January 22, 1914, House Diary, vol. 2, 23, box 296, folders 5–6, House Papers.

43. Edward House, interview by William Bullitt, May 7, 1930, notes on conversations about Woodrow Wilson, Bullitt Papers, box 148, folder 232.

44. Baker, *Wilson: Life and Letters,* 1: 30–31.

45. Merrill D. Peterson, *The President and His Biographer: Woodrow Wilson and Ray Stannard Baker* (Charlottesville: University of Virginia Press: 2007), 20–21.

46. Baker, *Wilson: Life and Letters,* 2: 23. Emphasis in original.

47. Woodrow Wilson to Ellen Axson Wilson, July 19, 1902, Baker, *Wilson: Life and Letters,* 2: 134.

48. William Bullitt, "Notes on Woodrow Wilson," vol. 1, 53, Bullitt Papers, box 148, folder 234.

49. Baker, *Wilson: Life and Letters,* 2: 162, 175–180.

50. Link, *Wilson: Road to the White House,* 44; Baker, *Wilson: Life and Letters,* 2: 202–203.

51. W. Barksdale Maynard, *Woodrow Wilson: Princeton to the Presidency* (New Haven, CT: Yale University Press, 2008), 158.

52. Henry W. Bragdon, *Woodrow Wilson: The Academic Years* (Cambridge, MA: Belknap Press of Harvard University Press, 1967), 188.

53. See Hale, *Wilson, The Story of His Life,* 125–129.

54. Woodrow Wilson, "President Wilson's Address to the Board of Trustees," news release, June 10, 1907, *Papers of Woodrow Wilson,* 17: 199–206.

55. Baker, *Wilson: Life and Letters,* 2: 257.

56. Bragdon, *Woodrow Wilson: The Academic Years,* 198.

57. Woodrow Wilson, "From the Minutes of the Board of Trustees of Princeton University," October 17, 1907, *Papers of Woodrow Wilson,* 17: 441–443.

58. William Bullitt, "Notes on Woodrow Wilson," vol. 1, 69, box 148, folder 236, Bullitt Papers. Sigmund Freud and William C. Bullitt, *Thomas Woodrow Wilson: A Psychological Study* (Boston: Houghton Mifflin, 1966), 130.

59. Stockton Axson, testimony to Ray Baker, n.d., Baker, *Wilson: Life and Letters,* 2: 266.

60. John Milton Cooper, *Woodrow Wilson: A Biography* (New York: Alfred A. Knopf, 2009), 94; Baker, *Wilson: Life and Letters,* 2: 267.

61. James Kerney, *The Political Education of Woodrow Wilson* (New York: Century, 1926), 450; Alexander L. George and Juliette L. George, *Woodrow*

Wilson and Colonel House: A Personality Study (New York: John Day, 1956), 38.

62. Woodrow Wilson to Moses Taylor Pyne, December 25, 1909, *Papers of Woodrow Wilson,* 19: 628–631; Link, *Wilson: Road to the White House,* 68.

63. *Papers of Woodrow Wilson,* 19: 631, 458, quoted in Maynard, *Princeton to the Presidency,* 215.

64. Woodrow Wilson to Pyne, December 25, 1909.

65. Link, *Wilson: Road to the White House,* 70–71.

66. Baker, *Wilson: Life and Letters,* 2: 325.

67. Freud and Bullitt, *Thomas Woodrow Wilson,* 139.

68. "Woodrow Wilson Is for True Democracy," news report of Wilson's address to Princeton alumni, Pittsburgh, *Gazette Times* (Pittsburgh), April 17, 1910, *Papers of Woodrow Wilson,* 20: 363.

69. John Blum, *Joe Tumulty and the Wilson Era* (Boston: Houghton Mifflin, 1951), 34, 41, 138.

70. Kerney, *Political Education of Woodrow Wilson,* 26.

71. William Bullitt, "Notes on Woodrow Wilson," vol. 1, 78, Bullitt Papers, box 148, folder 236.

72. Peterson, *The President and His Biographer,* 45–46.

73. House and Seymour, *Intimate Papers of Colonel House,* 1: 120.

7. Neurosis on the World Stage

1. Jerold S. Auerbach doubts that this conversation occurred. See Auerbach, "Woodrow Wilson's 'Prediction' to Frank Cobb: Words Historians Should Doubt Ever Got Spoken," *Journal of American History* 54, no. 3 (1967): 608–617. Arthur S. Link argues that it was a real conversation. See Link, "That Cobb Interview," *Journal of American History* 72, no. 1 (1985): 7–17.

2. Edward House, interview by William Bullitt, June 1, 1930, notes on conversations about Woodrow Wilson, box 148, folder 232, William C. Bullitt Papers, MS 112, Manuscripts and Archives, Yale University Library (hereafter Bullitt Papers).

3. Edward House, interview by William Bullitt, May 30, 1930, notes on conversations about Woodrow Wilson, Bullitt Papers, box 148, folder 232.

4. Edward House, diary, entry for September 5, 1925, vol. 9, 107–108, box 298, folders 1–2, Edward Mandell House Papers, MS 466, Manuscripts and Archives, Yale University Library (hereafter House Papers).

5. John A. Thompson, "Woodrow Wilson and World War I: A Reappraisal," *Journal of American Studies* 19, no. 3 (1985): 325–348, 333; John A. Thompson, *Woodrow Wilson* (Harlow, UK: Pearson Education, 2002), 112.

6. Charles E. Neu, *Colonel House: A Biography of Woodrow Wilson's Silent Partner* (New York: Oxford University Press, 2014), 194.

7. Edward House, diary, entry for November 14, 1914, vol. 2, 227, House Papers, box 296, folders 3–4.

8. Edward House, diary, entry for September 22, 1915, vol. 3, 228, House Papers, box 296, folders 5–6.

9. Arthur Walworth, *Woodrow Wilson,* 3rd ed. (New York: Norton, 1978), 2: 26.

10. Woodrow Wilson to Edward House, October 18, 1915, and Edward House, draft of memorandum to Edward Grey, October 17, 1915, Woodrow Wilson, *The Papers of Woodrow Wilson,* ed. Arthur S. Link et al., 69 vols. (Princeton, NJ: Princeton University Press, 1966–1993), 35: 80–81. Emphasis added.

11. Neu, *Colonel House,* 215–216.

12. See Edward Mandell House and Charles Seymour, *The Intimate Papers of Colonel House, Arranged as a Narrative by Charles Seymour,* 4 vols. (Boston: Houghton Mifflin, 1926), 3: 110, 117; Walworth, *Woodrow Wilson,* 2: 29.

13. Woodrow Wilson to Edward House, January 9, 1916, *Papers of Woodrow Wilson,* 35: 457.

14. "Not unfavorable" meant Alsace-Lorraine for France, Constantinople for Russia, restoration of Belgium and Serbia, Polish independence, cession of Italian-speaking regions of Austria to Italy, and establishment of the League of Nations. Germany would be compensated for its losses in Europe with gains in Africa. See House and Seymour, *Intimate Papers of Colonel House,* 2: 170.

15. See Philip Kerr to Charles Seymour, October 7, 1933, box 9, folder 522, Charles Seymour Papers, MSS 441, Manuscripts and Archives, Yale University Library (hereafter Seymour Papers); House and Seymour, *Intimate Papers of Colonel House,* 2: 201.

16. Sigmund Freud and William C. Bullitt, *Thomas Woodrow Wilson: A Psychological Study* (Boston: Houghton Mifflin, 1966), 178; and Neu, *Colonel House,* 244–245.

17. Woodrow Wilson to Mary Hulbert, August 3, 1913, quoted in Alexander L. George and Juliette L. George, *Woodrow Wilson and Colonel House: A Personality Study* (New York: John Day, 1956), 31.

18. See David Lawrence, *The True Story of Woodrow Wilson* (New York: George H. Doran, 1924), 334.

19. Robert Lansing, "An Appeal for a Statement of War Aims," *Papers of Woodrow Wilson,* 40, 273–276.

20. Philip Zelikow, *The Road Less Traveled: The Secret Battle to End the Great War, 1916–1917* (New York: PublicAffairs, 2021), 208.

21. William Bullitt, "Notes on Woodrow Wilson," vol. 1, 173, Bullitt Papers, box 148, folder 237. Woodrow Wilson, "Peace without Victory," address

to the U.S. Senate, January 22, 1917, *Papers of Woodrow Wilson,* 40: 535–538.

22. Holger Afflerbach and Gary Sheffield, "Waging Total War: Learning Curve or Bleeding Curve?" in *The Legacy of the Great War: Ninety Years On,* ed. Jay Winter, 61–90 (Columbia: University of Missouri Press, 2009), 75.
23. Joseph P. Tumulty, *Wilson as I Know Him* (Garden City, NY: Doubleday Page, 1921), 256–259.
24. Ray Stannard Baker, *Woodrow Wilson: Life and Letters,* 8 vols. (Garden City, NY: Doubleday, 1927–1939), 2: 28.
25. Ellis W. Hawley, *The Great War and the Search for a Modern Order: A History of the American People and Their Institutions, 1917–1933* (New York: St. Martin's Press, 1979), 17–18, 21, 448.
26. Beatrice Farnsworth, *William Bullitt and the Soviet Union* (Bloomington: Indiana University Press, 1967), 18.
27. House and Seymour, *Intimate Papers of Colonel House,* 3: 393–394.
28. William Bullitt to George Kennan, September 22, 1955, Bullitt Papers, box 44, folder 1062; George F. Kennan, *Soviet-American Relations, 1917–1920,* vol. 1: *Russia Leaves the War* (Princeton, NJ: Princeton University Press, 1956), 475–483.
29. Charles Seymour, memorandum of conversation with Edward House, March 31, 1922, Seymour Papers, box 52, folder 254.
30. Joseph Tumulty, interview by William Bullitt, September 30, 1930, notes on conversations about Woodrow Wilson, Bullitt Papers, box 148, folder 233.
31. A. Scott Berg, *Wilson* (New York: G. P. Putnam's Sons, 2013), 444.
32. William Bullitt, "Notes on Woodrow Wilson," vol. 2, 33, 36–37, Bullitt Papers, box 148, folder 238.
33. William Bullitt, "Notes on Woodrow Wilson," vol. 2, 55, Bullitt Papers, box 148, folder 238.
34. Joseph Tumulty, telegram to Cary Grayson, December 17, 1918, box 83, folder "Tumulty, Joseph P.," Cary T. Grayson Papers, MS 000465, Woodrow Wilson Presidential Library and Museum, Staunton, VA (hereafter Grayson Papers); James Kerney, *The Political Education of Woodrow Wilson* (New York: Century, 1926), 428.
35. George Bernard Noble, *Policies and Opinions at Paris, 1919: Wilsonian Diplomacy, the Versailles Peace and French Public Opinion* (New York: Macmillan, 1935), 40.
36. House and Seymour, *Intimate Papers of Colonel House,* 4: 300.
37. Paul Cambon, *Correspondance,* vol. 3: *1912–1924* (Paris: B. Grasset, 1946), 300.
38. Margaret MacMillan, *Paris 1919: Six Months That Changed the World* (New York: Random House, 2001), 382–388. Arthur Walworth, *Wilson and*

His Peacemakers: American Diplomacy at the Paris Peace Conference, 1919 (New York: Norton, 1986), 488, n. 21.

39. Walworth, *Wilson and His Peacemakers,* 54; and Charles Seymour, "Woodrow Wilson and Self-Determination in the Tyrol," *Virginia Quarterly Review* 38, no. 4 (1962): 567–587.

40. Neu, *Colonel House,* 401–402.

41. Cary Grayson, diary entry for March 13, 1919, Peace Conference, second trip, original copy, 22, series Grayson Diaries, box 2, Grayson Papers. House also agreed with André Tardieu, Clemenceau's representative, on a plan for a temporary Rhenish Republic but did not report it to Wilson before the president's return to France. See Arthur Walworth, "Considerations on Woodrow Wilson and Edward M. House: An Essay Letter to the Editor," *Presidential Studies Quarterly* 24, no. 1 (1994): 79–86. House's acceptance of the proposed temporary Rhenish Republic is confirmed in André Tardieu to Georges Clemenceau, March 7, 1919, War Archives (1914–1939), vol. 2, box 6N73, Georges Clemenceau Papers, French Ministry of Defense Archives, Vincennes.

42. Charles L. Swem, "Peace Conference + Going Abroad," unpublished ms., "Writings," box 87, folder 19, "Charles L. Swem (personal)," series 10: Papers of Others about Wilson, "Swem, Charles L.," Woodrow Wilson Collection, MC 168, Public Policy Papers, Special Collections, Princeton University Library.

43. Edward House to Charles Seymour, April 21, 1922, Seymour Papers, box 52, folder 255.

44. William Bullitt, memorandum of meeting with Ray Baker, October 11, 1931, "Thomas Woodrow Wilson" manuscript, notes, box 148, folder 231.

45. Bernard Baruch, interview by William Bullitt, October 4, 1930, notes on conversations about Woodrow Wilson, Bullitt Papers, box 148, folder 233.

46. William Bullitt, "Notes on Woodrow Wilson," vol. 1, 141, Bullitt Papers, box 148, folder 237.

47. William Bullitt, "Notes on Woodrow Wilson," vol. 1, 142–150, Bullitt Papers, box 148, folder 237.

48. Macmillan, *Paris 1919,* 283.

49. Wilson admitted to Baker, "I am sorry for that decision. I was ignorant of the situation when the decision was made." Ray Stannard Baker, diary entry for May 28, 1919, in Ray Stannard Baker, *A Journalist's Diplomatic Mission: Ray Stannard Baker's World War I Diary,* ed. John Maxwell Hamilton and Robert Mann (Baton Rouge: Louisiana State University Press, 2012), 398.

50. Neu, *Colonel House,* 416–417.

51. Noble, *Policies and Opinions,* 335.

52. Macmillan, *Paris 1919,* 466; Noble, *Policies and Opinions,* 362.

53. Bullitt, memo of meeting with Baruch, October 4, 1930.

54. Antony Lentin, *Lloyd George, Woodrow Wilson and the Guilt of Germany: An Essay in the Pre-History of Appeasement* (Baton Rouge: Louisiana State University Press, 1985), 96.

55. Robert Lansing to Frank Polk, June 4, 1919, box 9, folder 315, Frank Lyon Polk Papers, MS 656, Manuscripts and Archives, Yale University Library.

56. Sigmund Freud, "Introduction," in Freud and Bullitt, *Thomas Woodrow Wilson,* xii.

57. Freud and Bullitt, *Thomas Woodrow Wilson,* 355.

58. Edward House to Charles Seymour, September 29, 1930, box 101, folder 3492, House Papers.

8. Analyzing Wilson

1. Max Schur, *Freud: Living and Dying* (New York: International University Press, 1972), 424.

2. For example, Bullitt sought Philip Kerr's minutes of the Council of Four. Philip Kerr to William Bullitt, October 6, 1930, box 51, folder 1225, William C. Bullitt Papers, MS 112, Manuscripts and Archives, Yale University Library (hereafter Bullitt Papers).

3. William Bullitt, memorandum of conversation with Sigmund Freud, October 27, 1930, "Thomas Woodrow Wilson" manuscript, notes, Bullitt Papers, box 148, folder 231.

4. Bullitt, memo of conversation with Freud, October 27, 1930.

5. Sigmund Freud and William C. Bullitt, *Thomas Woodrow Wilson: A Psychological Study* (Boston: Houghton Mifflin, 1966), 86. The dates of Wilson's illnesses were: June 1874–October 1875, December 1880–June 1882, November 1883–March 1884, October 1887–June 1888, November 1895–August 1896, June–August 1899, summer of 1903, January–March 1905, September 1907–September 1908, February–March 1910, August 1914–February 1915, April 1919.

6. Ellen Axson Wilson to Florence S. Hoyt, June 27, 1906, Woodrow Wilson, *The Papers of Woodrow Wilson,* ed. Arthur S. Link et al., 69 vols. (Princeton, NJ: Princeton University Press, 1966–1993), 16: 430.

7. Alfred Stengel, interview by William Bullitt, August 11, 1930, notes on conversations about Woodrow Wilson, Bullitt Papers, box 148, folder 233.

8. Francis Dercum, interview by William Bullitt, July 7, 1930, notes on conversations about Woodrow Wilson, Bullitt Papers, box 148, folder 233.

9. William Allen White, *Woodrow Wilson: The Man, His Times, and His Task* (Boston: Houghton Mifflin, 1924), 276.

10. Cary Grayson, interview by William Bullitt, October 9, 1930, notes on conversations about Woodrow Wilson, Bullitt Papers, box 148, folder 233.

11. William Bullitt, draft of Foreword, n.d., "Thomas Woodrow Wilson" manuscript drafts, Bullitt Papers, box 146, folder 201.

12. Ray Stannard Baker, interview by William Bullitt, July 18, 1930, notes on conversations about Woodrow Wilson, Bullitt Papers, box 148, folder 232.

13. Cary T. Grayson, "The Colonel's Folly and the President's Distress," *American Heritage* 15, no. 6 (October 1964).

14. Baker, interview by Bullitt, July 18, 1930.

15. William Bullitt, "Notes on Woodrow Wilson," William Bullitt Papers, box 148, folders 234 to 247.

16. Sigmund Freud to William Bullitt, November 22, 1930, "Thomas Woodrow Wilson" manuscript, drafts, Freud ms fragments, Bullitt Papers, box 147, folder 222.

17. Sigmund Freud and William C. Bullitt, "Thomas Woodrow Wilson, Twenty-eighth President of the United States: A Psychological Study," unpublished original manuscript (1932), 12, 14, typescript in presentation binder, 389 pp, Bullitt Papers, Accession 2008-M-037, box 2, folder 10.

18. Freud and Bullitt, *Thomas Woodrow Wilson,* 40.

19. William Bullitt, memorandum of conversation with Sigmund Freud, December 12, 1930, "Thomas Woodrow Wilson" manuscript, notes, Bullitt Papers, box 148, folder 231. Emphasis in original.

20. Freud and Bullitt, *Thomas Woodrow Wilson,* 38.

21. Sigmund Freud, "Introduction," in Freud and Bullitt, *Thomas Woodrow Wilson,* xvi.

22. William Bullitt, note, n.d., "Thomas Woodrow Wilson" manuscript, drafts, Bullitt Papers, box 147, folder 228. Emphasis in original.

23. Sigmund Freud, additions to "draft of chapters 1 and 2," 42, n.d., "Thomas Woodrow Wilson" manuscript, drafts, Freud ms fragments, Bullitt Papers, box 147, folder 222. These additions of Freud appear in Freud and Bullitt, *Thomas Woodrow Wilson,* 54.

24. Freud and Bullitt, *Thomas Woodrow Wilson,* 53, 130–131. House noted Wilson's demand for adulation. Charles Seymour, memorandum of conversation with Edward House, April 28, 1922, box 52, folder 255, Charles Seymour Papers, MSS 441, Manuscripts and Archives, Yale University Library.

25. Woodrow Wilson to Ellen Axson Wilson, April 19, 1888, Baker, *Wilson: Life and Letters,* 1: 35.

26. Woodrow Wilson to Joseph Wilson, December 16, 1888, Freud and Bullitt, *Thomas Woodrow Wilson,* 99.

27. Woodrow Wilson to Joseph Wilson, March 20, 1890, Freud and Bullitt, *Thomas Woodrow Wilson,* 100.

28. Sigmund Freud, *Inhibition, Symptoms, and Anxiety* (1926), in Sigmund Freud, *The Standard Edition of the Complete Works of Sigmund Freud,* ed.

James Strachey with Anna Freud, 24 vols. (London: Hogarth Press, 1953–1974), 20: 102 (hereafter Freud, *Standard Edition*). Jean Laplanche and J.-B. Pontalis, *The Language of Psycho-analysis* (London: Hogarth, 1973), 28.

29. Sigmund Freud to Mrs. Lancaster, December 8, 1930, General Correspondence, box 36, folder Elizabeth G. Lancaster, Sigmund Freud Papers, MSS 39990, Library of Congress.

30. Freud and Bullitt, *Thomas Woodrow Wilson,* 69.

31. Anna Freud to Ernest Jones, January 31, 1954, Series C: Named Correspondence, P04-C-C-06: Anna Freud, Alfred Ernest Jones Collection, P04, Archives of the British Psychoanalytical Society, Institute of Psychoanalysis, London.

32. Sigmund Freud to Max Eitingon, March 20, 1931, Sigmund Freud, *Max Eitingon, Briefwechsel, 1906–1939,* 2 vols. (Tübingen: Edition Diskord, 2004), letter 638F, 2: 720. My translation.

33. Quoted in Schur, *Freud: Living and Dying,* 425.

34. Schur, *Freud: Living and Dying,* 427–428. Sigmund Freud to William Bullitt, April 22, 1931, "Thomas Woodrow Wilson" manuscript, drafts, Freud ms fragments, Bullitt Papers, box 147, folder 224.

35. Freud and Bullitt, "Thomas Woodrow Wilson," original manuscript (1932), 85–86, Bullitt Papers, Accession 2008-M-037, box 2, folder 10.

36. Sigmund Freud, handwritten note on "Wilson illnesses," "Thomas Woodrow Wilson" manuscript, drafts, Freud ms fragments, Bullitt Papers, box 147, folder 223; Freud's handwritten note, translated into English, "Thomas Woodrow Wilson" manuscript, partial drafts, Bullitt Papers, box 146, folder 197. Freud and Bullitt, "Thomas Woodrow Wilson," original manuscript (1932), 83–85, Bullitt Papers, Accession 2008-M-037, box 2, folder 10.

37. William Bullitt to Sigmund Freud, March 7, 1931, "Thomas Woodrow Wilson" manuscript, drafts, Freud ms fragments, Bullitt Papers, box 147, folder 224.

38. Baker, *Wilson: Life and Letters,* 1: 57, 71, 89.

39. Freud and Bullitt, "Thomas Woodrow Wilson," original manuscript (1932), 90–91, Bullitt Papers, Accession 2008-M-037, box 2, folder 10.

40. William Bullitt to Sigmund Freud, March 7, 1931, "Thomas Woodrow Wilson" manuscript, drafts, Freud ms fragments, Bullitt Papers, box 147, folder 224.

41. Arthur G. Hays to Louise Bryant, May 14, 1931, box 4, folder 46, Louise Bryant Papers, MS 1840, Manuscripts and Archives, Yale University Library (hereafter Bryant Papers).

42. Henry Brougham confirmed that the 1910 *New York Times* editorial emphasizing Wilson's principled battle at Princeton was in fact written in consultation with Wilson. Henry B. Brougham to William Bullitt, September 23, 1931, "Thomas Woodrow Wilson" manuscript, correspondence, Bullitt Papers, box 142, folder 127. See Arthur S. Link, *Wilson: The Road to the White House*

(Princeton, NJ: Princeton University Press, 1947), 77. Neil Burkinshaw confirmed to Bullitt that Wilson had ordered the suspension of US financial support to the Allies in April 1919. Neil Burkinshaw to William Bullitt, March 12, 1932, Bullitt Papers, Accession 2008-M-037, box 1, folder 37.

43. See Ray Baker, correspondence with William Bullitt, August and September 1931, box 101, folder Bullitt, Correspondence Relating to Woodrow Wilson, 1920–1939, Ray Stannard Baker Papers, MSS 11593, Library of Congress.

44. Cary Grayson, interview by William Bullitt, October 22, 1931, notes on conversations about Woodrow Wilson, Bullitt Papers, box 148, folder 233.

45. John Milton Cooper, *Woodrow Wilson: A Biography* (New York: Alfred A. Knopf, 2009), 587.

46. Grayson, interview by Bullitt, October 22, 1931.

47. William Bullitt, correspondence with Louise Bryant, August 29 and 31, 1931, Bullitt Papers, box 11, folder 241; Arthur Hays to Louise Bryant, October 16, 1931, Louise Bryant Papers, box 4, folder 47.

48. Arthur Hays to Louise Bryant, October 30, 1930, Louise Bryant Papers, box 4, folder 46; Mary V. Dearborn, *Queen of Bohemia: The Life of Louise Bryant* (Boston: Houghton Mifflin, 1966), 289.

49. Wambly Bald, *On the Left Bank, 1929–1933*, ed. Benjamin Franklin V (Athens: Ohio University Press, 1987), August 12, 1930, 22.

50. See Sigmund Freud to William Bullitt, February 22, 1932, "Thomas Woodrow Wilson" manuscript, drafts, Freud ms fragments, Bullitt Papers, box 147, folder 224.

51. William Shirer, *20th Century Journey*, vol. 1: *The Start, 1904–1930* (New York: Simon and Schuster, 1976), 441–447.

52. Bald, *On the Left Bank*, February 9, 1932, 119.

53. William Bullitt to Edward House, April 29, 1932, box 21, folder 684, Edward Mandell House Papers, MS 466, Manuscripts and Archives, Yale University Library.

9. Signing On with FDR

1. William Bullitt, memorandum of conversation with Sigmund Freud, October 27, 1930, box 148, folder 231, "Thomas Woodrow Wilson" manuscript, notes, William C. Bullitt Papers, MS 112, Manuscripts and Archives, Yale University Library (hereafter Bullitt Papers).

2. Charles E. Neu, *Colonel House: A Biography of Woodrow Wilson's Silent Partner* (New York: Oxford University Press, 2014), 482.

3. William Bullitt to Edward House, December 13, 1931, box 21, folder 685, Edward Mandell House Papers, MS 466, Manuscripts and Archives, Yale University Library (hereafter House Papers).

4. Edward House to William Bullitt, December 28, 1931, Bullitt Papers, Accession 2008-M-037, box 1, folder 50.
5. William Bullitt to Edward House, May 27, 1932, House Papers, box 21, folder 685.
6. Eugene Lyons, *Assignment in Utopia* (New York: Harcourt, 1937), 501.
7. Elliot A. Rosen, *Hoover, Roosevelt, and the Brains Trust: From Depression to New Deal* (Cambridge: Cambridge University Press, 1977), 23.
8. Edward House to Louis Wehle, February 19, 1932, House Papers, box 117, folder 4126.
9. Louis Wehle, *Hidden Threads of History: Wilson through Roosevelt* (New York: Macmillan, 1953), 110–113.
10. William Bullitt to Gardner Cowles, August 31, 1950, Bullitt Papers, box 21, folder 462.
11. Louis Wehle to William Bullitt, September 30, 1932, Bullitt Papers, Accession 2008-M-037, box 1, folder 65.
12. William Bullitt, handwritten addition to the unpublished transcript of Louis Wehle interview for the Columbia Center for Oral History, Columbia University, 145, Bullitt Papers, box 88, folder 2262.
13. Quoted in Robert Dallek, *Franklin D. Roosevelt: A Political Life* (New York: Viking, 2017), 115.
14. Wehle, *Hidden Threads,* 114–115.
15. William Bullitt to Gardner Cowles, August 31, 1950.
16. Wehle, *Hidden Threads,* 118.
17. Sigmund Freud to William Bullitt, December 13, 1932, Bullitt Papers, box 30, folder 681.
18. Will Brownell and Richard N. Billings, *So Close to Greatness: A Biography of William C. Bullitt* (New York: Macmillan, 1987), 123–124.
19. Sigmund Freud to Jeanne Lampl-de Groot, February 16, 1933, in Sigmund Freud, *Briefe an Jeanne Lampl-de Groot, 1921–1939,* ed. Gertie F. Bögels, transcription by Gerhard Fichtner (Giessen: Psychosozial-Verlag, 2017), 105.
20. "'Who Is Bullitt?' Echoes in the Senate," *New York Times,* February 3, 1933.
21. Sigmund Freud to Jeanne Lampl-de Groot, February 1, 1933, Freud, *Briefe an Jeanne Lampl-de Groot,* 102.
22. Arthur Schlesinger, Jr., *The Coming of the New Deal 1933–1935,* vol. 2: *The Age of Roosevelt* (Boston: Houghton Mifflin, 2003), 188–189.
23. William Bullitt to Raymond Moley, March 19, 1933, Raymond Moley Papers (68008), General Correspondence, box 63, folder 8, Hoover Institution Library and Archives, Stanford University.
24. Sigmund Freud to Jeanne Lampl-de Groot, March 9, 1933, Freud, *Briefe an Jeanne Lampl-de Groot,* 107.

25. Raymond Moley, *After Seven Years* (New York: Harper & Brothers, 1939), 135–136.

26. Anne O'Hare McCormick, "The Two Men at the Big Moment," *New York Times*, November 5,1932.

27. Ben Cohen, interview by Joseph Lash, May 6, 1970, Joseph P. Lash Papers, General Correspondence, Box 3, Franklin D. Roosevelt Presidential Library and Museum, Hyde Park, NY.

28. Franklin D. Roosevelt to Hugh S. Gibson, January 2, 1920, box 3, Hugh Gibson Collection, Herbert Hoover Presidential Library and Museum, West Branch, IA.

29. Robert Dallek, *Franklin D. Roosevelt and American Foreign Policy, 1932–1945* (New York: Oxford University Press, 1979), 35.

30. Rosen, *Hoover, Roosevelt, and the Brains Trust*, 269–270.

31. Raymond Moley, transcript of interview by Elliot Rosen, series 2, October 4, 1967, 54, box 21, Elliot A. Rosen Papers, Herbert Hoover Presidential Library and Museum, West Branch, IA.

32. "Reminiscences of James P. Warburg," 1952, transcript, p. 505, Columbia Center for Oral History, Columbia University.

33. Schlesinger, *The Coming of the New Deal*, 205.

34. Raymond Moley, speech at Columbia Broadcasting network, May 20, 1933, in Moley, *After Seven Years*, 209; Shepard Stone, "Anglo-American Economic Issues," *Current History* 38, no. 4 (1933): 399–405, 400.

35. Dallek, *Franklin D. Roosevelt and American Foreign Policy*, 38–39.

36. Schlesinger, *The Coming of the New Deal*, 215.

37. Moley, *After Seven Years*, Appendix F, 417–418. Patricia Clavin, "'The Fetishes of So-Called International Bankers': Central Bank Co-operation for the World Economic Conference, 1932–3," *Contemporary European History* 1, no. 3 (1992): 281–311, 281, 306.

38. President Roosevelt to the Acting Secretary of State, July 2, 1933, Foreign Relations of the United States, Diplomatic Papers, 1933, General, vol. 1, doc. 503.

39. Ramsay MacDonald, message to Thomas Lamont, July 5, 1933, folder "World Economic Conference: exchange of messages Lamont and Bullitt," PRO 30/69/597, James Ramsay MacDonald . . . Papers, British National Archives.

40. "Reminiscences of James P. Warburg," transcript pp. 233, 429.

41. William Bullitt to Franklin D. Roosevelt, July 8, 1933, Franklin D. Roosevelt, Papers as President, President's Personal File, file 1124: "Bullitt, William C.," Franklin D. Roosevelt Presidential Library and Museum, Hyde Park, NY.

42. "Recognition of the Soviet Union, 1933," Office of the Historian, US Department of State, n.d., https://history.state.gov/milestones/1921-1936/ussr (site retired and no longer maintained).

43. John Morton Blum, *From the Morgenthau Diaries,* 3 vols. (Boston: Houghton Mifflin, 1959–1967), 1: 21.

44. William Bullitt, "How We Won the War and Lost the Peace," part 1, *Life,* August 30, 1948, 83–97.

45. Katherine Siegel, *Loans and Legitimacy: The Evolution of Soviet-American Relations, 1919–1933* (Lexington: University Press of Kentucky, 1996), 137.

46. Siegel, *Loans and Legitimacy,* 137.

47. George F. Kennan, "The United States and the Soviet Union, 1917–1976," *Foreign Affairs* 54, no. 4 (1976): 670–690, 676; Moritz Schlesinger to William Bullitt, November 18, 1933, Bullitt Papers, box 74, folder 1865.

48. Cissy Patterson to William Bullitt, November 18, 1933, Bullitt Papers, box 65, folder 1592.

49. Steffens added: "The third is probably Litvinov." Lincoln Steffens to William Bullitt, November 25, 1933, Bullitt Papers, box 78, folder 2009.

50. William Bullitt, note regarding Roosevelt, no date, Bullitt Papers, box 73, folder 1830; William Bullitt to George Lansbury, Bullitt Papers, box 48, folder 1170.

10. Ambassador Bullitt Goes to Moscow

1. S. J. Woolf, "Bullitt Looks at the European Scene," *New York Times Magazine,* September 6, 1936.

2. Franklin D. Roosevelt and William C. Bullitt, *For the President, Personal and Secret: Correspondence between Franklin D. Roosevelt and William C. Bullitt,* ed. Orville H. Bullitt (Boston: Houghton Mifflin, 1972), 66–69.

3. Henry W. Brands, *Inside the Cold War: Loy Henderson and the Rise of the American Empire, 1918–1961* (New York: Oxford University Press, 1991), 51.

4. Elbridge Durbrow, interview with Virginia Gardner, January 23, 1973, box 5, folder 40, Virginia Gardner Papers, TAM.100, Tamiment Library, New York University (hereafter Gardner Papers).

5. William Bullitt to J. V. A. MacMurray, American ambassador to Riga, December 14, 1933, box 54, folder 1325; and George Kennan to William Bullitt, December 27, 1933, box 44, folder 1060, both in William C. Bullitt Papers, MS 112, Manuscripts and Archives, Yale University Library (hereafter Bullitt Papers).

6. Loy W. Henderson, *Question of Trust: The Origins of U.S.-Soviet Diplomatic Relations,* ed. with intro. by George W. Baer (Stanford, CA: Hoover Institution Press, 1986), 352–353.

7. Peter Gay, *Freud: A Life for Our Time* (New York: Norton, 1988), 592.

8. William Bullitt to Sigmund Freud, December 2, 1933, Bullitt Papers, box 30, folder 681.

9. William Bullitt to Julian W. Mack, February 3, 1934, Bullitt Papers, box 54, folder 1320.

10. Sigmund Freud to Hilda Doolittle, March 5, 1934, box 10, folder 341, H. D. [Hilda Doolittle] Papers, YCAL MSS 24, Beinecke Rare Book and Manuscript Library, Yale University Library (hereafter Doolittle Papers).

11. Sigmund Freud to E. Freud, March 11, 1934, in Gerhard Fichtner, "'Was ist doch menschliches Glück . . .': Ein Brief Freuds an Samuel Hammerschlag aus dem Jahre 1885," *Jahrbuch der Psychoanalyse* 55, no. 1 (2007): 167–175.

12. Julian W. Mack and Marie Bonaparte, correspondence, February–March 1934, box 66: 1934 G–Z, folder M, Fonds Marie Bonaparte, NAF28230, Bibliothèque nationale de France. See also Sigmund Freud to Hilda Doolittle, November 3, 1935, Doolittle Papers, box 10, folder 341.

13. See, e.g., William Bullitt to Louise Bryant, July 5, 1932, Bullitt Papers, box 11, folder 240.

14. Louise Bryant to Art Hays, November 14, 1932, box 4, folder 47, Louise Bryant Papers, MS 1840, Manuscripts and Archives, Yale University Library (hereafter Bryant Papers).

15. Louise Bryant to William Bullitt, December 27 and 28, 1933, January 24, 1934, Bullitt Papers, box 11, folder 240. Emphasis in original.

16. Samuel Putnam, *Paris Was Our Mistress: Memoirs of a Lost and Found Generation* (New York: Viking, 1947), 94, 137.

17. Putnam, *Paris Was Our Mistress,* 137; Clément Geslin to William Bullitt, December 5, 1933, Bullitt Papers, box 31, folder 707.

18. John Lewis Gaddis, *George F. Kennan: An American Life* (New York: Penguin, 2011), 81.

19. Loy Henderson to William Brownell, May 13, 1974, Correspondence, box 6, Loy W. Henderson Papers, MSS 53314, Library of Congress (hereafter Henderson Papers).

20. Roosevelt and Bullitt, *For the President, Personal and Secret,* 83.

21. U.S. recognition of Russia played a role in Japan's decision not to attack Russia in 1934. Joseph Grew, *Ten Years in Japan* (New York: Simon and Schuster, 1944), 108. July 18, 1933. Roosevelt's June 1933 executive order allocating $238 million for construction of new warships played a role, too. Beatrice Farnsworth, *William Bullitt and the Soviet Union* (Bloomington: Indiana University Press, 1967), 208n18.

22. Alexander Etkind, *Roads Not Taken, An Intellectual Biography of William C. Bullitt* (Pittsburgh: University of Pittsburgh Press, 2017), 130–133.

23. William Bullitt to Edward House, September 2, 1934, box 21, folder 686, Edward Mandell House Papers, MS 466, Manuscripts and Archives, Yale University Library. See also, Farnsworth, *William Bullitt and the Soviet Union,* 104.

24. Charles Wheeler Thayer, *Bears in the Caviar* (Philadelphia: Lippincott, 1951), 230.

25. Henderson, *Question of Trust,* 337–340.

26. [no author], "The Position of an American Ambassador in Moscow," memorandum, [n.d.], group "Ambassador to France, Soviet Union," Bullitt Papers, box 118, folder 524; "Reminiscences of Henry A. Wallace," 1951–1953, regarding May 20, 1942, transcript, 1598, Columbia Center for Oral History, Columbia University.

27. Jean-François Fayet, *Karl Radek (1885–1939), Biographie politique* (Bern: Peter Lang, 2004), 673; Warren Lerner, *Karl Radek: The Last Internationalist* (Stanford, CA: Stanford University Press, 2004), 156–157; Lerner, *Karl Radek,* 163.

28. "Reminiscences of Henry A. Wallace," regarding May 20, 1942, transcript, 1593.

29. Elbridge Durbrow, interview, January 23, 1973.

30. William Bullitt, correspondence with David Salmon, August 28–October 4, 1934, Bullitt Papers, box 74, folder 1853. Kennan confirmed Bullitt's pioneering role in the security of transmissions. George Kennan, *Memoirs 1925–1950* (Boston: Little Brown, 1967), 80.

31. GPU archives, quoted in Allen Weinstein and Alexander Vassiliev, *The Haunted Wood: Soviet Espionage in America—The Stalin Era* (New York: Random House, 1999), 36–37; John Earl Haynes, Harvey Klehr, and Alexander Vassiliev, *Spies, The Rise and Fall of the KGB in America* (New Haven, CT: Yale University Press, 2009), 156.

32. Thayer, *Bears in the Caviar,* 116–117.

33. William C. Bullitt, "A Talk with Voroshilov," in United States Congress, House, Committee on Un-American Activities, "The Great Pretense; A Symposium on Anti-Stalinism and the 20th Congress of the Soviet Communist Party," May 19, 1956, 18–19.

34. Thayer, *Bears in the Caviar,* 116–129.

35. Alexei Varlamov, *Mikhaïl Boulgakov,* trans. from Russian to French by Marie Starynkevitch (Paris: Éditions Louison, 2020), 940–942.

36. Elbridge Durbrow, interview with Brownell and Billings, December 6, 1983, in Will Brownell and Richard N. Billings, *So Close to Greatness: A Biography of William C. Bullitt* (New York: Macmillan, 1987), 157.

37. Frank Costigliola, "'Unceasing Pressure for Penetration': Gender, Pathology and Emotion in George Kennan's Formation of the Cold War," *Journal of American History* 83, no. 4 (1997): 1309–1339, 1317.

38. Charles Thayer to George Kennan, April 10, 1940, quoted in Robert D. Dean, *Imperial Brotherhood: Gender and the Making of Cold War Foreign Policy* (Amherst: University of Massachusetts Press, 2001), 121.

39. George Kennan to William Bullitt, February 13, 1935, Bullitt Papers, box 44, folder 1060.

40. Gaddis, *George F. Kennan,* 90; George Kennan to William Bullitt, April 15, 1935, Bullitt Papers, box 44, folder 1060.

41. William Bullitt to Walton Moore, May 11, 1935, box 3, folder "Bullitt," Walton Moore Papers, Franklin D. Roosevelt Presidential Library and Museum, Hyde Park, NY (hereafter Moore Papers). Emphasis in original.
42. William Bullitt to Hugh Wilson, June 6, 1938, Bullitt Papers, box 91, folder 2321.
43. Burton Hersh, *The Old Boys: The American Elite and the Origins of the CIA* (New York: Scribner's, 1992), 42–43.
44. Roosevelt and Bullitt, *For the President, Personal and Secret,* 135.
45. Orville Horwitz to William Bullitt, undated, Bullitt Papers, box 39, folder 921.
46. William Bullitt to Franklin D. Roosevelt, April 13, 1934, Roosevelt and Bullitt, *For the President, Personal and Secret,* 84.
47. William Bullitt to Missy LeHand, August 21 and September 21, 1933, Bullitt Papers, box 49, folder 1181. For the September dinner, see also "Reminiscences of James P. Warburg," 1952, transcript, 1550, Columbia Center for Oral History, Columbia University.
48. Missy LeHand to William Bullitt, June 3, 1934, Bullitt Papers, box 49, folder 1186. Emphasis in original; Missy LeHand to William Bullitt, undated [1934], Bullitt Papers, box 49, folder 1186; Missy LeHand to William Bullitt, April 21, 1934, Bullitt Papers, box 49, folder 1192.
49. Kathryn Smith, *The Gatekeeper: Missy LeHand, FDR and the Untold Story of a Partnership That Defined a Presidency* (New York: Touchstone, 2016), 151.
50. William Bullitt, memorandum on Thomas D. White, Chief of Staff of the Air Force, February 4, 1961, Bullitt Papers, box 210, folder 221.
51. The Secretary of State, telegram to William Bullitt, May 15, 1935, Department of State, division of international conferences, file 123: Bullitt William C./171, 1930–39 Central Decimal File, RG 59: General Records of the Department of State, U.S. National Archives and Records Administration (hereafter RG 59, NARA).
52. See Stanley Hornbeck, *The United States and the Far East: Certain Fundamentals of Policy* (Boston: World Peace Foundation, 1942).
53. William Bullitt to John Wiley, November 2, 1934, General Correspondence, box 6, "Bullitt," John Cooper Wiley Papers, Franklin D. Roosevelt Presidential Library and Museum, Hyde Park, NY.
54. William Bullitt to Cordell Hull, December 14, 1934, Bullitt Papers, box 111, folder 414; and Roosevelt and Bullitt, *For the President, Personal and Secret,* 100.
55. John Wiley to William Bullitt, January 2, 1935, and William Bullitt to John Wiley, March 13, 1935, files123 Bullitt William C./125, 142, 143, RG 59, NARA. The party cost $5,000, more than $100,000 in current (2022) dollars.

56. Irena Wiley, *Around the Globe in Twenty Years* (New York: David McKay, 1962), 31–34; Thayer, *Bears in the Caviar,* 110, 161–162; Elbridge Durbrow, interview, January 23, 1973.

57. Missy LeHand to William Bullitt, May 7, 1935, Bullitt Papers, box 49, folder 1187.

58. Loy Henderson to William Brownell, May 13, 1974, Correspondence, box 6, Henderson Papers.

59. William Bullitt to R. Walton Moore, May 11, 1935, Moore Papers, box 3, folder "Bullitt"; Donald G. Bishop, *The Roosevelt-Litvinov Agreements: The American View* (Syracuse, NY: Syracuse University Press, 1965), 169.

60. William Bullitt to Robert P. Browder, February 2, 1950, Bullitt Papers, box 11, folder 227.

61. See Thomas Maddux, *Years of Estrangement: America Relations with the Soviet Union, 1933–1941* (Tallahassee: University Presses of Florida, 1980), 40–41.

62. Stephen Kotkin, *Waiting for Hitler, 1929–1941* (New York: Penguin, 2017), 263.

63. Roosevelt and Bullitt, *For the President, Personal and Secret,* 110.

64. William R. Dodd, Jr., and Martha Dodd, eds., *Ambassador Dodd's Diary, 1933–1938* (New York: Harcourt, 1941), 277–278.

65. Robert H. Jackson, *That Man: An Insider's Portrait of Franklin D. Roosevelt,* ed. and intro. by John Q. Barrett (New York: Oxford University Press, 2003), 15.

66. Weinstein and Vassiliev, *The Haunted Wood,* 53.

67. Louise Bryant to Art Hays, May 27, 1935, Florence Corliss Lamont Letters from Various Correspondents, MS Eng 1457, Houghton Library, Harvard Library.

68. Anne Bullitt, interview by Conor Sweeney, in "The Turbulent Life and Lonely Death of Louise Bryant," *Sunday Tribune* (Dublin), October 10, 1982, 10.

69. Elbridge Durbrow, interview, January 23, 1973.

70. See, for example, Franklin D. Roosevelt to William Bullitt, April 21, 1935, Roosevelt and Bullitt, *For the President, Personal and Secret,* 113.

71. John M. Blum, *Roosevelt and Morgenthau: A Revision and Condensation of "From the Morgenthau Diaries"* (Boston: Houghton Mifflin, 1970), 134.

72. William Bullitt to R. Walton Moore, April 8, 1936, Moore Papers, box 3, folder "Bullitt."

73. William Bullitt to Cordell Hull, April 20, 1936, Bullitt Papers, box 135, folder 918.

74. Kennan, *Memoirs,* 79.

75. "Retreat from Moscow," *Time,* 28, no. 10, September 7, 1936, 12.

76. Samuel Rosenman, *Working with Roosevelt* (New York: Da Capo Press, 1952), 100–103.

77. Franklin D. Roosevelt, *The Public Papers and Addresses of Franklin D. Roosevelt,* 13 vols., compiled by Samuel I. Rosenman (New York: Random House, 1938–1949), 5: 235.

11. Diplomacy to the Rescue?

1. Jean Monnet, *Memoirs,* trans. Richard Mayne (Garden City, NY: Doubleday, 1978), 116.

2. Philip Kerr to Felix Frankfurter, March 25, 1936, box 117, Felix Frankfurter Papers, MSS 47571, Library of Congress.

3. William Bullitt to Franklin D. Roosevelt, October 24, 1936, Franklin D. Roosevelt and William C. Bullitt, *For the President, Personal and Secret: Correspondence between Franklin D. Roosevelt and William C. Bullitt,* ed. Orville H. Bullitt (Boston: Houghton Mifflin, 1972), 173.

4. Léon Blum, *La Prison, Le Procès, La Déportation: Mémoires et Correspondance* (Paris: Albin Michel, 1955), 27.

5. Janet Flanner, "Mr. Ambassador—I," *New Yorker,* December 10, 1938, 30–31.

6. William Bullitt, assorted correspondence, box 3WA56, Commune Verneuil Saint Firmin, folder Château Saint-Firmin: correspondance, devis et mémoires (1927–1929, 1937–1942), and correspondance, copie d'acte de vente, mémoire de travaux (1898–1945), Condé Museum Library and Archives, Château de Chantilly, France; Hubert P. Earle, *Blackout: The Human Side of Europe's March to War* (Philadelphia: J. B. Lippincott, 1939), 102–111.

7. Bullitt had probably spent all that he had inherited from his parents during the 1920s when he had no job, though he made some money from sales of *It's Not Done.* He was also lucky that his brother Orville, who managed his assets, sold all of his stocks in the summer of 1929, a few months before the crash. See Will Brownell and Richard N. Billings, *So Close to Greatness: A Biography of William C. Bullitt* (New York: Macmillan, 1987), 119.

8. Earle, *Blackout,* 107.

9. William Bullitt to Franklin D. Roosevelt, November 4, 1937, Roosevelt and Bullitt, *For the President, Personal and Secret,* 230.

10. William Bullitt, *The Sword Without,* unpublished manuscript, ca. 1948, 7–8, box 151, folder 309, William C. Bullitt Papers, MS 112, Manuscripts and Archives, Yale University Library (hereafter Bullitt Papers).

11. William Bullitt to Franklin D. Roosevelt, December 7, 1936, Roosevelt and Bullitt, *For the President, Personal and Secret,* 195; William Bullitt to

Franklin D. Roosevelt, January 10, 1937, Roosevelt and Bullitt, *For the President, Personal and Secret,* 203–207.

12. Jean-Baptiste Duroselle, *La Décadence, 1932–1939* (Paris: La Documentation française, 1979), 301; Annie Lacroix-Riz, *De Munich à Vichy: l'assassinat de la Troisième République, 1938–1940* (Paris: Armand Colin, 2008), 377–378.

13. William Bullitt to Franklin D. Roosevelt, April 7, 1935, Roosevelt and Bullitt, *For the President, Personal and Secret,* 103.

14. Earle, *Blackout,* 49. The Foreign Service had grown little since WWI, from 721 employees in 1921 to 753 in 1936. Zara S. Steiner, *The State Department and the Foreign Office: The Wriston Report, Four Years Later* (Princeton, NJ: Center for International Studies, Princeton University, 1958), 5.

15. Robert Dallek, *Franklin D. Roosevelt and American Foreign Policy, 1932–1945* (New York: Oxford University Press, 1979), 144–145.

16. James Farley, quoted in Roosevelt and Bullitt, *For the President, Personal and Secret,* 167.

17. Raymond G. Swing, "Diplomacy by Telephone," March 10, 1939, box 1, Raymond Swing Papers, MSS 42119, Library of Congress.

18. William Bullitt, correspondence with David Salmon, November 17–December 8, 1936, Bullitt Papers, box 74, folder 1853. Kenneth Weisbrode, *The Atlantic Century: Four Generations of Extraordinary Diplomats Who Forged America's Vital Alliance with Europe* (Cambridge, MA: DaCapo Press, 2009), 37.

19. Earle, *Blackout,* 106; and Burton Hersh, *The Old Boys: The American Elite and the Origins of the CIA* (New York: Scribner's, 1992), 65, 254.

20. William Castle diary, vol. 31: April 1–August 30, 1936, 380, William R. Castle Papers, MS AM 2021, Houghton Library, Harvard Library.

21. Missy LeHand to William Bullitt, March 20, 1940, Bullitt Papers, box 72, folder 1807.

22. Quoted in Dallek, *Democrat and Diplomat: The Life of William E. Dodd* (Oxford: Oxford University Press, 1968), 271.

23. Roosevelt and Bullitt, *For the President, Personal and Secret,* 181.

24. Max Schur, *Freud: Living and Dying* (New York: International University Press, 1972), 496.

25. John Wiley to William Bullitt, March 10, 1938, Bullitt Papers, box 90, folder 2301.

26. John Wiley to William Bullitt, March 15, 1938, file 363.6315/5, 1930–39 Central Decimal File, RG 59: General Records of the Department of State, U.S. National Archives and Records Administration (hereafter RG 59, NARA).

27. William Bullitt to John Wiley, March 16, 1938, 363.6315/8A, RG 59, NARA.

28. Irena Wiley, *Around the Globe in Twenty Years* (New York: David McKay, 1962), 81. See also Anna Freud to Ernest Jones, February 20, 1956, box 52, folder 5, Anna Freud Papers.

29. John Wiley, exchange of telegrams with State Department, March 15–22, 1938, 363 631 5 / 4, 5, 8, 8B, 10, 12, 17, 24, RG 59, NARA. Peter Gay, *Freud: A Life for Our Time* (New York: Norton, 1988), 625–626.

30. Max Schur, "The Problem of Death in Freud's Writings and Life," 30, Bullitt Papers, box 178, folder 737; Ernest Jones, *The Life and Work of Sigmund Freud*, vol. 3: *The Last Phase, 1919–1939* (London: Hogarth Press, 1957), 240.

31. David Cohen, *The Escape of Sigmund Freud* (London: JR Books, 2009), 144–146.

32. Schur, *Freud: Living and Dying*, 498–499. Jones, *Life and Work of Sigmund Freud*, 3: 237–238.

33. John Wiley to William Bullitt, March 25, 1938, and William Bullitt, draft letter to John Wiley, undated, both in Bullitt Papers, box 90, folder 2301.

34. William Bullitt to Bernard Baruch, June 7, 1938, Bullitt Papers, box 8, folder 157.

35. John Wiley to Secretary of State, March 15, 1938, file 363.6315 / 4, RG 59, NARA.

36. Jones, *Life and Work of Sigmund Freud*, 3: 237.

37. John Wiley, telegram to William Bullitt, March 22, 1938, file 363 6315 / 16, RG 59, NARA.

38. William Bullitt to Ernest Jones, March 30, 1956, Series C, Correspondence B, P04-C-F-02, Alfred Ernest Jones Collection, P04, Archives of the British Psychoanalytical Society, Institute of Psychoanalysis, London. John Wiley, telegram to State Department, March 31, 1938, file 363 6315 / 53, RG 59, NARA.

39. John Wiley to William Bullitt, April 8 and April 15, 1938, Bullitt Papers, box 90, folder 2301.

40. Michael Burlingham, *The Last Tiffany: A Biography of Dorothy Tiffany Burlingham* (New York: Atheneum, 1989), 264.

41. William Bullitt to John Wiley, May 27, 1938, Bullitt Papers, box 90, folder 2301.

42. John Wiley, telegram to William Bullitt, June 3, 1936, Bullitt Papers, box 90, folder 2301.

43. Anna Freud to Ernest Jones, February 20, 1956, box 52, folder 5, Anna Freud Papers, MSS 49700, Library of Congress.

44. Anna Freud, interview, in Robert Coles, *Anna Freud: The Dream of Psychoanalysis* (Reading, MA: Addison-Wesley, 1992), 19.

45. Anna Freud to Louise Theis, April 8, 1958, box 8, folder 163, Louise Morgan and Otto Theis Papers, GEN MSS 80, Beinecke Rare Book and Manuscript Library, Yale University Library.

46. William Bullitt to Bernard Baruch, June 7, 1938, Bullitt Papers, box 8, folder 157.

47. Schur, *Freud: Living and Dying,* 504.

48. Sigmund Freud to William Bullitt, Bullitt Papers, box 30, folder 681.

49. Sigmund Freud to Anna Freud, July 30, 1938, Sigmund Freud and Anna Freud, *Correspondence 1904–1938,* ed. Ingeborg Meyer-Palmedo, trans. Nick Sommers (Cambridge: Polity, 2014), 399. See also William Bullitt to Sigmund Freud, June 21, 1938, box 20, folder "Bullitt," Sigmund Freud Papers, MSS 39990, Library of Congress.

50. Robert Frankenstein, *Le prix du réarmement français* (Paris: Presses universitaires de la Sorbonne, 1982), 168–169.

51. John McVickar Haight Jr., "France's Search for American Military Aircraft: Before the Munich Crisis," *Aerospace Historian* 25, no. 3 (1978): 141–152, 142.

52. Joseph Vuillemin quoted in Haight, "France's Search," 145.

53. William Bullitt to Franklin D. Roosevelt, February 23, 1938, *Foreign Relations of the United States,* 1938, vol. 2 (Washington, DC: Government Printing Office, 1955), 303–304.

54. John McVickar Haight, Jr., *American Aid to France 1938–1940* (New York: Atheneum, 1970), 4–12.

55. Monnet, *Memoirs,* 117; Jean Monnet, interview with Alan Watson, for *Father of Europe,* broadcast on BBC2 on December 31, 1971, transcript in English, 53, Fonds Jean Monnet, series AML (discours, allocutions, interviews, etc.) 313/112, Fondation Jean Monnet pour L'Europe, Lausanne. Carmel Offie to Anne Bullitt, note on a draft of William Bullitt–Franklin D. Roosevelt correspondence, April 29, 1972, Bullitt Papers, box 213, folder 265; and William Bullitt to William Langer, March 14, 1950, Bullitt Papers, box 48, folder 1166.

56. Dallek, *Franklin D. Roosevelt and American Foreign Policy,* 171.

57. John Lukacs, *The Last European War, 1939–1941* (1976; New Haven, CT: Yale University Press, 2001), 26.

58. William Bullitt to the Secretary of State, October 3, 1938, *Foreign Relations of the United States,* 1938, vol. 1 (Washington, DC: Government Printing Office, 1955), 711–712.

12. After Munich

1. Barbara Farnham, *Roosevelt and the Munich Crisis: A Study of Political Decision-Making* (Princeton, NJ: Princeton University Press, 1997), 175–177; Mark Skinner Watson, *Chief of Staff: Prewar Plans and Preparations* (Washington, DC: Historical Division, Dept. of the Army, 1950), 131; Jean Monnet, *Memoirs,* trans. Richard Mayne (Garden City, NY: Doubleday,

1978), 117–118; Robert Dallek, *Franklin D. Roosevelt and American Foreign Policy, 1932–1945* (New York: Oxford University Press, 1979), 172.

2. James Forrestal, *The Forrestal Diaries*, ed. Walter Millis (New York: Viking, 1951), 121–122; Farnham, *Roosevelt and the Munich Crisis*, 158; Jean Monnet, *Memoirs*, 120.

3. William Bullitt to Guy La Chambre, October 25, 1938, Bullitt Papers, Box 48, folder 1153, William C. Bullitt Papers, MS 112, Manuscripts and Archives, Yale University Library (hereafter Bullitt Papers).

4. Jean Monnet, interview with Alan Watson, for *Father of Europe*, broadcast on BBC2 on December 31, 1971, transcript in English, 49, Fonds Jean Monnet, series AML (discours, allocutions, interviews, etc.) 313 / 112, Fondation Jean Monnet pour L'Europe, Lausanne.

5. Henry Morgenthau Diaries, dictated October 23, 1938, vol. 147, 185, Henry Morgenthau Jr. Papers, Franklin D. Roosevelt Presidential Library and Museum, Hyde Park, NY (hereafter Morgenthau Diaries).

6. "'American Power to Act,' Confidential Monnet Notes," undated, Fonds Jean Monnet, series AME (Seconde guerre mondiale), 1 / 2 (notes sur rapatriement des capitaux), folder 15, Fondation Jean Monnet pour L'Europe, Lausanne.

7. Morgenthau Diaries, dictated October 24, 1938, vol. 147, 187. Monnet wrongly attributed the idea to Bullitt. Monnet, *Memoirs*, 120.

8. Monnet, *Memoirs*, 121. See René Pleven, *L'Union européenne: une construction continue et irréversible* (Lausanne: Fondation Jean Monnet pour l'Europe, 1984), 22.

9. Jean Monnet to William Bullitt, November 19, 1938, Bullitt Papers, box 95, folder 2411.

10. John McVickar Haight, Jr., *American Aid to France 1938–1940* (New York: Atheneum, 1970), 39; Jean-Baptiste Duroselle, *La Décadence, 1932–1939* (Paris: La Documentation française, 1979), 454; and Haight, *American Aid to France*, 46.

11. Henry Harley Arnold, *Global Mission* (New York: Harper, 1949), 177; Dallek, *Franklin D. Roosevelt and American Foreign Policy*, 173; Farnham, *Roosevelt and the Munich Crisis*, 184.

12. William Bullitt to William Langer, March 14, 1950, Bullitt Papers, box 48, folder 1146.

13. John Morton Blum, *From the Morgenthau Diaries*, 3 vols. (Boston: Houghton Mifflin, 1959–1967), 2: 65–66.

14. Haight, *American Aid to France*, 96–97; John Morton Blum, *Roosevelt and Morgenthau: A Revision and Condensation of "From the Morgenthau Diaries"* (Boston: Houghton Mifflin, 1970), 281, 284.

15. Wesley Stout, memorandum of conversation with Herbert Feis, prepared for Joe Alsop, "H. F. March 8, 1939, Bullitt," box 1, folder "Alsop," Wesley Winans Stout Papers, MSS 41665, Library of Congress.

16. William Bullitt to the Secretary of State, September 27, 1938, Franklin D. Roosevelt and William C. Bullitt, *For the President, Personal and Secret: Correspondence between Franklin D. Roosevelt and William C. Bullitt*, ed. Orville H. Bullitt (Boston: Houghton Mifflin, 1972), 293.

17. Édouard Daladier, *Journal de captivité* (Paris: Calmann-Lévy, 1991), 69; and Édouard Daladier, speech in the Constitutive National Assembly, July 18, 1946, Journal Officiel de la République française, Débats de l'Assemblée nationale constituante, 2684.

18. Samuel Rosenman and Dorothy Rosenman, *Presidential Style: Some Giants and a Pygmy in the White House* (New York: Harper and Row, 1976), 276–277.

19. Arthur H. Sulzberger, notes taken in Bullitt Office, American Embassy, Paris, May 10, 1939, strictly and entirely confidential for personal guidance only, Arthur Hays Sulzberger Papers, series 1, box 9, folder 6, New York Times Company Records, MssCol 17782, Manuscripts and Archives Division, New York Public Library. The meeting is noted by two major Hitler biographers, Ian Kershaw and Volker Ullrich. Joseph Goebbels also confirmed the plan in his diary entry of March 11, 1939: "Decision: On Wednesday 15 March, we'll invade and destroy" Czechoslovakia. See Ian Kershaw, *Hitler, 1936–1945: Nemesis* (New York: Norton, 2000), 169; and Volker Ullrich, *Hitler: Downfall, 1939–45*, trans. Jefferson Chase (London: Bodley Head, 2016), 749–750.

20. Renaud Meltz, *Alexis Léger dit Saint-John Perse* (Paris: Flammarion, 2008), 553; William Bullitt, telegram to State Department, August 22, 1939, telegram 740.00/2106, 301–4, 1930–39 Central Decimal File, RG 59: General Records of the Department of State, U.S. National Archives and Records Administration (hereafter RG 59, NARA). See Duroselle, *La Décadence*, ch. 13.

21. Dallek, *Franklin D. Roosevelt and American Foreign Policy*, 137, 202–205.

22. William Bullitt to Harold Ickes, October 5, 1939, Bullitt Papers, box 41, folder 960.

23. William Bullitt to Alexander Kirk, September 28, 1939, Bullitt Papers, box 45, folder 1076.

24. Haight, *American Aid to France*, 133.

25. Jean Monnet to Edward Bridges, Secretary of the War Cabinet, London, October 19, 1939, Fonds Jean Monnet, series AME (Seconde guerre mondiale), 6/4 (Organisation de la coopération franco-britannique, etc.), folder 3, Fondation Jean Monnet pour L'Europe, Lausanne (hereafter Fonds Jean Monnet, AME 6/4). Louis Johnson, assistant secretary of war, conversation with Arthur Purvis, notes signed M. A., November 5, 1939, British National Archives, series Ministry of Aviation, ref. AVIA, box 38, folder 2.

26. William Bullitt to William Langer, March 14, 1950, Bullitt Papers, box 48, folder 1146.

27. John McVickar Haight Jr., "Jean Monnet and the American Arsenal after the Beginning of the War," in *French Society and Culture since the Old Regime,* ed. Evelyn M. Acomb and Marvin L. Brown (New York: Holt, Rinehart and Winston, 1966), 275.

28. Arthur Purvis to Jean Monnet, January 12, 1940, Fonds Jean Monnet, AME 6/4, folder 29; "Reminiscences of Henry A. Wallace," 1951–1953, regarding March 18, 1940, Joe Alsop on Henry Woodring, transcript, 941, Columbia Center for Oral History, Columbia University.

29. Jean Monnet, interview with Alan Watson, broadcast December 31, 1971, English transcript, 54; Monnet, *Memoirs,* 132.

30. William Bullitt, telegram to Franklin D. Roosevelt, January 9, 1940, Bullitt Papers, box 72, folder 1807.

31. Haight, *American Aid to France,* 279–281.

32. Jordan A. Schwarz, *Liberal: Adolf A. Berle and the Vision of an American Era* (New York: Free Press, 1987), 177–178.

33. David Reynolds, *The Creation of the Anglo-American Alliance, 1937–41: A Study in Competitive Cooperation* (Chapel Hill: University of North Carolina Press, 1981), 80.

34. William Bullitt to Franklin D. Roosevelt, April 18, 1940, Roosevelt Presidential Papers, Secretary's File, Series 3: Diplomatic Correspondence, box 31, folder "France–Bullitt (1940)."

35. Saul Friedlander, *Prelude to Downfall: Hitler and the United States 1939–41,* trans. Aline B. Werth and Alexander Werth (London: Chatto and Windus, 1967), 72–73.

36. Michael Fullilove, *Rendezvous with Destiny: How Franklin D. Roosevelt and Five Extraordinary Men Took America into the War and into the World* (New York: Penguin, 2013), chap. 1.

37. Friedlander, *Prelude to Downfall,* 75–77.

38. Susan Dunn, *1940: FDR, Willkie, Lindbergh, Hitler—The Election amid the Storm* (New Haven, CT: Yale University Press, 2013), 238.

39. William Castle diary, vol. 39: January 1–June 29, 1940, 138, William R. Castle Papers, MS AM 2021, Houghton Library, Harvard Library.

40. Jean Chauvel, *Commentaire,* vol. 1: *De Vienne à Alger* (Paris: Fayard, 1971), 83.

41. "M. Daladier's Attitude," War Cabinet, WM series, Confidential Annexes and Notes, CAB 65/56/150, Second World War Conclusions, British National Archives.

42. William Bullitt to Franklin D. Roosevelt, May 18, 1940, Roosevelt and Bullitt, *For the President, Personal and Secret,* 426.

43. Hélène Hoppenot, *Journal 1936–1940: Hitler sait attendre, Et nous?* (Paris: Claire Paulhan, 2015), 454.

44. A. D. Harvey, "The French Armée de l'Air in May–June 1940: A Failure of Conception," *Journal of Contemporary History* 25, no. 4 (1990): 447–465, 452.

45. Marc Bloch, *Strange Defeat,* trans. Gerard Hopkins (New York: Norton, 1968), 54–55.

46. Clara was the sister of Nicholas Longworth, Speaker of the House from 1925 to 1931, who was married to Alice Roosevelt.

47. René de Chambrun, *Mission and Betrayal 1940–1945: Working with Franklin Roosevelt to Help Save Britain and Europe* (Stanford, CA: Hoover Institute Press, 1993), 47–48.

48. William Bullitt to R. Walton Moore, June 7, 1940, box 3, folder "Bullitt," R. Walton Moore Collection, Franklin D. Roosevelt Presidential Library and Museum, Hyde Park, NY.

49. Chambrun, *Mission and Betrayal,* 52–53.

50. William Bullitt to Franklin D. Roosevelt, June 1, 1940, René de Chambrun Archives, Fondation Josée et René de Chambrun, Paris.

51. Chambrun, *Mission and Betrayal,* 68.

52. René de Chambrun's "Report to Secretary Morgenthau" is based on experiences at the front. "Report of Captain de Chambrun, June 19, 1940," Morgenthau Diaries, vol. 274, 32–40 (hereafter Chambrun, "Report to Secretary Morgenthau").

53. Chambrun, "Report to Secretary Morgenthau," 37.

54. Chambrun, *Mission and Betrayal,* 69, 71, 78, 98; "Chambrun Depicts Belgian Debacle," *New York Times,* June 17, 1940.

55. Reynolds, *The Creation of the Anglo-American Alliance,* 98; Blum, *Roosevelt and Morgenthau,* 321.

56. Watson, *Chief of Staff: Prewar Plans and Preparations,* 11; and Keith D. McFarland, *Harry H. Woodring: A Political Biography of FDR's Controversial Secretary of War* (Lawrence: University Press of Kansas, 1975), 224–225.

57. Richard M. Leighton and Robert W. Coakley, *Global Logistics and Strategy,* vol. 1: *1940–1943* (Washington, DC: Office of the Chief of Military History, Department of the Army, 1955), 33–34. The Nazi government was informed of these deliveries. See Friedlander, *Prelude to Downfall,* 120. Blum, *Roosevelt and Morgenthau,* 321.

58. "Bullitt Says All Pray for France," *New York Times,* June 10, 1940; Carmel Offie, memorandum of conversation with William Bullitt, March 2, 1942, Bullitt Papers, box 62, folder 1517. The main contributors were Thomas J. Watson, president of IBM; Henry R. Luce, publisher of *Time* and other magazines; and Francis J. Spellman, archbishop of New York. See Carmel Offie to Burke Walsh, June 13, 1940, Bullitt Papers, box 85, folder 2182.

59. Franklin D. Roosevelt, "Stab in the Back Speech," University of Virginia, June 10, 1940, Franklin D. Roosevelt, *The Public Papers and Addresses*

of Franklin D. Roosevelt, 13 vols., compiled by Samuel I. Rosenman (New York: Random House, 1938–1949), 9: 159–164.

60. Basil Rauch, *Roosevelt: From Munich to Pearl Harbor; A Study in the Creation of a Foreign Policy* (1950; New York: Barnes and Noble, 1967), 213.

61. François Darlan, handwritten notes taken during meeting of the French War Committee, May 25, 1940, François Darlan, *Lettres et Notes de l'Amiral Darlan,* compiled by Hervé Coutau-Bégarie and Claude Huan (Paris: Economica, 1992), 183–184.

62. Winston Churchill, *The Second World War,* vol. 2: *Their Finest Hour,* Book 1: *The Fall of France* (Boston: Houghton Mifflin, 1949), 157.

63. Anne Morrow Lindbergh, *War Within and Without: Diaries and Letters* (New York: Harcourt, Brace, Jovanovich, 1980), 107.

64. Alexander Kirk, chargé in Germany, to the Secretary of State, Berlin, June 13, 1940, Roosevelt and Bullitt, *For the President, Personal and Secret,* 471.

65. Carmel Offie, memorandum of conversation with William Bullitt, March 2, 1942, Bullitt Papers, box 62, folder 1517.

66. See Pierre Mendès-France, *Liberté, liberté chérie* (New York: Éditions Didier, 1943), 39.

67. William Bullitt to Franklin D. Roosevelt, June 12, 1940, Roosevelt and Bullitt, *For the President, Personal and Secret,* 465–466.

68. William Bullitt, correspondence with John Lukacs, June 1948, Bullitt Papers, box 48, folder 1149.

69. Maurice Dejean, Mémoires, undated, article 8, 61, Papiers Maurice Dejean, Papiers d'agents–Archives privées (PA-AP) 288, Ministère de L'Europe et des Affaires Étrangères, France.

70. Roosevelt and Bullitt, *For the President, Personal and Secret,* 472.

71. Cordell Hull, "Cataclysm in Europe," in *The Memoirs of Cordell Hull,* 2 vols. (New York: Macmillan, 1948), 1: 767; Haight, *American Aid to France,* 255.

72. Tony Judt, with Timothy Snyder, *Thinking the Twentieth Century* (New York: Penguin, 2012), 275.

73. Eric Roussel, *Le naufrage* (Paris: Gallimard, 2009), 230–233.

74. H. Freeman Matthews to Father Luke, August 14, 1940, series 1, box 2, folder 1, H. Freeman Matthews, Jr., Papers, MC 277, Public Policy Papers, Special Collections, Princeton University Library.

75. Churchill thanks Monnet in Churchill, *The Second World War,* vol. 2, book 1: *The Fall of France,* 189. See also H. Duncan Hall, *North American Supply* (London: Her Majesty's Stationery Office and Longmans, Green, 1955), 146–149.

76. William Shirer, *Berlin Diary: The Journal of a Foreign Correspondent, 1934–1941* (New York: Knopf, 1941), 411, 418.

77. William Bullitt to Secretary of State, July 5, 1940, file 125 Bullitt William C./ 663, RG 59, NARA.
78. William Bullitt, telegram to the Secretary of State and to the President, La Bourboule, July 1, 1940, 9 PM, Roosevelt and Bullitt, *For the President, Personal and Secret*, 481.
79. Bullitt, telegram to the Secretary of State and to the President, July 1, 1940, Roosevelt and Bullitt, *For the President, Personal and Secret*, 487.
80. Cordell Hull, telegram to William Bullitt, July 6, 1940, 123 Bullitt, William C./ 623, RG 59, NARA.
81. Henry Morgenthau Jr., "The Morgenthau Diaries: IV. The Story Behind Lend-Lease," *Collier's*, October 18, 1947.
82. Will Brownell and Richard N. Billings, *So Close to Greatness: A Biography of William C. Bullitt* (New York: Macmillan, 1987), 262; William Bullitt, Madrid, telegram 363 to Cordell Hull, July 13, 1940, Roosevelt and Bullitt, *For the President, Personal and Secret*, 490.
83. Paul Reynaud to Col. Fuller, secret, May 29, 1940, Bullitt Papers, box 69, folder 1746.
84. Léon Blum to William Bullitt, May 18, 1946, Bullitt Papers, box 10, folder 203. Bullitt gave the suitcase to the Library of Congress.
85. Later, in April 1941, the British grew concerned that the contents of the Blum letter might become a weapon for Nazi propagandists trying to convince the French that the British aimed "to restore the Front Populaire." The letter's "publication would certainly be used by the Germans and Vichy to our detriment," the Foreign Service argued. Correspondence with various advisers, Winston Churchill, Chartwell Papers, Prime Minister 1940–1945, CHAR 20, box 24, folder 81–86, Churchill Archives Centre, Churchill College, University of Cambridge.
86. William Bullitt, memo concerning Lafayette's pistols, June 28, 1940, Bullitt Papers, box 49, folder 1173.
87. "Bullitt, Back, Says France of Pétain Is No Fascist State," *New York Times*, July 21, 1940.
88. Felix Frankfurter to William Bullitt, August 6, 1940, Bullitt Papers, box 30, folder 669.

13. A Phony War

1. Jules Henry, French ambassador to Brazil, secret telegram 608 to Paul Baudouin, July 6, 1940, 129, box 4, folder 40, Papiers Baudouin, 386QO, Papiers 1940, Ministère de L'Europe et des Affaires Étrangères, Centre des Archives diplomatique de La Courneuve. William Bullitt, strictly confidential telegram to the President and Secretary of State, Madrid, (copy),

July 12, 1940, box 72, folder 1814, William C. Bullitt Papers, MS 112, Manuscripts and Archives, Yale University Library (hereafter Bullitt Papers).

2. Roscoe Hillenkoetter to William Bullitt, July 25, 1940, Bullitt Papers, box 38, folder 892.

3. "Bullitt at Camp in Woods," *New York Times,* August 9, 1940; William Bullitt, *The Sword Without,* unpublished manuscript, ca. 1948, 14, Bullitt Papers, box 151, folder 309; Charles Stanwood, unpublished history of Camp Pasqueaney, quoted in Will Brownell and Richard N. Billings, *So Close to Greatness: A Biography of William C. Bullitt* (New York: Macmillan, 1987), 268.

4. "Text of Ambassador Bullitt's Speech Warning America Is in Danger," *New York Times,* August 18, 1940.

5. Bullitt, *The Sword Without,* 14–15, Bullitt Papers, box 151, folder 309.

6. Willkie quoted in Robert Dallek, *Franklin D. Roosevelt and American Foreign Policy, 1932–1945* (New York: Oxford University Press, 1979), 249; Herbert Hoover to Hugh Gibson, October 4, 1940, box 45, folder "Hoover/1915–1941," Hugh Gibson Papers, coll. 56000, Hoover Institution Library and Archives, Stanford University.

7. William Bullitt, "How We Won the War and Lost the Peace," part 1, *Life,* August 30, 1948, 83–97, 88. David Reynolds, *The Creation of the Anglo-American Alliance, 1937–41: A Study in Competitive Cooperation* (Chapel Hill: University of North Carolina Press, 1981), 158. The genius Bullitt credited to Roosevelt was actually that of Harold Ickes, who suggested the rhetorical approach as a means of persuading Congress. Warren F. Kimball, *The Most Unsordid Act: Lend-Lease, 1939–1941* (Baltimore: Johns Hopkins Press, 1969), 77.

8. Robert Murphy, *Diplomat among Warriors* (Garden City, NY: Doubleday, 1964), 67–69.

9. William Bullitt to Missy LeHand, August 14, 1940, Marguerite A. (Missy) LeHand Papers, box 10, series 2, Grace Tully Collection, Franklin D. Roosevelt Presidential Library and Museum, Hyde Park, NY (hereafter LeHand Papers); Missy LeHand to William Bullitt, August 18, 1940, Bullitt Papers, box 49, folder 1185.

10. William Bullitt to Grenville Clark, March 4, 1948, Bullitt Papers, box 20, folder 426. This account seems plausible. See William Bullitt to Franklin D. Roosevelt, March 20, 1940, Franklin D. Roosevelt, Papers as President, President's Secretary's File, series 3: Diplomatic Correspondence, box 31, folder "France–Bullitt (1940)," Franklin D. Roosevelt Presidential Library and Museum, Hyde Park, NY.

11. William Bullitt to Missy LeHand, May 29, 1940, LeHand Papers, box 10.

12. Quoted in H. Duncan Hall, *North American Supply* (London: Her Majesty's Stationery Office and Longmans, Green, 1955), 42.

13. Harold Ickes, *The Secret Diary of Harold L. Ickes,* 3 vols. (New York: Simon and Schuster, 1953–1954), 3: 344.

14. George Biddle diary, September 25, 1940, 130, Diary 1933–1941 (revised typescript), box 2, George Biddle Papers, MSS 12674, Library of Congress; Offie quoted in Ickes, *Secret Diary,* 3: 343–344.

15. William Bullitt, correspondence with Thomas Mann, August–September 1940, Bullitt Papers, box 55, folder 1338.

16. William Bullitt, telegram to Robert Murphy, July 27, 1940, 123 Bullitt William C./641, 1930–39 Central Decimal File, RG 59: General Records of the Department of State, U.S. National Archives and Records Administration.

17. See Varian Fry, letters and telegrams to William Bullitt, July 25, 1940, November 16 and 17, 1940, and June 17, 1941, Bullitt Papers, box 29, folder 634.

18. Anna Freud to William Bullitt, April 28, 1940, Bullitt Papers, box 30, folder 677.

19. Harry Freud to William Bullitt, April 2 and April 9, 1941, Bullitt Papers, box 30, folder 680.

20. Alexander Freud, correspondence with Carmel Offie, September–October 1942, Bullitt Papers, box 30, folder 676; William Bullitt to W. Ernst Kris, August 22, 1940, Bullitt Papers, box 46, folder 1099.

21. Ernesta Drinker, autograph manuscript memoir, July 15, 1939–1940, 2–3, series 4, box 5, folder 1, Ernesta Drinker Barlow Papers, GTM-081118, Georgetown University Libraries.

22. Ernesta Drinker to William Bullitt, October 27, 1940, Bullitt Papers, box 12, folder 250.

23. Joseph Lash, memorandum on interview with Samuel Rosenman, May 4, 1970, Joseph P. Lash Papers, General Correspondence, box 16, Franklin D. Roosevelt Presidential Library and Museum, Hyde Park, NY (hereafter Lash Papers).

24. William Bullitt to Franklin D. Roosevelt, November 7, 1940, Franklin D. Roosevelt and William C. Bullitt, *For the President, Personal and Secret: Correspondence between Franklin D. Roosevelt and William C. Bullitt,* ed. Orville H. Bullitt (Boston: Houghton Mifflin, 1972), 504.

25. Roosevelt and Bullitt, *For the President, Personal and Secret,* 504–506.

26. James Farley, interview by Joseph Lash, November 15, 1968, Lash Papers, series 3, box 44: Transcripts of Interviews.

27. See "M. Roosevelt va désigner un nouvel ambassadeur en France en remplacement de William Bullitt," *Le Petit Parisien,* November 9, 1940, 1.

28. George Kennan to Elbridge Durbrow, January 7, 1971, series 1A, box 12, folder 10, George F. Kennan Papers, MC 076, Public Policy Papers, Special Collections, Princeton University Library.

29. Ickes, *Secret Diary,* 3: 338–339.

30. Joseph Alsop, memo on conversation with William Bullitt, December 20, 1940, box 32, Joseph Alsop and Stewart Alsop Papers, MSS 10561, Library of Congress; Ickes, *Secret Diary,* 3: 398.

31. The source of the message was Maxwell Blake, the US representative in Tangiers, who had an informant in the State Department. Roscoe Hillenkoetter to William Bullitt, July 25, 1940, Bullitt Papers, box 38, folder 892.

32. See Jules Henry, telegram 608 to Paul Baudouin, July 6, 1940.

33. William Bullitt to Cordell Hull, June 4, 1943, Bullitt Papers, box 40, folder 946.

34. Benjamin Welles, *Sumner Welles: FDR's Global Strategist: A Biography* (New York: St. Martin's Press, 1997), 275.

35. Hugh Wilson to Franklin D. Roosevelt, March 3, 1938, box 3, folder "Roosevelt," Hugh R. Wilson Papers, Herbert Hoover Presidential Library, West Branch, IA. On Sumner Welles's manner, see also Isaiah Berlin, *Washington Despatches, 1941–1945: Weekly Political Reports from the British Embassy,* ed. H. G. Nichols (London: Weidenfeld, 1981), 241.

36. William Bullitt to Sumner Welles, May 28, 1937, Bullitt Papers, box 88, folder 2265.

37. Sumner Welles, memo of conversation with William Bullitt, September 28, 1938, Europe Files 1933–1943, box 161, folder "France, 1935–1940," Sumner Welles Papers, Franklin D. Roosevelt Presidential Library and Museum, Hyde Park, NY.

38. "Welles Finds Hope in Will for Peace," *New York Times,* October 4, 1938; and Arnold A. Offner, *American Appeasement: United States Foreign Policy and Germany, 1933–1938* (Cambridge, MA: Belknap Press of Harvard University Press, 1969), 269.

39. Irwin F. Gellman, *Secret Affairs: Franklin Roosevelt, Cordell Hull, and Sumner Welles* (Baltimore: Johns Hopkins University Press, 1995), 56.

40. Jean Monnet, interview with Alan Watson, for *Father of Europe,* broadcast on BBC2 on December 31, 1971, transcript in English, 53, Fonds Jean Monnet, series AML (discours, allocutions, interviews, etc.) 313/112, Fondation Jean Monnet pour L'Europe, Lausanne. The epithet "arsenal of democracy" was originally Monnet's.

41. "Text of Bullitt's Statement," *New York Times,* January 26, 1941.

42. William Bullitt to Stanley Hornbeck, January 5, 1941, and Stanley Hornbeck to William Bullitt, January 6, 1941, box 41, folder "Bullitt, William C.," Stanley Kuhl Hornbeck Papers, coll. 67008, Hoover Institution Library and Archives, Stanford University.

43. Stephen Fletcher, "Ambassador William C. Bullitt Visits UNC, 1941," in "A View to Hugh: Processing the Hugh Morton Photographs," University of North Carolina Libraries, January 7, 2015, https://blogs.lib.unc.edu/morton/index.php/2015/01/ambassador-william-c-bullitt-visits-unc-1941; "Bullitt Appeals for Air Strength, Calls on Nation to Discard 'Business

as Usual' Policy to Speed Plane Output," *New York Times,* February 19, 1941; "Bullitt Calls U.S. to Wartime Effort," *New York Times,* February 28, 1941.

44. William Bullitt, memorandum of meeting with Roosevelt, April 23, 1941, Roosevelt and Bullitt, *For the President, Personal and Secret,* 512. See also Richard W. Steele, "Preparing the Public for War: Efforts to Establish a National Propaganda Agency, 1940–41," *American Historical Review* 75, no. 6 (1970): 1640–1653.

45. Benjamin Welles, *Sumner Welles,* 272. "Reminiscences of Henry A. Wallace," 1951–1953, regarding May 23, 1943, transcript, 2656, Columbia Center for Oral History, Columbia University.

46. William Bullitt, memorandum of conversation with the President, April 23, 1941, Bullitt Papers, box 210, folder 217.

47. R. Walton Moore, handwritten notes and typed copy, Bullitt Papers, box 210, folder 218.

48. Carmel Offie to Anne Bullitt, note on a draft of William Bullitt–Franklin D. Roosevelt correspondence, April 29, 1972, Bullitt Papers, box 213, folder 265.

49. Benjamin Welles, *Sumner Welles,* 273.

50. William Bullitt, memorandum of conversation with the President, April 23, 1941, Bullitt Papers, box 210, folder 217.

51. Suzanne Blum to William Bullitt, December 13, 1940, and July 31, 1941, Bullitt Papers, box 10, folders 204–205.

52. Roscoe Hillenkoetter to William Bullitt, July 25 and August 31, 1940, Bullitt Papers, box 38, folder 892.

53. Roosevelt and Bullitt, *For the President, Personal and Secret,* 258–259.

54. Saul Friedlander, *Prelude to Downfall: Hitler and the United States 1939–41,* trans. Aline B. Werth and Alexander Werth (London: Chatto and Windus, 1967), 237.

55. Edouard Daladier to William Bullitt, December 24, 1940, Bullitt Papers, box 24, folder 506.

56. Ickes, *Secret Diary,* 3: 486–487, 538.

57. Christopher O'Sullivan, *Harry Hopkins: FDR's Envoy to Churchill and Stalin* (Lanham, MD: Rowman and Littlefield, 2015), 63, 66–68.

58. On June 22, 1941, Bullitt cowrote with J. David Stern an editorial titled "A Plague on Both Their Houses." See Stern, *Memoirs of a Maverick Publisher* (New York: Simon and Schuster, 1962), 263. Roosevelt thought Stalin would have signed these agreements but would have then simply disregarded their terms. Bullitt, *The Sword Without,* 23, Bullitt Papers, box 151, folder 309.

59. Hervé Alphand, *L'étonnement d'être, Journal 1939–1973* (Paris: Fayard, 1977), 87.

60. William Bullitt to the President, July 1, 1941, Roosevelt and Bullitt, *For the President, Personal and Secret,* 522.

61. Harold Ickes, diary entry for September 20, 1941, vol. 38, 5905, "Ickes, Harold, diary excerpts," Bullitt Papers, box 119, folder 556.

62. "Bullitt Asks War Now, Tells Republicans at Philadelphia Roosevelt Is Lagging," *New York Times,* October 1, 1941.

63. Henry Stimson diary, entry for October 7, 1941, series XIV: Diaries, 1909–1945, box 74, vol. 36, Henry Lewis Stimson Papers, MS 465, Manuscripts and Archives, Yale University Library.

64. Mark A. Stoler, *The Politics of the Second Front, American Military Planning and Diplomacy in Coalition Warfare, 1941–1943* (Westport, CT: Greenwood Press, 1977), 12.

65. Churchill, *The Grand Alliance* (1950; Boston: Houghton Mifflin, 1986), 552.

66. "Reminiscences of Henry A. Wallace," 1951–1953, regarding February 12, 1946, transcript, 4537.

67. Carmel Offie to Secretary of State, March 26, 1942, Bullitt Papers, box 63, folder 1531.

68. William Bullitt, telegram to Franklin D. Roosevelt, December 21, 1941, Roosevelt and Bullitt, *For the President, Personal and Secret,* 533–535.

69. Roosevelt and Bullitt, *For the President, Personal and Secret,* 548–550; Dwight David Eisenhower, *The Papers of Dwight David Eisenhower,* ed. Alfred D. Chandler, Jr., 21 vols. (Baltimore: Johns Hopkins Press, 1970–2001), 1: 193–194.

70. William Bullitt to Franklin D. Roosevelt, April 20, 1942, Bullitt Papers, box 73, folder 1823; George F. Kennan, "Introduction," in Roosevelt and Bullitt, *For the President, Personal and Secret,* xii.

14. Liberating France, Confronting the "Red Amoeba"

1. Albert Barnes to William Bullitt, June 2, 1942, box 8, folder 148, William C. Bullitt Papers, MS 112, Manuscripts and Archives, Yale University Library (hereafter Bullitt Papers).

2. Harold Ickes, *The Secret Diary of Harold L. Ickes,* 3 vols. (New York: Simon and Schuster, 1953–54), 3: 615.

3. William Bullitt, correspondence with Franklin D. Roosevelt, June 13 and 17, 1942, Franklin D. Roosevelt and William C. Bullitt, *For the President, Personal and Secret: Correspondence between Franklin D. Roosevelt and William C. Bullitt,* ed. Orville H. Bullitt (Boston: Houghton Mifflin, 1972), 555.

4. Saint-John Perse, *Courrier d'exil: Saint-John Perse et ses amis américains, 1940–1970,* ed. Carol Rigolot (Paris: Gallimard, 2001), 88.

5. Henri Laugier to William Bullitt, February 4, 1941, and William Bullitt to Henri Laugier, July 23, 1941, Bullitt Papers, box 49, folder 1173.

6. Léon Blum, *L'Histoire jugera* (Montreal: Editions de L'Arbre, 1943).

7. See S. K. McKee, FBI Special Agent in Charge, to the Director of the FBI, September 24, 1942, Bullitt's FBI file, 62–59481, transmitted to author, September 11, 2019, following the Freedom of Information Act request no. 1446093-000.

8. Edward R. Stettinius, Jr., *The Diaries of Edward R. Stettinius, 1943–1946*, ed. Thomas M. Campbell and George C. Herring (New York: New Viewpoints, 1975), 240.

9. William Bullitt to Franklin D. Roosevelt, June 5, 1940, Roosevelt and Bullitt, *For the President, Personal and Secret*, 452.

10. William Bullitt, diary entry for July 20, 1942, Bullitt Papers, box 121, folder 592.

11. Julian Jackson, *De Gaulle* (Cambridge, MA: Belknap Press of Harvard University Press, 2018), 235.

12. William Bullitt, diary entry for July 20, 1942, Bullitt Papers, box 121, folder 592.

13. Churchill and Roosevelt had previously agreed to proceed with a North African operation. Winston Churchill, *The Grand Alliance* (Boston: Houghton Mifflin, 1986), 585–586.

14. William Bullitt to Franklin D. Roosevelt, November 29 and December 17, 1942, January 29, May 12, and August 10, 1943, Roosevelt and Bullitt, *For the President, Personal and Secret*, 572–600.

15. Anthony Sampson, *The Seven Sisters: The Great Oil Companies and the World They Shaped* (New York: Viking, 1974), 95–97.

16. Robert Dallek, *Franklin D. Roosevelt: A Political Life* (New York: Viking, 2017), 505–506.

17. In late summer 1942, Stalin shared these suspicions in a telegram to Ivan Maisky, his ambassador in London. Jonathan Haslam, "Litvinov, Stalin and the Road Not Taken," in *Soviet Foreign Policy, 1917–1991: A Retrospective*, ed. Gabriel Gorodetsky (London: Frank Cass, 1994), 58.

18. George F. Kennan, "Introduction," in Roosevelt and Bullitt, *For the President, Personal and Secret*, xiv.

19. Daniel Yergin, *Shattered Peace: The Origins of the Cold War and the National Security State* (Boston: Houghton Mifflin, 1977), 42.

20. Anthony Eden, *The Reckoning: The Memoirs of Anthony Eden* (Boston: Houghton Mifflin, 1965), 372–374; Robert Sherwood, *Roosevelt and Hopkins: An Intimate History* (New York: Harper and Brother, 1948), 315–320; and Memorandum of conversation Welles/Eden, March 16, 1943, Foreign Relations of the United States: Diplomatic Papers, 1943, The British Commonwealth, Eastern Europe, the Far East, vol. 3, 19–24, Office of the Historian, U.S. Department of State.

21. See Forrest Davis, "Roosevelt's World Blueprint," *Saturday Evening Post,* April 10, 1943, 20–21, 109–111; James McAllister, *No Exit: America and the German Problem, 1943–1954* (Ithaca, NY: Cornell University Press, 2002).

22. Todd Bennett, Culture, Power, and Mission to Moscow: Film and Soviet-American Relations during World War II, *The Journal of American History,* Sept. 2001, Vol. 88, No. 2, pp. 489–518, 495.

23. See Martin Weil, *A Pretty Good Club: The Founding Fathers of the U.S. Foreign Service* (New York: Norton, 1978), 139–141.

24. H. W. Brands, *Inside the Cold War: Loy Henderson and the Rise of the American Empire, 1918–1961* (New York: Oxford University Press, 1991), 110–111.

25. Loy W. Henderson, interview by Richard D. McKinzie, June 14 and July 5, 1973, transcript, 27, Oral History Interviews, Harry Truman Presidential Library, Independence, MO.

26. Quoted in Weil, *A Pretty Good Club,* 135.

27. Jordan A. Schwarz, *Liberal: Adolf A. Berle and the Vision of an American Era* (New York: Free Press, 1987), 192.

28. Isaiah Berlin, *Washington Despatches, 1941–1945: Weekly Political Reports from the British Embassy,* ed. H. G. Nichols (London: Weidenfeld, 1981), 163.

29. James G. Ryan, *Earl Browder: The Failure of American Communism* (Tuscaloosa: University of Alabama Press, 1997), 211–212. Edgar Hoover, memo to Harry Hopkins, October 24, 1942, *Documentary History of the Franklin D. Roosevelt Presidency,* ed. George McJimsey, 43 vols. (Bethesda, MD: University Publications of America, 2001–2009), 32: 604.

30. Carmel Offie to Thomas Bullitt, May 17, 1943, Bullitt Family Papers, Bullitt, Thomas W. (1914–1991), box 97, folder 1062, Filson Historical Society, Louisville, KY.

31. William Bullitt, memo of conversation with Ralph Brewster, April 27, 1943, Bullitt Papers, box 210, folder 219. See also Welles FBI files, series 5, box 6, folder "FBI and Sumner Welles," Barbara F. Gellman Papers, Franklin D. Roosevelt Presidential Library and Museum, Hyde Park, NY; Irwin F. Gellman, *Secret Affairs: Franklin Roosevelt, Cordell Hull, and Sumner Welles* (Baltimore: Johns Hopkins University Press, 1995), 313.

32. William Bullitt, memo of conversation with Cordell Hull, June 2, 1943, Bullitt Papers, box 210, folder 218.

33. William Bullitt, memo of conversation with Franklin D. Roosevelt, July 27, 1943, Bullitt Papers, box 210, folder 218.

34. Benjamin Welles, *Sumner Welles: FDR's Global Strategist: A Biography* (New York: St. Martin's Press, 1997), 346.

35. See Ted Morgan, *A Covert Life: Jay Lovestone, Communist, Anti-Communist, and Spymaster* (New York: Random House, 1999), 211.

36. William Bullitt, memo of conversation with Cordell Hull, June 21, 1944, Bullitt Papers, box 210, folder 219.

37. William Castle diary, vol. 46: July 9–December 31, 1943, 278, William R. Castle Papers, MS AM 2021, Houghton Library, Harvard Library (hereafter Castle Papers).

38. Walter Lowenfels, "Discredited in Washington, Bullitt Tries New Scheme," *The Worker*, August 15, 1943; and "William C. Bullitt, Vichy's Friend," *The Worker*, September 12, 1943.

39. Quoted in Benjamin Welles, *Sumner Welles*, 354.

40. William Castle diary, vol. 46: July 9–December 31, 1943, 278, Castle Papers.

41. Missy LeHand to William Bullitt, September 1943, Bullitt Papers, box 49, folder 1185.

42. William Bullitt to Archbishop Francis J. Spellman, February 26, 1944, Bullitt Papers, box 78, folder 1995.

43. Kathryn Smith, *The Gatekeeper: Missy LeHand, FDR and the Untold Story of a Partnership That Defined a Presidency* (New York: Touchstone, 2016), 263.

44. Missy LeHand to William Bullitt, April 25, 1944, Bullitt Papers, box 49, folder 1185.

45. William Bullitt to Charles de Gaulle, May 19, 1944, Bullitt's translation of his letter into English, Bullitt Papers, box 24, folder 527.

46. Charles de Gaulle to William Bullitt, May 25, 1944, Bullitt Papers, box 24, folder 527. My translation.

47. Jackson, *De Gaulle*, 306–308.

48. William D. Leahy, *I Was There: The Personal Story of the Chief of Staff to Presidents Roosevelt and Truman* (New York: Whittlesey House, 1950), 280.

49. William Bullitt, "The Future of France," *Life*, August 14, 1944, 75.

50. William Castle diary, vol. 46: July 9–December 31, 1943, 285, Castle Papers.

51. William Bullitt, "The World from Rome," *Life*, September 4, 1944, 101.

52. "Bullitt Denounced as 'Liar' by Pravda," *New York Times*, September 5, 1944.

53. William Bullitt to John Wiley, October 28, 1945, Bullitt Papers, box 90, folder 2307.

54. See Antoine Béchaux and Michel Lafuma, *Le 2e Choc: Bataillon Janson-de-Sailly, 1944–1945* (Paris: France-Empire, 1988), 160. See also interview of Simonne de Lattre de Tassigny, *L'Aurore*, March 6, 1968.

55. William Bullitt to Orville Bullitt, October 14, 1944, Roosevelt and Bullitt, *For the President, Personal and Secret*, 606.

56. William Bullitt to Jean de Lattre, December 17, 1949, Bullitt Papers, box 24, folder 532.

57. Jean de Lattre, *Histoire de la Première Armée Française: Rhin et Danube* (Paris: Plon, 1949), 344–345.

58. Pierre Pellissier, *De Lattre* (Paris: Perrin, 2009), 560.

59. William Bullitt, "The Most Unforgettable General I Have Known," undated manuscript, Bullitt Papers, box 151, folder 296, later published in French under the title "Un chevalier sans peur," in *Jean De Lattre, Maréchal de France Le soldat, l'homme, le politique* (Paris: Plon, 1953), 83–85.

60. Roosevelt and Bullitt, *For the President, Personal and Secret,* 612.

61. Charles de Gaulle, telegram to Jean de Lattre, April 14, 1945, De Gaulle, *Lettres, Notes & Carnets, Juin 1943–Mai 1945* (Paris: Plon, 1983), 409. The *New York Times* announced Bullitt's supposed nomination: "Bullitt Is Military Governor," *New York Times,* April 15, 1945.

62. "Le Général de Gaulle à Stuttgart," *Le Monde,* May 22, 1945; and "Le général De Gaulle en Autriche et à Stuttgart," June 1, 1945, video, Journal les Actualités Françaises, L'INA éclaire d'actu, https://www.ina.fr/video/AFE86003119/le-general-de-gaulle-en-autriche-et-a-stuttgart-video.html.

63. Roosevelt and Bullitt, *For the President, Personal and Secret,* 614. "Défilé militaire du 14 juillet 1945 à la Bastille," video, Journal les Actualités Françaises, L'INA éclaire d'actu, https://www.ina.fr/video/I17194347/defile-militaire-du-14-juillet-1945-a-la-bastille-video.html.

64. William Bullitt, memorandum of meeting with Pablo Picasso, February 21, 1966, Bullitt Papers, box 64, folder 1562.

65. "Miss Anne Bullitt Engaged to Marry," *New York Times,* October 13, 1943. George Biddle to William Bullitt, February 22, 1944, and William Bullitt to George Biddle, February 26, 1944, Bullitt Papers, box 9, folder 189. Anne Bullitt to William Bullitt, March 4, 1944, Bullitt Papers, box 13, folder 266.

66. For example, Bullitt accompanied Katherine Biddle and Alexis Léger to a reception at the Chilean Embassy in Washington, DC, on October 13, 1945. Katherine Biddle, *Saint-John Perse Intime: Journal inédit d'une amie américaine, 1940–1970,* ed. Carol Rigolot (Paris: Gallimard, 2011), 114.

67. William Bullitt, *The Sword Without,* unpublished manuscript, c. 1948, Bullitt Papers, box 151, folder 309, 18–19.

68. George F. Kennan, correspondence with William Bullitt, April–May 1944, Bullitt Papers, box 44, folder 1061.

69. William Bullitt to Carmel Offie, October 12, 1945, Bullitt Papers, box 63, folder 1532; William Bullitt to Maria Cuttoli, October 25, 1945, Bullitt Papers, box 22, folder 481.

70. William Bullitt, memo of conversation with Forrest Davis, January 25, 1946, Bullitt Papers, box 22, folder 488.

71. William C. Bullitt, *The Great Globe Itself: A Preface to World Affairs* (New York: C. Scribner's Sons, 1946), 17–19.

72. Daniel Kurtz Phelan, *The China Mission: George Marshall's Unfinished War 1945–1947* (New York: Norton, 2018), 252.

73. "X" [George F. Kennan], "The Sources of Soviet Conduct," *Foreign Affairs* 25, no. 4 (July 1947), 566–582.

74. John Foster Dulles, "Thoughts on Soviet Foreign Policy and What to Do about It," *Life*, June 3, 1946, 112–126, and June 10, 1946, 118–130.

75. Henry R. Luce to William Bullitt, June 16, 1946, Bullitt Papers, box 51, folder 1230.

15. America's Freelance Secretary of State

1. John Wiley to William Bullitt, April 13, 1946, box 90, folder 2301, William C. Bullitt Papers, MS 112, Manuscripts and Archives, Yale University Library (hereafter Bullitt Papers).

2. Will Brownell and Richard N. Billings, *So Close to Greatness: A Biography of William C. Bullitt* (New York: Macmillan, 1987), 308–309.

3. Hearing of William Bullitt, March 24, 1947, Hearings before the Committee on Un-American Activities, House of Representatives, Eightieth Congress, First Session, on H.R. 1884 and H.R. 2122 bills to curb or outlaw the Communist party of the United States, Washington, DC, March 24–28, 1947.

4. See "Contre mauvaise fortune . . ." *Le Monde*, May 9, 1947; and William Bullitt to Robert Lovett, May 13, 1947, Bullitt Papers, box 51, folder 1227.

5. William Bullitt to Henry Luce, September 15, 1948, Bullitt Papers, box 51, folder 1231; and William Bullitt to Robert Lovett, September 16, 1948, Bullitt Papers, box 51, folder 1227.

6. Quoted in Lionel Chassin, *The Communist Conquest of China* (Cambridge, MA: Harvard University Press, 1965), 61.

7. *Last Chance in Manchuria: The Diary of Chiang Kia-Ngau*, ed. Donald G. Gillin and Ramon H. Myers, trans. Dolores Zen (Stanford, CA: Hoover Institution Press, Stanford University, 1989), 13–14.

8. Alan Brinkley, *The Publisher: Henry Luce and His American Century* (New York: Alfred A. Knopf, 2010), 346–347.

9. William Bullitt, "A Report to the American People on China," *Life*, October 13, 1947. Time Inc. paid an unprecedented fee of $13,000 for Bullitt's article. John Shaw Billings, editor of *Life*, found the work "superficial and mediocre," but, due to Luce's eagerness to publish Bullitt, did not dare stand in the way. Brinkley, *The Publisher*, 339.

10. Robert Dallek, *Franklin D. Roosevelt and American Foreign Policy, 1932–1945* (New York: Oxford University Press, 1979), 517.

11. Joseph Keeley, *The China Lobby Man: The Story of Alfred Kohlberg* (New Rochelle, NY: Arlington House, 1969), 16, 217.

12. Bullitt, "Report to the American People on China," 35.

13. Albert Wedemeyer to Douglas MacArthur, October 20, 1947, in Albert C. Wedemeyer, *Wedemeyer on War and Peace,* ed. Keith E. Eiler (Stanford, CA: Hoover Institution Press, Stanford University, 1987), 199.

14. Ross Y. Koen, *The China Lobby in American Politics* (New York: Macmillan, 1960), 88–90.

15. William Bullitt, "The Saddest War," *Life,* December 29, 1947, 64–69.

16. Lucien Bodard, *La Guerre d'Indochine* (Paris: Grasset, 1997), 508. My translation.

17. Vincent Auriol, *Mon Septennat: 1947–1954, notes de journal,* ed. Pierre Nora and Jacques Ozouf (Paris: Armand Colin, 1970), 469–471.

18. Brownell and Billings, *So Close to Greatness,* 313–314.

19. Edward Rice-Maximin, "The United States and Indochina, 1946–1947," *Proceedings of the Meeting of the French Colonial Historical Society* 6/7 (1982): 119–128, 124.

20. See Georgette Elgey, *Histoire de la IVème République,* part 1: *La république des illusions, 1945–1951* (Paris: Fayard, 1965), 470.

21. John Foster Dulles to Herbert Brownell, Jr., August 4, 1948, Bullitt Papers, box 26, folder 569.

22. John Lewis Gaddis, *Strategies of Containment: A Critical Appraisal of Postwar American National Security Policy* (New York: Oxford University Press, 1982), 5. Carmel Offie to Robert Murphy, September 14, 1948, Robert D. Murphy Collection (78060), box 59, folder 6, Hoover Institution Library and Archives, Stanford University (hereafter Murphy Papers).

23. William Bullitt, "How We Won the War and Lost the Peace," part 1, *Life,* August 30, 1948, 83–97, 94. This conversation with Roosevelt occurred in 1943 and is reported in William Bullitt, *The Sword Without,* unpublished manuscript, c. 1948, 31, Bullitt Papers, box 151, folder 309.

24. William Bullitt to Margaret Biddle, October 7, 1948, Bullitt Papers, box 9, folder 192. "Bullitt Declares He Will Support Dewey; Assails Democrats as Appeasing Russia," *New York Times,* October 25, 1948, 13.

25. William Bullitt to Thomas Dewey, October 30, 1948, Bullitt Papers, box 25, folder 545.

26. Carmel Offie to Robert Murphy, October 31, November 9, and November 29, 1948, Murphy Papers, box 59, folder 6.

27. William Bullitt to Edna Millay, August 31, 1949, box 75, folder "Bullitt, William C.," Edna St. Vincent Millay Papers, MSS 32920, Library of Congress.

28. William Bullitt, draft of a poem, Bullitt Papers, box 163, folder 513.

29. Samuel Rosenman to William Bullitt, February 21, 1949, Bullitt Papers, box 73, folder 1841.

30. Franklin D. Roosevelt, "On Drought Conditions," Fireside Chat, September 6, 1936, *The Public Papers and Addresses of Franklin D. Roosevelt,* 13 vols., compiled by Samuel I. Rosenman (New York: Random House, 1938–1949), 5: 331.

31. William Bullitt to Samuel I. Rosenman, [n.d.] 1949, Bullitt Papers, box 73, folder 1841.

32. Samuel Rosenman to William Bullitt, June 23, 1949; William Bullitt to Samuel Rosenman, March 3, 1949, Bullitt Papers, box 73, folder 1841.

33. Franklin D. Roosevelt, "I Have Seen War . . . I Hate War," address at Chautauqua, NY, August 14, 1936, *The Public Papers and Addresses of Franklin D. Roosevelt,* 5: 289.

34. William Bullitt to Samuel Rosenman, [n.d.] 1949, Bullitt Papers, box 73, folder 1841.

35. William Bullitt, "The Shining Adventure" [memoir], 1, 1950, Bullitt Papers, box 141, folder 101.

36. William Bullitt to DeWitt Wallace, August 26, 1950, Bullitt Papers, box 87, folder 2227.

37. William C. Bullitt, *The Great Globe Itself: A Preface to World Affairs* (New York: C. Scribner's Sons, 1946), 176.

38. Bullitt to Wallace, August 26, 1950.

39. Guillain De Bénouville to William Bullitt, July 14, 1948, Bullitt Papers, box 24, folder 253.

40. See Gregor Mathais, *David Galula: Combattant-espion, maître à penser de la guerre contre-révolutionnaire* (Paris: Economica, 2012), 1–21.

41. Higher spending resumed in 1951, as national security expenditures rose to 12.7 percent of GDP in 1953 and remained around 10 percent until 1959. See Gaddis, *Strategies of Containment,* 359.

42. William Bullitt to Allen Dulles, December 28, 1948, Bullitt Papers, box 26, folder 568.

43. William Bullitt to Dean Acheson, March 13, 1950, Bullitt Papers, box 2, folder 21.

44. George H. Kerr, *Formosa Betrayed* (Boston: Houghton Mifflin, 1965; New York: Da Capo, 1976), 389.

45. Robert L. Miller and Dennis Wainstock, *Indochina and Vietnam: The Thirty-Five-Year War 1940–1975* (New York: Enigma Books, 2013), 77–91.

46. See André Kaspi, "La mission du général de Lattre aux Etats-Unis (13–25 septembre 1951)," *Revue française d'histoire d'outre-mer* 79, no. 295 (1992): 213–226.

47. Brinkley, *The Publisher*, 377.

48. William Bullitt and Herbert Hoover correspondence, June 1952, Bullitt Papers, box 39, folder 908; Timothy Walch, ed., *Herbert Hoover and Dwight D. Eisenhower: A Documentary History* (New York: Palgrave, 2013), 63–64, 77–78.

49. Stephen Ambrose, *Eisenhower: Soldier and President* (New York: Simon and Schuster, 1983), 401. For a contemporary view defending Eisenhower's lenience toward the USSR on the basis purely of military considerations, see Forrest Pogue, "Why Eisenhower's Forces Stopped at the Elbe," *World Politics* 4, no. 3 (April 1952): 356–368, 356–358. See, generally, James McAllister, *No Exit: America and the German Problem, 1943–1954* (Ithaca, NY: Cornell University Press, 2001), 26–73.

50. Carmel Offie to Robert Murphy, July 7, 1952, Murphy Papers, box 59, folder 6.

51. Richard M. Nixon, *Six Crises* (Garden City, NY: Doubleday, 1962), 3.

52. Alan Weinstein, *Perjury: The Hiss-Chambers Case* (New York: Random House, 1997; Stanford, CA: Hoover Institution Press, 2013), 370. "Hiss's Reputation Backed by Days," *New York Times*, December 14, 1949.

53. Quoted in Tony Judt, "An American Tragedy? The Case of Whitaker Chambers," in Judt, *Reappraisals: Reflections on the Forgotten Twentieth Century* (New York: Penguin, 2008), 307.

54. Ronald Steel, "I Had to Win," *New York Times*, April 26, 1987, review of Stephen Ambrose, *Nixon: The Education of a Politician, 1913–1962* (New York: Simon and Schuster, 1987).

55. Richard Nixon to William Bullitt, September 11, 1962, Wilderness Years (1962–1968) Collection, Series 1A, box 5, folder "Bullitt, William C.," Richard Nixon Presidential Library and Museum, Yorba Linda, CA (hereafter Nixon Library). Fawn M. Brodie, *Richard Nixon: The Shaping of His Character* (New York: Norton, 1983), 336.

56. Stanley Hornbeck to Secretary of State, January 9, 1942, box 41, folder "Bullitt, William C.," Stanley Kuhl Hornbeck Papers, coll. 67008, Hoover Institution Library and Archives, Stanford University.

57. Richard Nixon to William Bullitt, November 9, 1953, Bullitt Papers, box 62, folder 1510.

58. William Bullitt to Richard Nixon, November 28, 1953, Bullitt Papers, box 62, folder 1510.

59. Syngman Rhee to William Bullitt, January 19, 1954, Bullitt Papers, box 69, folder 1748.

60. William Bullitt, secret memoranda for himself, June 29 and 30, 1953, Bullitt Papers, box 135, folder 921.

61. "How Can We Stop Russia?" Georgetown University Forum, April 20, 1952. Bullitt, secret memorandum to himself, March 19, 1954, Bullitt Papers, box 135, folder 921.

62. Bullitt, secret memorandum to himself, March 19, 1954, Bullitt Papers, box 135, folder 921; William Bullitt to Syngman Rhee, November 1, 1955, Bullitt Papers, box 69, folder 1749; Anne Bullitt, comments on Edward Gulick, *Ambassador Bullitt and Ashfield,* galleys of an unpublished manuscript, 1992, 4, Bullitt Papers, box 212, folder 248.

63. William Bullitt, Certificate of Employment for Mr. Lee Yung-Kwei, his aide, July 28, 1963, Bullitt Papers, box 47, folder 1122.

64. George F. Kennan, "What Should We Do about Russia?" *U.S. News and World Report,* June 29, 1956, 72–73.

65. William C. Bullitt and George F. Kennan, "Two Former Ambassadors to Moscow Argue: 'What Should We Do about Russia?'" *U.S. News and World Report,* June 29, 1956, 68–77.

66. George Kennan, letter to unknown recipient, June 29, 1956. George Kennan sent a copy of the letter to Bullitt: Kennan to Bullitt, July 31, 1956, box 6, folder "Bullitt, William C.," Loy W. Henderson Papers, MSS 53314, Library of Congress.

67. Karl L. Rankin to William Bullitt, August 7, 1956, Bullitt Papers, box 69, folder 1723.

68. Richard Nixon to William Bullitt, January 20, 1958, Pre-Presidential Collection, Series 320: Correspondence 1946–1962, box 111, folder "Bullitt, William C.," Nixon Library.

69. William Bullitt, telegram to Richard Nixon, August 5, 1959, Pre-Presidential Collection, Series 320: Correspondence 1946–1962, box 111, folder "Bullitt, William C.," Nixon Library.

70. William Bullitt to Richard Nixon, October 21, 1960, Pre-Presidential Collection, Series 320: Correspondence 1946–1962, box 111, folder "Bullitt, William C.," Nixon Library.

71. Richard Nixon, memo to William Bullitt, undated and unsigned, Wilderness Years (1962–1968) Collection, Series 1A, box 5, folder "Bullitt, William C.," Nixon Library.

72. William Bullitt, dossier on Kennedy's illness and on presidential candidate's health, May 20 and June 1, 1960, Wilderness Years (1962–1968) Collection, Series 1A, box 5, folder "Bullitt, William C.," Nixon Library.

73. William Bullitt to Richard Nixon, November 15, 1960, Wilderness Years (1962–1968) Collection, Series 1A, box 5, folder "Bullitt, William C.," Nixon Library.

74. Richard Nixon to William Bullitt, January 18, 1961, Wilderness Years (1962–1968) Collection, Series 1A, box 5, folder "Bullitt, William C.," Nixon Library.

75. William Bullitt to Richard Nixon, August 16, 1961, Wilderness Years (1962–1968) Collection, Series 1A, box 5, folder "Bullitt, William C.," Nixon Library.

76. William C. Bullitt, *Report to the American People* (Boston: Houghton Mifflin, 1940), 28.
77. William Bullitt, memo of conversation with Francisco Franco, January 18, 1950, and William Bullitt to Roscoe Hillenkoetter, January 27, 1950, both in Bullitt Papers, box 210, folder 207.
78. Burton Hersh, *The Old Boys: The American Elite and the Origins of the CIA* (New York: Scribner's, 1992), 154.
79. Ted Morgan, *A Covert Life: Jay Lovestone, Communist, Anti-Communist, and Spymaster* (New York: Random House, 1999), 212–213.
80. See Carmel Offie, correspondence with Robert Murphy, 1944–1959, Murphy Papers, box 59, folder 6, and box 90, folder 4; Carmel Offie, correspondence with William Bullitt, 1949 to 1957, Bullitt Papers, box 63, folder 1534 to 1536.
81. Carmel Offie to William Bullitt, April 28, 1954, Bullitt Papers, box 63, folder 1535.
82. John Foster Dulles, memo of conversation with William Bullitt, March 26, 1958, JFD Chronological Series, box 15, John Foster Dulles Papers, Dwight D. Eisenhower Presidential Library, Abilene, KS.
83. Robert M. Pennoyer, *As It Was: A Memoir* (Westport, CT: Prospecta Press, 2015), 289.
84. William Bullitt, interview with Emily Wabeke, February 29, 1948, American Education Publications, "An Evening with William C. Bullitt," file "Bullitt, William C. (1891–1967)," box 111, folder 1390, Bullitt Family Papers, Filson Historical Society, Louisville, KY.
85. Orville Bullitt, interview by Virginia Gardner, March 30, 1973, box 5, folder 13, Virginia Gardner Papers, TAM.100, Tamiment Library, New York University.
86. Janet Flanner, *Darlinghissima, Letters to a Friend* (New York: Random House, 1985), 217.
87. William Bullitt to Ernesta Drinker Barlow, February 24, 1930, series 1, box 1, folder 7, Ernesta Drinker Barlow Papers, GTM-081118, Georgetown University Libraries.
88. Ernest Jones to William Bullitt, May 24, 1955, Bullitt Papers, box 42, folder 1001.
89. William Bullitt to Ernest Jones, July 22, 1955, Bullitt Papers box 42, folder 1001.
90. Ernest Jones to William Bullitt, April 4, 1956, Bullitt Papers, box 42, folder 1001.
91. Ernest Jones to Anna Freud, April 20, 1956, box 52, folder 5, Anna Freud Papers, MSS 49700, Library of Congress.
92. William Bullitt to Ernest Jones, June 18, 1955, Series C, Correspondence B, P04-C-F-02, Alfred Ernest Jones Collection, P04, Archives of the British Psychoanalytical Society, Institute of Psychoanalysis, London.

16. The Wilson Book, at Last

1. William Bullitt, correspondence with Henry A. Laughlin, February–March 1962, box 49, folder 1173, William C. Bullitt Papers, MS 112, Manuscripts and Archives, Yale University Library (hereafter Bullitt Papers).
2. William Bullitt to Anne Bullitt, February 1, 1962, Bullitt Papers, Accession 2014-M-013, box 1, folder 2.
3. John W. Frost to Barry Goldwater, August 10, 1964, Bullitt Papers, box 30, folder 683.
4. Max Schur to William Bullitt, May 8, 1964, box 2, correspondence re: *Thomas Woodrow Wilson,* Max Schur Papers, MSS 62040, Library of Congress (hereafter Schur Papers).
5. Max Schur to William Bullitt, May 8 and October 13, 1964, and January 25, 1965, Schur Papers, box 2, correspondence re: *Thomas Woodrow Wilson.* See also Max Schur, *Freud: Living and Dying* (New York: International University Press, 1972), 497.
6. William Bullitt to Anne Bullitt, October 10, 1964, Bullitt Papers, Accession 2014-M-013, box 1, folder 2. See also William Bullitt to Internal Revenue Service, May 9, 1958, "Thomas Woodrow Wilson" ms, publishing correspondence, Bullitt Papers, box 141, folder 113.
7. Helen Stewart, Rutgers University Press, to Max Schur, December 31, 1964, Schur Papers, box 2, correspondence re: *Thomas Woodrow Wilson.*
8. William Bullitt to Ernest Jones, June 25, 1956, Series C, Correspondence B, P04-C-F-02, Alfred Ernest Jones Collection, P04, Archives of the British Psychoanalytical Society, Institute of Psychoanalysis, London.
9. Charles Seymour, memorandum of conversation with Edward House, March 17, 1922, Charles Seymour Papers, MSS 441, Manuscripts and Archives, Yale University Library.
10. Irwin ("Ike") Hood Hoover, *Forty-two Years in the White House* (Boston: Houghton Mifflin, 1934), 87–89, 91–95.
11. David Lloyd George, *War Memoirs,* vol. 1: *1914–1915* (Boston: Little, Brown, 1933), 142.
12. Freud had wanted to include this paragraph in the manuscript. Freud manuscript fragments, "Thomas Woodrow Wilson" ms, partial drafts, Bullitt Papers, box 147, folder 222. It was reduced to one line in both the original (1932) manuscript and 1966 published book. Sigmund Freud and William C. Bullitt, "Thomas Woodrow Wilson, Twenty-eighth President of the United States: A Psychological Study," 52, unpublished original manuscript (1932), typescript in presentation binder, 389 pp, Bullitt Papers, Accession 2008-M-037, box 2, folder 10; Sigmund Freud and William C. Bullitt, *Thomas Woodrow Wilson: A Psychological Study* (Boston: Houghton Mifflin, 1966), 61.
13. Alexander L. George and Juliette L. George, *Woodrow Wilson and Colonel House: A Personality Study* (New York: John Day, 1956), 8–13; and Juliette L.

George and Alexander L. George, "Woodrow Wilson and Colonel House: A Reply to Weinstein, Anderson, and Link," *Political Science Quarterly* 96, no. 4 (1981): 641–665.

14. George and George, *Woodrow Wilson and Colonel House,* 114.

15. Philip Rich, notes on "Thomas Woodrow Wilson" manuscript, October 14, 1965, Houghton-Mifflin copy, undated, "Thomas Woodrow Wilson" ms, publishing correspondence, Bullitt Papers, box 142, folder 126.

16. William Bullitt to Harry Laughlin, February 23, 1965, "Thomas Woodrow Wilson" ms, publishing correspondence, Bullitt Papers, box 142, folder 118.

17. Anna Freud to William Bullitt, December 8, 1939, Bullitt Papers, box 30, folder 677.

18. Anna Freud to William Bullitt, May 3, 1965, "Thomas Woodrow Wilson" ms, publishing correspondence, Bullitt Papers, box 142, folder 116.

19. Ernst Freud to Edward Bernays, June 17, 1965, part III, box 1, folder "Freud, Ernst," Edward L. Bernays Papers, MSS 12534, Library of Congress.

20. Alick Bartholomew, memo of conversation with Anna Freud, October 14, 1965, box 53: Freud, Sigmund, Houghton Mifflin Company Correspondence, MA Am 2105 (92), folder 1, Houghton Library, Harvard Library (hereafter Houghton Mifflin Correspondence).

21. Ernst Freud to William Bullitt, December 28, 1965, "Thomas Woodrow Wilson" ms, publishing correspondence, Bullitt Papers, box 142, folder 119. Anna Freud claimed she suggested between fifty and one hundred amendments to the manuscript. Anna Freud to Erik Erikson, November 6, 1966, box 25, folder "Erikson, Erik H.," Anna Freud Papers, MSS 49700, Library of Congress (hereafter Anna Freud Papers). In fact she had proposed two hundred changes, though they were not very significant. See "Thomas Woodrow Wilson" version with Anna Freud's revisions, Bullitt Papers, box 144, folders 150–155.

22. Freud and Bullitt, *Thomas Woodrow Wilson,* 126. "Thomas Woodrow Wilson" version with Anna Freud's revisions, 137, Bullitt Papers, box 144, folder 152.

23. Freud and Bullitt, *Thomas Woodrow Wilson,* 128. "Thomas Woodrow Wilson" version with Anna Freud's revisions, 139, Bullitt Papers, box 144, folder 152.

24. Freud and Bullitt, *Thomas Woodrow Wilson,* 59.

25. "Thomas Woodrow Wilson" version with Anna Freud's revisions, 68, Bullitt Papers, box 144, folder 151.

26. "Thomas Woodrow Wilson" version with Anna Freud's revisions, 113, Bullitt Papers, box 144, folder 151, missing at Freud and Bullitt, *Thomas Woodrow Wilson,* 102.

27. Paul Roazen, notes of telephone interview with William Bullitt, October 15, 1966, box 25, folder 17, Paul Roazen Collection, Howard Gotlieb Archival Research Center, Mugar Memorial Library, Boston University.

28. John P. Tracey, Bullitt's lawyer, to Paul Brooks, president of Houghton-Mifflin, January 20, 1966, "Thomas Woodrow Wilson" ms, publishing correspondence, Bullitt Papers, box 142, folder 119.

29. Benjamin Tilghman to William Bullitt, July 26, 1966, "Thomas Woodrow Wilson" ms, publishing correspondence, Bullitt Papers, box 142, folder 124.

30. Benjamin Tilghman, memo, October 18, 1966, box 53, folder 4: Freud, Sigmund, Houghton Mifflin Correspondence.

31. Benjamin Tilghman, memo "Thomas Woodrow Wilson," November 9, 1966, box 53, folder 5: Freud, Sigmund, Houghton Mifflin Correspondence.

32. Lawrence J. Friedman, *Identity's Architect: A Biography of Erik H. Erikson* (New York: Scribner, 1999), 354–355.

33. Erik Erikson to Anna Freud, October 31, 1966, Anna Freud Papers, box 25, folder "Erikson, Erik H."

34. Benjamin Tilghman to William Bullitt, October 24, 1966, Bullitt Papers, Accession 2014-M-013: Additional Materials, box 1, folder 5.

35. Benjamin Tilghman, memo "Thomas Woodrow Wilson," November 9, 1966.

36. Erik Erikson to William Bullitt, October 31, 1966, Bullitt Papers, box 26, folder 581.

37. Anna Freud to Erik Erikson, November 6, 1966, Anna Freud Papers, box 25, folder "Erikson, Erik H."

38. Max Schur to Erik Erikson, November 9, 1966, Schur Papers, box 2, correspondence re: *Thomas Woodrow Wilson.*

39. Sigmund Freud and William C. Bullitt, "Thomas Woodrow Wilson," *Look,* December 13, 1966, 36–49.

40. Benjamin Tilghman to William Bullitt, December 15, 1966, box 53, folder 5: Freud, Sigmund, Houghton Mifflin Correspondence.

41. Orville Bullitt to Virginia Gardner, June 1, 1977, Virginia Gardner Papers, TAM.100, box 5, folder 13, Tamiment Library, New York University.

42. Anne Bullitt, comments on Edward Gulick, *Ambassador Bullitt and Ashfield,* galleys of an unpublished manuscript, 1992, 14, Bullitt Papers, box 212, folder 248.

43. Richard Nixon, telegram to William Bullitt, February 9, 1967, Wilderness Years (1962–1968) Collection, Series 1A, box 40, folder "Bullitt, William C.," Richard Nixon Presidential Library and Museum, Yorba Linda, CA (hereafter Nixon Library).

44. Hunter Guthrie to William Bullitt, February 6, 1967, Robert D. Murphy Collection (78060), box 137, folder 5, Hoover Institution Library and Archives, Stanford University.

45. Anne Bullitt, comments on Edward Gulick, *Ambassador Bullitt and Ashfield,* galleys of an unpublished manuscript, 1992, 4, box 212, folder 248, Bullitt Papers.

46. "Nixons and Farley Attend Funeral Service for Bullitt," *New York Times,* February 21, 1967, 44.

47. Charles de Gaulle to Anne Bullitt, February 16, 1967, Bullitt Papers, box 24, folder 527.

48. Chip Bohlen to Orville Bullitt, March 2, 1967, Bullitt Papers, box 213, folder 263.

49. "Death of a Friend," editorial, *Ma'ariv,* February 20, 1967, originally Hebrew, English translation in Bullitt, William C. (1891–1967) file, box 111, folder 1390 (Miscellaneous), Bullitt Family Papers, Filson Historical Society, Louisville, KY.

50. Alden Whitman, "Energetic Diplomat, William C. Bullitt, First U.S. Envoy to Soviet, Dies," *New York Times,* February 16, 1967, 1, reprinted in Alden Whitman, *The Obituary Book* (New York: Stein and Day, 1971), 9. Whitman quotes Janet Flanner, "Mr. Ambassador—I," *New Yorker,* December 10, 1938.

51. Richard Nixon to Alden Whitman, February 21, 1967, Wilderness Years (1962–1968) Collection, Series 1A, box 40, folder "Bullitt, William C.," Nixon Library.

17. The Return of the Father

1. Paul Roazen, "The Doctor and the Diplomat: The Mysterious Collaboration between Freud and Bullitt," unpublished manuscript, 9, box 17, folder 6, Paul Roazen Collection, Howard Gotlieb Archival Research Center, Mugar Memorial Library, Boston University (hereafter Roazen Collection).

2. Anna Freud to Paul Roazen, March 15, 1967, Roazen Collection, box 25, folder 5; Roazen, "The Doctor and the Diplomat," 11, Roazen Collection, box 17, folder 6; Anna Freud to Erik Erikson, November 6, 1966, box 25, folder "Erikson, Erik H," Anna Freud Papers, MSS 49700, Library of Congress (hereafter Anna Freud Papers).

3. Anna Freud to Max Schur, February 15, 1967, letter translated by Paul Roazen, Roazen Collection, box 25, folder 17; Burness Moore, American Psychoanalytic Association, to Edward Bernays, March 7, 1967, part III: General Correspondence, box 11, folder "March–April 1967," Edward L. Bernays Papers, MSS 12534, Library of Congress.

4. Robert Sussman Stewart to Anna Freud, December 14, 1966, and January 18, 1967, box 97, folder "Sussman-Stewart, Robert," Anna Freud Papers. Robert Sussman Stewart, "Posthumous Analysis," *New York Times* book review, January 29, 1967, 42.

5. Roazen, "The Doctor and the Diplomat," 129, Roazen Collection, box 17, folder 6; Paul Roazen, *Encountering Freud: The Politics and History of Psychoanalysis* (New Brunswick, NJ: Transaction, 1990), 158; David Rapaport, "A Historical Survey of Psychoanalytic Ego Psychology," introduction to Erik Erikson, *Identity and Life Cycle* (New York: International Universities Press, 1959), 5–17.

6. After completing the manuscript with Bullitt, Freud ridiculed those who argued for exact correspondence between the three characteristics of consciousness—conscious, preconscious, and unconscious—and the three provinces of mental apparatus: id, ego, and superego. Freud compared his interlocutors to, of all people, Wilson. Sigmund Freud, *New Introductory Lectures in Psycho-Analysis* (1933), in Freud, *The Standard Edition of the Complete Works of Sigmund Freud,* ed. James Strachey with Anna Freud, 24 vols. (London: Hogarth Press, 1953–1974), 12: 73.

7. Theodor Reik, preface to *Thomas Woodrow Wilson,* undated, box 1, folder "Anna Freud, 1966–69," Max Schur Papers, MSS 62040, Library of Congress.

8. Anna Freud to Max Schur, January 15, 1968, Max Schur Papers, box 1, folder "Anna Freud, 1966–69"; Max Schur to Miss Legru, Houghton Mifflin, January 19, 1968: Schur Papers, box 2, correspondence re: *Thomas Woodrow Wilson.*

9. William Bullitt, interview by Paul Roazen, October 15, 1966, Roazen Collection, box 25, folder 17.

10. Orville Bullitt, interview by Virginia Gardner, March 30, 1973, box 5, folder 13, Virginia Gardner Papers, TAM.100, Tamiment Library, New York University (hereafter Gardner Papers); Virginia Gardner, memo on Orville Bullitt, March 30, 1973, 16, Gardner Papers, box 5, folder 13.

11. Ted Morgan, *A Covert Life: Jay Lovestone, Communist, Anti-Communist, and Spymaster* (New York: Random House, 1999), 232.

12. Robert M. Pennoyer, *As It Was: A Memoir* (Westport, CT: Prospecta Press, 2015), 289, 291; Mark Solms, "'Freud' and Bullitt: An Unknown Manuscript," *Journal of the American Psychoanalytic Association* 54, no. 4 (2006): 1263–1298, 1266; Paul Roazen, "Oedipus at Versailles: New Evidence of Freud's Part in a Study of Woodrow Wilson," *Times Literary Supplement,* April 22, 2005; Solms, "'Freud' and Bullitt: An Unknown Manuscript," 1263.

18. The Secret

1. Sigmund Freud to William Bullitt, September 20, 1931, "Thomas Woodrow Wilson" manuscript, drafts, Freud ms fragments, box 147, folder 222, William C. Bullitt Papers, MS 112, Manuscripts and Archives, Yale University Library (hereafter Bullitt Papers). Roazen described Freud's

document in German as an "addition" to a work in progress but at the same time suggested it was perhaps the "general part." Paul Roazen, "Oedipus at Versailles: New Evidence of Freud's Part in a Study of Woodrow Wilson," *Times Literary Supplement*, April 22, 2005.

2. Paul Roazen, "The Doctor and the Diplomat: The Mysterious Collaboration between Freud and Bullitt," unpublished manuscript, 127, box 17, folder 6, Paul Roazen Collection, Howard Gotlieb Archival Research Center, Mugar Memorial Library, Boston University (hereafter Roazen Collection); Mark Solms, "'Freud' and Bullitt: An Unknown Manuscript," *Journal of the American Psychoanalytic Association* 54, no. 4 (2006): 1263–1298, 1280. The original text was published in German as Sigmund Freud, "Ohne Titel. Ein bislang unbekannter Text," *Neue Rundschau* (Frankfurt am Main: S. Fischer, 2006), 9–26. The French publication is Sigmund Freud, *Abrégé de Théorie Analytique*, intro. by Elisabeth Roudinesco, trans. Jean-Pierre Lefebvre (Paris: Seuil, 2017).

3. Freud to Bullitt, September 20, 1931, Bullitt Papers, box 147, folder 222.

4. Sigmund Freud, translation of draft of chapter 1, handwritten, Sigmund Freud manuscripts (oversize), Bullitt Papers, box 245, folder 38. The typed version with Bullitt's corrections is in "Thomas Woodrow Wilson" manuscript, partial drafts, Bullitt Papers, box 146, folder 192; the final typed version is in "Thomas Woodrow Wilson" manuscript, partial drafts, Bullitt Papers, box 146, folder 191.

5. Sigmund Freud and William C. Bullitt, "Thomas Woodrow Wilson, Twenty-eighth President of the United States: A Psychological Study," unpublished original manuscript (1932), 28, typescript in presentation binder, 389 pp, Bullitt Papers, Accession 2008-M-037, box 2, folders 10–12; Sigmund Freud and William C. Bullitt, *Thomas Woodrow Wilson: A Psychological Study* (Boston: Houghton Mifflin, 1966), 47.

6. Solms, "'Freud' and Bullitt: An Unknown Manuscript," 1295.

7. Freud to Bullitt, September 20, 1931, Bullitt Papers, box 147, folder 222.

8. These suggestions are in excerpts of drafts: "Thomas Woodrow Wilson" manuscript, drafts, Freud ms fragments, Bullitt Papers, box 147, folder 222.

9. William Bullitt to Edward House, April 29, 1932, box 21, folder 684, Edward Mandell House Papers, MS 466, Manuscripts and Archives, Yale University Library.

10. Freud's and Bullitt's signatures appear in a draft of the original manuscript on pages 31, 54, 69, 87, 94, 105, 116, 123, 132, 147, 160, 173, 184, 200, 205, 213, 220, 225, 237, 244, 252, 260, 266, 275, 293, 306, 314, 325, 337, 344, 359, 366, 372, 383, 389, "Thomas Woodrow Wilson" manuscript, drafts, Freud ms fragments, Bullitt Papers, box 147, folder 222. This manuscript does not include the introduction by Freud, the foreword by Bullitt, or the digest of biographical data that appears in the published book.

11. Sigmund Freud to Arnold Zweig, December 7, 1930, *The Letters of Sigmund Freud and Arnold Zweig,* ed. Ernst Freud, trans. Elaine Robson-Scott and William Robson-Scott (New York: Harcourt, Brace and World, 1970), 25.

12. Sigmund Freud, introductions in German and English, undated, "Thomas Woodrow Wilson" manuscript, drafts, Freud ms fragments, Bullitt Papers, box 147, folder 222.

13. Sigmund Freud, undated fragment, "Thomas Woodrow Wilson" manuscript, drafts, Freud ms fragments, Bullitt Papers, box 147, folder 222.

14. Sigmund Freud, handwritten introduction in German, undated, Sigmund Freud manuscripts (oversize), Bullitt Papers, box 245, folder 39.

15. Contract signed by Sigmund Freud and William Bullitt for a book tentatively titled *Thomas Woodrow Wilson, Twenty Sixth President of the United States, A Psychological Study,* January 20, 1932, Bullitt Papers, box 141, folder 110.

16. Sigmund Freud to Abraham Brill, January 31, 1932, General Correspondence, box 19, "Brill, A. A.," folder "from Freud, originals, 1930–1933," Sigmund Freud Papers, MSS 39990, Library of Congress.

17. Sigmund Freud to Max Eitingon, November 20, 1932, Sigmund Freud, *Max Eitingon, Briefwechsel, 1906–1939,* 2 vols. (Tübingen: Edition Diskord, 2004), 2: 838. Marie Bonaparte to Sigmund Freud, December 7, 1933, quoted in Max Schur, *Freud: Living and Dying* (New York: International University Press, 1972), 449. Emphasis added.

18. Sigmund Freud to Paul A. Hill, November 16, 1934, box 1, folder "Sigmund Freud," Paul A. Hill Collection (69075), Hoover Institution Library and Archives, Stanford University.

19. Anna Freud to William Bullitt, November 21, 1939, and William Bullitt to Anna Freud, November 28, 1939, both in Bullitt Papers, box 30, folder 677.

20. Carmel Offie to William Bullitt, July 1, 1946, Bullitt Papers, box 63, folder 1531.

21. Brooks Atkinson, "Drama about League of Nations and Woodrow Wilson Opens at the Mansfield," *New York Times,* December 29, 1941, 20.

22. "Wilson Birthplace to Become a Shrine," *New York Times,* April 13, 1941, 38.

23. Winston Churchill, Address to Congress, December 26, 1941, *Senate Journal,* 77th Cong., 1st sess., 515–517.

24. Bosley Crowther, "Wilson: An Eminent Screen Biography, Barring Some Distressing Oversights," *New York Times,* August 6, 1944.

25. William Castle diary, vol. 27: January 1–March 29, 1935, 139–140, William R. Castle Papers, MS AM 2021, Houghton Library, Harvard Library.

26. Cary Grayson, interview by William Bullitt, October 9, 1930, notes on conversations about Woodrow Wilson, Bullitt Papers, box 148, folder 233.

27. William Bullitt, signed private will, Ashfield, September 10, 1953, "Thomas Woodrow Wilson" ms, publishing correspondence, Bullitt Papers, box 141, folder 113.

28. William Bullitt, draft of Foreword, undated, "Thomas Woodrow Wilson" manuscript drafts, Bullitt Papers, box 146, folder 201.

29. Orville Bullitt to Alexander George, December 6, 1973, (copy), box 21, folder 10, "Freud research and leads," Peter J. Gay Papers, MS 2934, Manuscripts and Archives, Yale University Library.

30. William Bullitt, Appointment Books, August 9, 1939, visit to London, Bullitt Papers, box 193, folder 12. On October 29, 1962, Bullitt signed a note describing three minor changes he and Freud agreed to, such as replacing the term "Notes" with "Data" in "Digest of Data." William Bullitt, note, October 29, 1962, Bullitt Papers, box 146, folder 202.

31. William Bullitt, note, November 21, 1941, Bullitt Papers, Accession 2008-M-037, box 2, folder 10. Emphasis in original.

32. Orville Bullitt, interview by Virginia Gardner, March 30, 1973, box 5, folder 13, Virginia Gardner Papers, TAM.100, Tamiment Library, New York University. In his 1953 will, Bullitt also confirmed that "the manuscript contained in the Viennese Tooled leather case, . . . each chapter of which is signed by both Freud and myself, is not to be published." Signed in Ashfield, September 10, 1953, "Thomas Woodrow Wilson" ms, publishing correspondence, Bullitt Papers, box 141, folder 113.

33. William Bullitt, note introducing a 1956 draft of the manuscript, handwritten and signed, November 1, 1956, Bullitt Papers, Accession 2008-M-037, box 2, folder 13.

34. William Bullitt to Anne Bullitt, February 1, 1962, Bullitt Papers, Accession 2014-M-013, box 1, folder 3.

35. Otto Fenichel, *The Psychoanalytic Theory of Neurosis* (New York: W. W. Norton, 1945), 12.

36. See Jean Laplanche, *Life and Death in Psychoanalysis,* trans., with an introduction by Jeffrey Mehlman (Baltimore: Johns Hopkins University Press, 1976), 9–10; Jonathan Lear, *Freud,* 2nd ed. (London: Routledge, 2015), 77–78.

37. Freud and Bullitt, *Thomas Woodrow Wilson,* 26.

38. Freud and Bullitt, "Thomas Woodrow Wilson," original manuscript (1932), 279, 306, 324, Bullitt Papers, Accession 2008-M-037, box 2, folders 10–12.

39. Freud and Bullitt, "Thomas Woodrow Wilson," original manuscript (1932), 12–14, 18, 39, 47, Bullitt Papers, Accession 2008-M-037, box 2, folders 10–12.

40. William Bullitt, memorandum of conversation with Sigmund Freud, November 1, 1930, "Thomas Woodrow Wilson" manuscript, notes, Bullitt Papers, box 148, folder 231.

41. William Bullitt, "The Tragedy of Woodrow Wilson," Act I, 28–29, undated (copyright registered March 1, 1927, at the Library of Congress), Writings: Plays, Bullitt Papers, box 163, folder 506.

42. Charles Swem, "re: War," unpublished ms., "Writings," box 87, folder 19, "Charles L. Swem (personal)," series 10: Papers of Others about Wilson, "Swem, Charles L.," Woodrow Wilson Collection, MC 168, Public Policy Papers, Special Collections, Princeton University Library.

43. Dudley Malone, interview by William Bullitt, July 9, 1930, notes on conversations about Woodrow Wilson, Bullitt Papers, box 148, folder 233. On romantic masculine friendships in the nineteenth century, see E. Anthony Rotundo, *American Manhood: Transformations in Masculinity from the Revolution to the Modern Era* (New York: Basic Books, 1983), 82–88.

44. Freud and Bullitt, *Thomas Woodrow Wilson,* 66.

45. Freud and Bullitt, "Thomas Woodrow Wilson," original manuscript (1932), 61, 65, Bullitt Papers, Accession 2008-M-037, box 2, folders 10–12.

46. Bullitt and Freud, 1956 draft of the manuscript, "Digest of Data," 8, November 1, 1956, Bullitt Papers, Accession 2008-M-037, box 2, folder 13.

47. Freud and Bullitt, "Thomas Woodrow Wilson," original manuscript (1932), 35, Bullitt Papers, Accession 2008-M-037, box 2, folders 10–12.

48. Gordon Auchincloss, memorandum of conversation with Mrs. Reid, author of *Life of Woodrow Wilson,* May 22, 1939, Special Correspondence, box 2, folder "Auchincloss, Gordon, 1939–1941," Stephen Bonsal Papers, MSS 13193, Library of Congress.

49. Henry Van Dyke, interview by Ray Baker, November 17, 1970, Correspondence Related to Woodrow Wilson, box 116, folder "Van Dyke, Henry," Ray Stannard Baker Papers, MSS 11593, Library of Congress.

50. David Lawrence, *The True Story of Woodrow Wilson* (New York: George H. Doran, 1924), 27.

51. Freud and Bullitt, "Thomas Woodrow Wilson," original manuscript (1932), 304, Bullitt Papers, Accession 2008-M-037, box 2, folders 10–12.

52. Freud and Bullitt, "Thomas Woodrow Wilson," original manuscript (1932), 30, 56, 59, 64 (twice), 68, 69, 78, 114, 150, 153, Bullitt Papers, Accession 2008-M-037, box 2, folders 10–12.

53. Freud and Bullitt, "Thomas Woodrow Wilson," original manuscript (1932), 56, Bullitt Papers, Accession 2008-M-037, box 2, folders 10–12.

54. Freud and Bullitt, "Thomas Woodrow Wilson," original manuscript (1932), 8, 57, Bullitt Papers, Accession 2008-M-037, box 2, folders 10–12.

55. Sigmund Freud, unpublished letter to Sandor Ferenczi, October 17, 1910, quoted in Jeffrey M. Masson, "Introduction," *The Complete Letters of Sigmund Freud to Wilhelm Fliess* (Cambridge, MA: Harvard University Press, 1985), 4.

56. Sigmund Freud, "Letter to an American Mother," *American Journal of Psychiatry* 107, no. 10 (1951): 787.

57. Freud and Bullitt, "Thomas Woodrow Wilson," original manuscript (1932), 26, Bullitt Papers, Accession 2008-M-037, box 2, folders 10–12.
58. William Bullitt, foreword to "The Tragedy of Woodrow Wilson," Bullitt Papers, box 163, folder 509.
59. Freud and Bullitt, "Thomas Woodrow Wilson," original manuscript (1932), 76, Bullitt Papers, Accession 2008-M-037, box 2, folders 10–12.
60. Freud and Bullitt, "Thomas Woodrow Wilson," original manuscript (1932), 79–80, Bullitt Papers, Accession 2008-M-037, box 2, folders 10–12. In the published book, the sentence "and the miracle . . . mere mortal" was suppressed. Freud and Bullitt, *Thomas Woodrow Wilson,* 78.
61. Freud and Bullitt, "Thomas Woodrow Wilson," original manuscript (1932), 24–25, Bullitt Papers, Accession 2008-M-037, box 2, folders 10–12.
62. Anna Freud to Erik Erikson, November 6, 1966, box 25, folder "Erikson, Erik H.," Anna Freud Papers, MSS 49700, Library of Congress.
63. William Bullitt, "The Shining Adventure" [memoir], 1950, 12, Bullitt Papers, box 141, folder 101.
64. Freud and Bullitt, "Thomas Woodrow Wilson," original manuscript (1932), 323, Bullitt Papers, Accession 2008-M-037, box 2, folders 10–12.
65. William Bullitt, "Review of John Maynard Keynes, *The Economic Consequences of the Peace* (London: Macmillan, 1919)," *The Freeman,* March 17, 1920, 19.
66. Adolf A. Berle, *Navigating the Rapids, 1918–1971,* ed. Beatrice Bishop Berle and Travis Beal Jacobs (New York: Harcourt, Brace, Jovanovich, 1976), 829.
67. William Bullitt to Alexander Kirk, September 28, 1939, Bullitt Papers, box 45, folder 1076.
68. William Bullitt to Reverend C. Leslie Glenn, January 20, 1949, Bullitt Papers, box 33, folder 760.
69. William Bullitt, "The World from Rome," *Life,* September 4, 1944, was subtitled: "The Eternal City Fears a Struggle between Christianity and Communism."
70. Alexis de Tocqueville, *Democracy in America,* trans. Arthur Goldhammer (New York: Library of America, 2004), 338.
71. Peter Gay, *A Godless Jew: Freud, Atheism, and the Making of Psychoanalysis* (New Haven, CT: Yale University Press, 1987), 125.
72. Anna Freud Bernays (Sigmund Freud's sister), excerpts, other papers article about Sigmund Freud, undated, part III: Family Papers, 1831–1993, box 1, Edward L. Bernays Papers, MSS 12534, Library of Congress.
73. Sigmund Freud to Arnold Zweig, September 30, 1934, in *Letters of Sigmund Freud 1873–1939,* selected and ed. Ernst L. Freud, trans. Tania Stern and James Stern (London: Hogarth Press, 1961), no. 276, 418.

74. Sigmund Freud to Lou Andreas-Salomé, March 11, 1935, in *Sigmund Freud and Lou Andreas-Salomé Letters,* ed. Ernst Pfeiffer, trans. William Robson-Scott and Elaine Robson-Scott (London: Hogarth Press, 1972), 205. In addition, Freud thought his essay needed more work.

75. John Wiley to William Bullitt, March 10, 1938, Bullitt Papers, box 90, folder 2301.

76. Peter Gay, *Freud: A Life for Our Time* (New York: Norton, 1988), 644.

77. Will Brownell and Richard N. Billings, *So Close to Greatness: A Biography of William C. Bullitt* (New York: Macmillan, 1987), 323.

78. "Thomas Woodrow Wilson" manuscript, drafts, Freud ms fragments, Bullitt Papers, box 147, folder 222; Freud and Bullitt, "Thomas Woodrow Wilson," original manuscript (1932), Bullitt Papers, Accession 2008-M-037, box 2, folders 10–12.

19. Wilson in Retrospect

1. Woodrow Wilson, "An Address to the Senate," July 10, 1919, Woodrow Wilson, *The Papers of Woodrow Wilson,* ed. Arthur S. Link et al., 69 vols. (Princeton, NJ: Princeton University Press, 1966–1993), 61: 434.

2. Wilson used the word "enforce" in the draft of his December 1916 peace note but replaced it with "ensure" in the final version. John M. Cooper, *Breaking the Heart of the World: Woodrow Wilson and the Fight for the League of Nations* (Cambridge: Cambridge University Press, 2001), 19n18.

3. Woodrow Wilson, *Woodrow Wilson's Case for the League of Nations* (Princeton, NJ: Princeton University Press, 1923), 67, quoted in Nicholas Mulder, *The Economic Weapon: The Rise of Sanctions as a Tool of Modern War* (New Haven, CT: Yale University Press, 2022), 1.

4. Ralph A. Stone, *The Irreconcilables: The Fight against the League of Nations* (Lexington: University Press of Kentucky, 1970), 41. Lloyd E. Ambrosius, "Wilson, the Republicans, and French Security after World War I," *Journal of American History* 59, no. 2 (1972): 341–352. Ralph A. Stone, "The Irreconcilables' Alternatives to the League of Nations," *Mid-America,* July 1967, 167–173, cited in Ambrosius, "Wilson, the Republicans."

5. William C. Widenor, *Henry Cabot Lodge and the Search for an American Foreign Policy* (Berkeley: University of California Press, 1980), 295–297.

6. Henry Cabot Lodge to Henry White, April 8, 1919, Paris Peace Conference File, box 41, Henry White Papers, MSS 45328, Library of Congress.

7. "From the Diary of Dr. Grayson," *Papers of Woodrow Wilson,* 61: 375–376.

8. Woodrow Wilson, "An Address to the Senate," July 10, 1919, *Papers of Woodrow Wilson,* 61: 436.

9. John M. Cooper, *Breaking the Heart of the World: Woodrow Wilson and the Fight for the League of Nations* (Cambridge: Cambridge University Press, 2001), 120.

10. Ray S. Baker, memorandum of conversations with Admiral Grayson, February 18 and 19, 1926, Correspondence Related to Woodrow Wilson, box 106, folder "Grayson, Cary T.," Ray Stannard Baker Papers, MSS 11593, Library of Congress.

11. Cary Grayson, interview by William Bullitt, October 2, 1931, notes on conversations about Woodrow Wilson, box 148, folder 233, William C. Bullitt Papers, MS 112, Manuscripts and Archives, Yale University Library (hereafter Bullitt Papers).

12. Grayson, interview by Bullitt, October 2, 1931.

13. Alexander L. George and Juliette L. George, *Woodrow Wilson and Colonel House: A Personality Study* (New York: John Day, 1956), 8.

14. Jessie Bones Brower to Ray Stannard Baker, May 9, 1926, Correspondence Related to Woodrow Wilson, box 101, folder "Brower, Jessie B.," Ray Stannard Baker Papers, MSS 11593, Library of Congress.

15. Arthur Walworth, interview and correspondence with Helen Woodrow Bones, box 1, folder 4, Arthur Clarence Walworth Papers, MS 532, Manuscripts and Archives, Yale University Library (hereafter Walworth Papers).

16. Helen Woodrow Bones to Arthur Walworth, October 18, 1949, Walworth Papers, box 1, folder 4.

17. See Arthur Link, "Introduction," in Stockton Axson, *"Brother Woodrow": A Memoir of Woodrow Wilson*, ed. Arthur Link (Princeton: Princeton University Press, 1993), xii.

18. Axson, *"Brother Woodrow": A Memoir*, 214–215.

19. Stockton Axson, "Mr. Wilson: An Appreciation and a Bit of Analysis," n.d., box 49, folder 4, "Works: Axson, Stockton," series 10: Papers of Others about Wilson, "Family (1837–1962)," Woodrow Wilson Collection, MC 168, Public Policy Papers, Special Collections, Princeton University Library.

20. Abram Kardiner, *My Analysis with Freud* (New York: Norton, 1977), 58.

21. Axson, *"Brother Woodrow": A Memoir*, 217.

22. Woodrow Wilson to Colonel House, December 21, 1911, quoted in Ray Stannard Baker, *Woodrow Wilson: Life and Letters*, 8 vols. (Garden City, NY: Doubleday, 1927–1939), 3: 250.

23. Hiram Johnson to Hiram Johnson, Jr., and Arch M. Johnson, August 23, 1919, in *The Diary Letters of Hiram Johnson*, ed. Robert Burke, 7 vols. (New York: Garland, 1983), vol. 3, at August 23, 1919.

24. Charles Seymour, memorandum of conversation with Edward House, March 17, 1920, Charles Seymour Papers, MSS 441, Manuscripts and Archives, Yale University Library (hereafter Seymour Papers).

25. "Thomas Woodrow Wilson" manuscript, partial drafts, "Chapters I and II [annotated by Freud and Bullitt]," 40, Bullitt Papers, box 146, folder 193. This passage did not appear in the 1932 original manuscript or in the 1966 published version. Sigmund Freud and William C. Bullitt, "Thomas Woodrow Wilson, Twenty-eighth President of the United States: A Psychological Study," unpublished original manuscript (1932), typescript in presentation binder, 389 pp, Bullitt Papers, Accession 2008-M-037, box 2, folders 10–12. Sigmund Freud and William C. Bullitt, *Thomas Woodrow Wilson: A Psychological Study* (Boston: Houghton Mifflin, 1966).

26. Woodrow Wilson to John Hibben, January 26, 1907, Baker, *Wilson: Life and Letters,* 2: 252. Emphasis in original.

27. Woodrow Wilson to John Grier Hibben, July 10, 1907, *Papers of Woodrow Wilson,* 17: 269.

28. Freud and Bullitt, *Thomas Woodrow Wilson,* 124.

29. Margaret Randolph Axson Elliott, *My Aunt Louisa and Woodrow Wilson* (Chapel Hill: University of North Carolina Press, 1944), 237.

30. Edward House to Dudley Malone, July 31, 1917, box 76, folder 2562, Edward Mandell House Papers, MS 466, Manuscripts and Archives, Yale University Library (hereafter House Papers).

31. See, for example, Woodrow Wilson to Dudley Malone, October 10, 1918, Baker, *Wilson: Life and Letters,* 8: 471.

32. Freud and Bullitt, *Thomas Woodrow Wilson,* 181. See also Cary Grayson, interview by William Bullitt, October 2 and October 22, 1931, notes on conversations about Woodrow Wilson, box 148, folder 233, Bullitt Papers.

33. Arthur C. Walworth to Charles Seymour, March 19, 1955, Seymour Papers, box 14, folder 854.

34. Walworth to Seymour, March 19, 1955.

35. Baker, *Wilson: Life and Letters,* 1: 172–173.

36. Woodrow Wilson, *Congressional Government: A Study in American Politics,* 15th ed. (Boston: Houghton Mifflin, 1900), 21, 22, 307.

37. James Kerney, *The Political Education of Woodrow Wilson* (New York: Century, 1926), 375–376.

38. Freud and Bullitt, *Thomas Woodrow Wilson,* 181.

39. James E. Watson, *As I Knew Them: Memoirs of James E. Watson* (Indianapolis, IN: Bobbs-Merrill, 1936), 200.

40. Woodrow Wilson to Rolland Cotton Smith, December 29, 1916, and January 5, 1917, *Papers of Woodrow Wilson,* 40: 354, 412.

41. Watson, *As I Knew Them,* 202. On one occasion in 1921, after mentioning Lodge's name in a conversation, Wilson suffered a spasm that lasted fifty minutes. According to House, those present "thought he would surely die." Edward House, diary entry for April 3, 1921, vol. 8, 14, House Papers, box 299, folders 1–2.

42. Arthur Walworth, *Woodrow Wilson,* vol. 2: *World Prophet* (New York: Longmans, Green, 1958), 368.

43. Jean Laplanche and J.-B. Pontalis, *The Language of Psycho-analysis* (London: Hogarth, 1973), 79n1; Sigmund Freud, *Analysis of a Phobia in a Five-Year-Old Boy* (1909), in Sigmund Freud, *The Standard Edition of the Complete Works of Sigmund Freud,* ed. James Strachey with Anna Freud, 24 vols. (London: Hogarth Press, 1953–1974), 10: 122.

44. Ray Baker, interview by William Bullitt, undated, notes on conversations about Woodrow Wilson, Bullitt Papers, box 148, folder 233.

45. Freud and Bullitt, "Thomas Woodrow Wilson," original manuscript (1932), 306, Bullitt Papers, Accession 2008-M-037, box 2, folders 10–12; Freud and Bullitt, *Thomas Woodrow Wilson,* 234.

46. See Edwin A. Weinstein, "Woodrow Wilson's Neurological Illness," *Journal of American History* 57, no. 2 (1970): 324–351. Edwin A. Weinstein, James W. Anderson, and Arthur W. Link, "Woodrow Wilson's Political Personality: A Reappraisal," *Political Science Quarterly* 93, no. 4 (1978): 585–598, 594.

47. Alan Sharp, *David Lloyd George* (London: Haus, 2008), 108.

48. Antony Lentin, *The Last Political Law Lord: Lord Sumner (1859–1934)* (Newcastle: Cambridge Scholars, 2008), 101.

49. Cary Grayson, diary entry for March 26, 1919, Peace Conference, second trip, original copy, 22, series Grayson Diaries, box 2, Cary T. Grayson Papers, MS 000465, Woodrow Wilson Presidential Library and Museum, Staunton, VA (hereafter Grayson Papers).

50. Antony Lentin, *Lloyd George, Woodrow Wilson and the Guilt of Germany: An Essay in the Pre-History of Appeasement* (Leicester: Leicester University Press, 1984), 56.

51. Jan Smuts to David Lloyd George, June 8, 1918, in *Selections from the Smuts Papers,* ed. W. K. Hancock and Jean Van der Poel, 7 vols. (Cambridge: Cambridge University Press, 1966–1973), no. 833, 3: 662–663.

52. Woodrow Wilson, note to Edward House, January 29, 1919, House Papers, box 121, folder 4294; Walworth, *Woodrow Wilson,* vol. 2: *World Prophet,* 250.

53. Cary T. Grayson, memo of conversation with General Jan Christian Smuts, January 14, 1930, "1913–1920[1930]: various typed diary entries and notes," series Grayson Diaries, box 1, Grayson Papers.

54. Jan Smuts to M. C. Gillett, March 31, 1919, Smuts, *Selections from the Smuts Papers,* no. 925, 4: 95, no. 925.

55. J. R. M. Butler, *Lord Lothian (Philip Kerr) 1882–1940* (London: Macmillan, 1960), 73. Philip Kerr, memorandum to Charles Seymour, October 7, 1933, 3–4, Seymour Papers, box 9, folder 522.

56. "A Memorandum by Jan Christiaan Smuts," Note on Reparation, March 31, 1919, *Papers of Woodrow Wilson,* 56: 480–482.

57. Walworth, *Woodrow Wilson*, vol. 2: *World Prophet*, 293.
58. Woodrow Wilson to Robert Lansing, February 24, 1919, series 1, "Lansing, Robert," box 2, folder 1919, John Foster Dulles Papers, MC 016, Public Policy Papers, Special Collections, Princeton University Library (hereafter Dulles Papers).
59. John Foster Dulles, memorandum of conference held at President Wilson's hotel, Paris, April 1, 1919, 2 PM, series 1, "Lansing, Robert," box 2, folder 1919, Dulles Papers.
60. Bernard Baruch, interview by William Bullitt, October 4, 1930, notes on conversations about Woodrow Wilson, Bullitt Papers, box 148, folder 233.
61. Lentin, *Lloyd George, Woodrow Wilson and the Guilt of Germany*, 128.
62. Arthur S. Link, *Woodrow Wilson: Revolution, War, and Peace* (Arlington Heights, IL: AHM, 1979), 91.
63. Irwin H. (Ike) Hoover, "The Illness of Woodrow Wilson," *Saturday Evening Post*, July 21, 1934.
64. Cary Grayson, diary entry for April 8, 1919, Peace Conference, second trip, 91, series Grayson Diaries, box 2, Grayson Papers. Edith Helm to her husband, March 28, 1919, (copy), box 7, folder "Corres. March 14–April 15, 1919," Edith Benham Helm Papers, MSS 25700, Library of Congress.
65. Gilbert Close to Helen Close, April 7, 1919, series 1, box 1, folder 1, Gilbert F. Close Papers, MC 202, Public Policy Papers, Special Collections, Princeton University Library.
66. Raymond B. Fosdick, "Scholar in Action," *Saturday Review*, March 29, 1958, 17. See also Walworth, *Wilson and His Peacemakers*, 156–162; and Charles E. Neu, *Colonel House: A Biography of Woodrow Wilson's Silent Partner* (New York: Oxford University Press, 2014), 401, 666n43.
67. Edward House, interview by Charles Seymour, March 21, 1922, Seymour Papers, box 2, folder 254.
68. James Kerney, notes on visit to Woodrow Wilson, October 23, 1923, box 1, folder 3, James Kerney Collection on Woodrow Wilson, MC 169, Public Policy Papers, Special Collections, Princeton University Library.
69. Jan Smuts, interview by Roy Harrod, June 8, 1948, in Roy Harrod, *Life of John Maynard Keynes* (New York: Macmillan, 1951), 260n4.

Conclusion: Personality in History

1. Margaret MacMillan, *Paris 1919: Six Months That Changed the World* (New York: Random House, 2002), 190.
2. Antony Lentin, *Lloyd George, Woodrow Wilson and the Guilt of Germany: An Essay in the Pre-History of Appeasement* (Leicester: Leicester University Press, 1984), 150–151.

3. John M. Keynes, *Les Conséquences économiques de la paix*, trans. Paul Frank (Paris: Gallimard, 1920), Préface à l'édition française par l'auteur, 10.
4. John Maynard Keynes, *The Economic Consequences of the Peace* (London: Macmillan, 1919), 28.
5. On contact with the German government, see Georges-Henri Soutou, "La France et l'Allemagne en 1919," in *La France et l'Allemagne entre les deux guerres mondiales*, ed. J. Bariéty, A. Guth, and J.-M. Valentin (Nancy: Presses universitaires de Nancy, 1987), 9–19. On the possible meeting with Hindenburg, see Stephen Bonsal, "What Manner of Man Was Clemenceau?" *World's Work*, February 1930, 72.
6. Keynes, *Economic Consequences of the Peace*, 52–53.
7. Bernard M. Baruch, *The Making of the Reparation and Economic Sections of the Treaty* (New York: Harper and Brothers, 1920), 19.
8. John Maynard Keynes to Harold Temperley, October 24 and November 10, 1920, series CO: "Comments by JMK . . . 1910–1946," file 11, docs. 203, 206, Papers of John Maynard Keynes, GBR/0272/JMK, Archive Centre, King's College, University of Cambridge (hereafter Keynes Papers).
9. Bernard Baruch, memo, December 9, 1921, Subseries 1B: Selected Correspondence, 1919–1921, box 45, Bernard M. Baruch Papers, MC006, Public Policy Papers, Special Collections, Princeton University Library.
10. John Maynard Keynes to Harold Temperley, September 29, November 10, and November 14, 1920, Harold Temperley to John Maynard Keynes, November 27, 1920, Keynes Papers, series CO, file 11, docs. 201, 206, 220, 233.
11. Bernard Baruch, *The Public Years* (New York: Holt, Rinehart and Winston, 1960), 124.
12. Jordan A. Schwarz, *Liberal: Adolf A. Berle and the Vision of an American Era* (New York: Free Press, 1987), 402.
13. Harold Nicolson to Edward House, April 18, 1934, box 12, Harold Nicolson Papers, GEN MSS 614, Beinecke Rare Book and Manuscript Library, Yale University Library. Philip Kerr, memorandum to Charles Seymour, October 7, 1933, box 9, folder 522, Charles Seymour Papers, MSS 441, Manuscripts and Archives, Yale University Library.
14. François Charles-Roux, memorandum of conversation with Georges Clemenceau, March 5, 1925, article 9, 9 handwritten notes, note G, Papiers François Charles-Roux, Papiers d'agents–Archives privées (PA-AP) 37, Ministère de L'Europe et des Affaires Étrangères, France.
15. Henry Cabot Lodge to Henry White, April 8, 1919, Paris Peace Conference File, box 41, Henry White Papers, MSS 45328, Library of Congress.
16. See correspondence sent to Stephen Bonsal before, during, and after Clemenceau's 1922 trip. Special Correspondence, box 2, folder "Edward House," and Subject File, box 5, folder "Clemenceau, Georges, 1922–1972," both in Stephen Bonsal Papers, MSS 13193, Library of Congress.

17. Jean-Jules Jusserand to French Ministry of Foreign Affairs, December 1 and 3, 1919, volume 2, box 6N138, Georges Clemenceau Papers, War Archives (1914–1939), French Ministry of Defense Archives, Vincennes.

18. Thomas A. Bailey, *Woodrow Wilson and the Great Betrayal* (New York: Macmillan, 1945), 277.

19. Bailey, *Wilson and the Great Betrayal,* quoted in Lloyd E. Ambrosius, "Woodrow Wilson's Health and the Treaty Fight, 1919–1920," *International History Review* 9, no. 1 (1987): 73–84.

20. Sigmund Freud, "Introduction," in Sigmund Freud and William C. Bullitt, *Thomas Woodrow Wilson: A Psychological Study* (Boston: Houghton Mifflin, 1966), xiii.

21. Allen Dulles, "The Real Woodrow Wilson," *Look,* December 13, 1966, 50–99, quoted in Jean M. White, "Woodrow Wilson: Oedipus Complex? World Affairs at Peace Talks May Have Been Affected," *Washington Post,* November 26, 1966.

22. Frank C. Waldrop, letter to the editor, *Washington Post,* November 30, 1966. After sending the letter to the *Post,* Waldrop had second thoughts, expressing a desire to read the whole book first. The *Post* editor objected: "it is a mistake to suppress indignation. Like fish it is only good when it is fresh." James Russell Wiggins to Frank Waldrop, December 7, 1966, Correspondence, box 12, folder "Aug.–Dec. 1966," Frank C. Waldrop Papers, Herbert Hoover Presidential Library and Museum, West Branch, IA.

Acknowledgments

Without the invitation I received in 2008 to teach at Yale Law School, this book would not exist. I want to thank Deans Harold Koh, Robert Post, and Heather Gerken, as well as all my colleagues and friends on the faculty, most sincerely and deeply. When I discovered, in the summer of 2014, that the William C. Bullitt papers were housed at Yale's Sterling Memorial Library, all I had to do to visit the manuscripts room was walk across the street. Over the months and years that followed, I was able to explore not only every box in the Bullitt collection but also many other resources held at the Sterling and Beinecke Libraries. Special thanks to Bill Landis and all the archivists who helped me in the United States, France, the United Kingdom, and Switzerland.

My thanks as well to Yale University Library; Robert, Christy, and Tracy Pennoyer; Alice Ballard and Ellen Saltonstall; and Daniel Heller-Roazen, who authorized me to quote precious archival documents from the archives of William Bullitt, Ernesta Drinker Barlow, and Paul Roazen.

At Yale I have benefited greatly from discussions with Bruce Ackerman, Howard Bloch, Owen Fiss, John Gaddis, Oona Hathaway, Alice Kaplan, Paul Kahn, Judith Resnik, Scott Shapiro, Ellen Spitz, James Whitman, and Jay Winter. Over the years, several Yale Law School students have assisted me with critical tasks: Joe Chatham, Nick Kilstein, Robert Nelson, Eric Parrie, Alexandra Perloff-Giles, Ilana Rice, Thomas Scott-Railton, Mattie Wheeler. Monika Piotrowicz offered invaluable assistance beginning with my arrival in 2008. The Centre d'histoire sociale des mondes contemporains, my research facility at the University of Paris 1, has provided unfailing support.

I wish to thank Alexandre Berlinski for numerous conversations and illuminating ideas. Thanks are also owed to Raffael Fasel and Birthe Mühlhoff, who translated some of Freud's manuscript notes from German.

Robert Dallek, Georges-Henri Soutou, and Brad Snyder provided me with important information. I am also grateful for the insights, support, and encouragement I received from Julien Charnay, Daniel Cohen, Jon Colcord, Pamela Druckerman, Romain Enriquez, Laurent Ferri, Marc Flandreau, Nick Frisch, Gilles Grin, Nicolas Guilhot, Yves-André Istel, Laurent Joly, Gabriel Kachuck, Adam Kuper, Victor Louzon, Alison MacKeen, Margaret MacMillan, Pierre Marlière, Rahsaan Maxwell, James McAuley, Sara McDougall, Nicholas Mulder, Ramona Naddaff, Olivier Nora, Noah Rosenblum, Peter Sahlins, Emmanuelle Sidem, Robert Skidelsky, Kathryn Smith, Jacob Soll, Tristan Storme, Dominique Trudel, Pierre Vesperini, Frederic Viguier, Sam and Sherry Wells, Winthrop Wells, Stephen Wertheim, Lila Azam Zanganeh, Philip Zelikow, and Alex Zevin.

A truly special thanks to Georges Borchardt, my indefatigable agent who guided my steps over the years and has become a dear friend.

I am very grateful to my editor Sharmila Sen and her assistant Samantha Mateo at Harvard University Press, and to my copyeditors Simon Waxman and Anne McGuire, for their remarkable work and support.

Grey Anderson, Chantal de Rudder, and Eugene Rusyn know how much I owe them.

Index